A LEVEL
LAW

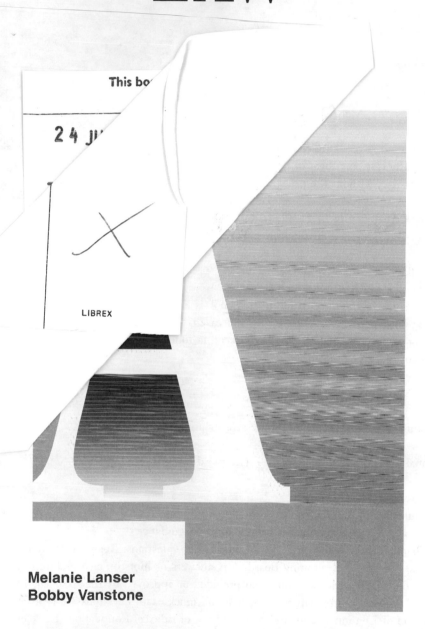

Melanie Lanser
Bobby Vanstone

Letts
EDUCATIONAL

Every effort has been made to trace copyright holders and to obtain their permission for the use of copyright material. The authors and publishers will gladly receive information enabling them to rectify any reference or credit in subsequent editions.

First published 1997
Reprinted 1998

Letts Educational
Aldine House
Aldine Place
London W12 8AW
0181 740 2266

Text © Bobby Vanstone, Melanie Lanser, 1997

British Library Cataloguing in Publication Data
A CIP record for this book is available from the British Library

ISBN 1 85758 603 4

Note for readers: Some of the information in this book is liable to change, particularly that which is directly influenced by new legislation and case law. Such information is correct at the time of going to press but the reader should keep in touch with current affairs to ensure an up-to-date knowledge of the subject.

Typeset by Kai, Nottingham

Printed and bound in Great Britain by Progressive Printing UK Ltd

Letts Educational is the trading name of BPP (Letts Educational) Ltd

Acknowledgements
The authors would like to thank Denis Lanser specifically for contributing parts of the text for chapters 3, 5 and 8 and generally, for his support and guidance.
Questions in Chapters 1, 2, 3, 4, 5, 6, 7, 9 and mock exam questions: Reproduced by kind permission of the Associated Examining Board. Any answers or hints on answers are the sole responsibility of the authors and have not been provided or approved by the Associated Examining Board. Questions in Chapters 3, 5, 6, 8 and mock exam questions are reproduced by kind permission of London Examinations, A division of Edexcel Foundation. Edexcel Foundation, London Examinations accepts no responsibility whatsoever for the accuracy or method of working in the answers given. Questions in Chapters 1, 2, 4, 5, 6, 7 and mock exam questions: Reproduced by kind permission of the Northern Examinations and Assessment Board. The authors are responsible for the solutions given to these questions and they may not necessarily constitute the only possible solutions. Questions in Chapters 1, 4, 5, 6, 7, 9 and mock exam questions: UODLE material is reproduced by permission of the University of Cambridge Local Examinations Syndicate. University of Cambridge Local Examinations Syndicate bears no responsibility for the example answers to questions taken from past UODLE question papers which are contained in this publication.

CONTENTS

STARTING POINTS

In this section:

How to use this book
   The structure of this book
   Using your syllabus checklist

Syllabus checklist and paper analysis

Examination board addresses

Studying and revising Law
   The difference between GCSE and A level
   Studying strategies and techniques
   Subject-specific skills
   Effective revision

The examination
   Question styles
   Understanding the terminology of the question
   Examination techniques
   Final preparation

HOW TO USE THIS BOOK

THE STRUCTURE OF THIS BOOK

The key aim of this book is to guide you in the way you tackle A Level Law. It should serve as a study guide, work book and revision aid throughout your course. This book, by its very nature, is a condensed version of the more detailed law textbooks which are available. It is not intended to be a complete guide to the subject and should be used as a companion to your textbooks. It is designed to complement rather than duplicate. The law is stated at July 1997 though in some places more recent developments have been incorporated.

The study guide is divided into three sections. Section One, Starting Points deals with study and revision skills plus advice on planning your revision and tips on how to tackle the exam itself. Use the Syllabus Checklists to find out exactly where you can find the study units which are relevant to your particular syllabus.

Section Two, the main body of the text, contains the key information which you will need to tackle in A Level Law. It has been devised to make study as easy as possible and has been divided into chapters which cover the topics you will encounter on your syllabus. The Chapter Objectives direct you towards the key points of the chapter you are about to read. To reinforce what you have just read and learned, there are Illustrative Questions at the end of each chapter. All questions are actually taken from those recently set by the examination boards. The tutorial notes and suggested answers provided give you practical guidance on how to answer A Level questions. There are also Practice Questions, which are further examples of A Level exam questions for you to attempt, with the key points and potential pitfalls emphasised.

Finally, in Section Three, Test Run, you will find a mock exam to help prepare you for your examination. This will give you invaluable examination practice and, together with the specimen answers provided by the authors, will help you to judge how close you are to achieving your A Level pass.

USING YOUR SYLLABUS CHECKLIST

Whether you are using this book to work step-by-step through the syllabus or to structure your revision campaign, you will find it useful to use the checklist to record what you have covered — and how far you still have to go.

The checklist for each examination is in two parts. First, there is a list of topics covered by this book which are part of the syllabus. Although the checklists are detailed, it is not possible to print entire syllabuses. *You are strongly recommended to obtain an official copy of the syllabus for your examination and consult it when the need arises.* The examination board addresses are given after the syllabus checklists.

When you have revised a topic tick the box in the column provided and, if there are questions on it elsewhere in the book, try to answer these too.

The second part of the checklist gives you information about the examination, providing useful details about the time allocated for each paper and the weighting of the questions. The different types of questions which may be set are explained in detail later in this section under the heading The Examination (page 12).

SYLLABUS CHECKLISTS AND PAPER ANALYSIS

ASSOCIATED EXAMINING BOARD
(A Level) (0625)

Syllabus topic	Covered in Unit No	✓
The idea of law Section 1		
Nature and functions of law	3.1	
Sources of law	2	
Law and justice	3.3	
Law and morals	3.2	
Social aspects of law Section 2		
Balancing conflicting interests	3.1	
Legal personality	3.4	
Liability in law	9.1; 9.2	
Protection and restraint of individual freedom	8	
Judicial review	1.8	
Parliamentary law-making Section 3		
Legislative process	2.1	
Delegated legislation	2.1	
Influences on Parliament	2.1	
The European Union	2.3	
Judicial law-making Section 4		
Judicial precedent	2.2	
Judicial creativity and policy	2.2	
Statutory interpretation	2.1	
Development and role of equity	2.4	
Dispute solving in English law Section 5		
Structure of the courts	1.1; 1.6	
Alternatives to courts	1.6	
Legal personnel	1.2	
Judiciary	1.3	
Laypersons	1.4	
Legal aid/unmet need for legal services	1.7	
Criminal law Section 6		
Nature and aims	5.1	
Persons involved in the criminal trial	1.5	
Actus reus and *mens rea*	5.2	
Strict liability	5.4	
Vicarious and corporate liability	5.4	
General defences	5.3	
Unlawful homicide	5.7	
Offences against the person	5.8	
Sanctions	4.1	
Sentencing	4.2	
Tort Section 7		
Nature and aims	7.1	
Negligence	7.2	
Occupiers' liability	7.3	
Nuisance	7.4	
Strict and vicarious liability	7.5; 7.10	
General defences	7.9	

Syllabus topic	Covered in Unit No	✓
Remedies	4.3; 4.5	
Contract *Section 8*		
Nature and aims	6.1; 6.8	
Formation	6.2	
Terms	6.4; 6.5; 6.6	
Vitiating elements	6.3	
Discharge	6.7	
Remedies	4.3; 4.4	

Paper analysis

Paper 1	*3 hours*	50% of the total marks
		Any four essay questions out of a choice
		of ten (based on Sections 1 – 5 above)
Paper 2	*3 hours*	50% of the total marks
		Two questions out of six chosen from
		either one *or* two of three sections
		(criminal law, tort and contract law)

LONDON EXAMINATIONS, EDEXCEL
(A Level) (9345); (Advanced supplementary) (8345)

Syllabus topic	Covered in Unit No	✓
Paper 1		
The nature of law *Section A*		
Rules, law and morality	3.2	
Principal legal theories	3.1	
Nature and role of law	3.1	
Legal reasoning and analysis	Not covered	
The effect of law on the individual *Section B*		
Rights, duties, liabilities and privileges	8.1; 8.2	
Common law and equitable remedies	4.3; 4.4; 4.5	
Sanctions for criminal wrongs	4.1; 4.2	
Judicial review	1.8	
Legal personality	3.4	
The sources of law *Section C*		
Legislation	2.1	
Binding precedent	2.2	
European Community law	2.3	
Law reform	2.5	
Law enforcement and administration *Section D*		
Civil and criminal cases	1.5; 1.7	
Dispute settlement	1.6	
Role of the police	1.5; 1.8	
The legal profession	1.2	
The role of the lay person	1.4	
Paper 2		
The Market *Section A*		
Contract	6.1; 6.2; 6.3; 6.4; 6.5; 6.7; 4.4; 6.6	
Liability in negligence	7.2; 7.8	
Criminal liability	Not covered	
Outline of consumer credit legislation	6.6	
Extra judicial approaches	Not covered	

Syllabus topic	Covered in Unit No	✓
The workplace Section B		
Duties of employers and employees	6.6	
Restraint of trade	6.3	
Discrimination and equal pay	6.6	
Termination	6.6	
Health and safety at work	Not covered	
Trade unions	Not covered	
The family Section C	Not covered	
The criminal offender Section D		
Reasons for criminal liability	5.1	
Inchoate offences	5.6	
General defences	5.3	
Law protecting the person	5.7; 5.8	
Theft and dishonesty	5.10	
Criminal damage	5.10	
The individual Section E		
Basis of civil liberties	8.1; 8.2; 8.5	
Freedom of assembly and association	8.3; 7.6; 7.4	
Freedom of speech	7.7	
Freedom of person and property	Not covered	
Freedom of information	Not covered	

Paper analysis
A level (9345)

Paper 1　　3 hours　　50% of the total marks
The paper consists of ten essay questions set on
Sections A to D of the Paper 1 content in two Parts.
Answer four questions, two from Part I (Sections A
and B) and two from Part II (Sections C and D)

Paper 2　　3 hours　　50% of the total marks
The paper consists of five sections A to E,
each containing four problem questions. Answer four
questions, choosing two from each of two sections.

AS level (8345)

Paper 1　　1¹/₂ hours　　50% of the total marks
The paper consists of five essay questions set on
Sections C and D of the Paper 1 content. Answer two
questions.

Paper 2　　1¹/₂ hours　　50% of the total marks
As Paper 2 A level, but answer two questions from
any one section.

WELSH JOINT EDUCATION COMMITTEE

Syllabus topic	Covered in Unit No	✓
The nature of law	3.1, 3.2	
History	2.4	
Sources and legal reasoning		
Law reform	2.5	
Judicial precedent and legal reasoning	2.2	
Legislation	2.1	
European Union law	2.3	

Syllabus topic	Covered in Unit No	✓
Machinery of justice		
Settlement of disputes	1.5; 1.6	
Civil, criminal and specialist courts	1.1	
Tribunals	1.6	
European courts	2.3; 8.5	
Personnel of the law	1.2; 1.3	
The lay element	1.4	
Legal process	1.5	
The provisions of legal services	1.7	
Sanctions and remedies		
Punishment and compensation	4.1; 4.2	
Civil remedies	4.3; 4.4; 4.5	
The consumer and the law		
Importance of contract and tort	6.1; 6.2; 6.3; 6.4; 6.5; 6.6; 6.7 7.2; 7.8; 4.4	
Criminal law and the consumer	Not covered	
Travel	Not covered	
Credit and hire agreements	6.6	
Fair trading and voluntary regulation	Not covered	
The European Union and the consumer	Not covered	
The worker and the law	Partly covered in 6.6	
Civil liberties, the individual and the law	Partly covered in 8.3; 8.5 and 1.8	
Criminal justice and public order	Partly covered in 8.3	

Paper analysis

Paper 1   *3 hours*   50% of the total marks
                        Any four essay questions out of a choice of ten
Paper 2   *3 hours*   50% of the total marks
                        Candidates study **one** of four topics:
                          The Consumer and the Law
                          The Worker and the Law
                          Civil Liberties, the Individual and the Law
                          Criminal Justice and Public Order
                        The paper is divided into two sections: Section A
                        comprises six essay questions; Section B comprises
                        four problem questions. Answer four questions, at
                        least *one* from *each section*

OCEAC
(A Level) (9949); (Advanced Supplementary) (8849)

Syllabus topic	Covered in Unit No	✓
Paper 1 and Paper 2		
Sources of law		
Doctrine of precedent	2.2	
Equity	2.4	
Legislation	2.1	
European Law	2.3	
Law reform	2.5	
Civil courts and other methods of dispute resolution		
Civil Courts	1.5; 1.4; 1.8	
Tribunals	1.6	
Arbitration	1.6	
Alternative methods of dispute resolution	1.6	

Syllabus topic	Covered in Unit No	✓
European Court of Justice	2.3	
Criminal process and the criminal courts		
Police powers	Not covered	
Criminal courts	1.5; 1.4	
Legal profession		
Barristers and solicitors	1.2; 1.5	
Judiciary	1.3	
Provision of legal services	1.7	
Penal system		
Principles of sentencing	4.2	
Powers of courts	4.1	
Paper 3		
General principles of criminal law		
Principles of criminal liability		
Actus reus and *mens rea*	5.2	
Strict liability	5.4	
Participation	5.5	
General defences	5.3	
Preliminary crimes	5.6	
Offences against the person		
Homicide	5.7	
Non-fatal offences against the person	5.8	
Defences	5.3	
Offences against property	5.10	
Paper 4		
General principles of the law of contract		
Formation of a contract	6.2	
Contents of a contract		
Contractual terms	6.4	
Capacity	6.3	
Privity	6.2	
Vitiating factors	6.3	
Discharge of contracts	6.7	
Remedies	4.4	
Paper 5		
General principles of the law of tort		
General principles	7.1	
Defences	7.9	
Remedies	4.5	
Negligence	7.2; 7.3	
Defamation	7.7	
Trespass to land	7.6	
Nuisance	7.4	
Rylands v Fletcher	7.5	
Trespass to the person	7.6	
Vicarious liability	7.10	
Joint and several tortfeasors	Not covered	

Paper analysis

Paper 1	$2^1/_4$ hours	70% of marks for papers 1 and 2 Any three essay questions out of a choice of seven
Paper 2	$2^1/_4$ hours	30% of marks for papers 1 and 2 One of two data questions

Papers 1 and 2 comprise the AS level examination. For the A level, candidates must, in addition, take one of the papers 3, 4 or 5 during the same examination session or within four years.

| Papers 3, 4 and 5 | *3 hours* | 50% of marks for the A level |
| | | The papers are divided into two sections: Section A comprises four essay questions, Section B comprises four problem questions. Answer four questions, at least *one* from *each section*. |

NORTHERN EXAMINATIONS AND ASSESSMENT BOARD

(A Level) (4381; 4382) (Advanced Supplementary) (3381; 3382)

Syllabus topic	Covered in Unit No	✓
The institutions of the English legal system *Section 1*		
Common law and equity	2.4	
Parliament and legislation	2.1	
Delegated legislation and judicial review	2.1; 1.8	
The Lord Chancellor and the law officers of the Crown	1.3	
Court structure	1.1	
Judiciary and the magistracy	1.3; 1.4	
Statutory tribunals; ombudsman	1.6; 8.3	
The European Union	2.3	
Human rights treaties	8.3	
Legal profession	1.2	
Law reform	2.5	
Legal concepts and methods of legal reasoning *Section 2*		
Law and fact	1.5; 1.4	
Precedent	2.2	
Interpretation of statutes	2.1	
Evidence	1.5	
Legal personality	3.4	
The operation of the legal system *Section 3*		
Law enforcement by the police	1.5; 8	
Prosecuting authorities	1.5	
Mode of trial	1.5	
Bail	1.5	
Juries	1.4	
Sentencing	4.1; 4.2	
Civil proceedings	1.5; 1.6	
Arbitration	1.6	
Legal aid and advice	1.7	
Criminal law *Section 4*		
Nature and extent of crime	5.1	
Actus reus and *mens rea*; strict liability	5.2; 5.4	
Participation	5.5	
Inchoate offences	5.6	
General defences	5.3	
Unlawful homicide	5.7	
Non-fatal offences	5.8	
Sexual offences (rape and indecent assault)	5.9	
Offences against property	5.10	
Sentencing powers in homicide and rape cases	5.7; 5.9; 4.1; 4.2	

Syllabus topic	*Covered in Unit No*	✓
Law of contract *Section 5*		
Nature and functions of the law of contract	6.1	
Freedom of contract	6.8	
Formation	6.2	
Terms	6.4; 6.5; 6.6	
Vitiating factors	6.3	
Discharge	6.7	
Remedies	4.4	
Consumer protection	6.6; 6.8; 7.8	
Small claims procedure	1.6	
Law of tort *Section 6*		
Nature and functions of the law of tort	7.1	
Forms of liability	9.1; 9.2; 7.10	
General defences	7.9	
Remedies	4.5	
Negligence (including occupiers' liability)	7.2; 7.3	
Trespass to the person	7.6	
Defamation	7.7	
Nuisance	7.4	
The rule in *Rylands* v *Fletcher*	7.5	
Trespass to land	7.6	

Paper analysis

A Level: 4381 *(end of course)*

Paper 1	*3 hours*	50% of the total marks
(LW01)		The paper consists of two sections: Section A
English legal system		comprising four source questions;

Section B comprising six essay questions, based on Sections 1 - 3 above. Answer four questions, at least *one from each section*

AND one Paper from Papers 2, 3 and 4

Paper 2	*3 hours*	50% of the total marks
(LW02)		The paper consists of two sections: Section A
Criminal law		comprising four problem questions;

Section B comprising six essay questions. Answer four questions, at least *one from each section*

Paper 3
(LW03)
Contract

See Paper 2

Paper 4
(LW04)
Tort

See Paper 2

A Level: 4382 *(modular)*

An advanced award requires the assessment of *two* modules. Candidates must offer module LW01 and *either* LW02 *or* LW03 *or* LW04. Modules are assessed in June in each year.

AS: 3381; 3382 *(end of course/modular)*

An advanced supplementary award requires the assessment of any *one* module. Candidates following the modular route may choose to carry their module test marks forward to contribute towards an advanced award by completing a further module (in which case one module must be LW01).

EXAMINATION BOARD ADDRESSES

AEB   The Associated Examining Board
                    Stag Hill House, Guildford, Surrey GU2 5XJ
                    Tel: 01483 506506

LONDON   London Examinations, EDEXCEL
                    Stewart House, 32 Russell Square, London WC1B 5DN
                    Tel: 0171 331 4000

NEAB   Northern Examinations and Assessment Board
                    Devas Street, Manchester M15 6EX
                    Tel: 0161 953 1180

UODLE   University of Oxford Delegacy of Local Examinations
(*part of OCEAC*)   Ewert House, Summertown, Oxford OX2 7BZ
                    Tel: 01865 554291

WJEC   Welsh Joint Education Committee
                    245 Western Avenue, Cardiff CF5 2YX
                    Tel: 01222 561231

STUDYING AND REVISING LAW

THE DIFFERENCE BETWEEN GCSE AND A LEVEL

Law as a subject is probably new to you, unlike some of the other A Levels you may have chosen to study. In particular, the study of law requires you to be able to apply your knowledge of the law to given factual situations, in order to reach a conclusion. The key differences between A Level studies and GCSE studies are:

❶ A *quantitative difference*: generally speaking, A Levels involve more than GCSEs: more hours in the classroom, more work at home, longer essays, more, and longer examinations.

❷ A *qualitative difference:* the most important change from GCSE work is that A Levels require a thoughtful and critical approach rather than simply churning out a previously learned set of facts. The emphasis is on understanding. Detailed knowledge is required and you are expected to be able to apply your knowledge to both essay questions and problems. You are expected to be able to evaluate legal institutions and legal rules and provide evidence to support your arguments.

STUDY STRATEGIES AND TECHNIQUES
General hints

The examination is designed to test your understanding and knowledge. During your course you will be preparing for this examination. To pass it, you have to make notes throughout the course, read around the subject, file the notes systematically, and carry out regular revision. The amount and nature of this revision is influenced by the time available and the demands made by the examination. In all A Level law examinations, you will have to write essays and apply your knowledge of law to factual scenarios. Therefore, as you revise, you should refer to past papers and the Illustrative and Practice Questions provided in this book, and practise answering the questions.

You are advised to think about revision at the start, rather than towards the end of the course. Many A Level courses include a form of 'revision' as part of learning. Frequently you will revisit material learned already, and build upon this prior knowledge, when learning a new topic. For example, if your A Level requires you to have knowledge of criminal law, you will probably revisit topics such as criminal procedure and sources of law. You will be revising and building on previous learned content by having to relate it to new content being studied. Most A Level law courses can be compared to completing a jigsaw puzzle. As each piece slots into place you gain a fuller picture of the subject as a whole. When the 'jigsaw' is finished you should have a clear understanding of how the different topics are interrelated.

You should aim to plan some active revision sessions during the course. Probably the structure of your course will enable you to do this. You may have regular tests and examinations and a mock examination to prepare for. You should use school or college holidays to organise and revise work recently covered. This should:

- take some pressure and anxiety off you at examination time, by spreading your workload;
- identify any learning problems and subject-matter difficulties in time for you to seek advice and help from your teacher;
- lead to a more thorough learning of new law topics because you have a better foundation of knowledge on which to build.

SUBJECT-SPECIFIC SKILLS

All A Level Law examinations assess the following:

Content

Factual information is always required on the subject matter of the question. For example, a question on juries will usually expect detail on the selection and composition of juries, and their role in the legal system. Preferably you should learn more than the minimum amount of content on every subject. Too little or inaccurate factual information creates a bad impression in an essay. You should always try to include relevant cases and statutes in your answer in order to illustrate the points made.

Examples

Lawyers always state the sources of legal principles and rules. You should learn and quote, where relevant, cases and statutes. Merely citing the *names* of cases or statutes is pointless. You must provide a *brief* explanation of the facts and principle of law and indicate why it is relevant. Lengthy descriptions of facts of cases does not improve the quality of your answer, and probably means you will run out of time. Learn to summarise cases succinctly. Try to include any recent cases or statutes or proposals for law reform in your discussion. Knowledge of new law, although not essential, indicates that you are aware of law as a dynamic subject.

Evaluation

This is as important as content. Facts alone are not sufficient. You should be aware of standard comments and criticisms and should refer to these, including sensible comments of your own opinion. Criticism should be supplemented with evidence of recent research. Evaluation must be of a constructive nature and be based on evidence. It is not advisable to write 'I don't think the jury is a good thing'. Instead, you could write 'The jury may be in need of reform because...' or 'The jury should be replaced with...because...'.

Analysis

You must be able to work out what content and evaluation is required for a particular question. Analysis is particularly important for a complex essay title (e.g., a long quotation) or a problem question. You must be able to select and organise your content and evaluation. Use of relevant material throughout an answer indicates a correct analysis of the subject.

Communication

Examiners are looking to see whether you understand what information they are asking for and whether you can clearly explain that information in written form. Poor grammar (for example, long rambling sentences) and poor punctuation may obscure your meaning. A good communicator presents information in a logical and coherent way. Spelling need not be 100% accurate, but if you consistently mis-spell common *legal* words, the examiner may reasonably conclude that you are unfamiliar with them. Spelling, punctuation and grammar now form part of your assessment at A Level.

EFFECTIVE REVISION

There are various methods of revising, and what suits one person does not suit another. As a general principle reading through your notes is not of much benefit. You will not remember very much of what you have read, and you will probably find it a rather unstimulating exercise. You must aim to *actively* revise. You should aim to follow certain steps:

❶ **Summarise your notes**. Once your notes are organised (and until this is done you will not achieve a great deal) you may find it of great benefit to reduce your notes (again and again). Try to summarise a topic meaningfully on one or two sheets of paper. Use a technique which works for you. You do not necessarily have to write linear notes. Instead you could write key words on a flowchart or spidergram, for example. The study of law *always* requires you to learn cases. You must devise a method of achieving this early in your course. You may choose to write case notes on index cards, perhaps colour coding them by topic, and keeping them safe.

❷ **Learn your notes**. Once you have actively reduced your notes, you must learn them. You must know the topic thoroughly. Just because you have read your file and reduced your notes, you do not necessarily *know* the information.

❸ **Look at past examination papers**. Always keep a check on how your examiner treats a topic. Keep referring to past questions on a topic. If you are unable to answer a particular question, it may mean you have not anticipated a particular angle, and need to go back to the note-taking stage. If you do this *before* the examination, you are unlikely to be 'caught out' in the examination.

❹ **Write some timed answers**. It is often useful to meet with a friend who is also studying A Level Law and discuss your revision and test each other. Once you have thoroughly learned a topic, set some time aside to do a timed essay or problem to ensure that you can answer questions in the time available. Perhaps you can ask your teacher if he or she will mark your timed answers.

If you propose to use this Study Guide as the basis of a revision programme, you should concentrate on one or two topic areas only at each revision session. Try the following:

* read the topic detail;

* summarise what you have read on one sheet of paper, without referring to the book;

* check your summary with the topic detail and add any further detail needed;

* attempt one or more of the questions provided by drafting out a planned answer;

* check your answer with the one provided;

* identify any differences or omissions;

* go back quickly over the topic again to reinforce your knowledge and to correct any misunderstandings.

THE EXAMINATION

Question styles

There are three types of A Level Law questions. These are:

* Essays
* Problems
* Stimulus response.

Essays

These are used by all Examination Boards. They require you to write a significant length essay in which the question set is fully answered. Good essay technique depends on the following:

❶ **Planning**: You should always plan your essays, so that when you are writing them, you concentrate on clarity of style and quality of answer. If you simply start writing and hope to produce a relevant and coherent answer then nine times out of ten you will write a muddled essay. Your plan should not be lengthy and complex, but simply list the key words and cases/statutes. If you believe you 'can't plan' or your plans are almost as long as your essay, it is advisable to practice this skill frequently during your revision period.

❷ **Introduction**: Always write an introduction which defines key terms and sets out how you propose to answer the question set.

❸ **Content**: Each piece of relevant information should be put into separate paragraphs. One of the most off-putting things for a marker is to see a 'wall' of writing without breaks. Paragraphs also help you to see quite clearly how your essay is progressing and whether your have missed any points from your plan. Ensure you connect your paragraphs. Do not write a number of unconnected points in separate paragraphs and expect your examiner to make sense of them. Each paragraph should be clearly related to the ones preceding and following it.

❹ **Conclusion**: Every essay must have a conclusion which answers the question. In two part essays, conclude each part. It is a good idea to refer back to the question at this point, and using the words in the question, summarise the main points and arguments. Do not introduce any new material into a conclusion. At this stage, you may be required, or choose, to give your own opinion. For example, if the question has asked whether you agree that juries should be abolished, you should state, with reasons, your opinion in your conclusion (not introduction). Only at this point, after examining all the arguments and evidence, can you legitimately decide.

Problems

Problem-solving is an essential skill in law. All A Level Law examinations require you to be able to analyse a factual situation and select the relevant law in order to solve it. Problem questions, in particular, test your knowledge of substantive law. This is a skill which can be learned, and improved with practice. The key steps are often referred to as I D E A (identify, define, explain, apply):

❶ **Identification**: Identify the relevant area of law.

❷ **Definition**: Define the relevant area of law.

❸ **Explanation**: Explain the rules of law. Use of cases and statutes as evidence is often the weakest part of candidates' answers. It is essential to identify and explain relevant legal authority.

❹ **Application**: Apply the law to the problem and reach a conclusion. If the relevant law is found in cases, you must compare the facts in the problem with the facts in those cases. If they are sufficiently similar, you can conclude that the problem you are dealing with will have a similar outcome; if the facts are different, you may distinguish the case. If the relevant law is found in a statute, explain the provisions of the statute and any cases which assist in its interpretation. You need not be completely certain in your conclusion. For example, you do not need to say 'A will be guilty of...'. Instead you could write 'On the evidence given, A appears to be guilty...'.

Stimulus response

Some A Level Law examinations require you to answer stimulus questions. In such questions stimulus material is provided. This may be an extract from a book, newspaper, official report, case or statute or similar such material. A number of questions are then asked which can be answered partially by reference to the source(s) and partially from wider knowledge and understanding of the topic. Your wider knowledge needs to be applied in a relevant way to the answers. When answering such questions, you should:

❶ Read the stimulus material thoroughly. Read it a number of times so that you fully understand it.

❷ Read all the questions which follow, noting what each one requires you to do, and how many marks are available for each. If you do this you will avoid answering, for example, part (b) in part (a). You will also avoid the mistake of providing a lengthy answer to a question with only a few marks available. Allocate your time accordingly.

❸ Plan each answer briefly.

❹ Write clearly and concisely and ensure, where necessary, that you **refer to the source material**. Justify your answer partly be reference to that material, if appropriate.

❺ The question will always provide you with an opportunity to **apply your wider knowledge** of the topic. If you don't have a wider knowledge, then do not attempt the question. You will not be able to gain good marks merely by using the source material.

UNDERSTANDING THE TERMINOLOGY OF THE QUESTION

Examination questions use a variety of words of instruction. If you are to answer the question set, it is vital that you understand the different words. Generally speaking there are two types of instruction: description (for which fewer marks are normally awarded) and evaluation. Some of the more common words are considered below:

Outline/describe

Outline simply means to describe in minimum detail. It is rarely asked for, and only a few marks will usually be awarded for this type of question. Describe means to write uncritically about the features of an institution or law. It is usually necessary to describe something before you begin to evaluate it.

Account for

This goes one stage further than describe, as it also requires an explanation. It is often used when there is some historical element.

Explain

This requires you to describe a topic clearly and intelligibly paying attention to detail. Explanations are often asked for in connection with a difficult or complicated area of law.

Analyse

This term is usually used where a fairly complex issue is the subject of the question. A detailed and accurate break down of the issues involved is required.

Examine

This is very similar to analyse, but often is linked to a statement which may be controversial or only one of a number of possible opinions. The implication for you is to be aware of alternative explanations and criticisms.

Discuss

This means to look in detail at a number of different explanations and/or opinions and point out their strengths and weaknesses. Often the examiners say 'critically discuss', to add weight to the point that you should not simply present textbook arguments.

Assess and evaluate

These words are similar to 'discuss'. These are usually used when the examiner wants you to examine the strengths and weaknesses of a particular institution or principle of law, and to give your opinion on the topic.

EXAMINATION TECHNIQUES

- Do not tire yourself out the night before the examination with intensive revision. If you do not know it by now, you will not learn much extra. It may be worthwhile looking at your summary notes briefly in order to boost your confidence and reinforce short-term learning.

- Arrive in plenty of time. Ensure you have all the necessary equipment with you. Take a number of pens, in case one runs out or doesn't work properly.

- When you are allowed to start, take your time and read carefully through all the instructions on the examination paper. Make sure you understand them.

- Read each question carefully and choose all those you feel that you might be able to do. Re-read these carefully and narrow your choice down. Do not panic if everyone else is writing. It is more important that you carefully choose your questions. If you think you can only answer one or two questions, and you are supposed to answer four, do not panic. Very often you find that once in the swing of the examination you become less nervous and can see possibilities of answering questions which at first seem impossible.

- Do not start a question without first constructing a plan. This provides a source against which you can check that all points are included.

- Keep an eye on the clock *at all times*. Do not spend a disproportionate amount of time on any one answer. One question answered in great depth earns fewer marks than two questions answered competently. Most examiners would agree that the higher marks are 'won and lost' on the fourth essay question (if four are required) and full answers to the problem questions. If you do mismanage your time, you must try to recover the situation. This can be done by summarising your answer to one question as a series of points. Though not ideal, it will earn you some marks. Remember, no writing, no marks!

- Answer the question asked, not the one you wish had been asked. A key cause of low marks is failing to answer the question. Writing all you know on a topic is pointless and gains few marks. Check carefully to see if the question focuses on one or two aspects of a topic. If it does, the examiner expects you to select and apply relevant details from this topic.

- Avoid repeating points. There is nothing to be gained by repeating information which you have already explained clearly and fully. The examiner always prefers to mark clear and concise essays, rather than over-long, repetitive and rambling ones.

- Write legibly in black or blue ink. Do not use correction fluid, red or green ink on your paper. No Examination Boards allow this. If your handwriting is reasonably easy to read, your examiner will be able to mark your paper more effectively. If you make a mistake, merely put a line through it.

- Try to set some time aside at the end of the examination to read through your answers. You can correct minor mistakes and add one or two points if necessary.

FINAL PREPARATION

The confidence you now have in your subject knowledge will be of great advantage to you. Try to view the examination positively. Treat it as an opportunity to demonstrate *what you know*. In the final days, running up to the examination, you should:

- Check the time, date and place of the examination.

- Check you have all necessary things (for example, pens, watch etc).

- Make sure you are know the exact requirements of the examining board. How many questions are there on the paper(s)? Is there a choice? What type(s) of questions do you have to answer? How many sections are there in each paper? What is the time limit for each section and paper? What overall weighting do the papers have?

- Take some physical exercise before the exam to relieve tension and clear the mind.

- Arrive in good time.

- Practise relaxation techniques while waiting for the exam to start.

LEGAL TOPICS

In this section:

Each chapter features:

- *Units in this chapter:* a list of the main topic heads to follow.

- *Chapter objectives:* a brief comment on how the topics relate to what has gone before, and to the syllabus. Key ideas and skills which are covered in the chapter are introduced.

- *The main text*: this is divided into numbered topic units for ease of reference.

- *Worked questions:* typical exam questions, with tutorial notes and our suggested answers.

- *Question bank:* further questions, with comments on the pitfalls to avoid and points to include in framing your own answers.

THE ENGLISH LEGAL SYSTEM

Units in this chapter

Chapter objectives

This chapter deals with the people who work in the law, both lawyers and laypeople. It explains which courts deal with which type of legal case, how cases are handled by the courts and other bodies and how this work may be financed.

1.1 THE COURTS

1.1.1 CRIMINAL COURT HIERARCHY AND APPEALS

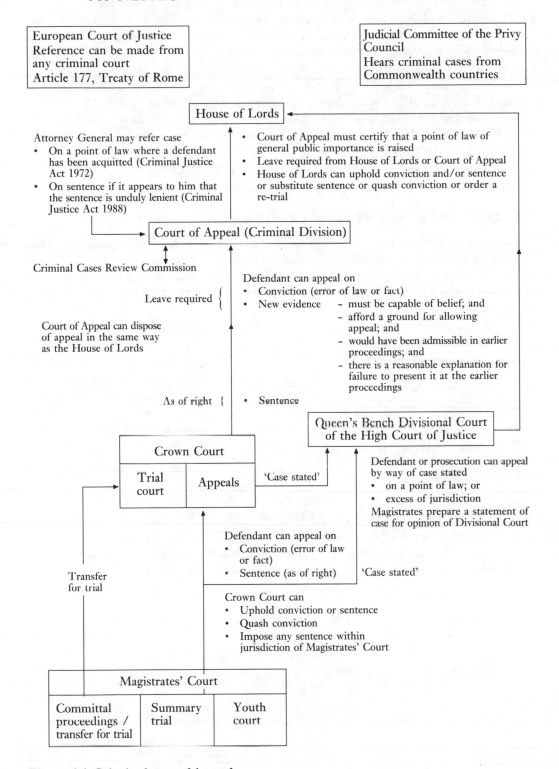

European Court of Justice
Reference can be made from
any criminal court
Article 177, Treaty of Rome

Judicial Committee of the Privy
Council
Hears criminal cases from
Commonwealth countries

House of Lords

Attorney General may refer case
• On a point of law where a defendant
  has been acquitted (Criminal Justice
  Act 1972)
• On sentence if it appears to him that
  the sentence is unduly lenient (Criminal
  Justice Act 1988)

• Court of Appeal must certify that a point of law of
  general public importance is raised
• Leave required from House of Lords or Court of Appeal
• House of Lords can uphold conviction and/or sentence
  or substitute sentence or quash conviction or order a
  re-trial

Court of Appeal (Criminal Division)

Criminal Cases Review Commission

Leave required {

Court of Appeal can dispose
of appeal in the same way
as the House of Lords

As of right {

Defendant can appeal on
• Conviction (error of law or fact)
• New evidence   - must be capable of belief; and
                  - afford a ground for allowing
                    appeal; and
                  - would have been admissible in earlier
                    proceedings; and
                  - there is a reasonable explanation for
                    failure to present it at the earlier
                    proceedings

• Sentence

Queen's Bench Divisional Court
of the High Court of Justice

Crown Court

| Trial court | Appeals |

'Case stated'

Defendant or prosecution can appeal
by way of case stated
• on a point of law; or
• excess of jurisdiction
Magistrates prepare a statement of
case for opinion of Divisional Court

Defendant can appeal on
• Conviction (error of law
  or fact)
• Sentence (as of right)   'Case stated'

Crown Court can
• Uphold conviction or sentence
• Quash conviction
• Impose any sentence within
  jurisdiction of Magistrates' Court

Transfer
for trial

Magistrates' Court

| Committal proceedings / transfer for trial | Summary trial | Youth court |

Figure 1.1 Criminal court hierarchy

Criminal Appeal Act 1995

The Criminal Appeal Act 1995 has significantly altered the provisions for appeal in criminal cases. It has amended the Criminal Appeal Act 1968. The main changes can be identified as:

- All appeals against conviction to the Court of Appeal now require the leave of the Court of Appeal or a certificate from the trial judge.

- There are simplified grounds for allowing an appeal. The Court of Appeal '*(a) shall allow an appeal against conviction if they think that the conviction is unsafe; and (b) shall dismiss such an appeal in any other case*'.

- The test for the admission of fresh evidence has been amended. The Court of Appeal must now consider whether the evidence appears to be 'capable of belief' rather than 'likely to be credible'. The court must, in addition, have regard to whether the evidence may afford any ground for allowing the appeal, whether it would have been admissible in the earlier proceedings and whether there is a reasonable explanation for failure to present it in these proceedings.

- The power of the Home Secretary to make references to the Court of Appeal is abolished. This role has been given to the Criminal Cases Review Commission.

The Criminal Cases Review Commission

The Commission is a corporation wholly independent of the Crown. It is comprised of not less than 11 members. At least one third must have a 10 year legal qualification (s. 71 Courts and Legal Services Act 1990) and at least two thirds must be persons with knowledge or experience of any aspect of the criminal justice system. The major rights, powers and duties of the Commission are:

- To investigate and report on any matter referred to it by the Court of Appeal in connection with an appeal.

- To refer the matter of a conviction and/or sentence to the Crown Court (conviction after summary trial) or to the Court of Appeal (conviction after trial on indictment) in any case. Before the Commission make such a reference, they must consider that there is a real possibility that the original decision would not be upheld, and an appeal against conviction or sentence must have been determined or appeal must have been refused.

- To consider and report on any matter referred by the Home Secretary in which he seeks their assistance in connection with the exercise of the prerogative of mercy in relation to a conviction.

- To initiate and supervise investigations, accompanied by a power to appoint an investigating officer, for example, a Chief Constable.

The Commission was established in an attempt to minimise the occurrence of miscarriages of justice by providing for independent, broad ranging review and investigations of cases where conviction and/or sentence raise doubts.

1.1.2 CIVIL COURT HIERARCHY AND APPEALS

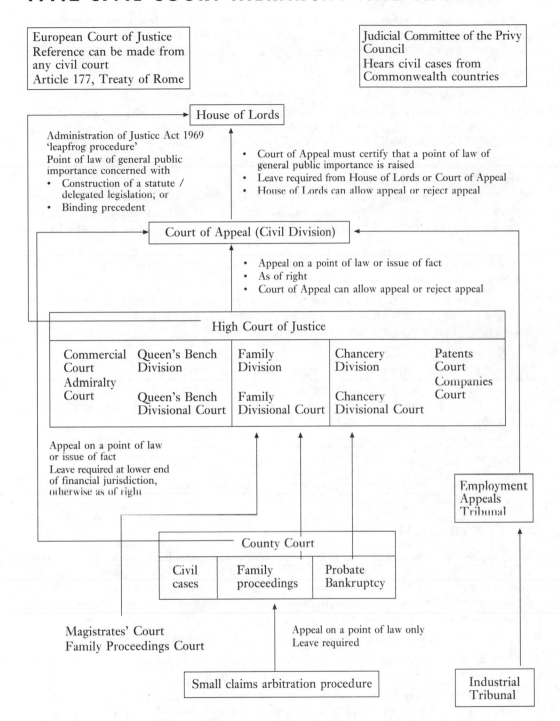

Figure 1.2 Civil court hierarchy

1.1.3 FUNCTIONS AND JURISDICTION OF THE COURTS

The jurisdiction of a court refers to its capacity to hear and determine particular cases and its capacity to impose specific remedies or sanctions. Courts that hear cases for the first time, such as the magistrates' court or county court, are called **courts of first instance**. Courts, such as the Court of Appeal or House of Lords, which hear appeals from lower courts are called **appellate courts**. Some courts, such as the Crown Court, have both first instance and appellate functions.

The magistrates' court

Magistrates' courts are the lowest level of criminal court. All criminal cases commence in this court and approximately 96% of cases are disposed of by the magistrates. The magistrates' court has a limited geographical jurisdiction hearing cases in its local area.

Criminal jurisdiction

- Magistrates hear less serious cases, known as **summary** offences.

- They may also try summarily an offence which is '**triable either way**' (triable summarily or on indictment). The magistrates' court may pass a sentence of up to six months' imprisonment or a maximum fine of £5,000. However, if the case involves two or more triable either way offences, they may pass a maximum of two six-month sentences of imprisonment, to run consecutively.

- In a case of a person charged with an indictable offence, the magistrates' court must decide whether to transfer the case for trial to the Crown Court. A single magistrate can perform this function and must decide if there is sufficient evidence to warrant a Crown Court trial.

- Magistrates are able to issue search and arrest warrants to the police. They also consider applications for bail (where police bail has not been granted).

- The magistrates' court also sits as a separate **Youth Court** to deal with children and young persons (aged between 10 - 17) charged with criminal offences. In such cases, the bench must comprise at least one person of each sex.

Civil jurisdiction

Although primarily a criminal court, magistrates also hear a variety of civil matters.

- They have the jurisdiction to hear an assortment of family law matters, including applications for maintenance, residency orders, supervision and care of children, adoption and guardianship of children.

- They deal with licensing matters.

- They can enforce certain debts, such as council tax.

Cases are heard by lay magistrates or stipendiary magistrates. They are assisted by the clerk of the court (see Unit 1.4.2).

The Crown Court

Crown Courts hear more serious criminal cases, known as indictable offences. The Criminal Justice Act 1988 reclassified many indictable and triable either way offences as summary offences in order to relieve the workload of the Crown Court. Cases are heard by a judge and a jury. The Crown Court may impose any sentence allowed in law. There are four classes of offence:

- Class 1 offences are tried by a High Court judge (e.g. murder).

- Class 2 offences are also tried by a High Court judge unless released by the presiding judge for trial by a Circuit judge or Recorder (e.g. manslaughter).

- Class 3 offences may be heard by a High Court judge or Circuit judge or Recorder and comprise all offences triable only on indictment not in Classes 1, 2 or 4.

- Class 4 offences are tried by a Circuit judge or Recorder normally (e.g. wounding or causing grievous bodily harm with intent, robbery, all offences triable either way).

The county court

County courts were created in 1846 to deal with small claims. Subject to some restrictions, a case can be commenced in any county court. Each court is staffed with a Circuit judge and a District judge. The Circuit judge normally sits alone but may call a jury of eight. The Courts and Legal Services Act 1990 provided for a reallocation of business in the civil courts. The county courts' jurisdiction has gradually been expanded, and covers nearly all aspects of civil law within prescribed financial limits. *All* county courts have the jurisdiction to hear:

- *Actions in tort and contract*. Most claims under £25,000 will be dealt with in the county court although it may transfer the proceedings to the High Court if, for example, a particularly complex question of law or fact is involved, or the case raises an issue of general public interest. Generally all claims concerning *damages for personal injury* where the plaintiff is claiming less than £50,000 will commence in the county court. However, claims between £25,000 and £50,000 will be heard by the court best able to deal with the case. Actions of which the value is £50,000 or more are to be tried in the High Court unless they are deemed more suitable for trial in the county court. However, cases involving professional negligence, fatal accidents, allegations of fraud or undue influence, defamation, malicious prosecution or false imprisonment and claims against the police should be heard in the High Court (*Practice Direction 1991*).
- *Actions for the recovery of land.*
- *Family proceedings* under the Children Act 1989 and injunctions against molestation and domestic violence.
- *Contentious probate disputes* where the net value of the estate is under £30,000.
- *Equity matters*, such as trusts, mortgages, dissolution of partnerships, where the amount of fund or value of property does not exceed £30,000.
- *Unlawful sexual discrimination* other than in the field of employment.

Certain county courts, designated by the Lord Chancellor, have the jurisdiction to hear:

- bankruptcy and insolvency proceedings where the paid up capital is less than £120,000;
- undefended divorce petitions, nullity and judicial separation;
- unlawful racial discrimination other than in the field of employment.

Small claims arbitration procedure in the county court

The District judge deals with administrative and pre-trial matters, and has jurisdiction to hear cases involving less than £3,000 (*small claims arbitration procedure*). Where the sum is for less than £3,000, the dispute will automatically be referred to arbitration, although in certain circumstances the case may be heard by a county court if the District judge is satisfied that:

- a difficult question of law or exceptionally complex facts are involved; or
- fraud is alleged; or
- the parties agree the dispute should be heard in the county court; or
- it is unreasonable to proceed by arbitration, for example, where one party is funded to be represented (e.g. by an insurance company), resulting in an imbalance (*Pepper* v *Healey* (1982)).

The District judge is empowered to refer any disputes (those exceeding £3,000) to arbitration if the parties agree.

The High Court of Justice

The High Court was created in 1873 and now has three administrative divisions. Normally the High Court sits in London, although it is possible for it to sit anywhere in England or Wales. The High Court judiciary comprises the Lord Chancellor (who is technically president of the Chancery Division but never sits), the Lord Chief Justice who presides over the QBD, the President of the Family Division and High Court judges.

- The **Queen's Bench Division** deals with the greatest number of cases and handles any work not allocated to one of the other divisions. The majority of its cases are actions in tort or contract. The Commercial Court is part of this division, dealing with banking and insurance matters. The QBD also includes an Admiralty Court to deal with issues of law relating to shipping.
- The **Chancery Division** is the modern successor to the old Court of Chancery. Its jurisdiction includes matters relating to the sale or partition of land, redemption or foreclosure of mortgages, trusts, administration of the estates of the dead where the value

exceeds £30,000, bankruptcy, contentious probate business (over £30,000), company law and partnerships and revenue law. The Chancery Division contains specialist courts; these are the Patents Court and the Companies Court.

- The **Family Division** deals with all matrimonial matters both first instance and on appeal, proceedings under the Children Act 1989 including wardship proceedings, legitimacy, adoption and proceedings under the Domestic Violence and Matrimonial Proceedings Act 1976 and the Human Fertilisation and Embryology Act 1990.

The Divisional Courts of the High Court of Justice

The Divisional Courts exercise appellate jurisdiction. Two, or sometimes three, judges sit to hear appeals:

- The **Queen's Bench Divisional Court** hears appeals on a point of law by way of case stated from the magistrates' courts, tribunals and the Crown Court. It exercises judicial review of the decisions made by governmental and public authorities and inferior courts and tribunals and determines applications for the writ of *habeas corpus*.

- The **Chancery Divisional Court** hears appeals from the Commissioners of Inland Revenue on income tax cases and from county courts on certain matters like bankruptcy.

- The **Family Divisional Court** hears appeals from decisions of magistrates' courts and county courts in family matters.

The Court of Appeal

There are two divisions of the Court of Appeal:

- The **Civil Division** is headed by the Master of the Rolls. It hears appeals from the county courts and High Court on matters of law or fact. It also hears appeals on questions of law from the Employment Appeals Tribunal.

- The **Criminal Division** is headed by the Lord Chief Justice. It hears appeals from the Crown Court on issues of conviction and sentencing.

Three Lord Justices of Appeal normally sit to hear an appeal. Appeals are heard on the basis of transcripts of the original trial and arguments from barristers. The Court has a heavy workload dealing with about 1,000 cases per year.

The House of Lords

The House of Lords is the final court of appeal in civil and criminal law. Appeals are heard by Lords of Appeal in Ordinary, known as 'Law Lords'. For most cases, five Lords will sit to hear the appeal. Cases are heard in relative informality, with the Lords unrobed. They hear appeals from the Court of Appeal and the Divisional Court of the Queen's Bench Division, and occasionally, in civil matters, from the High Court under the 'leapfrog' procedure. The Lords deliver their judgments as speeches. A majority decides the case. The House of Lords hears approximately 50 cases per year.

The Judicial Committee of the Privy Council

This court dates from 1833 and has the same membership as the House of Lords. It is the final court of appeal for cases from the Channel Islands, the Isle of Man, the Colonies and certain Commonwealth countries, for example, Jamaica. It also hears appeals from certain English courts and tribunals, for example, the ecclesiastical courts and the General Medical Council.

The European Court of Justice

The European Court of Justice (ECJ) is the ultimate authority on EC law. It is a court of reference. The ECJ attempts to provide uniformity and consistency in interpretation of EC law by member states. It is *not* an appellate court but a court to which, by **Article 177** of the **Treaty of Rome,** any court or tribunal of a member state may refer a question if it considers that a '*decision on that question is necessary to enable it to give judgment*'. English courts are bound by the ruling, and must apply it to the case in question (see Unit 2.3).

The European Court of Human Rights

The United Kingdom has ratified the European Convention on Human Rights, although it has not been incorporated into our law (unlike the Treaty of Rome 1957). The European Convention on Human Rights was established in an attempt to protect fundamental human rights. Article 25 of the Convention provides the individual with a right of petition to the Commission. If the application is deemed admissible, and a 'friendly settlement' is not reached between the individual and the member state, the case will be heard by the European Court of Human Rights. Decisions are not binding on the UK government. However, our law *may* be changed in order to comply with the decision (see Chapter 8).

1.2 LEGAL PERSONNEL

The legal profession in England and Wales consists of solicitors and barristers. There are, in addition, para-legals: legal executives who work in solicitors' offices, and licensed conveyancers.

1.2.1 FUNCTIONS

Solicitors may work for central or local government or in industry but most are in private practice. They:

1. advise on the law;
2. negotiate on behalf of clients;
3. prepare documents and conduct litigation in a wide variety of areas of law:

- conveyancing (purchase and sale of land),
- probate (wills and the administration of estates),
- divorce,
- personal injury,
- criminal,
- company, partnership and commercial,
- housing,
- welfare,
- immigration.

Solicitors may represent clients in magistrates' and county courts and before tribunals and in matters heard in chambers. The Qualification Regulations 1992, following the Courts and Legal Services Act 1990, provide that a solicitor may qualify to appear in higher courts in civil matters, criminal cases or both. The qualification is open to solicitors who have practised for at least three years, gaining suitable experience in advocacy and the preparation of cases for higher courts. There are written tests in evidence and procedure and a practical course.

Barristers:

- give advice,
- draft documents,
- appear in court.

Barristers cannot be approached directly by the public but must be instructed by a solicitor or appropriate professional. Each barrister is self-employed. Groups of barristers come together to form 'chambers', contributing to rent and other expenses. The chambers is run by a clerk who is not legally qualified but is an administrator who runs the office, distributes work sent by solicitors and negotiates and collects fees. The modern trend is to pay the clerk a salary but many are paid a percentage of all fees paid to the barristers.

There is no longer a rule prohibiting barristers from working from home and clerking for themselves. Over the past few years the rules of professional conduct have been relaxed but barristers are still not allowed to advertise or to take instructions directly from the client, unless the client is a professional person such as an accountant.

Barristers may also be employed in industry, commerce, the Crown Prosecution Service or government departments but such barristers have no rights of audience in court, so a barrister in private practice has to be instructed to conduct any advocacy.

Queen's Counsel (QC's) are senior advocates who command higher fees and do not take pupils. High Court judges are generally appointed from among QCs. Barristers and solicitors can apply to the Lord Chancellor to be appointed as a QC: the first solicitor QCs were appointed in 1997.

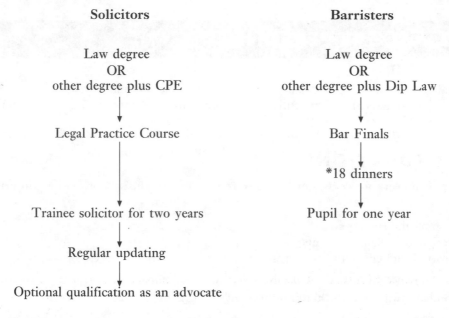

* Each Barrister belongs to an Inn. A traditional part of qualifying as a barrister has been a requirement to eat a number of dinners at the Inn. The Inns of Court have proposed that this requirement be replaced by attendance at educational functions to be organised by the Inns.

Table 1.1 A summary of the routes to qualification

1.2.2 EARNINGS

Solicitors are paid during their two years' training. They then become assistant solicitors and may expect to earn anything from about £15,000 upwards, depending on the job they do, the area of the country and the size of the firm. Partners take a share of profits and generally earn more than assistants.

Some chambers now pay their pupils, but barristers generally earn only the fees they are paid. This means that new barristers struggle financially as they build a practice but successful barristers can be very high earners.

Both branches of the profession complain of low rates of pay for legal aid work.

1.2.3 CONTROL AND DISCIPLINE

The **Law Society** is responsible for control and discipline of solicitors. Each solicitor has to:

• have a practising certificate, renewed annually by the Law Society on payment of a fee;

• be insured against negligence claims through the policy held by the Law Society.

Disciplinary matters are dealt with by the **Solicitors Disciplinary Tribunal**. For example:

- the obligation to keep accounts;
- the rules governing advertising;
- rules preventing formation of multi-disciplinary partnerships.

The Disciplinary Tribunal is independent of the Law Society. It can fine up to £5,000, reprimand, suspend from practice or strike a solicitor off the roll.

Complaints about delay, incompetence or dishonesty are handled by the **Office for the Supervision of Solicitors** (OSS) (which replaced the Solicitors Complaints Bureau), run by the Law Society. The OSS will attempt conciliation between the parties but appoints an investigation officer if conciliation fails. It can order return or waiver of fees, payment of compensation, or that errors be put right free of charge.

The **Bar Council** is responsible for professional discipline of barristers, covering matters such as:

- honesty;
- duty to the client;
- duty to the court.

Complaints against barristers are handled by the **Professional Conduct Committee** which may resolve the matter informally or pass it on to the **Disciplinary Committee**. The Disciplinary Committee can fine, admonish, suspend or disbar.

The **Legal Services Ombudsman**, appointed by the Lord Chancellor but not a lawyer, oversees the way the Law Society and the Bar deal with complaints and issues an annual report.

The **Lord Chancellor's Advisory Committee on Legal Education and Conduct** reviews the rules of professional conduct for both branches of the profession.

If a solicitor or barrister has been negligent, the client's only recourse is to sue through the courts because negligence is not regarded as a disciplinary matter. The **Courts and Legal Services Act 1990** provides that there cannot be a negligence action against a person in respect of something said or done whilst acting as an advocate. It is possible, however, to sue barristers or solicitors for negligent paperwork.

For example, in *Saif Ali* v *Sydney Mitchell & Co* (1977) the plaintiff had been wrongly advised that he had no claim in respect of an injury sustained in a road accident. By the time he found out the advice was wrong he was 'out of time' (see Unit 4.6) and unable to sue the person who had caused his injury. He therefore sued the firm of solicitors who had advised him and they joined to the action the barrister who had advised them. It was held that whilst a barrister could not be sued in respect of negligent advocacy, it was possible to sue a barrister for negligent advice. The distinction lies in the fact that in giving written advice a barrister has the opportunity to reflect and to research points of law.

1.2.4 REFORM

The legal profession has been the subject of much criticism, review and change over the past 20 years.

The **Royal Commission on Legal Services** (the Benson Commission) reported in 1979. Its major conclusions were that the legal profession generally provided a good service but had an 'indifferent' public image. Benson was against **fusion** of the professions (that is, having one legal profession instead of two: barristers and solicitors). The fusion argument has been running for years and continues.

The arguments against fusion are:

- The present high quality of advocacy would be threatened.
- The pool of specialist barristers would be lost.
- Specialists would cease to be available on the cab-rank principle.
- Two heads are better than one.

The arguments in favour of fusion are:

- Economy: it is cheaper to pay one lawyer than to pay two.
- Less danger of confusion and delay if one person deals with the case.
- No obligation for lawyers to choose a specialisation at the beginning of their career.
- There would be a wider pool from which to choose judges.

Over the years the Bar has been steadily against fusion whilst the Law Society has taken a softer line, advocating some changes whilst maintaining support for two separate professions. The **Law Society Discussion Paper** in 1986 recommended:

- all lawyers would train in the same way, essentially as solicitors are trained;
- lawyers could then choose to take a specialist qualification;
- rights of audience in higher courts would be restricted to specialists;
- access to specialists would usually be through a lawyer;
- specialists in one firm would be available for consultation by another firm.

The Bar responded that:

- lawyers would be unwilling to take the financial risk of specialising;
- the proposals would effectively put an end to an independent Bar.

The **Marre Committee** reported in 1988, making recommendations on legal aid, legal education and the structure of the profession.

Threads from all these sources were drawn together and can be identified in the provisions of the Courts and Legal Services Act 1990: advocacy rights for solicitors, multi-disciplinary practices, wider access to the Bar, for example.

1.3 JUDGES

1.3.1 FUNCTION

The judge's primary duty is to ensure a fair trial of the matter. The English system has traditionally been **adversarial**, which means the judge acts as a referee, making sure that the rules of evidence and procedure are followed and deciding who wins. In an **inquisitorial** system, common in European courts and in some tribunals, the judicial role is much more active and involves asking questions to determine the truth of the matter, rather than leaving it to the parties to formulate their arguments.

The implementation of Lord Woolf's proposals (see Unit 1.5) will make English judges more active in determining the course of civil cases.

Judges always decide issues of law. If there is a jury, the judge directs them as to the law and they determine issues of fact. If there is no jury, the judge decides issues of fact.

1.3.2 APPOINTMENT

Historically, most judges were appointed from among barristers. The Courts and Legal Services Act 1990 provided for solicitors and academic lawyers to be appointed as High Court judges.

All appointments are very much influenced by the Lord Chancellor's Department, even if they are not, strictly, made on his advice. The rules about appointment are as follows:

❶ Assistant Recorders and Recorders	<ul><li>barristers or solicitors for ten years</li><li>usually at least 38 years' old</li><li>part-time</li><li>sit in Crown Court</li></ul>

		• appointed by the Crown on recommendation of Lord Chancellor
		• appointments renewable every three years
		• retire at 70
❷	District judges	• barristers or solicitors for seven years
		• administer county courts, hear small claims and pre-trial matters
		• appointed by the Crown on recommendation of Lord Chancellor
		• retire at 70
❸	Circuit judges	• advocates for ten years, or district judge for three years
		• sit in county courts and Crown Court
		• appointed by the Crown on recommendation of Lord Chancellor
		• retire at 70
❹	High Court judges 'puisne judges'	• advocates for ten years
		• knighted on appointment (Sir Christopher French, Dame Ann Ebsworth)
		• appointed by the Crown on recommendation of Lord Chancellor
		• sit in High Court, Crown Court, Divisional Courts and Court of Appeal (Criminal Division)
		• retire at 70
❺	Lords Justices of Appeal	• advocates for fifteen years, usually previously High Court judges
		• appointed by the Crown on recommendation of Prime Minister
		• sit in Court of Appeal
		• retire at 70
❻	Lords of Appeal in Ordinary	• advocates for fifteen years,
		• usually previously Lords Justices of Appeal
		• created Life Peers on appointment (Lord Nolan)
		• appointed by the Crown on recommendation of Prime Minister
		• sit in Judicial Committee of the House of Lords and Judicial Committee of the Privy Council
		• retire at 70

The Lord Chancellor is usually a politician. He or she is appointed and dismissed by the Prime Minister and loses office if the government loses office. The Lord Chancellor is head of the Judiciary.

The Lord Chief Justice presides over the Court of Appeal (Criminal Division) and is head of the Queen's Bench Division. The Chancery Division is headed nominally by the Lord Chancellor, but there is a Vice-Chancellor who effectively does the job. The Family Division is headed by a President.

The Master of the Rolls is head of the Court of Appeal (Civil Division) and is nominal head of the solicitors' profession.

Other important figures in the legal system are the Director of Public Prosecutions, who heads the Crown Prosecution Service, and the Attorney-General who acts as the government's legal advisor. The Attorney-General is a politician.

There are very few women judges and very few judges from ethnic minorities.

1.3.3 TRAINING

Judges are trained by the Judicial Studies Board. They receive some initial training, especially in sentencing, and observe experienced judges working. Updating courses are provided.

1.3.4 DISMISSAL

Senior judges enjoy great security of tenure. The object of this is to be sure that they are not under political pressure when they make their decisions. A judge of High Court rank or above can be dismissed only if both Houses of Parliament request the Crown to remove him or her. This procedure dates back to the Act of Settlement 1701 and has been used only once, in 1830.

Circuit judges can be removed by the Lord Chancellor for misbehaviour or incapacity. A criminal conviction, sexual impropriety or racist or sexist behaviour would be considered misbehaviour.

There appears to be little control over the quality of judges' work. Criticism by the Court of Appeal is the only sanction for poor quality work which falls short of evidence of inability or incapacity.

1.3.5 PROTECTION OF JUDGES

Judges enjoy **absolute privilege** for anything they say in their judicial capacity and cannot, therefore, be sued in libel or slander. In addition, judges have power to fine or imprison under the law of **contempt of court**. It is contempt to:

- publish material which may be prejudicial to a fair criminal trial or fair civil proceedings;

- scandalise the court;

- disrupt proceedings.

The law is now largely contained in the Contempt of Court Act 1981 and the County Court (Penalties for Contempt) Act 1983.

1.3.6 JUDGES AND POLITICS

In doing their work, judges must be seen to be without political bias. They cannot, therefore, taken an active part in politics. Those who sit in the House of Lords take part in debate only if the issues are legal rather than political.

The Lord Chancellor is an exception to this rule. He is a member of the Cabinet and head of the Lord Chancellor's Department. He is speaker of the House of Lords. He is responsible for the appointment of magistrates and judges and can dismiss junior judges. He may sit as a member of the Judicial Committee of the House of Lords.

Montesquieu advocated keeping the three functions of government — legislative, executive and judicial — in separate hands so that they could balance each other and prevent too much power accruing in one place. The Lord Chancellor's position can be criticised because he has functions in each of these three areas. It has been suggested that the office of Lord Chancellor should be abolished and replaced with a Minister of Justice who would also take on those functions of the Home Secretary which relate to the legal system. A compromise position has been reached by appointing a junior minister who sits in the House of Commons and deals with questions relating to the Lord Chancellor's Department.

As all judicial appointments are made by the Lord Chancellor, it may be asked how free from political bias those appointments can be. Further, Professor Griffith argues in his book, *Politics of the Judiciary*, that judges have a vested interest in the status quo and are therefore inherently conservative. He argues they therefore have problems with socialist legislation, such as giving rights to trade unionists, because it goes against their ideology and culture. It is true that most judges are from a public school/Oxbridge background and that, combined with the traditions of the Bar from which they are almost all drawn, tends to make them upper-middle class by the time they become judges.

The process of judicial review (see Unit 1.8), by which High Court judges review decisions made by government to ensure that the correct procedures have been followed, brings judges into conflict with politicians and lays them open to charges of political bias.

1.4 LAYPERSONS IN THE ENGLISH LEGAL SYSTEM

A layperson is a person involved in the administration of justice who has no formal legal qualifications. A variety of laypersons are used in the administration of criminal and civil law. These are lay magistrates, juries, arbitrators, conciliation officers, lay assessors and lay members of a tribunal panel.

1.4.1 THE MAGISTRACY

Lay and stipendiary magistrates

The use of magistrates in the English legal system dates back to the Justices of the Peace Act 1361. Today two types of magistrates are used in the English legal system. These are **lay** and **stipendiary** magistrates. Lay magistrates are unqualified in law. Stipendiary magistrates are qualified as either a solicitor or barrister (of at least seven years' standing). Lay magistrates are part-time and unpaid. Stipendiary magistrates are full-time and paid. At least two lay magistrates must sit together to hear a case (normally they sit in benches of three). Stipendiary magistrates sit alone. The majority of our magistrates are laypersons. There are approximately 30,000. However, there are only approximately 100 stipendiaries hearing cases in larger cities.

Magistrates are assisted by a legally-qualified clerk. The clerk is a solicitor or barrister of at least five years' standing. The clerk is the administrator of the court. The clerk calls cases, reads the charge, takes the plea, determines the defendant's eligibility for criminal legal aid, liaises with the lawyers and generally keeps the court running smoothly. In addition to these administrative functions, the clerk advises lay magistrates on points of law and sentencing powers. However, the clerk must not influence the magistrates' verdict. The independence of Justices' Clerks is guaranteed by the Police and Magistrates' Courts Act 1994. They are not subject to directions from anyone.

Role of the magistracy

Magistrates preside over the magistrates' courts. The functions of the magistrates' court are diverse. The magistrates' court has both criminal and civil jurisdiction (see Unit 1.1).

Appointment and removal of lay magistrates

The Justices of the Peace Act 1979 as amended by the Police and Magistrates' Courts Act 1994 sets outs the procedure for appointment. The Lord Chancellor officially appoints lay magistrates in the name of the Crown. He generally accepts recommendations from the Local Advisory Committees. Members of the Local Advisory Committees are also appointed by the Lord Chancellor. They are expected to have good local knowledge and to represent a balance of political opinion. Their identity used to be kept secret, but since 1993, in order to have a more open procedure, names are available to the public. Members of the public may be nominated (e.g. by existing magistrates, voluntary groups or trade unions) or apply by filling in an application form, available from the court. The use of application forms is currently being encouraged in order to increase the diversity of people on the bench. Appointments are made on the basis of both individual qualities and any requirements needed to balance the existing bench. Political affiliations are taken into account, in the quest for a balanced bench. The qualities expressly sought are:

- to be of good character;
- to have integrity;
- to have an understanding of the role;
- to be an 'upstanding member of the community';
- to be local (the magistrate must live within a 15 mile radius of the court he or she is to serve).

Those disqualified include:

- undischarged bankrupts;
- those with serious criminal convictions;
- members of the armed forces;
- police, traffic wardens and others involved in the administration of law;
- those with serious infirmity.

Magistrates retire at 70. Occasionally they may be compulsorily retired before this age for reasons of age, infirmity, that they cannot do the job, or neglect to do so. Magistrates may be removed from office by the Lord Chancellor for misbehaviour (e.g. commission of a serious criminal offence) or because they have acted in a way inconsistent with the office (e.g. sexual harassment, causing offence on racial grounds etc).

Training of lay magistrates

Lay magistrates are not expected to be experts in law. Upon appointment, magistrates attend an initial eight hour training course, followed by a further eight hours later in the year. During the training, the new appointees judge simulated cases, visit local penal institutions and observe other magistrates at work. The Justices' Clerk assists in this training. The aim of the training is to familiarise them with court procedure, to learn the technique of chairing, and to understand the theory and practice of sentencing. Training is continuous. Lay magistrates are required to attend a 12 hour training course every three years after appointment. Lay magistrates involved in the youth or domestic court receive additional training.

1.4.2 THE JURY

Role of the jury

A jury is a group of between 7–12 lay persons who decide issues of fact. Juries are used in both criminal and civil cases.

In the *Crown Court* a jury comprising 12 jurors determines guilt or innocence based on the facts. Since only approximately 5% of criminal trials involve indictable offences, and many defendants plead guilty, the jury is used in around 1% of all criminal cases. However, it is used in the most serious trials. Although it is desirable that a jury reach a unanimous verdict, the Criminal Justice Act 1967 allows the judge to accept a majority verdict (11:1 or 10:2) after at least two hours of deliberations.

Use of a civil jury, comprising 8 laypersons in the *county court* and 12 persons in the *High Court* (Queen's Bench Division), has gradually declined since the middle of the nineteenth century. Now less than 1% of civil cases are tried by a jury. The role of the jury is to determine liability and, more controversially, award damages if it finds the defendant liable. Today the Supreme Court Act 1981 gives a qualified right to jury trial of civil cases in four types of cases:

- libel and slander (defamation);
- malicious prosecution;
- false imprisonment; and
- fraud.

A jury will be used in these cases unless, for example, the court decides that there will be prolonged examination of complicated documents or accounts. The right has been exercised most frequently in relation to defamation, although the Defamation Act 1996 introduces a new summary disposal procedure (see Unit 7.7) heard and determined without a jury. In all other cases the right to a jury is at the discretion of the court.

A jury may also be used in the *coroners' court*. The coroner has jurisdiction to inquire into violent or unnatural deaths, sudden deaths where the cause is unknown, and deaths in prison. This is essentially a question of fact. Under the Coroners Act 1981 the coroner has a discretion to summon a jury to the inquest in most cases. The jury consists of between 7 and 11 persons.

Selection of jurors

Jurors are chosen at random from the electoral roll by a court officer. Any person summoned is legally required to attend as specified in the notice, unless he or she does not qualify or is excused. The Juries Act 1974, as amended, sets out the criteria for qualification (see Table 1.2).

Qualification	A juror must be aged between 18 and 70; A juror must have been resident in the UK for 5 or more years since the age of 13; A juror must be registered to vote.
Disqualification	Those who have been sentenced to five or more years' imprisonment are disqualified for life; Those who have been sentenced to three or more months' imprisonment or probation are disqualified for 10 years.
Ineligibility	Any person who is or has been involved in the administration of justice (e.g. lawyers, judges, police officers, traffic wardens etc); Any person diagnosed as suffering from a mental disorder; Members of the clergy.
Excusal as of right	Members of Parliament, Members of the European Parliament and Peers; The armed forces; Doctors, vets, nurses and midwives; Any person who has served as a juror in the past two years; Any person who is aged between 65 and 70.
Discretionary excusal	Any person may be excused at the discretion of the court officer (e.g. for reasons of pregnancy, pre-paid holidays, examinations, illness etc).

Table 1.2 Criteria for jury qualification

Jury vetting

A jury is supposed to be a random selection of people. Before a jury is sworn in, the defence and prosecution have a right to challenge any potential jurors for cause. This may not be because of race, religion, occupation or politics (*R* v *Ford* (1989)). Counsel should not ask potential jurors any questions. Any challenge for cause is tried as a preliminary matter by the trial judge. The Criminal Justice Act 1988 removed the defence's right to peremptory challenge (challenge without cause). This right was abolished for fear that it was being abused by the defence in order to secure as sympathetic jury as possible in terms of age, gender, race and general appearance.

In general, jury vetting (checking the background of potential jurors) is not allowed except in only two special cases under guidelines issued in 1988: those involving terrorism and national security. In these cases, it is felt that a potential juror's political beliefs might be so biased as to interfere with:

- the fair assessment of the facts,
- to exert undue pressure on fellow jurors, or
- reveal evidence given *in camera* (not in open court).

Such vetting must be authorised by the Attorney-General, acting on advice from the Director of Public Prosecutions. For a juror to be excluded, the vetting must reveal a very strong reason.

1.4.3 OTHER LAY PARTICIPATION IN THE ENGLISH LEGAL SYSTEM

In the administration of the civil justice system laypersons are used in a range of roles. What distinguishes these laypersons from magistrates and jurors, is that, although they are not legally qualified, they are usually experts within their field.

- In the formal court system, lay assessors and scientific advisors may be used. The Supreme Court Act 1981 empowers a judge to appoint people with special expertise in a particular area to sit with them in cases involving scientific or technical evidence. Their role is to assist the judge in interpreting the evidence and help him or her form a judgment, although the judge still makes the final decision.

- Laypersons are also used in tribunals (see Unit 1.6). Specific issues are dealt with by persons with an intimate knowledge and experience of the problems involved. The Tribunals and Inquiries Act 1971 requires the chair to be legally qualified. However, he or she is normally assisted by laypersons.

- Commercial arbitration may be conducted by a layperson. The arbitrator may have expertise in the relevant field. Similarly, conciliation officers supplied by ACAS may not be legally qualified. The Family Law Act 1996 promotes mediation as a means of settling disputes arising in divorce proceedings. This may be conducted by specially trained personnel, but not necessarily legally trained.

1.4.4 ISSUES IN EVALUATION

There are a great number of issues to consider in evaluating the contribution of laypersons to the administration of criminal and civil justice. It is always essential to support criticism with evidence. It is recommended that you use topical evidence collected during your course. If you conclude that disadvantages outweigh advantages, and therefore recommend that juries and/or lay magistrates should be abolished, you must identify and justify a more suitable alternative.

Use of laypersons: common factors

- They have the understanding of the 'ordinary' person.
- Criminal law often involves the judgment of the reasonable person.
- Lack of legal knowledge requires legal language to be moderated making justice more accessible.
- Laypersons tend to be involved in fact-finding which requires common sense rather than legal knowledge.
- Use of laypersons demonstrates that people are willing to stand in judgment of each other and partake in society's condemnation of offenders.
- Justice is seen to be done.

Juries

- Juries are randomly selected but there is no intelligence testing. Use of jury vetting and discretionary excusals may affect the supposed random nature of a jury. There is no requirement for a racially balanced jury (*R* v *Ford* (1989)) although the **Runciman Commission** (1993) recommended that there should be at least three jurors representing the ethnic minorities where the accused is from an ethnic minority.

- Trial by jury gives ordinary members of the public an opportunity to contribute to the criminal justice system, and to a lesser extent, the civil justice system. Ordinary people are given a chance to voice an opinion on the law but juries can make a decision which is unjustifiable in law reaching a 'perverse' verdict (*R* v *Ponting* (1985) or *R* v *Kronlind and others* (1996)). Jurors may make decisions based on their emotions rather than being objective. Ordinary people may be over-awed by the formality of the court room and legal procedure. Members of a jury may be influenced by a particularly good barrister, the judge *(R* v *Whybrow & Saunders* (1994)) or by media reports. Jurors may be incompetent at understanding some complex evidence, e.g. in fraud trials (*Roskill Committee recommendations*, 1986). Jurors may not be sufficiently experienced to decide upon a sum of damages when performing their civil function (*Sutcliffe* v *Pressdram Ltd* (1991); *John* v *Mirror Group Newspapers Ltd* (1996)).

- Twelve persons reaching a verdict encourages impartiality and anonymity. No one person can be blamed for a decision but jury decision-making is conducted in private so it is difficult to evaluate the process (s. 8 Contempt of Court Act 1981), so research into the decision-making process is difficult (see use of shadow/simulated juries; *Baldwin & McConville's research*, 1976).

Magistrates

- Magistrates are respected in the community they serve but criteria for appointment are vague. The typical magistrate does not necessarily represent the community in terms of age, race and social class. This has led to allegations of magistrates being 'prosecution-minded', i.e., relying on police evidence unfairly (the Runciman Commission Report 1995 found that the chances of acquittal in the magistrates' court is 30% compared with 57% in the Crown Court). Lay magistrates may be unable to set aside their individual biases.

- Use of lay magistrates is a cheap form of justice. They receive training and are assisted by a legally-trained clerk on any points of law but the training is short and, it could be argued, inadequate for the diversity of work they are expected to perform. Their lack of legal knowledge may result in them relying on their clerk too much. Is this cheap form of justice 'amateur justice'?

1.5   CIVIL AND CRIMINAL PROCEDURE

1.5.1 CIVIL PROCEDURE

Most civil disputes are settled before they come to court.

Outline of civil procedure

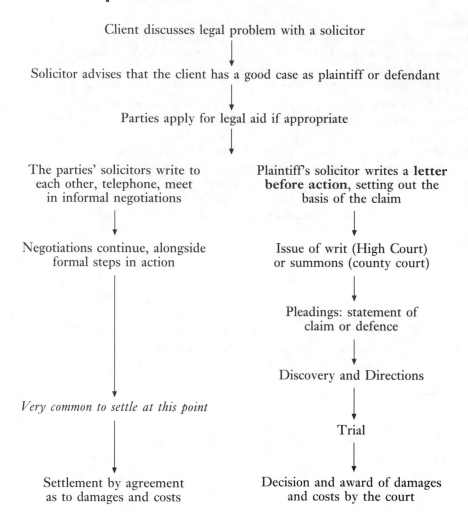

Client discusses legal problem with a solicitor

↓

Solicitor advises that the client has a good case as plaintiff or defendant

↓

Parties apply for legal aid if appropriate

↓

The parties' solicitors write to each other, telephone, meet in informal negotiations | Plaintiff's solicitor writes a **letter before action**, setting out the basis of the claim

Negotiations continue, alongside formal steps in action | Issue of writ (High Court) or summons (county court)

Pleadings: statement of claim or defence

Discovery and Directions

Very common to settle at this point

Trial

Settlement by agreement as to damages and costs | Decision and award of damages and costs by the court

Table 1.3 Civil procedure

Pleadings set out the issues between the parties in a formal way. Any point that is not included in the pleadings cannot be raised at the trial and, for that reason, pleadings are often written by a barrister.

Discovery is the process by which each side tells the other what relevant documents it has in its possession. Some of these will be **privileged**, so the other side has no right to see them, but most will be available for inspection by the other side and it is usual to ask for photocopies of the documents one wishes to inspect.

Directions are instructions to the parties from the court about how the matter will be tried and the steps each party has to take before the trial.

This procedure is criticised for being:

❶ Slow: there are time limits for each step in the formal process but they are routinely ignored or the parties voluntarily allow each other more time.

❷ Complex: the rules of procedure are contained in the **Rules of the Supreme Court** and the **County Court Rules**. Both sets of rules are long and complex and much of the art of litigation lies in knowing these rules thoroughly and using them to the advantage of one's client — rather than to allow the issues to be dealt with promptly.

❸ Expensive: this follows from the complexity and lack of speed.

Reform of civil procedure

The **Civil Justice Review** was conducted by the Lord Chancellor's Department. Its terms of reference were: '*to improve the machinery of civil justice in England and Wales by means of reforms in jurisdiction, procedure and court administration and in particular to reduce delay, cost and complexity*'. It reported in June 1988 and recommended, among other things:

- one set of court rules, instead of separate rules for the High Court and county courts;
- the end to financial limits on county court jurisdiction;
- all personal injury cases to begin in the county court;
- the High Court should deal with issues of public law and other specialist issues and cases of 'importance, complexity and substance';
- advice agencies should provide duty representatives at courts, funded by legal aid;
- small claims litigants should be allowed to be represented by lay advisers;
- court administrators should keep litigants to time limits in pre-trial matters, rather than it being left to one party to complain that the other is guilty of delay;
- more pre-trial disclosure of evidence;
- the small claims limit should be raised to £1,000 (from the current limit of £500);
- use of contingency fees should be considered.

Some items on this list were implemented by the Courts and Legal Services Act 1990:

- the small claims limit was raised to £3,000 rather than £1,000;
- conditional fee agreements were allowed;
- the Lord Chancellor was given power to order that in consumer, housing and small claims actions in the county court there should be no restriction on who could exercise a right of audience — so advice workers would be able to represent people.

The system was again reviewed by a committee led by Lord Woolf, which reported in July 1996. Lord Woolf's solution to the continuing problems of cost, delay and complexity was to introduce judicial management of cases. Although solicitors would still be responsible for running their clients' cases, the court would take ultimate control and lay down the timetable to be followed.

As at present, claims for below £3,000 would be dealt with through the *small claims procedure* (also known as arbitration in the county court). Claims below £10,000 would be heard under the *fast track procedure*. There would be a period of between 20 and 30 weeks between the issue of the summons and the trial. There would be no expert oral evidence and limited use of discovery and lay witnesses in a trial heard by a District judge and lasting no more than half a day. Costs would be limited: Lord Woolf suggested a figure of £2,500.

The *multi track procedure* would be used for cases which were more complex or of public importance or for over £10,000. They would be heard by a Circuit judge or a High Court judge.

Under the Civil Procedure Act 1997 a Civil Court Rule Committee has been set up to make a single set of rules for the High and county courts and there is also an advisory body on civil procedure, the Civil Justice Council. The Labour government that came to power in May 1997 ordered a brief review of Lord Woolf's proposals and, following a report by Professor Middleton, accepted them. As implementation proceeds, the culture of the courts is changing with judges taking a more active role and expecting parties to make use of ADR whenever the law is clear.

1.5.2 CRIMINAL PROCEDURE

The major premise of English criminal law is that the defendant is innocent until proven guilty. Thus, it is for the prosecution to prove its case **beyond reasonable doubt**. In considering police powers and court procedure, there is a balance to be struck between the right of the defendant to be regarded as innocent until proved guilty and the interests of society in convicting those guilty of offences. The Police and Criminal Evidence Act 1984 (PACE) has been criticised for giving the police extensive powers which are open to abuse: alternatively, it has been said that PACE defines what the police may do, so making identification and control of abuse easier. The provisions of the Criminal Justice and Public Order Act 1994, allowing inferences to be drawn from silence, and the Criminal Procedure and Investigations Act 1996, requiring the defendant to give notice of his or her defence, have been criticised as changing the traditional bias in favour of the defendant in criminal cases to a bias in favour of the prosecution.

The powers of the police during investigations are discussed in Chapter 8. This Unit deals with procedure in the courts.

Classification of offences

Summary offences are triable in a magistrates' court; for example, drunk and disorderly, careless driving, assaulting a police officer. **Indictable offences** are the most serious and must be tried at a Crown Court. Many offences are **hybrid offences**, which may be tried either by a magistrates' court or a Crown Court: the magistrates first take the defendant's plea. If the defendant pleads not guilty he or she has the choice between trial by magistrates or trial by a jury. If the plea is guilty, the magistrates choose whether they can sentence the defendant or whether the Crown Court must do so.

Procedure in magistrates' courts

97% of all criminal charges are dealt with entirely by magistrates. There are no juries in magistrates' courts. All questions of guilt or innocence are decided by either lay magistrates or a stipendiary magistrate. Lay magistrates sit with a legally-qualified clerk, who advises on questions of law, procedure and sentencing.

If a case is to be tried summarily, the Criminal Procedure and Investigations Act 1996 requires the prosecution to disclose to the defence any prosecution material which 'might undermine the case for the prosecution'.

The clerk to the magistrates reads out the charge. The clerk asks the defendant whether he or she pleads guilty or not guilty. The magistrates then decide where the defendant will be tried: all guilty pleas are dealt with by magistrates unless the case is too serious.

If the plea is guilty, the prosecutor gives the facts of the offence and antecedents.

Antecedents concern the whole of the defendant's life: past convictions, present domestic circumstances, work record. The defence makes a plea in mitigation. **Mitigation** means anything that explains why the defendant committed the offence and the circumstances surrounding the offence. The magistrates then pass sentence.

If the plea is not guilty and there is a right to elect trial by jury, the option is put to the defendant.

If the defendant is to be tried by the magistrates, the prosecutor gives a summary of the evidence and calls and examines prosecution witnesses, who may be cross-examined by the defence. The defence may then submit that there is no case to answer or call defence witnesses and make a speech.

If the defence makes a speech both before and after the defence evidence *or* a point of law is raised, the prosecution has a right of reply. The magistrates then decide on matters of fact and law, taking advice from the clerk on the law.

If the defendant is found guilty, the prosecution then give evidence of antecedents, the defence may make a plea in mitigation and the clerk advises the magistrates on what sentences are available. The magistrates decide on sentence.

If the defendant is to be tried by the Crown Court, magistrates hold **committal proceedings** to decide whether there is a *prima facie* case against the defendant. The prosecution has to establish that there is enough evidence against the defendant for there to be a case to answer. The Criminal Procedure and Investigations Act 1996 abolished oral committals, so committal now consists of the magistrates reading the prosecution witnesses' statements. If the defendant is represented, committal may be by consent and the magistrates do not then have to read the statements.

Procedure in the Crown Court

The Criminal Procedure and Investigations Act 1996 requires the defendant to give a **defence statement** to the court and the prosecutor, setting out the nature of the defence and the points on which the defendant takes issue with the prosecution. The prosecutor then has to disclose to the defendant any prosecution material not previously disclosed which might be reasonably expected to assist the defence. If the defendant fails to comply with the disclosure rules the jury may draw 'such inferences as appear proper in deciding whether the accused is guilty of the offence concerned'.

A **preparatory hearing** takes place before a judge sitting alone. The judge gives directions on the timetable to be followed in preparing the case for trial. Trial in the Crown Court is conducted by a Recorder, a Circuit judge or a High Court judge, depending upon the complexity and severity of the case, plus a jury. The judge is responsible for conducting the trial in accordance with the rules of evidence and procedure and for deciding any issues of law that arise; the jury decides issues of fact.

The clerk of the court reads out the indictment, which may consist of more than one 'count'. The defendant pleads guilty or not guilty. If the plea is guilty the prosecution gives a summary of the evidence and evidence of antecedents. The defence then makes a plea in mitigation and the judge passes sentence.

If the plea is not guilty a jury is sworn in. The prosecution open by summarising their case and outlining the matters it is intended to prove. Prosecution witnesses are then called and examined. The defence may cross-examine the prosecution witnesses. Defence witnesses are called, examined and cross-examined. The defendant may give evidence and be cross-examined, or may choose not to give evidence (though inferences may be drawn from such a refusal, following the Criminal Justice and Public Order Act 1994).

Each side makes a final speech. The judge sums up, summarising the evidence for both sides and telling the jury what the relevant legal issues are. The judge then asks the jury to reach a verdict on which they are all agreed and the jury retires to consider its verdict in private. If the jury has deliberated for at least two hours and cannot agree on a verdict, they may return a majority verdict, provided at least ten of them are agreed.

1.6 DISPUTE RESOLUTION

The formality, cost and delay associated with the formal court system have led to a range of other methods being used for solving disputes.

1.6.1 TRIBUNALS

There have been special courts for particular purposes for centuries, e.g. courts martial. Towards the end of the nineteenth century, as more regulation of activities was introduced through a movement away from the laissez faire philosophy, tribunals were created to hear appeals, e.g. Railway and Canal Commission (1888). This trend continued modestly until an explosion of social legislation after the Second World War caused many more tribunals to be created.

Tribunals may be used instead of courts whenever there are large numbers of disputes to be settled. *The jurisdiction of a tribunal is laid down by the statute that creates it.* That is to say, individuals cannot choose whether to use a tribunal — if Parliament has created one to deal with the type of dispute in which a person is involved, then the person must use the tribunal.

A tribunal consists of a legally-qualified Chair and two other members who are experts in the subject-matter of the tribunal. The law on tribunals is now contained in the Tribunals and Inquiries Act 1992 (which succeeded the Acts of 1958 and 1971).

There are three types of tribunal:

❶ those dealing with disputes involving a government department, e.g. social security appeals, rating valuation appeals, general and special commissioners of income tax;

❷ those dealing with disputes between individuals, e.g. rent tribunals, industrial tribunals;

❸ domestic tribunals, which enforce professional discipline, e.g. Solicitors' Disciplinary Tribunal, General Medical Council.

The **Franks Committee** (the Committee on Administrative Tribunals and Enquiries) reported in 1957. Its recommendations, and the practices that have flowed from those recommendations, are as follows:

❶ All tribunals should display the characteristics of **openness, fairness and impartiality**.

2 There should be a **Council on Tribunals**, appointed by the Lord Chancellor. This is a part-time, advisory body which keeps tribunals under review and must be consulted before procedural rules for any tribunal are made. The Council publishes an annual report.

3 That tribunal members should not be appointed by ministers as this puts their impartiality in doubt. Tribunal Chairs have to be selected by the appropriate minister from a panel selected by the Lord Chancellor. Other members are chosen by the minister, but no tribunal member may be dismissed except by the Lord Chancellor.

4 That tribunals should **give reasons** for their decisions. This is essential if a party wishes to appeal.

5 That **legal representation should be allowed** before all tribunals. Legal aid is not available for tribunals generally, so parties have to represent themselves or pay for their lawyer themselves. Under the Green Form Scheme (see Unit 1.7), up to two hours worth of advice may be obtained from a lawyer and this can be used to get help in preparing a case for a tribunal.

The Lord Chancellor's Department commissioned a report by Genn and Genn on 'The Effectiveness of Representation at Tribunals'. It was published in 1988.

The Franks Committee regarded representation at tribunals as unnecessary because they were informal, accessible and dealt with simple issues. The report found that the success rate was greater for represented appellants. Unrepresented appellants often had an imperfect understanding of the rules and powers of the tribunal, lacked advocacy skills and were uncomfortable with tribunal procedures. The subject matter was sometimes legally complex.

The tribunals studied varied in their style: the Immigration Adjudicators had a formal, adversarial style; the Social Security Appeal Tribunal and Industrial Tribunal tended towards the inquisitorial style and the Mental Health Review Tribunal was inquisitorial. Of the last, Genn and Genn say: '*They are inclined to be more concerned to do whatever is best for the patient (as they see it) than to ensure that decisions are made strictly in accordance with law. Tribunal members view the hearing as essentially inquisitorial and many members resent attempts by patients' representatives to conduct cases in an adversarial fashion.*'

The report concluded that it would be desirable to increase representation but noted that there were several different ways of achieving this: an increase in legal aid funding, an increase in funding for lay agencies or an increase in funding for law centres.

The Legal Aid Act 1988 enables the Lord Chancellor to contract work out, so lay representation through legal aid funding is a possibility. Lay representation has been criticised as being 'second rate' but it should be noted that the word 'lay' here means 'not a lawyer' and the lay representative at a tribunal will often be an expert in the work of the particular tribunal, e.g. accountants, valuers, trade union officials, social workers, members of the United Kingdom Immigrants Advisory Service.

A law centre might be well placed to provide representation since an appellant's problems are often multi-faceted, not clear cut and involving only one area of law.

6 Generally, tribunal hearings should be **open to the public**, but some tribunals sit in private to protect the privacy of applicants, e.g. tax commissioners, mental health review tribunals.

Appeals

There may be a right of appeal to another tribunal and/or the ordinary courts, for example:

- Industrial Tribunal *to* Employment Appeal Tribunal *to* Court of Appeal *to* House of Lords
- Domestic Tribunals *to* Judicial Committee of the Privy Council

Rights of appeal are governed by the Tribunals and Inquiries Act 1992 and the particular statute that created each tribunal. However, *all* tribunals are subject to supervision by the Queen's Bench Division of the High Court by way of judicial review (see Unit 1.8), which considers the way the decision was reached, rather than the issues of law or fact involved.

The advantages of tribunals are:

❶ they can deal with a lot of small disputes more efficiently than a court;

❷ the less formal procedure may make legal representation unnecessary and so reduce costs;

❸ costs are not generally awarded against a losing party;

❹ the specialist tribunal members provide technical expertise so that complex issues can be handled quickly and efficiently;

❺ precedent is not rigidly adhered to, so there can be more emphasis on working justice in the particular case.

The disadvantages are:

❶ there is less publicity of tribunal decisions and thus less public confidence;

❷ the absence of legal aid means legal representation may not be available, even if·the points under discussion are complex;

❸ the rights of appeal may be limited;

❹ decisions are less predictable than those of courts, because of the different attitude to precedent.

1.6.2 ALTERNATIVE DISPUTE RESOLUTION

ADR is a term that covers a range of alternatives to the courts and tribunals for the resolution of disputes.

Arbitration

Arbitration may be defined as a reference of a dispute or difference between not less than two persons for determination after hearing both sides in a judicial manner by another person, other than a court.

Many trade associations have provision for arbitration between their members and customers. In banking, insurance and related industries, disputes may be heard by an ombudsman, an independent expert. Lord Woolf has recommended that the retail sector be encouraged to develop similar private ombudsman schemes to cover consumer complaints.

At present, consumer claims for below £3,000 are dealt with by arbitration in the county court (see Unit 1.5).

In business, it is common practice to provide in contracts that any dispute will be referred to arbitration, rather than be dealt with by a court. Such arbitrations are governed by the Arbitration Act 1996.

Arbitrators are obliged to follow the rules of natural justice and the arbitrator's award is enforceable through the courts. Parties may represent themselves but, in commercial disputes, the sums involved are often considerable and it is more usual for lawyers to be involved. Appeal is by way of judicial review. Arbitrations are held in private.

The advantages of arbitration are:

❶ the technical knowledge of the arbitrator, who is not a lawyer but a specialist in the field concerned who has been trained as an arbitrator;

❷ speed and, therefore, lower costs;

❸ lack of publicity;

❹ the convenience of the parties is a prime consideration, they are treated like customers — compare this with the court system, which tends to be run for the convenience of judges.

Conciliation/mediation

The purpose of conciliation and mediation is to allow the parties to a dispute to identify, discuss and resolve the issues between them. The difference between the two is that the third party involved (the conciliator or mediator) takes a more active role in conciliation, perhaps suggesting a solution, than in mediation. The technique has been used for some time in industrial relations through the Advisory Conciliation and Arbitration Service (ACAS) and is now widely used in matrimonial causes to handle the ancillary issues concerning children and financial arrangements. Groups of family law practitioners have come together in the National Family Conciliation Council to further the practice of conciliation in preference to the previous adversarial style.

The object of conciliation is to reduce conflict between the parties and to assist them in reaching lasting and satisfactory agreements.

The Family Law Act 1996 will make mediation compulsory in divorce. Parties to a divorce will become responsible for settling the issues between them, with the assistance of a mediator, before they are granted a divorce. There is concern among lawyers that this may result in weaker parties agreeing to settlements that are not in their long-term interests. If the settlements that are made *are* more satisfactory to the parties, they should result in savings in court time and yield long-term benefits relating to the health of the parties and the happiness of the children of the family.

Mediation is also being used by voluntary groups to settle neighbour disputes and there are schemes for the use of mediation between offenders and victims of crime. Lord Woolf has recommended that: '*In the review of legal aid, the funding of voluntary organisations providing mediation services should be considered.*'

The Woolf Report recognised a place for ADR in the civil justice system: '*Where there is a satisfactory alternative to the resolution of disputes in court, use of which would be an advantage to the litigants, then the courts should encourage the use of this alternative.*' Parties to litigation are now *obliged* to consider alternative dispute resolution before taking their case to court.

1.7   LEGAL AID, ADVICE AND ASSISTANCE

1.7.1 THE 'UNMET NEED'

The '*unmet need for legal services*' suggests that there is a need for legal services which is not being met by current provision. It is a concept which developed during the 1970s. Research has shown that advice is sought in only a fraction of potential legal matters (*Zander 1979*). In 1973 *Richard White* offered a number of reasons for the 'unmet need':

- an individual does not recognise that the problem may be resolved by law, so does not seek legal advice;
- an individual realises that the problem may be resolved by law but is unaware of the appropriate legal service or entitlement to use it;
- an individual realises that the problem may be resolved by law and knows of the available services, but does not make use of it for some reason, such as fear of expense and ignorance of the legal aid scheme;
- an individual realises that the problem may be resolved by law and wants advice, but cannot find a developed legal service.

The *Consumer Association* carried out further research in 1997. Of 1,892 people interviewed, more than half who had a potential legal dispute did not seek any advice about how to resolve it. There findings show that there is still an 'unmet need'.

1.7.2 SOURCES OF LEGAL ADVICE

There are a whole range of sources of free legal advice. Particularly important are:

- **Citizens' Advice Bureaux** which exist in most towns and are well known. They are staffed by trained volunteers. Some branches have solicitors who attend once a week to give advice on legal matters. Generally, CABx provide advice to anyone on a variety of issues, including legal matters.

- **Law Centres** which aim to provide free legal advice (and sometimes representation) in areas where there are few solicitors. They are staffed by a mixture of lawyers and volunteers. Common areas of work include housing, welfare rights, employment, children's rights and juvenile crime, immigration, discrimination and planning law. They are funded by a mixture of central and local government funds and charity donations. Cuts in funding have resulted in many law centres closing.

Free legal advice may also be obtained at: Consumer Advice Centres; Housing Advice Centres; legal advice helplines; insurance companies; claims assessors; trading standards; trade unions.

1.7.3 PAYING FOR ADVICE

If a person needs to consult a solicitor and/or barrister, there are several options in how the advice may be paid for:

- Legal expenses insurance: many house and car policies offer this insurance as part of the policy or as an add-on. Alternatively, an individual can purchase a policy specifically to cover legal expenses.

- Pro bono unit: the Bar launched this unit in June 1996. It is run on a charitable basis, holds a register of barristers offering up to three days of their time to deserving cases in any field of law. Assistance will be available if the applicant would otherwise be unable to afford legal advice or representation.

- Conditional fees (no win, no fee): these were introduced under the Courts and Legal Services Act 1990 and have operated since 1995. Presently, if a claim involves personal injury litigation, European human rights or insolvency, many lawyers will be prepared to enter a "no win, no fee" agreement. A lawyer may charge a client 100% more than his usual fee (although 50% is more normal) subject to his total fee not exceeding 25% of the damages awarded. Effectively, this means the lawyer is paid twice – by the other party and by his client. If the client loses the case, he does not have to pay his own legal costs, although he remains liable for his opponent's legal costs. Therefore the client must insure himself against this loss. The Law Society has introduced the Accident Line Protect insurance scheme for this purpose and an average policy costs around £150, although it may be substantially higher in high risk cases.

- Paying personally.

- Qualifying for the statutory scheme for legal advice, assistance and aid.

1.7.4 THE STATUTORY SCHEME

Legal aid, advice and assistance are schemes where the state provides a person with free or subsidised help from a solicitor and/or barrister. Such schemes provide for equality and justice in law. The state helps people with their legal costs, enabling people to have access to the law and, therefore, enforce their legal rights. This should not depend upon how wealthy someone is. The current scheme is governed by the Legal Aid Act 1988, which consolidates previous law. It came into force on 1 April 1989. Section 1 sets out the purpose: '*to establish a framework for the provision of advice, assistance and representation which is publicly funded with a view to helping persons who might otherwise be unable to obtain advice, assistance or representation on account of their means....*'.

The Act established the **Legal Aid Board**, which took over the administrative functions previously performed by the Law Society. The Legal Aid Board is sub-divided into local area committees, which consider applications. The Act sets out a framework which is supplemented by detailed regulations made under the authority of the Act by the Lord Chancellor, who has very wide powers to make regulations as appear to him necessary or desirable for giving effect to the Act or for preventing abuses of it.

There are two possible tests that an applicant may need to satisfy in order to qualify for a particular scheme:

❶ Means testing is where an applicant's income and savings are assessed. Such testing ensures the most needy are assisted. The applicant's disposable income (a person's gross income less certain deductions for income tax, national insurance payments and an allowance for each dependant) and disposable capital (the value of the applicant's savings and possessions less his house up to the value of £100,000, household furniture and effects, articles of personal clothing and the tools of his trade, if the applicant has his own business) will be assessed.

2 Merits testing is where the applicant's case is examined and assessed in order to determine whether public money should be spent on it. Various specific merits tests have been developed in relation to certain schemes.

There has been a steady decrease in the real value of the means test limits. The middle-income groups are particularly excluded, yet are unable to pay for proceedings themselves. Regulations have further tightened the means test in relation to disposable capital and given the Legal Aid Board greater discretion, for example, to take into account factors such as the applicant's 'wealthy lifestyle' or assets of friends, relatives or children. Legal Advice and Assistance no longer allows for contributions. Therefore this scheme is limited to those on very low incomes only and contributions an applicant may be required to pay for civil legal aid have extended from a maximum of 12 months to the full duration of the case.

The merits test for civil legal aid requires someone to pre-judge a case and the merits test for criminal legal aid grants the clerk much discretion when applying s. 22 Legal Aid Act 1988. The grant rates in different magistrates' courts range from 35% to 100% (*Lord Chancellor's Department*, 1990). Clerks differ in their interpretation of the Widgery criteria and many do not apply the criteria at all (*Young, Maloney and Saunders*, 1992).

Legal Advice and Assistance has resulted in a growing number of fraudulent uses being made of it by solicitors. Investigation of solicitors' use of the scheme over a period of two years found that certain solicitors were involved in defrauding the Scheme of £3 million. The scheme has been attacked as providing a 'blank cheque' to solicitors who fiddled the scheme by tricking people into agreeing to take advice they did not need (*House of Commons Public Accounts Committee*, 1995).

In 1992 only 94% of police stations had a 24 hour Duty Solicitor Scheme operating. The scheme relies on enough local firms volunteering (*Lord Chancellor's Department*, 1992). Studies show that use of telephone advice rather than advice in person is common, solicitors are slow to respond and sometimes leave before interrogation, and there is frequent use of unqualified solicitors/para-legals (*Sanders*, 1989). Further research has shown that duty solicitors are mainly passive during police interrogation. In 75% of interviews observed, the duty solicitor was silent or played only a nominal role (*John Baldwin*, 1992). Such criticisms have led to the Law Society to introduce a qualification, *Police Station Accreditation Schemes*, for non-lawyers giving advice in police stations, which aims to improve quality of advice. The introduction of standard fees for solicitors for criminal legal aid work, whereby solicitors are paid 'per job' rather than 'per hour' has resulted in a decline of solicitors offering such services.

Civil legal aid in not available in a number of proceedings, such as defamation, where costs are particularly high, or before tribunals, or the small claims arbitration procedure resulting in an imbalance between parties in such proceedings. The statutory charge means that some of the applicant's compensation may be swallowed up by the Legal Aid Board before he or she receives it. The Legal Aid Board have first charge over it (*Hanlon* v *Law Society* (1981)).

1.7.5 LEGAL AID, ADVICE AND ASSISTANCE SCHEMES

SCHEME	CIVIL, CRIMINAL OR BOTH?	WHAT DOES IT COVER?	IS IT MEANS TESTED?	IS IT MERITS TESTED?
LEGAL ADVICE AND ASSISTANCE (Green Form Scheme)	• Civil and criminal	• A solicitor may give any advice or help up to two hours (or three hours in matrimonial matters) which stops short of actual court work. • It covers pre-trial work in both criminal and civil matters. This could be legal advice, or help such as the writing of letters, making telephone calls, drawing up papers and the filling in of documents, and requesting a barrister's opinion.	• The applicant must pass a means test. His or her disposable income and disposable capital will be assessed.	• The scheme is NOT merits tested.
DUTY SOLICITOR SCHEME	• Criminal	• Any person suspected or charged with a criminal offence, who is at the police station, may request to see the 'duty solicitor'. It is a scheme which operates 24 hours per day. • The duty solicitor is a local solicitor who will come to the police station to assist the person by giving advice, and being present during interrogation.	• The scheme is NOT means tested.	• The scheme is NOT merits tested.
CIVIL LEGAL AID	• Civil	• This scheme provides financial help to an applicant for the conducting of a case in the civil courts, including appeals. • Civil legal aid is not available for defamation cases, or most tribunal proceedings, or undefended divorce cases, or proceedings before a coroner's court or the small claims arbitration procedure.	• The applicant must pass a means test. His or her disposable income and disposable capital will be assessed by DSS Assessment Officers, who specialise in civil legal aid. • The finances of both the applicant and his or her partner must be added together for these purposes. • The applicant may be given some financial assistance, but have to make regular contributions (on a rising scale) for the duration of his or her case.	• The Legal Aid Board Area Committee must be satisfied that the applicant has reasonable grounds for suing or defending, i.e, if he or she were not financially assisted, a solicitor would advise that he or she has a reasonable chance of success. • If civil legal aid is refused, the applicant has the right to appeal to the Area Committee.

SCHEME	CIVIL, CRIMINAL OR BOTH?	WHAT DOES IT COVER?	IS IT MEANS TESTED?	IS IT MERITS TESTED?
CRIMINAL LEGAL AID	• Criminal	• Financial help is granted to an applicant for the conducting of a case in the criminal courts, including appeals.	• The applicant must pass a means test, similar to civil legal aid, although in more serious criminal cases it tends not be enforced as rigorously. • The applicant may be asked to pay contributions towards his or her costs as a condition.	• It must also be in 'the interests of justice' that legal aid be granted. • Under s. 21 of the Legal Aid Act 1988 criminal legal aid *must* be granted if the applicant is charged with *murder*. • Otherwise, under s. 22 Legal Aid Act 1988, one or more of the '*Widgery criteria*' apply: – a conviction may result in imprisonment or loss of livelihood; – a difficult question of law is involved; – the accused is unable to follow or conduct his own case because of inadequate English, mental illness or some other disability; – the case will involve the tracing or interviewing of witnesses, or expert cross-examination of prosecution witnesses; – legal representation is desirable in the interests of someone other than the accused, e.g. in a rape case it is not in the interests of justice that the accused cross-examines the victim.
ASSISTANCE BY WAY OF REPRESENT-ATION (ABWOR)	• Civil and criminal	• The Lord Chancellor has been given the power to extend ABWOR to '*any proceedings he thinks fit*'. Currently ABWOR is available for: • representation in civil proceedings in the magistrates' court; • representation before the Mental Health Review Tribunal (a tribunal which hears appeals from patients who have been 'sectioned' under the Mental Health Acts) • representation for prisoners facing some disciplinary charges before the Board of Visitors; • representation by a solicitor at a defendant's first hearing at the magistrates' court, if he or she is unrepresented and there is a court duty solicitor available for such representation, and the magistrates agree that such representation is desirable.	• Generally the applicant must pass a means test (the same means test as the Green Form Scheme applies, except the disposable capital limits are more generous). • However the availability of ABWOR in criminal proceedings is NOT dependant upon a means test.	• The applicant must also pass a merits test (identical to the civil legal aid merits test) except for criminal proceedings.

1.7.6 PROPOSED REFORM

- Legal aid expenditure has been rising steadily. Over the past seven years, the cost of civil and family aid has tripled to £671 million, representing an increase of 53% above inflation, yet the number of people funded by legal aid fell by 39,000. The fact that more and more public money is being spent on fewer and fewer people has stimulated debate. In March 1998, the Lord Chancellor issued a Consultation Paper *"Access to Justice with Conditional Fees"*. The broad aims behind the proposals are to control expenditure; target legal aid where there is the greatest need and where it will do more good; and obtain good value for money.

The key proposals in the Consultation Paper are:

- to allow conditional fee arrangements to be used in all cases, except family and criminal cases;

- to remove all personal injury actions from the legal aid system by July 1998, except for medical negligence actions. A number of other action will also be removed, such as cases pursued in the course of a business, inheritance, partnership or trust disputes. It is estimated that such a reform will remove 60% of money and damages claims will be removed from the scope of legal aid;

- to use only experienced lawyers in medical negligence cases. The Legal Aid Board will award contracts to those lawyers who can demonstrate sufficient competence in this area of law;

- gradually to transfer most cases currently supported by legal aid to conditional fee arrangements during the next few years;

- to focus taxpayers' money where it is most needed – social welfare matters and judicial review, and those defending claims against them for payment of money or damages;

- to encourage a wider use of legal expenses insurance.

The Government are planning to introduce a Bill in the Autumn of 1998 in order to bring about modernisation of legal aid and services. The Bar, Law Society, and consumer groups have expressed concerns about the expansion of conditional fees. In particular, there is the concern that lawyers will have too great a financial interest in the outcome of a case, compromising their independence. Conditional fees may not be suitable for all civil cases involving damages, such as defamation, or large commercial cases where, perhaps, solicitors would have to work for some years before being paid. People with complicated cases may not be able to find a solicitor who is able to take the case on a no win, no fee basis, or an insurer willing to provide affordable insurance, resulting in some people being denied access to justice. Nevertheless, an expansion of conditional fees will certainly enable people to bring cases without public funding.

1.8 JUDICIAL REVIEW

Judicial review is the process by which a judge examines the way in which an inferior court, tribunal, government department or other public body has made a decision. The subject matter must be in the realm of *public*, as opposed to private, law. For example, a local authority will be subject to judicial review of its decision-making processes but would be sued for negligence in maintaining the highway or for breach of contract. The question is whether the body has acted appropriately in exercising a public duty.

Professor Yardley has described judicial review as: *'the ultimate safeguard for the ordinary citizen against unlawful action by .... the more powerful administration'*. This is demonstrated by the case of *M* v *Home Office* (1993). M had applied for political asylum. He was refused and applied for judicial review. He was due to be deported and the Home Office barrister agreed he would not be deported that night, as had been intended, pending a decision from the judge the next day. The Home Secretary ordered that M be deported as arranged and was held to be in contempt of court.

Judicial review is a *review* not an appeal. It is concerned with the *process* by which a decision was reached, not the subject matter of the dispute.

The applicant must first obtain leave to bring an action for judicial review. The applicant has to demonstrate a '**sufficient interest**' in order to obtain leave. In *Inland Revenue Commissioners* v *National Federation of Self-Employed and Small Businesses Ltd* (1982) Lord Wilberforce explained how this question should be determined: ' *... it will be necessary to consider the powers or the duties in law of those against whom the relief is asked, the position of the applicant in relation to those powers or duties, and to the breach of those said to have been committed.'* In this case, the Federation was complaining that the Inland Revenue was failing to assess and collect tax from Fleet Street casual labour. The House decided the Federation did not have sufficient interest because the Federation's members were not directly affected by how the Revenue dealt with individual taxpayers who were not members of the Federation.

1.8.1 GROUNDS FOR JUDICIAL REVIEW

In the *GCHQ* case (below) Lord Diplock said: ' *... one can conveniently classify under three heads the grounds on which administrative action is subject to control by judicial review. The first ground I would call "illegality", the second "irrationality" and the third "procedural impropriety".'*

❶ **Illegality** (or **want of jurisdiction**): the body has acted *ultra vires*, that is, beyond its powers.

❷ **Irrationality** (or *Wednesbury* **unreasonableness**): in *Associated Provincial Picture Houses Ltd* v *Wednesbury Corporation* (1948) Lord Greene MR explained that a body is obliged to reach a decision on reasonable grounds, taking account of the appropriate legal rules and relevant facts and excluding irrelevant issues.

   In *Council of Civil Service Unions* v *Minister for the Civil Service* (1985) (the *GCHQ* case) in which employees of the Government Communication Headquarters challenged a government decision to deprive them of the right to be members of a trade union, Lord Diplock described an unreasonable decision as: *'a decision which is so outrageous in its defiance of logic or of accepted moral standards that no sensible person who had applied his mind to the question to be decided could have arrived at it.'*

❸ **Procedural impropriety** (or **denial of natural justice**).

The rules of natural justice fall within three principles:

❶ **No person is to be condemned unheard** (*audi alteram partem*). In *Ridge* v *Baldwin* (1964) R was the Chief Constable of Brighton. He had been acquitted on a charge of conspiracy to obstruct the course of justice. The Brighton Watch Committee then dismissed him, using a statutory power to dismiss 'any constable whom they think negligent in the discharge of his duty or otherwise unfit for the same'. He was not given the opportunity to appear before the Watch Committee or otherwise state his case. His dismissal was held to be void. R had a right to be heard in his own defence.

   Prior to *Ridge* v *Baldwin* it was thought that the rules of natural justice applied only to court proceedings. This case makes it clear that they also apply to administrative decision making. As Professor Yardley has written, the rules of natural justice *'are the practical reminders of that somewhat abstract concept, the Rule of Law'*.

   There are two rights: to know the case against you; and to put your side of the argument. There must also be time to prepare a case: *R* v *Thames Magistrates' Court, ex parte Polemis* (1974). A summons was served at 10.30 am. Magistrates refused an adjournment, merely putting the case back from 2.00 pm to 4.00 pm the same day. The defendant was convicted and appealed to the Divisional Court, which quashed the conviction because natural justice requires that a party shall have a reasonable opportunity to prepare a case before being required to present it.

   The right to be heard generally includes a right to legal representation: *Enderby Town Football Club* v *Football Association* (1971) (but there are exceptions: *Maynard* v *Osmond* (1976) police officers involved in disciplinary proceedings are not entitled to a lawyer).

2 **No person may be a judge in his or her own cause** (*nemo judex in causa sua*). In *Dimes* v *Grand Junction Canal Proprietors* (1852) the Lord Chancellor confirmed orders, including an injunction in favour of the canal company of which he was a shareholder. It was held that the orders should be quashed, not because the Lord Chancellor had *actually* been influenced by his financial interest but because no one having a financial interest should be involved in making a judicial decision.

The interest involved must be direct and substantial. It does not have to be financial.

In *R* v *Sussex Justices, ex parte McCarthy* (1924) Lord Hewart CJ said '*it is ... of fundamental importance that justice should not only be done but should manifestly and undoubtedly be seen to be done.*'

In *R* v *Altrincham Justices, ex parte Pennington* (1975) the applicants supplied vegetables to schools. They were prosecuted and convicted for Weights and Measures offences. The Chair of the bench of magistrates was a member of the Education Committee and a governor of two schools. The conviction was quashed because the magistrate's interest was sufficient to raise the possibility of bias.

Lord Denning MR said in *Metropolitan Properties* v *Lannon* (1969): '*Justice must be rooted in confidence: and confidence is destroyed when right-minded people go away thinking: "The judge was biased".*'

3 **Legitimate expectation.** This issue arises, for example, in cases where the Inland Revenue have advised a taxpayer that a certain course of action will have certain tax consequences and have then changed their mind. The court will not prevent a body from enforcing the law but it will prevent unfair behaviour which does not provide any benefit to the public.

In the *GCHQ* case (1985) it was argued that the workers had a legitimate expectation of being allowed to be union members. Lord Diplock said: '*even where a person claiming some benefit or privilege has no legal right to it, as a matter of private law, he may have a legitimate expectation of receiving the benefit of privilege, and, if so, the courts will protect his expectation by judicial review as a matter of public law ... Legitimate, or reasonable, expectation may arise either from an express promise given on behalf of a public authority or from the existence of a regular practice which the claimant can reasonably expect to continue.*' The House of Lords decided that this legitimate expectation was outweighed by national security considerations.

The courts have also begun to adopt the principle of **proportionality**, borrowed from EC law. A judge will decide whether what was done was so bad in proportion to the whole issue as to require that the decision be declared void. In *R* v *Legal Aid Board, ex parte Donn & Co* (1996) the Legal Aid Board were awarding a contract to a firm of solicitors to conduct litigation on behalf of people claiming they were suffering from Gulf War Syndrome. The court found that there had been procedural irregularities and decided that, even though quashing the Board's decision and requiring them to go through the procedure correctly would delay the litigation, this was not disproportionate.

1.8.2 REMEDIES

The remedies available are the prerogative orders of:

* certiorari (quashing a decision);
* prohibition (forbidding a proposed course of action);
* mandamus (ordering that something be done);
* declaration (the court decides and declares what the law is);
* injunction (usually interlocutory);
* discovery (see Unit 1.5);
* damages.

Illustrative questions

1 Discuss critically the similarities in, and differences between, the work of barristers and solicitors. (25)
(NEAB)

Tutorial note
Despite its brevity, this question has several components. The *work* of barristers and solicitors must be described and the similarities and differences highlighted and discussed in a critical manner. A common mistake candidates make is to include accounts of training or professional organisations in this kind of question. It is very important to look at the particular aspect of a topic required and to restrict your answer to that aspect.

Suggested answer
Barristers and solicitors are qualified lawyers who, collectively, do a wide range of legal work: civil and criminal litigation, probate, conveyancing, company and commercial and family, for example. Individually, each lawyer specialises to a greater or lesser extent.

Barristers are usually self-employed, working with other barristers in a 'set'. They rent chambers and employ a clerk to deal with the administration. Some barristers work from home clerking for themselves. Each barrister does work sent to him or her by solicitors and is paid a fee, negotiated between the solicitor and the clerk, for that work. The work may be to advise on a point of law, or on the evidence needed in a case, or whether a payment into court should be accepted; or it might be to draft pleadings or other documents or it might be to appear in court. A barrister spends a lot of time waiting within the court buildings for his or her case to come on or for a jury to deliberate; it is important, therefore, to have low overheads so that this waiting time is not too expensive.

Solicitors in private practice work in firms, either as partners or as assistant solicitors. They draw a salary, so there is not a direct connection between each piece of work they do and their income. Solicitors take instructions from clients, write letters, prepare documents, negotiate, prepare cases for court, instruct barristers and appear in court. They have to maintain offices for clients to visit and employ staff to deal with the considerable amount of paperwork.

Traditionally, solicitors saw clients and barristers appeared in court, but this distinction has become less pronounced. There have always been barristers who concentrated on advice and drafting and made very few court appearances and solicitors who spent a great deal of time in court, usually the magistrates' court doing either family or criminal work. The Courts and Legal Services Act 1990 allowed solicitors to qualify as advocates in the higher courts. Solicitors who do so may then appear in the Crown Court and High Court, instead of instructing barristers to do so.

Several hundred solicitors have qualified as advocates, but few are making much use of the qualification. Research shows this is because of the expense of running a solicitor's office, which makes 'waiting time' in court prohibitively expensive, and because of the fear that judges and juries have a prejudice against solicitor advocates and the client's best interests would thus be served by instructing a barrister. Solicitors who have qualified as advocates may become QCs and High Court judges; formerly, a solicitor could become a District judge, Recorder or Circuit judge but could go no further up the judicial hierarchy.

The Courts and Legal Services Act also permitted barristers to take instructions direct from professional clients, such as accountants, without going through a solicitor.

Barristers and solicitors may be employed in industry or by the public sector. Their work is then indistinguishable: they provide advice to their employer, draft documents and conduct correspondence but may not appear in court except in very limited circumstances. So, for example, the Crown Prosecution Service has to instruct barristers, it cannot use its own staff as advocates.

It therefore appears true to say that, whilst it is still possible to discuss in general terms the differences between the work of barristers and solicitors, the work of two individual lawyers, one a barrister and one a solicitor, may be very similar.

2 (a) What provision exists in the English legal system to ensure the participation of laypersons in the formal resolution of civil and criminal cases? (12)

(b) How far is such participation desirable? (13)

(AEB)

Tutorial note

This question is asked in two parts. It is therefore important to answer it in two parts. It is split by the examiner to help you focus on what is required, so it makes sense to use that help. In addition, the marking scheme will be written in two parts and you will help the person marking your work by answering each part separately. When planning your answer, note how many marks are given to each part. Here, the split is almost even, so your answers should be of about the same length.

Note that you are being asked about 'laypersons'— so this will include magistrates, jurors and tribunal members. The reference to 'formal' dispute resolution precludes mention of ombudsmen, mediators and conciliators. The examiner is asking about civil and criminal cases.

The intelligent approach to this question is to describe the role of laypeople, and to explain briefly who they are in (a) and then to use that description as the basis for your evaluation in (b). That evaluation has to be specific, related to each kind of layperson individually. There are different points to be made in each case and it is not wise to try to deal with laypeople as if they were an amorphous mass.

Suggested answer

(a) Lay magistrates sit in the magistrates' court to deal with civil issues such as judicial separation, licensing of pubs and clubs and non-payment of certain debts. The larger part of their work is criminal. They hear committal proceedings, ensuring that there is a case to answer before a defendant is committed for trial by jury. If a defendant is charged with a summary offence or has elected to be tried by magistrates for a hybrid offence, magistrates hold a summary trial, hearing evidence, deciding on guilt and, if the defendant is found guilty, passing sentence. Magistrates also sit in the Crown Court, with a Recorder or Circuit judge, to hear appeals from the decisions of magistrates. Magistrates are appointed by the Lord Chancellor from people of good character between the ages of 21 and 60.

Jurors are selected at random from the electoral register. Service is a public duty and a person who refuses, without good reason, to serve commits contempt of court. People may be excused either as of right or at the discretion of the court. Some people are ineligible for jury service and others, notably those who have been sentenced to imprisonment, are disqualified. Otherwise, a jury consists of 12 people aged between 18 and 70, drawn from the local population. Only 2% of all criminal cases are heard by jury in the Crown Court. They are either indictable offences or hybrid offences for which the defendant has chosen jury trial. The job of the jury is to listen to all the evidence and, having had advice from the judge as to the law, to decide whether the defendant is guilty or not guilty.

The role of juries in civil cases is very restricted. They are usually found only in defamation cases, in which they have to decide whether the words complained of would lower the plaintiff in the estimation of right thinking members of society.

Tribunal members are appointed to apply their expert knowledge to the cases that come before the tribunal. There is a legally qualified chairperson, but he or she sits with two non-lawyers who are experts in their field. For example, an industrial tribunal will have someone who has been nominated by a trade union and someone nominated by an employers' organisation, both of whom will have significant industrial experience.

(b) The major argument in favour of the use of magistrates is that they are cheap. They receive only expenses and yet deal with 98% of all criminal cases from start to finish. If there were no lay magistrates, their work would probably be done by stipendiary magistrates, who are qualified lawyers, at present appointed only in large towns. Many lawyers are sceptical about the competence and impartiality of magistrates, who have limited training and are said to be more likely to convict than jurors.

Jurors were widely used in civil matters until the 1930's. Since that time, their role has been restricted and the character of juries has been changed dramatically by the abandonment of a property qualification for jurors. They are now used almost entirely in criminal trials. Jurors receive an introduction to their work, but no training and there is no test as to intelligence or literacy. Their strength lies in their ability to apply the standards of the average person in reaching a judgment. Occasionally, a jury will defy a legally correct but morally unacceptable course: in the trial of Clive Ponting, a civil servant who passed secret information to an MP and was thus clearly in breach of the Official Secrets Act, was found not guilty by the jury. Juries are useful when it is necessary to decide what the 'reasonable man' would have done in a particular situation. It is to be hoped that, because there are 12 jurors, personal prejudices do not influence jury decisions. Juries are very expensive because their use prolongs trials and they receive payments for loss of earnings and expenses.

Theoretically, laypersons who give their expertise to tribunals should be very useful. Unfortunately, the legally qualified chairperson often dominates proceedings; he or she will have accumulated some expertise in the subject-matter by serving on the tribunal and there is a tendency to consult with other members of the tribunal as a matter of courtesy, rather than because their opinions are needed.

In conclusion, it would appear that a very important role of laypeople in courts and tribunals is to demonstrate that justice is not monopolised by lawyers and that the standards of ordinary people count. The use of laypeople forces lawyers to explain themselves in ordinary language, instead of legal jargon. The legal system could operate without jurors and lay tribunal members, but it may well not then command the respect of the population as a whole. Expense would probably prevent the abolition of lay magistrates.

3 Harriet has been injured in a road traffic accident caused by Angela's negligence and wishes to claim damages for her pain and suffering.

(a) Advise Harriet as to where and how she should start civil proceedings against Angela. (15)

(b) If she is dissatisfied with the result of her case, what appeals are open to her? (15)

(c) To what extent have the changes in jurisdiction under the Courts and Legal Services Act 1990 improved the court as a forum for personal injury disputes? (20)

(UODLE)

Tutorial note
This style of question is very typical of the Oxford Board. It allows the examiner to ask about several different aspects of the legal system. This one is concerned with different aspects of jurisdiction, but you will find the examiner combining questions on courts with legal aid or the role of lawyers. Again, pay close attention to the distribution of marks between the parts. The 20 marks in (c) are not so much because you need to write more, but because the question being asked is more sophisticated and requires more thought. The key to the whole question is that no amount of damages has been specified, so you have to discuss different possibilities.

It is likely that examiners will turn their attention to the effect of the Civil Procedure Act 1997 and you should always be sure that you understand recent legislation and are able to comment on its effect.

Suggested answer

(a) The amount of damages Harriet is likely to be awarded will determine the court in which she should begin her case. Damages in personal injury cases are made up from different elements, of which pain and suffering is one. For a fairly minor injury, the award for pain and suffering may be only a few hundred pounds; for a very significant injury causing long-term disability and pain, the amount might be many thousands. The decision as to which court is appropriate is made on the basis of the total amount of damages Harriet's solicitor believes she is likely to recover.

Most claims below £3,000 are referred for arbitration in the county court, but this does not apply to personal injury claims, which will be referred only if they are below £1,000. All personal injury cases below £50,000 must begin by issuing a summons in a county court. The summons may be issued in any county court; if Angela wanted the case moved to a different county court she could put her case for doing so to a District judge. It is also possible for either party to ask the judge to transfer the case to the High Court if there is a complex issue of law involved. If Harriet is likely to recover over £50,000 she should begin her case by issuing a writ in the High Court. If the case is simple, even though there is a lot of money involved, the High Court judge can transfer the case to the county court to be heard.

(b) If the case is heard by a District judge acting as arbitrator, there is a right of appeal only if it can be shown that he or she acted as no reasonable judge could have acted. The appeal is heard by a Circuit judge.

If the case is heard in a county court or the High Court, appeal is to the Court of Appeal (Civil Division). Harriet might appeal against the decision reached, on the ground that the judge was wrong in law or made a mistake as to a fact. She can then appeal to the House of Lords if there is a point of law of general public interest involved and either the Court of Appeal or the House of Lords gives leave to appeal. Alternatively, it may be possible to 'leapfrog' the Court of Appeal and go straight to the House of Lords if there is an important point of law at issue and the Court of Appeal would be bound by previous decisions. Harriet might also appeal on the ground that the damages awarded are too low, but the award would have to be wrong in principle for there to be any chance of having it increased by the Court of Appeal or the High Court.

(c) The Courts and Legal Services Act 1990 changed the financial jurisdiction limits on county courts. Before that Act, the jurisdiction of county courts in personal injury cases was limited to £5,000. The effect of the Act has been a massive increase in the number of personal injury cases being dealt with in county courts. In turn, this means that solicitors have been able to complete cases, if they wish, without instructing a barrister. This, and the lower scale of charges applicable to county court work, should have reduced the costs in personal injury cases, which are notoriously inefficient in terms of the relationship between the average sum awarded to defendants and the average costs: on average, costs exceed the sum awarded. This does not affect plaintiffs, since they are awarded their costs in addition to damages, but it does increase insurance premiums, as most defendants are insured.

There is still a view that courts are not appropriate for many personal injury actions. If there is a dispute as to liability, it often turns on technical evidence which might be better heard by an arbitrator or a specialist tribunal.

More far-reaching changes are likely to follow from the Civil Procedure Act 1997 and the introduction of case management by judges. The delays inherent in personal injury work are likely to be diminished and it is likely that it will become very rare for more than one expert in any field to be heard by the court, as parties will be encouraged to agree experts' reports before the trial.

Practice questions

1 Two months ago Spenders Ltd purchased machinery for use in their factory from Whizz Electrics. The machinery cost £35,000 but is defective and has gone wrong several times. Spenders wish to claim compensation from Whizz Electrics.

(a) In which courts could a claim be made? (10)

(b) What other methods of resolving the dispute might be used? (15)

(c) Advise Spenders Ltd on the advantages and disadvantages of the various methods of dispute resolution, including the courts, which are available to them. (25)

(*UODLE*)

Pitfalls

Remember that this is a question about the legal system, don't get involved in a discussion of contract law. Take each section by itself and keep an eye on the mark distribution as a guide to the length and complexity of the answers expected.

Key points

(a) County court or High Court — this claim is in the £25,000 to £50,000 band, where the decision will rest on the complexity of the case.

(b) Negotiation/mediation or commercial arbitration: explain each of these alternatives, but leave evaluation of them to part (c).

(c) A logical consideration of the advantages and disadvantages of a county court, the High Court, commercial arbitration and negotiation with or without a mediator.

2 Access to legal advice and representation may be very expensive.

(a) What provisions have been made to ensure that, nonetheless, persons suspected of committing **criminal offences** can be properly advised and represented at all stages of investigation and trial? (13)

(b) How satisfactory are these provisions? (12)

(*AEB*)

Pitfalls

Take note of the help the examiner is giving. The expectation is that your answers to each part will be of about the same length — you can see that from the mark allocation. The examiner has also stressed that this is a question about criminal, not civil, provision.

A common error is to assume the question is *only* about funding. It is about the availability and quality of advice and representation as well.

Key points

Part (a)

❶ Describe the advice that is available: the right to have a solicitor present at the police station, the role of solicitors and barristers in advising and representing defendants.

❷ Funding of advice, through the Green Form scheme, and of representation, through ABWOR and legal aid. Describe means and merits tests, as appropriate.

Part (b)

An evaluation of the material in points 1 and 2 of (a). Is the quality of the advice good? Is the funding adequate? Could the funding be better arranged or administered?

SOURCES OF LAW

Units in this chapter

Chapter objectives

This chapter critically examines the different sources of English law. This is a fundamental part of any A Level Law syllabus and is crucial to the understanding of areas of substantive law.

First, the creation of legislation is critically examined. Legislation which is made by other bodies or persons with permission from Parliament, known as delegated legislation, is described and evaluated. The approach of judges in applying the words in statutes to individual cases, known as statutory interpretation, is examined.

The operation of the doctrine of precedent is explained, and the flexibility of precedent considered. You are strongly advised to refer to cases learned as part of your option, such as crime, contract or tort, to illustrate case-law development.

The United Kingdom is a member of the European Union, and this has become an important source of law. An outline of the institutions and sources of EC law is provided, together with an examination of the affects of membership on English law and law-making.

The historical development of equity, a subsidiary source of law, is outlined and suggestions of areas of law which may be used to illustrate its modern significance are given.

Finally, we take a critical look at the broad process of law reform, paying particular attention to the law reform agencies.

2.1 LEGISLATION, DELEGATED LEGISLATION AND THE INTERPRETATION OF STATUTES

2.1.1 LEGISLATION

Parliament

There are three organs of Parliament:

1 The **House of Commons** is an elected chamber made up of 659 MPs, elected by simple majority to represent constituencies.

2 The **House of Lords** is an unelected chamber consisting of hereditary peers, i.e. those who have inherited a title, and life peers, i.e. those who are granted a title for life (for example, former MPs; Law Lords; Bishops; persons from industry, commerce and the academic world).

3 The **Queen in Parliament**. The monarch's powers are severely limited by the Bill of Rights 1688 and consist of duties such as signing Bills and opening Parliament.

Parliament has legislative sovereignty. It is the supreme law-maker and has ultimate powers to make and repeal law. If an Act has gone through the correct constitutional process, then the validity of the Act cannot be questioned. In particular, the *courts* have no power to question the validity of an Act (*Pickin* v *British Railway Board* (1974)). However, UK membership of the European Union raises the difficult issue of competing supremacies, and some would argue that Parliament is no longer fully sovereign (see Unit 2.3).

Public and Private Acts

Statutes can be divided into two categories. Public Acts concern the general law and affect the general public. Most Acts are public Acts. Private Acts only affect a local community or a particular person or body. They do not affect the general law.

Government and Private Members' Bills

Most Acts of Parliament which are passed are introduced into Parliament by the government of the day, and when going through Parliament are known as Government Bills. However, some public Acts are introduced by individual Members of Parliament or individual Peers and are known as Private Members' Bills. Private Members' Bills are used for a variety of purposes including matters of social reform (e.g. the Abortion Act 1967), on which public opinion may be too sharply divided for the government to wish to take the initiative. They are frequently used in matters of special interest to minority groups, for example, consumer issues or animal rights, and also issues of law reform which have too low a priority to find a place in the government's programme. In a normal Parliamentary session, 110 days are set aside for public legislation and the government uses around 100 of these to push through its own legislation. The rest of the time may be used by 'private members' who can introduce legislation through one of two procedures:

- The Ballot. Any MP may enter by placing his or her name in the Ballot Box. Before the Parliamentary session starts, 20 names are picked out at random and listed. The first chosen has the first chance to introduce the Bill of their choice, and so on down the whole 20. In practice, only the first three or four stand any real chance of success due to the lack of Parliamentary time allocated to such Bills.

- The 'Ten Minute' rule. Any MP may, on two days a week, make a ten minute speech in support of a Bill. A ten minute speech opposing this may be made and, if the House agrees, a date for a second reading may be set. This method is very unlikely to succeed, again due to lack of Parliamentary time.

The legislative process

The following briefly describes the key stages of the creation of legislation. The first three stages are often referred to as the 'informal process'. The passage of a Bill through Parliament is referred to as the 'formal process'.

❶ The idea stage: Ideas for new legislation come from a range of sources, including:

- *The Government*.

- *Pressure Groups*: pressure groups can influence the government sufficiently to take up their cause. Interest pressure groups operate to protect their own interests (interest groups) and can exert enormous pressure on governments (who are dependent upon their co-operation). Promotional pressure groups focus on particular issues and have a wide variety of people campaigning. Most of these promotional groups have no access to Parliament and insufficient funds to employ MPs as consultants to promote their interests. They tend to wield little power.

- *Official Law Reform Bodies* (see Unit 2.5).

- *The Media*: media campaigns can influence the government to change the law. Sometimes the media can generate a 'moral panic' which results in hasty and poorly thought out legislation, e.g. the Dangerous Dogs Act 1991.

- *European Union* (see Unit 2.3).

❷ Consultation: The ideas of government and private members are often discussed by the media, especially if they are politically or socially controversial, in order to 'sound out' the public opinion. A more formal method of consultation is to publish the proposed reforms in the form of a Green or White Paper:

- *Green Papers* are occasionally used and indicate the general ideas which the government is considering. Any interested person or group may respond in writing.

- *White Papers* are a common form of discussion document and include the detailed proposals which the government wish to introduce.

❸ Drafting: In English law, statutes are drafted as fully as possible, and the draftsman attempts to foresee every possible situation which may arise under the statute. Government ideas are sent to parliamentary counsel. Private members' ideas are drafted by ordinary lawyers, although the government may make parliamentary counsel available if it supports the Private Members' Bill. Once the ideas have been drafted in a form to be presented to Parliament, it is known as a *Bill*.

❹ Most Bills are introduced in the House of Commons. The stages are as follows:

- **First Reading**: This Reading is a mere formality.

- **Second Reading**: The general principles of the Bill are debated and if 20 or more MPs object to the Bill, a vote is taken on whether or not to proceed.

- **Committee Stage**: The Bill is sent to a 'standing committee' of 20–30 MPs who examine the Bill and make amendments to the detail.

- **Report Stage**: All amendments by the committee are reported back to the whole House and a vote may be taken on each amendment.

- **Third Reading**: The Bill is again discussed but no further amendments can be made. If there are objections, a vote will be taken.

- **House of Lords**: The Bill is sent to the House of Lords where it goes through a very similar procedure to that of the House of Commons. The Parliament Acts 1911 and 1949 restrict the power of the House of Lords to delay or to stop Bills. If the Bill is a 'money bill' the House of Lords may only delay it for one month. Any other Bill can only be delayed by one year. The Bill could then be re-introduced into the House of Commons the following year and it would not be passed to the House of Lords for amendments (e.g. War Crimes Act 1991). In effect, the power of the House of Lords is to amend Bills, not to veto them.

- **Royal Assent**: The Bill is sent to the Queen for her assent. Although the Queen retains the right to object to any Bill, by convention she never does. From the moment the Royal Assent is given the Bill is known as an *Act*.

Issues in evaluation

1 *Criticisms of Parliament as a democratic law-making body*: electoral reform of House of Commons; power of the government; reform of the unelected House of Lords; influence of the House of Lords.

2 *The generation of ideas*: influence of promotional pressure groups; lack of opportunity for Private Members' Bills; many Private Members' Bills are narrow and specialist and can be poorly drafted because of lack of parliamentary draftsmen; influence of media and panic legislation.

3 *Research and consultation with experts*: for example, in the Dangerous Dogs Act 1991 the pit bull terrier is singled out but there is considerable disagreement amongst vets as to whether such a breed exists and most attacks are by German Shepherds and Rottweilers which are not singled out.

4 *Drafting and interpretation*: problems in drafting emerge when judges come to interpret statutes.

5 *The passage through Parliament*: slow; layout of Houses encourages confrontation rather than debate; House of Commons is too small to accommodate all MPs comfortably; complex process; is it a democratic process?

2.1.2 DELEGATED LEGISLATION

Meaning and historical background

Delegated legislation is the result of law-making powers conferred under Acts of Parliament. Parliament, as the sovereign body, can grant to some other body or person the power to make laws. In theory, this can be reconciled with the doctrine of parliamentary sovereignty as law making is carried on with Parliament's express sanction.

Forms of delegated legislation

Parliament passes an enabling Act (otherwise known as a parent Act) which

grants law-making powers to

Ministers	Local authorities	Privy Council
Ministers may be given powers to make laws which concern the area over which their ministry has control, for example, the Minister for Education may make certain **regulations** in relation to education or the Home Secretary may make regulations on immigration or prisons. The laws are issued in the form of a '**Statutory Instrument**' which is signed by the appropriate minister.	Each local authority is given the power to make **bye-laws** which apply to its geographical area. Examples of local authority by-laws include restrictions on parking, litter, dogs and smoking in public places.	The Privy Council consists of all Cabinet Ministers and other prominent persons from various walks of life, whose role is to advise the monarch. In practice it is the Cabinet which drafts **Orders in Council** and the 'Queen in Council' who merely 'rubber-stamps' them. Examples include emergency powers, for example, in times of war or states of emergency.

Controls over delegated legislation

There are a large number of bodies and persons making law through powers delegated to them by Parliament. Various controls have emerged which attempt to keep a check upon both the quality of the laws and possible abuse of the law-making process. These controls are of two main types:

1 **Parliamentary controls**. Parliament can control the delegated body by:

- Repealing the enabling Act, and revoking the delegated power. This is Parliament's ultimate control. It could also vary the delegated power.

- Requesting the delegated legislation to be 'laid before Parliament'. Usually this will be for Parliament's information. Parliament may question the Minister and debate the law, but not vote on it. Occasionally the enabling Act may require that there is an affirmative or negative resolution from one or both Houses.

- The Scrutiny Committees which were set up to keep under review all delegated legislation and report to Parliament on their findings. The Joint Committee on Statutory Instruments was created in 1974, with the duty to consider all instruments laid before both Houses of Parliament. It reports to both Houses. Also in 1974, each House set up a Committee on European secondary legislation and have a duty to bring to the attention of Parliament the more important Community proposals.

- Requiring, in the enabling Act, the delegated body to consult with, or submit a draft instrument for approval to, experts both within and outside their departments. For example, road traffic legislation may involve consultation with such interest groups as local authorities, police, AA, RAC, and motor car manufacturers.

2 **Judicial controls**. Judges retain some control over delegated bodies through judicial review. The courts cannot declare an Act of Parliament *'ultra vires'* (beyond power). However, they can and do declare the exercise of *delegated* powers invalid under the *ultra vires* rule. There are two grounds upon which the courts can declare delegated legislation to be void:

- the **procedural ground**: here the instrument is invalid because the Minister has failed to follow the procedure laid down in the enabling Act, for example, he or she has not consulted with a specified advisory body;

- the **substantive ground**: here the delegated body has made law not authorised by the enabling Act (excess of power) or made law not intended by the Act (abuse of power) or has acted unreasonably. If the delegated legislation is *ultra vires*, it is void and ceases to exist. The delegated body must re-draft the law. (See Unit 1.8.)

Issues in evaluation

- Granting law-making powers to others saves much Parliamentary time. Parliament could not possibly make all these laws.

- Parliament concerns itself with only the broad framework of the legislation leaving experts or those with local knowledge to add the detail, resulting in better-informed and specialised laws. Delegated legislation is often concerned with technical matters, such as safety of consumer goods, safety in factories and road traffic laws.

- Laws can be made quickly, e.g. in emergencies, and changed or repealed quickly, making it a more flexible source of law.

- So much law is made in this way (around 2,000 ministerial regulations are issued each year) that it becomes impossible for the ordinary layperson to keep abreast of new laws, yet 'ignorance of the law is no defence'. The rule of law implies, amongst other things, that a citizen should be able to ascertain fairly easily what the law is on a particular matter.

- This law making lacks debate and publicity.

- It is a less democratic source of law.

- The sheer quantity makes it difficult to control. Parliamentary controls are not always effective. The Scrutiny Committees cannot keep *all* delegated legislation under review. Not *all* delegated legislation could be laid before Parliament since this would defeat the object of it. Judicial controls depend on a member of the public taking legal action which is time-consuming and expensive.

- There is a real danger of sub-delegation, reducing parliamentary control of new law since Parliament may only be aware of the original enabling Act. For example, regulations may be made under the statute, orders made under the regulations and directions made under the orders.

- It could be argued that the process of delegated legislation is a direct contradiction to the theory of the separation of powers. The executive (Ministers) are making laws. This is a function which should be confined to the legislature (Parliament).

- The doctrine of parliamentary sovereignty is, in practice, eroded, since Parliament (the supreme law-maker) cannot supervise and control the vast amount of delegated legislation.

2.1.3 STATUTORY INTERPRETATION

Role of the judge

Statutory interpretation is the process where a judge applies a statute to a case. The judge must interpret the words in the statute in order to decide what they mean and how they should be applied to the case. The role of the judge when interpreting statutes is to put into effect the wishes of Parliament. Since Parliament is our supreme law-maker, the court cannot question an Act of Parliament. The judges must give effect to Parliament's intentions. Views conflict on whether the intention of Parliament is to be found in the words of the statute alone, or whether judges should enquire into the purpose of the Act, and then interpret the words in the light of that knowledge.

Difficulties in interpreting statutes

The words in a statute may be difficult to interpret. Although statutes in English law are drafted narrowly and, compared to continental codes of law, precisely, judges still face problems when applying the statute to cases before them. Two key problems are:

- Uncertainty: it is impossible for Parliament to foresee every possible factual situation which can occur and to provide for every eventuality. Even if it could, this would lead to impossibly long Acts of Parliament, which would be totally impractical.

- Language: one word can have several meanings. Ambiguity can lead to a situation where a word used by a Parliamentary draftsman was meant to convey one meaning but has an equally plausible second meaning which is quite different to the intended meaning.

Intrinsic and extrinsic aids

Intrinsic aids include anything in the Act which have been approved by Parliament. This does not include margin notes, which are added after Royal Assent. Aids which may be of assistance include:

- the preamble (a long, introductory paragraph which states the purposes for which the Act has been passed, only found in older statutes);

- schedules (found at the rear of the Act, normally providing information in the form of lists and illustrations, specimen forms and transitional provisions);

- the interpretation section (many Acts contain a section in which various words that are found in the Act are defined).

Extrinsic aids are any references which are not contained within the Act. Key extrinsic aids include:

- the dictionary;

- Interpretation Act 1978, which lists the definitions of many words and phrases commonly found in Acts;

- previous and subsequent Acts;

- Reports of Commissions and Committees can be referred to in order to discover what the old law was and what defects it had which led to the Act being passed;

- precedent decisions on the meaning of a word or phrase;

- *Hansard* may now be referred to. In the important case of *Pepper* v *Hart* (1993) the

House of Lords finally permitted the courts to refer to *Hansard* in interpreting the words of a statute, but only if:

- the legislation is ambiguous or obscure or the literal meaning leads to an absurdity; and

- the material relied on consists of statements made by a minister or other promoter of the Bill which led to the enactment of the legislation, together with any other parliamentary material necessary to understand such statements; and

- the statements relied upon are clear.

This relaxation of the former prohibition on the use of such materials was utilised by the House of Lords in *Warwickshire County Council* v *Johnson* (1993) in interpreting s. 20 of the Consumer Protection Act 1987 and in *Stubbings* v *Webb* (1993).

Presumptions

Over the centuries, as the courts have been called upon to interpret legislation, they have developed certain presumptions. These are basic principles which the courts presume that Parliament must have intended when passing a particular statute, even though Parliament has not actually stated them in the statute. The following are examples of presumptions that will be deemed to be in the statute unless Parliament expressly states otherwise:

- presumption against alteration of the existing law;

- presumption against the imposition of liability without fault;

- presumption against retrospective legislation. Statutes only apply to situations occurring after they become law, unless the statute specifically says otherwise, for example, the War Crimes Act 1991.

Rules of language

These have been developed by lawyers over time. Examples include:

- *ejusdem generis*: general words which follow specific ones are taken to include only things of the same kind;

- *expressio unius est exclusio alterius*: express mention of one thing implies the exclusion of another;

- *noscitur a sociis*: a word draws meaning from the other words around it.

Judicial approaches

Various guidelines or canons of construction have been developed by the judges in order to assist them in their task of statutory interpretation. These are guidelines for judges, not strict rules. The main approaches are:

❶ **The mischief rule:** This is the oldest approach, dating from *Heydon's Case* (1584). In this case the judges decided it was proper to look beyond the four corners of the Act itself. They said that when the words in the statute were not absolutely clear in a literal sense, it was permissible to consider:

- what was the common law before the Act;

- what was the defect for which the common law did not provide a remedy;

- what remedy had Parliament decided upon to cure the defect; and

- what was the true reason for the remedy.

This has come to be known as the 'mischief' rule. In *Smith* v *Hughes* (1961) the mischief rule was used to interpret the meaning of 'soliciting in a public place' as stated in the Street Offences Act 1959. The court held these words to include in a private building but in view of the public (at a window), declaring the 'mischief' in the old common law to be harassment of men by prostitutes. In *DHSS* v *Royal College of Nursing* (1981), concerning the Abortion Act 1967, nurses were carrying out early abortions under the supervision of doctors. The Act stated that only a doctor should perform abortions. However, the court held that the 'mischief' in the old common law was to prevent back-street abortions, and, at the time of passing the Act, Parliament could not have anticipated medical advancements in abortion techniques. Therefore, they held that there was nothing illegal in the practice of nurses performing abortions.

❷ **The literal rule:** This judicial approach became increasingly popular during the nineteenth century. The intention of Parliament is to be found in the ordinary and literal meaning of the words or phrase in the statute. If the result of the literal interpretation is not what Parliament intended, it can always change the law by passing another Act. This is precisely what happened in *Fisher* v *Bell* (1961) concerning the interpretation of the Restriction of Offensive Weapons Act 1959. The Act stated it was an offence to '*offer for sale*' certain weapons. The court held that a shopkeeper, displaying flick knives in his window, was not 'offering for sale' the weapons, but making an invitation to treat, and he was therefore acquitted. Parliament passed an amending Act soon after this case, making it an offence to *display* offensive weapons for sale.

❸ **The golden rule:** This judicial approach is an extension of the literal rule. If the literal meaning of the words in the statute results in an absurdity, the judge should attempt to look further than the actual words and discover and apply the intention of Parliament in passing the statute. This approach was seen in *R* v *Allen* (1872). The Offences Against the Person Act 1861 created the offence of bigamy. It stated '*Whosoever being married ... shall marry another ... commits an offence ...*'. The defendant claimed that it was impossible to legally marry another whilst already married, since such a marriage is void. On a literal interpretation of the words, this is a valid argument. However, this would have meant that Parliament had created an offence that no-one could ever be convicted of, which was absurd. They therefore interpreted the words as '*Whosoever being married ... shall go through a ceremony of marriage with another ... commits an offence*' and the defendant was convicted.

❹ **The purposive approach:** This approach is becoming more popular. It rejects the restrictions of the literal rule and suggests that the interpretative role of the judge should include, where necessary, the power to look beyond the words of the statute, in pursuit of the reason for its enactment. Such an approach is typical of civil law systems, such as those operating on the Continent, where legislation is set out as general principles leaving the fine details to be filled in later by the judges. EC law tends to be drafted in the Continental manner and, therefore, our membership of the European Union has required our judges to adopt a purposive approach to its interpretation. The need to interpret EC legislation in such a manner has forced a change in the interpretation of domestic legislation. In *Attorney-General's Reference (No. 1 of 1988)* (1989) the House of Lords, interpreting the Insider Dealing Act 1985, used the purposive approach to hold that the words '*obtain information*' meant both *seeking out* and passively *acquiring* the information. They stated that judges should not be bound by dictionary definitions and encouraged them to seek out the intention of Parliament in passing the Act, and apply the words in the statute to the case before them in the light of that knowledge. The effect of *Pepper* v *Hart*, permitting access to *Hansard*, further supports the purposive approach.

Issues in evaluation

❶ **The literal and golden rules:** The literal rule is a strict application of the doctrine of parliamentary sovereignty. It could be argued that if judges depart from the plain and ordinary meaning they are not merely interpreting the Act, they are altering it. This approach may promote certainty. However, it is based on the false premise that words have a 'plain and ordinary meaning' apart from their context. The court may say that the meaning of a word is obvious yet then disagree as to its interpretation. Counsel may have engaged in lengthy debate over the meaning of a word. Such an approach makes little allowance for the natural ambiguities of language and the impossibility of Parliament foreseeing future developments. Some may argue that such an approach encourages judges to be lazy. The golden rule protects the court from absurdities resulting from a literal construction but 'absurdity' is a concept which is vague and therefore unpredictable. It is difficult to predict when a judge will hold that a result is so absurd as to necessitate some other construction.

2 **The mischief and purposive rules:** Such approaches encourage the court to consider why the Act was passed and apply that knowledge. In view of the problems with drafting statutes, it can be argued that this is the most sensible and fairest way of approaching the task. However, it gives judges much freedom and, perhaps, allows them to make law rather than just interpret the statute, if the judge were to make a mistake as to Parliament's intentions. It places great reliance on extrinsic aids, which are limited in value, although *Pepper* v *Hart* may indicate a new era where judges really are seeking out the intentions of Parliament. It is debatable whether a purposive construction can be reconciled with the doctrine of Parliamentary sovereignty, if judges do create law under the auspices of this approach.

3 **Judicial discretion:** The approach adopted in a particular case depends upon the individual judge. There is a large discretionary element in the process of statutory interpretation. Some judges believe that the only legitimate approach, according to the doctrine of parliamentary sovereignty, is to apply the literal construction. At the other end of the scale, other judges consider it their duty to 'fill in the gaps' and ensure that foolish interpretations are avoided, and will apply a purposive construction.

2.2 THE DOCTRINE OF PRECEDENT

2.2.1 DEFINITION

The doctrine of precedent is a source of law whereby judges create law. The doctrine of precedent may also be known as '*stare decisis*' (let the decision stand) or common law. The doctrine of precedent may be defined as the practice whereby a previous decision of a court may be binding on future courts in a similar case. The circumstances which make a previous decision binding depend upon the position of the court in the court hierarchy and whether the material facts of the case are similar. The doctrine of precedent depends upon three essential elements, detailed below.

2.2.2 ELEMENTS OF THE DOCTRINE OF PRECEDENT

Court hierarchy

There are clear rules on the status of each court's decisions. As a general rule, lower courts are bound by the decisions of higher courts. The court hierarchy depends upon a centralised court system. In English law, there is only one House of Lords, Court of Appeal (two divisions) and High Court. There are many trial courts (other than the High Court) and, therefore, they are generally not bound by their own decisions. There are too many decisions from these courts which are largely unreported. The system of precedent would become unworkable if they had to take notice of their own decisions. The rules governing the operation of the court hierarchy in relation to the doctrine of precedent can be summarised in a diagram (see Figure 2.1 below). Further information is given on the House of Lords and Court of Appeal.

The House of Lords

Decisions of this court are binding upon all other courts. In the past, the House was bound by its own decisions (*London Trammays* v *London County Council* (1898)). However, the *Practice Statement* (1966) allowed for the House of Lords to depart from their previous decisions. Their reasons can be found within the *Statement*:

> '*Their Lordships regard the use of precedent as an indispensable foundation upon which to decide what is the law and its application to individual cases. It provides at least some degree of certainty upon which individuals can rely on the conduct of their affairs, as well as a basis*

for orderly development of legal rules. Their Lordships nevertheless recognise that too rigid adherence to precedent may lead to injustice in a particular case and also unduly restrict the proper development of the law. They propose, therefore, to modify their present practice and, while treating former decisions of this House as normally binding, to depart from a previous decision when it appears right to do so. In this connection they will bear in mind the danger of disturbing retrospectively the basis on which contracts, settlements of property and fiscal arrangements have been entered into and also the special need for certainty as to the criminal law...'

An example of its use occurs in *Herrington* v *British Railway Board* (1972) concerning occupiers' duty to trespassers. The House chose to overrule their own previous decision in *Addie* v *Dumbreck* (1929) on the grounds that there has been social change over the years, and in particular, since 1929, the tort of negligence had been developed, imposing general liability for negligent behaviour. However, since the *Practice Statement* was issued, it is evident that the House has been reluctant to depart from its own decisions. It must be convinced that great injustice or hardship would be experienced, and will always thoroughly consider the possible effect on established principles. In *Jones* v *Secretary of State for Social Services* (1972) the House refused to overrule its own previous decision although four of the Law Lords clearly felt that their previous decision in *Re Dowling* (1967) was wrong. They agreed that the mere finding that an earlier decision was wrong would not, in itself, be enough to justify departure.

The Court of Appeal

❶ **Civil Division:** The Court of Appeal (Civil Division) is bound by the decisions of the House of Lords, and binds lower courts. In *Young* v *Bristol Aeroplane Co Ltd* (1944) it declared that it was bound by its own previous decisions except for three instances. These restrictions on the Court of Appeal have been rigorously enforced. In *Davis* v *Johnson* (1976), a case concerning domestic violence, Lord Denning adopted the *Practice Statement*, stating, *'... while the court should regard itself as normally bound by a previous decision of the court, nevertheless it should be at liberty to depart from it if it is convinced that the previous decision was wrong'*. On appeal, the House of Lords unanimously re-affirmed that the rule laid down in *Young* v *Bristol Aeroplane Co Ltd* was still binding upon the Court of Appeal.

❷ **Criminal Division:** The Court of Appeal (Criminal Division) does not so strictly adhere to its own previous decisions, particularly where the liberty of the subject is at stake. This was confirmed in the case of *R* v *Taylor* (1950), concerning the offence of bigamy. Lord Goddard stated *'In its criminal jurisdiction ... the Court of Appeal does not apply the doctrine of stare decisis with the same rigidity as in its civil jurisdiction. If on due consideration we were to be of the opinion that the law has been either misapplied or misunderstood in an earlier decision of this court ... we should be entitled to depart from ... the earlier decision notwithstanding that the case could not be brought within any of the exceptions laid down in Young v Bristol Aeroplane Co Ltd...'*.

Law reporting

If previous decisions are potentially binding, it is essential that an effective system of reporting cases operates. Our current system of law reporting dates from 1865 when the Council of law reporting was set up. This became the Incorporated Council of Law Reporting in 1870. It publishes the official law reports. Private reports still exist. The All England Law Reports, published weekly and started in 1936, are the only general reports existing in the private sector. However, there are a vast number of private law reports covering specialist areas of law. Therefore many cases are duplicated in different sets of law reports. The system is expensive, complex and time-consuming, although computerised databases are having an impact. The LEXIS computer retrieval system records around 3,000 Court of Appeal decisions per year (whereas the All England and Weekly Law Reports only contain some 350 cases per year). Cases can also be accessed on CD Roms now.

House of Lords

Decisions bind all lower courts but the House is not bound by its own decisions (*Practice Statement* (1966))

Court of Appeal (Criminal Division)

Decisions bind all lower courts but it is not bound by its own decisions since the reputation and/or liberty of the subject is at stake (*R* v *Taylor* (1968))

Court of Appeal (Civil Division)

Decisions bind all lower courts and it is bound by its own decisions, unless any of the exceptions in *Young* v *Bristol Aeroplane Co Ltd* (1944) apply:

- the previous decision is *per incuriam* (in error of law);
- there has been a subsequent House of Lords decision, which must be followed;
- there are two conflicting Court of Appeal decisions (only one can be followed)

Divisional Court of the QBD

It is not bound to follow its own decisions for the same reasons as the Court of Appeal (Criminal Division). Decisions are binding on lower courts

Divisional Courts of the High Court

Decisions bind lower courts and they are bound to follow their own previous decisions unless *Young* v *Bristol Aeroplane Co Ltd* applies

Crown Court

They are not bound by their own decisions and neither do they bind lower courts

High Court

They are not strictly bound by their own decisions, although in practice, previous decisions are highly persuasive. Likewise, their decisions are highly persuasive on lower courts

magistrates' courts

They are not bound by their previous decisions

county courts

They are not bound by their previous decisions

Figure 2.1 The court hierarchy

The *ratio decidendi*

It is essential that the binding rule of law within a precedent case can be identified. This is known as the *ratio decidendi*. The *ratio decidendi* may be defined as *the principle of law based on the material facts of the case*. This is not stated clearly within the judgment. Whether facts in a case are 'material' to the decision is a question of interpretation by judges, when reaching their decision in a subsequent case. This is the process of reasoning by analogy. The *ratio* of a decision may be narrowed or widened by a subsequent judge before whom the case is cited as an authority. Thus the eventual and accepted *ratio* of a case may not be the *ratio* that the judge who decided the case would himself have chosen, but the one which has been approved by subsequent judges. The essence of widening or narrowing a *ratio* is in the level of abstraction that the material facts are expressed. Any statements made by the judge which are not material to the decision are known as *obiter dicta* (things said in passing) and they do not have binding force. Such statements of legal principle, are, however, of some persuasive power, particularly the *dicta* of the House of Lords.

Policy considerations may influence a judge when deciding on how to interpret the *ratio* in a previous case. The possible effects of a decision will be considered. A judge may decide that the social and economic effects of '*opening the floodgates*' would be detrimental to society. In such a situation the judge may interpret a previous decision narrowly, arresting the development of a particular area of law. Conversely, at times, judges have interpreted previous decisions very widely and extended the law. This is particularly well illustrated when examining the development of the tort of negligence (see Unit 7.2).

2.2.3 ISSUES IN EVALUATION

There are a number of possible angles in an A Level Law precedent question. Some of the fundamental issues are outlined below:

Is the doctrine of precedent a rigid or flexible source of law?

It is useful to consider this question by examining the court hierarchy (*stare decisis*) and the nature of the *ratio*. The court hierarchy indicates a rigid and inflexible system, on the whole. However, a close examination of the nature of *ratio decidendi*, together with examples of case law development drawn from any aspect of substantive law, reveals a great deal of flexibility.

Examination of the court hierarchy
The House of Lords may overrule its own previous decisions by virtue of the *Practice Statement* (1966). However, it seldom invokes the *Practice Statement*. Flexibility is achieved within the Court of Appeal (Criminal Division) but the Court of Appeal (Civil Division) is rarely able to depart from its own decisions. Higher courts may reverse or overrule the decisions of lower courts but lower courts are bound to follow higher court decisions.

Examination of ratio
The material facts of a previous case are open to wide interpretation and, therefore, a judge can choose to expand a previous decision. For example, the cases of *Alcock* v *Chief Constable of Yorkshire* (1991), *McLoughlin* v *O'Brian* (1982) and *Bourhill* v *Young* (1942) show gradual expansion of the law on duty of care to secondary victims suffering psychiatric injury as a result of the defendant's negligence. The definition of 'appropriation' in the offence of theft can be traced through cases such as *R* v *Lawrence* (1971), *R* v *Morris* (1983) and *R* v *Gomez* (1993).

Alternatively, cases may be distinguished on their material facts. For example, *Cambridge Water* v *ECL* (1994) limited the scope of *Rylands* v *Fletcher* (1868) in relation to the occupiers' liability for escaping 'things'. However, there are cases which suggest irrational distinguishing. It could be argued that *Williams* v *Roffey* (1990) (whether performance of an existing contractual duty is good consideration) should have overruled *Stilk* v *Myrick* (1807), rather than distinguishing it. Similarly, there is little difference in the material facts of *Lewis* v *Averay* (1972) and *Ingram* v *Little* (1961) on the effect of mistaken identity on the validity of a contract, yet they were decided differently by the Court of Appeal.

Should judges create law?

It is particularly useful to consider the appointment, training and social background of the judiciary when answering this question. Relevant issues include:

- It is undemocratic since judges are unelected.
- It is an unpredictable way of making new law. Judges respond to new situations quickly and individually. There is little scope for discussion, debate and reasoning.
- The appointment of judges has been heavily criticised.
- The social background of our judiciary is, on the whole, homogenous.
- There is a need to keep abreast of changing circumstances and incremental development of the law is useful.
- Parliament is unable to make all the necessary laws.
- There is a need to intervene where no clear rules exist.

Advantages and disadvantages of the doctrine of precedent

Advantages

- Following a previous decision allows a degree of certainty in the law, enabling a lawyer to predict the outcome of a client's case.

- The large number of reported cases has led to an enormous store of legal facts and decisions which is constantly being referred to and added to, thus providing a rich source of information to discover what the law is.

- Precedent is flexible enough to allow change in the law as society changes and new situations arise. It is a living system of adaptable law which develops as society develops.

- Treating similar cases in similar ways embodies justice and fairness.

Disadvantages

- The practice of distinguishing by judges has led to many apparently conflicting decisions where the facts of cases are similar, making the system confusing and unpredictable.

- The volume of law contained in law reports makes research of a particular point of law cumbersome and expensive for clients.

- The process of being legally bound to follow previous decisions can lead to a too rigid system of law since a bad or harsh precedent must be followed.

- Reform of the law through this method can be slow, since the right cases must present themselves to the right court, and since it is responsive and spontaneous, reforms may be poorly thought out.

2.3   EC LAW

2.3.1 THE ORIGINS AND DEVELOPMENT OF THE EUROPEAN COMMUNITY

The origins of the European communities date back to 1946 when Winson Churchill made a crucial speech in Zurich. He suggested '*a kind of United States of Europe*' and proposed '*a partnership between France and Germany*'. This resulted in three communities being established:

- the European Coal and Steel Community with the signing of the Treaty of Paris 1951;

- the European Economic Community with the signing of the Treaty of Rome 1957; and

- the European Atomic Energy Community with the signing of the Treaty of Rome (No. 2) (1957).

Today, the European communities are a unique grouping of 15 sovereign European member states committed to the development of closer economic and political co-operation. The *Single European Act 1986* followed by the *Treaty of Maastricht 1992* provided for a European Union based on the European Economic Community, but provided for closer integration across a wide range of activities, including economic and monetary union and a common social policy. In November 1993 the European Community officially became known as the European Union (although it is still common to refer to 'EC law' rather than 'EU law').

2.3.2 THE INSTITUTIONS OF THE EUROPEAN COMMUNITY

The Council of Ministers

This is the supreme legislative body of the Community. It rarely initiates legislation but usually acts upon proposals from the Commission. For the most part, voting on such proposals is by qualified majority. Only in a small number of instances do the Treaties provide for unanimous voting.

The Commission

The Commission is the executive arm of the Community. The Commission performs a number of functions, including:

- formulating policy and initiating proposals for new law;
- enforcing the application of EC law, investigating breaches and instituting proceedings before the European Court of Justice; and
- representing the EC in maintaining relations with international obligations.

It is important to understand that commissioners are required to be independent of all government influence. They represent the EC, not their state.

The Parliament

The elected European Parliament does not possess legislative powers, and is essentially a consultative body but its influence is strong and on the increase. The *Single European Act 1986* has introduced a new procedure for much legislation which requires the Council to act '*in co-operation with*' the Parliament following a proposal from the Commission. By virtue of this procedure, the Council is obliged to be unanimous in adopting any proposals to which Parliament has expressed its objection. The Parliament does have ultimate power to dismiss the Commission, and is in charge of the budget.

The European Court of Justice

The European Court of Justice (ECJ) is pre-eminent in the interpretation of EC law, which means that on questions of interpretation national courts, however important in their own system, must give way. The major heads of jurisdiction are:

- to rule upon allegations that a member state has failed to fulfil Treaty obligations;
- to supervise appeals against decisions (of the Council or Commission);
- to review the legality of acts of the institutions;
- to give preliminary rulings on the interpretation of EC law at the request of national courts by virtue of the Article 177 procedure;
- to rule upon actions for compensation for damage caused by the institutions;
- to rule upon disputes between the EC and its servants.

2.3.3 SOURCES OF EC PRIMARY LAW AND SECONDARY LEGISLATION

Primary law

The primary sources of EC law are the treaties creating the Communities and Union, establishing the institutions and their powers and creating the rights and duties for member states. The basic source of EC law is the *Treaty of Rome 1957*. Treaties are created directly by the Heads of State of member states. They only lay down a framework. They set out the objectives of the EC, establish its mechanisms and lay down a timetable within which the objectives are to be achieved.

Secondary legislation

In order to 'fill in the gaps' and supplement the framework set out in the Treaties, Article 189 of the *Treaty of Rome* provides that '... *the Council and the Commission ... shall make regulations, issue directives, take decisions*'.

Regulations

A Regulation has general application and is binding in its entirety and is directly applicable to all member states immediately. This can be illustrated by *The Commission* v *UK* (*Re Tachographs)* (1979). Regulations can bring about swift and immediate law reform amongst *all* member states.

Directives

Directives are addressed to member states and require the state to change their law in order to incorporate the Directive into national law. Directives are binding in *policy* but leave the choice of form and method of implementation to the member states. Directives have to be incorporated by a member state within a specified time. In the UK this is done through either an Act of Parliament or by issuing delegated legislation (s. 2 European Communities Act 1972). Examples of Directives which have been implemented include:

- the *Product Liability Directive 1985* which was incorporated as the Consumer Protection Act 1987 (see Unit 7.8); and
- the *Unfair Contract Terms Directive 1993* which was incorporated as the Unfair Contract Terms Regulations 1995 (see Unit 6.5).

Directives allow for gradual harmonisation of the laws of member states and enable member states to educate those affected, and fund and implement the reforms.

Decisions

Decisions are binding in their entirety upon those to whom they are addressed which could be one member state, one company or even one individual. Decisions are to be found, for example, where the Commission orders a company to discontinue an anti-competitive practice. Decisions bring one state, corporation or individual into line with EC policy and law.

2.3.4 THE EUROPEAN COMMUNITIES ACT 1972 AND THE SUPREMACY OF EC LAW

The UK became a member of the European Community with the signing of the Treaty of Accession. Treaties are not part of English law. Therefore, the UK had to incorporate EC law into its own law, and therefore, it was necessary to pass the European Communities Act 1972.

The 1972 Act makes provision for the immediate and direct incorporation of EC law and gives powers to introduce delegated legislation so as to achieve compliance. Section 2 incorporates all EC law into the UK and, under the doctrine of parliamentary sovereignty, judges must refer to it in their decision making.

Section 2 also states that where there is a conflict arising between UK law and EC law in a particular case, the court should follow EC law, unless our Parliament has expressly stated that UK law should prevail (which is most unlikely). Indeed, it seems that even when there is the *possibility* of conflict, the court should set aside our law, and follow EC law, whilst awaiting a ruling from the ECJ. In *R* v *Secretary of State for Transport, ex parte Factortame* (1990), concerning whether the Merchant Shipping Act 1988 conflicted with Article 7 of the Treaty of Rome 1957, the ECJ held that:

> 'National courts can disapply an Act even where it has not yet been proved that Community rights have been infringed if they can make out a prima facie case that the Act conflicts with European law...'

2.3.5 DIRECT EFFECT OF EC LAW

Meaning and scope

The ECJ created this doctrine in the *Van Gend en Loos* (1963) case. The essence of the doctrine is that some provisions of EC law can be directly relied upon by individuals in the courts of member states, irrespective of any action taken (or not taken) by the member state to implement the provision. The Treaties do not just create rights and duties between member states: they create rights and duties between individuals and member states. In *Van Gend en Loos*, the ECJ declared that EC law could have direct effect, if:

- the law was clear and unambiguous;
- it is unconditional and not dependent on the exercise of discretion; and
- it is not dependent on further action by the EC or a member state, which would seem to prevent Directives from having direct effect. However, the ECJ has evolved an interpretation which avoids this conclusion in many instances.

Vertical and horizontal effect

If EC law satisfies the conditions in *Van Gend en Loos*, it will certainly have vertical effect. This means it can be relied upon by individuals against governments or institutions of government. Some EC laws have horizontal effect too. They can be relied upon by individuals against other individuals. They give individuals rights against each other.

Which EC laws have direct effect?

Treaties, Regulations and Decisions
Treaties and Regulations can be directly relied upon by individuals in their national courts. They have vertical and horizontal effect (subject to the *Van Gend en Loos* conditions). Decisions can be relied upon against the addressee (i.e. the state, company or individual) since they are binding immediately on the addressee.

Directives
Directives require member states to incorporate them into their own law. Because of this, it was thought, for some time, that they could not have direct effect. In *Marshall* v *Southampton and South West Hampshire AHA* (1986), concerning discrimination between men and women on grounds of age, the ECJ held that, since a health authority is a government institution, Mrs Marshall was able to rely on the unimplemented Directive. It had vertical effect. The reasoning behind this was explained in *Publico Ministerio* v *Ratti* (1980), where the ECJ pointed out that member states could not be allowed to rely on their own wrongful failure to implement Directives as a means of denying individual rights. However, had Mrs Marshall been employed by a private company, she would not have been able to rely on the Directive in the same way. In *Duke* v *GEC Reliance* (1988), Mrs Duke was unable to rely on a Directive against her employer, as her employer was a private company. Directives do not have horizontal effect. However, the case of *Italy* v *Francovich* (1992) established that where a government fails to implement a Directive within the specified time limit, a person who is caused loss by that failure can sue the state for damages.

2.3.6 THE PRELIMINARY RULINGS PROCEDURE

Purpose

Article 177 of the *Treaty of Rome 1957* gives the ECJ the power to give preliminary rulings on the interpretation of the Treaties and secondary legislation. The purpose of Article 177 is to ensure uniformity of interpretation of EC law throughout the courts of the member states. Instead of an *appeal* court being established, the Treaty of Rome provided for a *reference* court. In this way, two separate spheres of jurisdiction are preserved. The ECJ rules on the meaning of EC law but does not rule on its application. The national court must accept the ECJ's interpretation and then apply it to the case before them. It is, essentially, a co-operative procedure.

Reference by a court

Article 177 provides that it is for the court or tribunal to refer, not the parties. The ECJ, as a reference court, has had considerable impact on our legal system.

Courts or tribunals which must refer

Where the court or tribunal is the *final* court or tribunal it *must* refer the matter to the ECJ. In English law the final court will always be the House of Lords, but in some matters, so might lower courts. Reference must be made if the court is satisfied that:

- the question of EC law is relevant to the decision made by the national court;
- no previous interpretation of the provision of EC law has been made by the ECJ;
- the interpretation is not *acte clair*, meaning that a ruling is not necessary as interpretation is so obvious that it leaves no scope for reasonable doubt.

Courts or tribunals which may refer

Any other court or tribunal *may* refer if it considers that a decision is necessary to enable it give judgment. The reference is discretionary. In many cases, it may be advisable for lower courts to avoid references since the issues will often become clearer at later stages in the process. However, this will not assist where appeals are not made. When deciding whether or not to refer, Lord Denning, in *Bulmer* v *Bollinger* (1974), suggested the following factors should be considered by the court or tribunal: time, delay and expense; the need not to overburden the ECJ; the need to be clear as to the question to be put; the difficulty and importance of the point; and the wishes of the parties.

2.3.7 THE DOCTRINE OF PARLIAMENTARY SOVEREIGNTY AND COMMUNITY MEMBERSHIP

Membership of the Community has resulted in some EC law becoming part of our law without reference to Parliament. It could be argued, therefore, that EC law is a higher source of law. Section 2(4) European Communities Act 1972 provides that English law should be interpreted and have effect subject to the principle that EC law is supreme. It is debatable whether Parliament is still supreme is some areas of law. However, strictly speaking it could be argued that Parliament has merely incorporated EC law into our law by passing the 1972 Act, and therefore, in exercising its sovereignty, need only repeal it, and reclaim its entire sovereignty. Therefore Parliament has *delegated* part of its sovereignty for an unspecified amount of time. The weight of these arguments can only be assessed by reference to economic and practical arguments about whether the UK is in a position to withdraw from the Community, or whether, after so many years, it is dependent upon membership.

2.4   EQUITY

2.4.1 HISTORICAL DEVELOPMENT

The old common law system

Historically, equity must be distinguished from the old common law. The common law emerged as the product of the Normal Conquest of England in 1066. Initially the courts were no more than part of the King's Council, the *Curia Regis*, but gradually the common law courts began to take on a distinct identity. Actions could only be brought in the courts upon purchase of a writ issued by the Chancellor's office. There were many problems with the common law:

- Writs were expensive, sometimes costing more than the amount of the plaintiff's claim.
- There was also excessive emphasis on procedural and formal matters and an action could fail on the smallest error in a writ, such as describing a mare as a stallion.
- The only common law remedy for a civil wrong was damages, and sometimes this was not appropriate.

- The common law did not recognise the concept of the trust.

- In relation to mortgages, the property became the property of the lender as soon as the last date for repayment passed. The borrower forfeited all money paid up to that date. Sometimes a lender would 'disappear' so that payment could not be made by the required date.

- As more and more new writs were created by the Chancellor's office in response to new problems, Parliament's powers to make new law were eroded. In response to this Parliament passed the **Provisions of Oxford 1258** which prevented new writs from being created. Effectively, this halted further development of the common law. These features of the common law system often lead to injustice.

The Court of Chancery

Increasingly, as plaintiffs were unable to obtain justice in the common law courts, they petitioned the King directly, requesting that he grant a remedy. Even though the courts of common law had been established, the King retained powers '*to do equal and right justice and discretion in mercy and truth*'. The King began to grant remedies on an ad hoc basis. As the common law courts became more formalistic and correspondingly more inaccessible, pleas to the King increased. Eventually he delegated his power to his first Chancellor. Gradually, people began to petition the Lord Chancellor directly. Remedies were granted according to what was fair or equitable. Such unsystematic granting of remedies lead to the well-known accusation that '*equity varies with the length of the Chancellor's foot*'.

To remedy this allegation the Court of Chancery was established by the Lord Chancellor in 1474 to administer equity and create some consistency. The Court proceeded according to the dictates of 'conscience' which transcended fixed rules. Common law and equity were separate, both in theory and procedure, each with their own courts.

Conflict between equity and common law

In theory, common law and equity were a perfect partnership, with equity providing a gloss on common law. In practice, common law and equity were administered side by side in separate courts in an uneasy alliance. Sometimes decisions in the common law courts and the Court of Chancery openly conflicted. Difficulties arose over which was the superior decision that had to be followed. This was resolved in the *Earl of Oxford's Case* (1615) which brought common law and equity into open conflict and resulted in the ruling of James I that '*where common law and equity are in conflict, equity should prevail*'.

The Judicature Acts 1873–75

Problems remained with the dual systems of equity and common law. Plaintiffs would have to bring two separate actions, entailing expense and delay. The Judicature Acts 1873–75 set up a new structure of courts known as the Supreme Court of Judicature. Matters previously dealt with by the Court of Chancery were assigned to the Chancery Division of the High Court. These Acts fused the *administration* of common law and equity. Equity and common law were to be administered side by side in all courts and all courts could award common law and equitable remedies. This is the position today.

Maxims of equity

The essence of equity was to act as a corrective to the rigour of common law. It was not to be tied to rules. However, if no rules at all were observed, and cases were dealt with entirely on matters of conscience, it could be alleged that '*conscience varied according to every individual Chancellor*'. As the Chancellor began to deal with more and more petitions, it was inevitable that standard practices would develop. The Chancellors of the seventeenth century began to give reasons for their decisions. Maxims of equity began to develop in order to maintain the justice and fairness notion and to bring some consistency and predictability to equity. These are broad statements of principle and were designed to ensure that decisions were morally fair. Examples of maxims include:

- *'He who comes to equity must come with clean hands'*. This means that plaintiffs who have themselves been in the wrong in some way will not be granted an equitable remedy (see *D & C Builders* v *Rees* (1966)).
- *'He who seeks equity must do equity'*. Anyone who seeks equitable relief must be prepared to act fairly towards their opponent (see *Chappell* v *Times Newspapers Ltd* (1975)).
- *'Delay defeats equity'*. Where a plaintiff takes an unreasonably long time to bring an action, equitable remedies will not be available (see *Leaf* v *International Galleries* (1950)).

Alongside these maxims, greater weight was given to precedent. By the nineteenth century, equity had a developed case law and recognised principles, and was no less rigid than the common law.

2.4.2 MODERN SIGNIFICANCE OF EQUITY

Although equity was developed many years ago in response to the old common law system, it still has much relevance in our law today. Equity has shown itself capable of adapting and expanding to meet new needs. Areas of law which could be used to illustrate its modern significance include:

- Equitable remedies: equity has substantially increased the number of remedies available to a wronged party. Equitable remedies include injunctions, specific performance, rectification and recission (see Units 4.4 and 4.5). Relatively new remedies have been developed under equity such as the *Mareva* injunction and the *Anton Piller* order.
- Trusts and mortgages.
- Development of equitable principles: these include the doctrines of promissory estoppel (see Unit 6.2) and undue influence (see Unit 6.3) and the duty of confidentiality.

2.5   LAW REFORM

2.5.1 INTRODUCTION

An effective legal system must adapt and change with society. There are many reasons why laws must be reformed. These include:

- to achieve different political aims;
- to respond to scientific and technological developments in society (such as the development of surrogacy and embryology or the impact of computers);
- to remedy problems which have arisen when the law has been applied to cases (to close loopholes);
- to meet the UK's international obligations (such as obligations imposed by our membership of the European Community);
- to respond to public opinion on a matter;
- to repeal old or obsolete laws.

2.5.2 AN OVERVIEW

Law reform is brought about in a number of ways. In essence, these methods are the sources of law discussed previously in this chapter and reference should be made to the relevant parts.

Judges

Judges can bring about law reform through the doctrine of precedent. Much of the law of tort and contract, and to a lesser extent criminal law, has been both created and reformed by judges developing precedent decisions (see Unit 2.2). In practice, major reforms are rarely produced by the courts (although see *R* v *R* (1991) on marital rape). Judges would not be adequate as the sole agency of reform. Some advantages and disadvantages of judicial law reform can be identified as:

Advantages

- It is an adaptable method. It can respond to situations immediately.
- Reform of the law takes effect immediately.
- It is relatively predictable. The vast amount of cases allow lawyers to predict possible reforms.

Disadvantages

- Law reform is retrospective, affecting something that happened before the judges decided what the law was.
- Judges are unelected, and therefore, it could be argued, they should not make decisions which change the law in areas of great social or moral controversy.
- It is reactive and haphazard means of law reform. The judges can only deal with such points as they arise in the cases before them, and this depends on the parties involved having sufficient finance, determination and interest to take their case up through the courts.
- Judges have to make decisions on the basis of the issues presented to them. They cannot commission research, or consult with interested bodies to find out the possible effects of a decision on society.
- Judges are constrained by *stare decisis*, and in general this prohibits any really radical reforms.

Parliament and delegated bodies

The majority of law reform is carried out by Parliament, directly or through delegated bodies.

Advantages

- Reform of the law is made by an elected body, making it more democratic.
- Ideas come from a range of people and groups (see Units 2.1.1 and 2.1.2).
- There are opportunities to consult with experts and to consider the effects of reform on society.
- Public opinion can be taken into account.
- There are official law reform bodies providing expertise and advice (see Unit 2.5.3).
- Parliament may delegate their law-making powers to others when necessary, enabling experts or those with specialist knowledge to reform the law.

Disadvantages

- It is generally a slow and inflexible method of reforming the law. If a Bill is rushed through, problems with its interpretation and application often arise (such as the Dangerous Dogs Act 1991).
- Poor drafting and problems with subsequent interpretation can frustrate the aims of the reform.
- The government dominate the legislative agenda. There is little scope for MPs and pressure groups to contribute ideas in reality.

The European Community

It is important to note that more reform of the law is being brought about by the European Community, particularly in the spheres of employment law, environmental law, consumer law and commercial law.

2.5.3 LAW REFORM AGENCIES

The Law Commission

The Law Commission was established by the Law Commissions Act 1965. The Commission's terms of reference are wide. They are set out in s. 3. It is the Commission's duty *'to take and keep under review all the law ... with a view to its systematic development and reform ...'*

The Law Commission is comprised of five full-time members, all of whom must be lawyers. The chairman will have been a judge. There is a staff of about 25 lawyers. The annual agenda of the Law Commission is approved by the Lord Chancellor. It issues annual reports which are laid before Parliament by the Lord Chancellor. When the Commission is working on substantive law reform, it produces a 'working paper', detailing the present law on the relevant subject, criticisms of it, and options for change. This is circulated to a wide range of interested parties, and their views are sought. Following this, a final report is produced, with a draft Bill.

The work of the Law Commission is large and varied. Many of its proposals are eventually implemented in the form of Acts of Parliament. As far as general law reform is concerned, the Commission has made over 100 proposals for major reforms, around 70% of which have been adopted. The Law Commission has instigated major family law reforms. Examples of statutes instigated by the Law Commission include the:

- Criminal Law Act 1967;
- Criminal Attempts Act 1981;
- Matrimonial and Family Proceedings Act 1984; and
- Occupiers' Liability Act 1984.

Royal Commissions

These are set up periodically to study particular areas of law reform, usually as a result of criticisms and concerns about the area in question. An eminent judge is appointed as chairperson and academics, lawyers, and other appointed persons conduct a detailed investigation and make recommendations. The Commission produces a final report detailing its recommendations, which the government can then choose to act upon or not. Royal Commissions are expensive to fund and have met with mixed success. The most recent Royal Commissions are:

- Royal Commission on Civil Liability and Compensation for Personal Injury (the Pearson Commission) 1978 (not implemented);
- Royal Commission on Legal Services (the Benson Commission) 1979;
- Royal Commission on Criminal Procedure (the Phillips Commission) 1981 (Police and Criminal Evidence Act 1984);
- Royal Commission on Criminal Justice (the Runciman Commission) 1993 (Criminal Justice and Public Order Act 1994; Criminal Appeal Act 1995).

The Advisory Committees

The Advisory Committees are part-time bodies and include:

❶ The Law Reform Committee, established in 1952 to *'consider, having regard especially to judicial decisions, what changes are desirable in such legal doctrines as the Lord Chancellor may from time to time refer to the Committee'*. It comprises judges, practising barristers, solicitors and academic lawyers. It focuses on fairly narrow issues requiring technical solutions rather than radical changes. Examples of law reform include the:

- Misrepresentation Act 1967;
- Occupiers' Liability Act 1957;
- Latent Damage Act 1986.

② The Criminal Law Revision Committee was established in 1959. It reports to the Home Secretary on criminal law. Examples of law reform instigated by the Committee include the Theft Acts 1968 and 1978. The Committee has not met since 1985 and seems to have fallen into disuse. Much of its work has been taken over by the Law Commission.

Temporary committees and public inquiries

From time to time the government sets up a temporary body to investigate a controversial area of law. One of the best examples of such a body is the Warnock Committee leading to the Surrogacy Arrangements Act 1985 and the Human Fertilisation and Embryology Act 1990. Another example is the Civil Justice Review which reported in 1986 and formed the basis of the Courts and Legal Services Act 1990.

Major disasters, such as the Hillsborough football stadium and events such as the Brixton riots, prompted public inquiries. Public inquiries are independent of government, often with experts in the particular area of law. They consult interested groups, and attempt to reach a consensus between them, conducting their investigation as far as possible in a non-political way. The inquiry into Hillsborough, headed by Lord Taylor, brought about changes in safety requirements at sports venues. The inquiry into the Brixton riots, headed by Lord Scarmen, led to some of its proposals on police accountability being incorporated into the Police and Criminal Evidence Act 1984.

Issues in evaluation

* There is no obligation for governments to consult with law reform bodies or set up Royal Commissions.

* Governments have no obligation to follow recommendations, and may reject them on political grounds.

* Governments may radically alter the detailed proposals.

* Royal Commissions and temporary committees are disbanded after they have reported, taking no further part in the implementation of the law. This could be regarded as a waste of expertise.

* There is no single ministry for law reform, such as a Ministry of Justice, so no member of government makes it their priority.

Illustrative questions

1 'Statute law consists of the words that Parliament has enacted. It is for the courts to construe those words and it is the court's duty in so doing to give effect to the intention of Parliament in using those words.'

(Lord Browne-Wilkinson in *Pepper* v *Hart* (1992))

How do the courts go about discovering the intention of Parliament when interpreting Acts of Parliament? (50)

(*UODLE*)

Tutorial note
It is important to refer to the words in the quote throughout your essay. Some explanation of Lord Browne-Wilkinson's words are required, with an account of the rule in *Pepper* v *Hart*. Ensure that the question set is answered, rather than a general discussion of everything you know about statutory interpretation.

Suggested answer
A definition of statutory interpretation should be given and identification of the problems judges face when carrying out this task. Your introduction should also include some discussion indicating that the role of the judge in interpreting statutes is to apply the words to cases before them, giving effect to the intention of Parliament. Some

reference could be made to the doctrine of parliamentary sovereignty. The fundamental issue in this question is how to discover the intention of Parliament. Some judges, such as Lord Browne-Wilkinson, believe that the intention of Parliament must be discovered. An explanation of the *purposive* approach and *mischief rule*, together with case illustrations should be given. Details of the instrinsic and *extrinsic* aids which judges may refer to, in order to assist them, require description and evaluation. This discussion should include the significance of the *Pepper* v *Hart* decision. On the other hand, other judges believe that the intention of Parliament is to be found in the plain and ordinary meaning of the words of the statute, even if this results in an absurdity. The literal rule should be explained and illustrated with a case. The golden rule which, although based on the literal rule, modifies its excesses, must also be described and illustrated. The answer should also include some discussion of presumptions and rules of language. Having described the various approaches, your answer should attempt to evaluate these. Your conclusion should summarise how the courts have set about discovering the intention of Parliament, emphasising key evaluative points.

2 Evaluate the statement that 'precedent is a useful tool but a bad master'.   (50)
(UODLE)

Tutorial note
Is important to explain the meaning of this quote, rather than launching into a description of the doctrine of precedent. The quote is suggesting that the doctrine of precedent must not be followed blindly, so that it becomes a 'master' and case law ceases to develop. Instead it should be used intelligently by judges. The law may develop through the process of reasoning by analogy. Therefore it is a 'useful tool'.

Suggested answer
The doctrine of precedent should be defined, and an explanation of the meaning of the quote offered. Your answer should explain the notion of binding precedent, examining the court hierarchy in detail. At this stage, the notion of precedent as a 'master' could be explored, since the court hierarchy appears rigid, with, in general, only the House of Lords being able to depart from their previous decisions. You should then explore how precedent operates, emphasising the interpretative nature of *ratio decidendi*, and distinguishing it from *obiter dicta*. Since the *ratio* is based on material facts, these can be expressed at different levels of abstraction. Sometimes the judges will distinguish a case on its material facts and, therefore, choose not to follow it. Examples of case law should be given to illustrate this. At other times, judges will interpret the material facts of a previous case widely, and so expand the law on a case by case basis (e.g., the nervous shock decisions). In this way, the law is allowed to develop, but within a framework, which offers an element of certainty. Therefore, precedent is a 'useful tool'.

3 What has been the effect on English law and law making of United Kingdom membership of the European Union (Community)?   (25)
(AEB)

Tutorial note
Since the question demands a broad approach, you are not expected to write in huge amounts of detail on the various ways EC membership has affected English law, otherwise you would run out of time in the examination. A common error in answering questions on Europe, is to give vast amounts of detail on the institutions and little else. Clearly that sort of information is not demanded by this question. The important issue in tackling broad questions, is to incorporate breadth into your answer. It is important to structure your answer carefully.

Suggested answer.
It would be useful to start your essay with a brief account of the origins and purpose of the European Community. Sources of EC law (primary and secondary legislation) must be described, carefully distinguishing between Regulations, Directives and

Decisions. Some detail on the UK becoming a member of the Community, together with an account of the provisions of the European Communities Act 1972 is essential. The supremacy of EC law over domestic law must be emphasised. The key ways membership of the EC has affected English law should be identified. These are through direct effect, preliminary rulings procedure and issues of sovereignty. The meaning and scope of direct effect, as created in *Van Gend en Loos* must be described and an analysis of which EC laws have direct effect. Your discussion should distinguish between vertical and horizontal effect. Cases should be used to illustrate the concept. When considering the impact of Article 177 preliminary rulings procedure, an explanation of the purpose of Article 177 and how it operates is necessary. Its impact on the court hierarchy and its effect on individuals must be assessed and illustrated with a case. Arguments should be presented as to whether membership has affected the doctrine of parliamentary sovereignty. In your conclusion, you should attempt to summarise the effect of UK membership of the Community on English law and law making, distinguishing between the two.

Practice questions

1 (a) Comment on why equity was found to be necessary.

(b) Describe the equitable remedies which are available to the court today. Comment on the circumstances in which they can be granted. (30)

(*NEAB*)

Pitfalls

This is a two-part question and the answer must be divided accordingly. In part (a) it is common error for students to give only a vague account of the old common law. Part (b) is prescriptive. The examiner wants an account of equitable remedies. No marks would be awarded for an explanation of other areas of law, such as promissory estoppel, no matter how well learned and accurate an account is given. It would be foolish to attempt this question unless you have good knowledge of remedies and can use cases to illustrate the remedies.

Key points

Part (a)

❶ Explanation and evaluation of old common law system leading to the growth of equity.

❷ Establishment of the Court of Chancery, maxims of equity and *stare decisis*.

❸ Impact of *Earl of Oxford's* case and dealing with conflict between equity and common law.

❹ Impact of Judicature Acts and the merging of the administration of the courts.

Part (b)

❶ Description and illustration with appropriate cases of equitable remedies available to the court today:
  • specific performance;
  • injunction;
  • recission;
  • rectification;
  • restitution.

❷ Circumstances in which they can be granted, including reference to their discretionary element.

2 Give a critical account of the legislative process.

(25)
(*AEB*)

Pitfalls

The key word in this question is 'critical'. Students often choose to describe (at length) the legislative process, suggesting one or two problems in the last paragraph. It makes much more sense to evaluate and illustrate the processes as you describe them. Failure to make use of examples of Acts which illustrate any critical comments is a common pitfall in this type of question too. Another common weakness in answers is to solely concentrate on the formal passage of a Bill through Parliament, without considering the informal processes at all, resulting in a narrow answer.

Key points

❶ A definition of legislation, together with some discussion of its purpose.

❷ Critical explanation of Parliament and the doctrine of parliamentary sovereignty.

❸ Explanation of types of Bill (public/private) and sponsors of Bills (government /private members).

❹ Critical discussion of the generation of ideas for legislation.

❺ Critical discussion of mechanisms for consultation and the drafting processes.

❻ Critical discussion of the formal passage of a Bill through Parliament.

❼ Reference to appropriate examples to illustrate the criticisms made.

LEGAL THEORY

Units in this chapter

Chapter objectives

The chapter considers:

- Positive and naturalist approaches to understanding the phenomenon of law and the issue of obedience.
- The distinction between law and morals.
- The meaning of 'justice' and some general theories.
- The extent to which legal rules and institutions may be said to pursue, promote or obstruct the interests of justice.
- The concept of legal personality.
- The meaning of natural and artificial personality.

3.1 NATURE OF LAW

3.1.1 APPROACHES TO UNDERSTANDING LAW

It is natural to think of law as consisting of rules of law which:

- may forbid things to be done or oblige things to be done and lay down what will happen if these instructions are not followed;

- may also enable things to be done (for instance, creating a company or getting married).

However, the phenomenon of law cannot be understood simply as a collection of independent, self-contained rules. To the extent that law does consist of rules (some commentators have argued that 'rules' merely masks the choices that judges make in practice, or that 'principles' and 'policies' are also vital components of law), those rules can only be fully understood in their social, economic and political context and in relation to the ways in which, and by whom, they are interpreted, administered and applied. Additionally, since rules of law share certain characteristics with other rules which people tend to obey, such as rules of morality, explanations of law have generally sought to establish some criteria to enable legal rules to be distinguished from other rules.

Thus, attempts to understand and explain the phenomenon of law draw on a variety of perspectives. Two broad approaches form a useful starting point:

❶ The **positivist** approach seeks to describe law as it *is* rather than considering what it *ought* to be. The main concern is with formal criteria for identifying authoritative law and distinguishing law from other phenomena, such as morals. Versions attributable to **Bentham** and **Austin** viewed law as a command from a sovereign power reinforced by a coercive sanction. This theory explained some of the characteristics of law but did not convey any notion of the true sense of obligation normally associated with law; that law is obeyed because it is thought to be right rather than because there is force to compel obedience. **Hart's** more recent modified positivist theory expressed law as a system of primary and secondary rules. Primary rules imposed the duties whilst secondary rules enabled primary rules to be recognised and adapted. Hart argued that the obligation to obey the primary rules arose not from the threat of coercive sanctions but from the perception (achieved after critical reflection and even against self-interest) that demands for conformity to certain patterns of behaviour as a common standard (embodied in the rules) were justified.

❷ The **naturalist** (natural law) approach seeks to understand law by reference not only to formal criteria but also moral or ethical criteria. It is overtly concerned not only with describing the law as it is but also with questions about what it ought to be in the light of authoritative criteria of validity. Of course, the claim to assess the validity of laws properly made according to formal criteria calls into question the higher authority on which the claim relies. Proponents of this approach have purported to find this higher authority in reason (**Plato, Aristotle**) and in morality derived from religion (**Aquinas** – though reason played a prominent part too). The social contract theories of **Hobbes, Locke** and **Rousseau** (rights and obligations derived from a notional 'contract' with the state or with the people) owed something to the 'reason' approach. Naturalist approaches were given fresh impetus during the twentieth century by the gross abuses of law and violation of human rights in Nazi Germany and other totalitarian regimes and a powerful version has been developed by **Finnis**, in which not only duties but also natural rights feature prominently.

This discussion leads conveniently to the question, can it be right to disobey the law? Though positivist thinking tends to argue that the validity of a law is to be established only by formal criteria, implying that it must be obeyed if valid by such criteria (in the UK, properly enacted by Parliament or laid down in the common law), positivist theorists were not generally addressing that question and even they might concede that some laws could be so unjust as to merit disobedience. Conversely, naturalist thinking does not inevitably lead to the conclusion that all laws perceived as somehow wrong or unjust may be disobeyed. Even in the unlikely event that everyone agreed on the moral or ethical criteria by which laws might be judged and whether any law was or was not valid by those criteria, commonplace law-breaking could only be to the detriment of society. It is not unreasonable to argue that if there are procedures for changing the law, and realistic possibilities of using them to do so, then disobedience should not be the first resort. However, it may be that some laws are so universally repugnant that all right-minded people would consider that they should be disobeyed. In these circumstances, both positivists and naturalists might concede that even law according to the formal criteria should be disobeyed.

In reality, those who deliberately disobey laws because they perceive them to be wrong are often in a minority. Yet disobedience may have significant practical consequences. For instance, an issue may be publicly scrutinised for the first time and the dominant perspective challenged. Legislative change may be brought about. Thus, the scale of protest about the poll tax in the early 1990's, including significant acts of civil disobedience, clearly influenced the government's decision to abandon it.

3.2   LAW AND MORALS

3.2.1 DEFINITIONS OF LAW AND MORALITY

The relationship between law and morality is complex. Law is often defined as a set of rules and principles which enforce particular types of behaviour. A society's code of morality may be defined as a set of beliefs, values, principles and standards of behaviour. The morals of individuals will vary from person to person. Morality, in this context, is the consensus reached in society in relation to different activities and standards of behaviour. However, there are many issues over which it is difficult or impossible to reach consensus in a pluralistic society. The main focus in this topic is how far the law *does* and *should* enforce moral rules. What should the relationship between the two be?

3.2.2 THE DISTINCTION BETWEEN LEGAL RULES AND MORAL RULES

LAW	MORALS
Laws are made by some formal institution, for example, Parliament or judges.	Morals evolve as a feeling within society. No formal creation exists.
Laws can be instantly made and instantly cancelled. For example, an Act can be repealed or a previous case decision overruled.	Morals form slowly and change slowly with society's opinions and attitudes. There is usually a slow transitional period, for example, society's attitude to pre-marital sex or Sunday trading.
Generally, a law either exists or it does not exist. Its existence can be established.	Morals are much vaguer in their definition. Although society is generally agreed that certain activities are immoral, such as murder or theft, on many issues society's opinion is divided, e.g. on abortion or homosexuality.
Breach of the law leads to some form of punishment or remedy enforced by the state.	Breach of a moral may lead to some form of social condemnation, but the state is not involved.
Laws are rules to which society's attitude is basically irrelevant. A law exists even if the vast majority disobey it (although often the law will be changed in such circumstances).	Morals are rules which reflect society's values and beliefs. Therefore these values and beliefs are vital for the existence of morals.

3.2.3 THEORIES ON THE RELATIONSHIP BETWEEN LAW AND MORALITY

There are many theories of how far the law should seek to enforce moral rules. Much of the debate concerns the use of criminal law to enforce morality. Key theories include:

The liberal view

This theory of the relationship between law and morality derives from **John Stuart Mill**, in his *Essay on Liberty* (1859). He wrote *'the only purpose for which power can be rightfully exercised over any member of a civilised community against his will is to prevent harm to others. His own good, either physical or moral, is not a sufficient warrant'*. Mill believed that the law should be used not to uphold a particular morality but rather to prevent harm to citizens. The 1957 Report of the *Wolfenden Committee on Homosexual Offences and Prostitution* recommended the decriminalisation of homosexual acts between consenting adults in private. The Wolfenden Committee endorsed Mill's statement, stating that the function of the criminal law *'... is to preserve public order and decency to protect citizens from what is offensive or injurious and to provide sufficient safeguards against exploitation and aggravation of others ... It is not, in our view, the function of the law to intervene in the private lives of citizens'*.

Mill's harm-to-others principle gives rise to a number of problems:

- What is harm? Physical harm is clearly intended, but does it also include mental, moral, emotional and spiritual harm? If it includes non-physical harm, it allows intervention in practically all circumstances.

- Who counts as others? Clearly this includes human beings, but does it also include the foetus? The debate over whether the foetus deserves legal protection is not clarified by this theory.

- How much 'harm' is sufficient for legal intervention?

- Why should we accept the harm-to-others principle as the exclusive justification for intervention? Why shouldn't society be concerned to protect individuals from their own folly, particularly vulnerable people, such as children?

The Hart/Devlin debate

During the 1950s and 1960s **Lord Devlin** and **Professor Hart** developed the debate about Mill's harm-to-others principle and the Wolfenden Report.

Lord Devlin's 'legal moralism'

The essence of Lord Devlin's theory is that a recognised morality is essential to societal existence. This justifies limiting individual liberty in order to protect the fabric of society. Lord Devlin argued that the criminal law can justifiably seek to enforce moral standards since morality is the *'cement of society'*. Devlin stated that *'society may use the law to preserve morality in the same way it uses it to safeguard anything else that is essential to its existence'*. The theory is based on the premise that there is an 'objective morality'. Society should tolerate what the reasonable man would tolerate, and where conduct is so immoral that the reasonable man would feel disgust, society should ban that activity. Devlin sets some limits on the law's intervention. There should be maximum freedom consistent with the integrity of society and privacy should be respected as far as possible. Laws should be concerned with the *minimum* not the *maximum* standards. Examples of the use of this theory can be seen in:

- *Shaw* v *DPP* (1962) (conspiracy to corrupt public morals in publishing details of services offered by prostitutes);

- *R* v *Brown & Others* (1993) (*consensual* sado-masochistic activities causing personal injury – no defence to offences under the Offences Against the Person Act 1861).

Criticisms of Devlin's theory include:

- The argument that *'morality is the cement of society'* is assumed and unqualified. Devlin has not proved that every act of immorality threatens the survival of society. Professor Hart (see below) pointed out that there is no evidence to support, and much to refute, the theory that those who deviate from conventional sexual morality are in other ways hostile to society.

- An objective standard of morality is difficult, if not impossible, to ascertain. Sometimes the morality of the masses may not necessarily be sound, for example, apartheid or Nazism.

- Legal moralism does not allow for changing moralities. The development of society may be held back by law perpetuating a particular moral rule.

Professor Hart's 'paternalism'

Professor Hart developed Mill's harm-to-others principle so as to include physical harm to oneself (as well as others) as a ground for legal intervention. The law may intervene not because the conduct is wrong, but because it is harmful. This can be characterised as a *paternalistic* approach. He acknowledged the problem of defining 'harm' and stated that it did not include moral harm to oneself. Hart's focus is on the individual, whereas Devlin's focus is on society. An example of the use of this theory can be seen in the laws concerning the possession of prohibited drugs.

Criticisms of Hart's theory include:

- Should the law seek to prevent adults causing harm to themselves? Perhaps people do not want to be 'looked after'.

- The argument that the law is entitled to show a paternalistic interest and decide for others what is in their best interests could be legitimately extended to showing a paternalistic interest in the morals of society.

- 'Harm' is not clearly defined by Professor Hart, yet the involvement of the law depends upon this.

3.2.4 EXAMPLES

There are many contexts in which the relationship between law and morality may be explored. Many examples focus on issues where there is no real consensus in society as to what the law should be, particularly sexual morality. However, traditionally some laws are inextricably bound up with morality. For example, the law of tort, and in particular, negligence, is related to the moral principle that 'you should not harm your neighbour', and if you do so, you should compensate him or her. The rationale for the law's intervention into contracts, for example, by enacting consumer legislation, is protection of the weaker party, which is a moral principle.

Any area of interest may be considered, but when analysing the issue, it is important that the legal rule(s) are explained, the theories are applied, and the moral arguments are considered. The following example illustrates this:

Euthanasia

The law does not allow us to authorise our own humane death, for example, by lethal injection, when suffering from a painful terminal disease. Any doctor who is involved in a 'mercy killing' may be prosecuted for murder or manslaughter (*R* v *Cox* (1992)). There have been many attempts to bring about reform of this law, and recently debate has centred on recognition of a 'living will'. Presumably the rule is based on morality. However, it is difficult to reach consensus on this issue. A national opinion poll in 1993 found that 79% of people supported the legalisation of euthanasia, suggesting a divergence of law and morality. When considering whether this is an area which the law should intervene, different conclusions are reached depending on the particular theory applied:

- Presumably, Mill's harm-to-others principle would not advocate intervention, since the intention is to harm oneself not others. The individual is best able to decide when and how he or she should die. This is an issue of individual freedom. The law should allow us to die proudly.

- However, Hart's paternalism would not allow euthanasia to be legalised, since the law must protect people from harming themselves.

- If Devlin's legal moralism theory is applied, it would depend on whether, objectively, this is a conduct which is so immoral that it justifies legal intervention to preserve society; society must prevent intentional killing in all circumstances since it is too fundamental to society to be negotiable on any terms. However, if the masses are in favour of euthanasia, perhaps, objectively, it is an area in which the law should not be involved.

3.3   LAW AND JUSTICE

Clearly, there is a close connection between the ideas of law and justice. We talk, for instance, of civil justice and criminal justice, of courts and judges dispensing justice, and examples of miscarriages of justice. We expect law and the legal system to promote justice and might doubt their claims upon us if they failed to do so. Yet none of this provides us with any clear understanding of what we mean by 'justice'.

3.3.1 FORMAL AND SUBSTANTIAL JUSTICE

The requirements of **formal** justice would be satisfied by the consistent and impartial application of rules and procedures without reference to questions of fairness or rightness of outcome. The requirements of **substantial** justice would be satisfied only if the outcome of the application of rules and procedures conformed to some higher principle of fairness. Thus, a rule that men and women were entitled to equal rates of pay for the same work could be applied so as to achieve formal justice simply by ensuring that all men and women doing the same work were paid at equal rates. Yet this might offend our ideas of true fairness (substantial justice) if it turned out that most of the higher paid jobs went only to men (or only to women). Here, substantial justice might require some way of ensuring a more equitable distribution between men and women of higher and lower paid jobs.

There is obviously some parallel here between positivist and naturalist approaches to understanding law and it might be expected that naturalists would be very concerned with issues of substantial justice. Essentially, the pursuit of substantial justice requires some theory of how the relations within a community between individuals (as individuals and as a group or groups) should be organised, and how the benefits and the burdens should be distributed. Law will play an important part in that organisation and distribution and will be perceived as just to the extent that it implements the theory and unjust to the extent that it prevents implementation or makes it more difficult.

3.3.2 DISTRIBUTIVE AND CORRECTIVE JUSTICE

Theories of justice are sometimes expressed in terms of a distinction between distributive and corrective justice. **Distributive** justice concerns distribution of the benefits and burdens amongst members of a society according to some theory of values (one of which, for instance, might be that differences of sex, race or religion are not significant in any distribution). The values which lie behind the distribution are the yardstick of substantial justice. **Corrective** justice repairs any disturbance to the balance achieved by distributive justice, as when a victim loses property by theft or suffers loss by another's breach of contract.

3.3.3 SOME SPECIFIC THEORIES OF JUSTICE

Theories of justice have been propounded for centuries. **Aristotle**, for instance, asserted notions of distributive and corrective justice, though his ideas of equal distribution of honours, wealth and other assets amongst 'equals' were designed to preserve *inequalities* between individuals which would be unacceptable to current thinking.

Theories of justice of broad scope are inevitably influenced by political philosophy; for instance, whether an individualist or collectivist approach is adopted. Leaving aside the latter, the flavour of some modern thinking can be conveyed by brief description, without critical evaluation, of two markedly different theories, those of **John Rawls** and **Robert Nozick**.

Perhaps the most fully articulated theory of justice is that proposed by *Rawls*. His first principle of justice is that each person should have the maximum amount of liberty consistent with the maximum amount for every other person. His second principle is that inequalities in social and economic distribution are only fair so far as they work to the advantage of the least advantaged people in society. He argues that these two principles would be chosen on grounds of rational self-interest by people deprived of key bits of information about themselves (for instance, their identity, jobs, intelligence and abilities and their conception of what is the 'good' life), so that they could not simply assume that they would already have lots of property, good jobs, intelligent children, and so on, or be able to get them. Rawls envisages the creation of a constitutional system dealing with powers of government and rights of citizens in the light of these principles, and then their progressive implementation by the legislators, judges, administrators, and in the actions of people generally.

Obviously, the state has a large role in the above theory. By contrast, *Nozick* argues against distributive justice and for a minimal role for the state. This role limits the function of the state to protection, which is the only justification for taking property (for example, by taxation) from individuals. Instead of a notion of distribution, Nozick argues for 'just entitlement', involving justice in acquisition and transfer of assets, and in rectifying any injustice resulting from their breach. Essentially, Nozick's theory proposes a free market model in which assets gained by an individual's effort are available to that individual and cannot be taken away to give to others without the individual's consent.

3.3.4 PRACTICAL APPLICATIONS

In considering the relevance of the meaning and theories of justice to an understanding of law and its operation in society, it will obviously help to try to relate legal rules and institutions to notions of formal and substantial justice and distributive and corrective justice. However, it is important not to become obsessed with such distinctions, which merely serve the purpose of analysis. Thus, legal rules and institutions may operate in such a way as to satisfy criteria of formal justice but not achieve substantial justice; achieve substantial justice but not satisfy formal justice criteria; or fulfil both or neither!

Distributive and corrective justice

Rules of law can be made and enforced with the aim of making large scale adjustments to the way benefits and burdens fall on individuals and groups within society. All modern UK governments have used legislation to engage in 'social engineering', for instance by manipulation of tax and benefits systems, access to health provision, regulation of the environment and consumer protection.

Rules of law supported by appropriate procedures exist to correct imbalances which arise. For instance, criminal law and sanctions exist to deter and punish those who seek to disturb the distribution, as do civil law rules and remedies in, say, contract and tort.

Formal justice

The whole structure for interpreting and applying rules of law and enforcing decisions can be seen as the pursuit of formal justice. Thus, equality in treatment is preserved, for instance, by:

- rules of evidence and procedure;
- access to legal advice and representation;
- access to financial support for legal advice and representation;
- impartial adjudication by judges and others;
- the general application of rules to all individuals.

These procedures are also supplemented by others designed to cope with initial errors in implementation, for instance:

- a system of appeals;
- judicial review, in which only the *method* of decision making is challenged, not the *substance* of the decision.

Moreover, most substantive rules of law have exceptions or modifications which recognise that true equality of treatment has to acknowledge the possibility of initial *inequality*. For example, criminal law rules on lack of mental capacity may excuse one person from liability for conduct which, if committed by a different person, would result in conviction.

Even so, uncorrected errors will occur in any system. For example:

- The spectacular 'miscarriages of justice' evident in the convictions of the Birmingham six and Guildford four and in the Carl Bridgwater case were in part the result of failure to apply rules of evidence and procedure properly.
- The rapid rejection of 'unit fines' (introduced in 1991 and abandoned in 1993) in magistrates' courts ensures that financial burdens in the imposition of fines for criminal offences continue to bear disproportionately on poorer defendants.

Substantial justice

The criteria for substantial justice must relate to some broad theory of justice or, at any rate, to some higher values by which legal rules may be judged, even if of a more limited nature. Failures in formal justice will probably, but not inevitably, result in failures in substantial justice.

Evidence of substantial justice or its breach should be sought in the application of specific rules of law (for instance, in crime, contract, tort etc.). Also on a limited scale, judges may seek to promote substantial justice through their decisions:

- judges have an inherent, albeit limited, flexibility in the way in which they interpret and apply rules of law (precedent is never a complete constraint);
- more formally, principles of equity developed to promote fairness in response to the rigidity and corruption which formerly existed in the common law, are still available to be adapted to changing circumstances.

3.4 LEGAL PERSONALITY

3.4.1 DEFINITION

Legal personality may be defined as *'an entity to which rights and duties attach'*. Every legal system has a set of rules (laws) which give rights, duties and liabilities to persons governed by that system. In order to pursue these rights a person must be a recognised person within the legal system – *legal personality*.

The law imposes various rights and duties. Duties can be divided into two categories. Correlative duties correspond with rights. This is particularly relevant in civil law. For example, I have a duty not to trespass on your land, and you have a right not to have trespassers on your land. Absolute duties exist irrespective of rights, for example, the duty not to break the criminal law. If I were to drive at 50 mph in a 30 mph zone I have breached a duty, but there is no corresponding right.

In English law, as in most legal systems, two types of legal person exist: *natural persons* and *artificial persons*.

3.4.2 NATURAL PERSONS

A natural person is any human being born alive. From birth to death, a person has legal rights and duties.

The moment of birth

In English law the accepted moment of birth is when the child is physically detached from its mother and the child exists in its own right. The key issue arising from this definition is whether a foetus has any legal personality. This question was raised in the *thalidomide tragedy*. After the out-of-court settlement Parliament attempted to deal with the legal issue by enacting the **Congenital Disabilities (Civil Liability) Act 1976** which enables only those children born alive, who were damaged whilst developing in their mother's womb, to sue *if*, for example, the drug manufacturer is clearly negligent to the mother.

Since the foetus is not recognised in law as having any rights, abortion is allowed in law in limited circumstances (**Abortion Act 1967** (as amended)). The decision to have an abortion is entirely the mothers, since legally, the child is regarded as part of her. The father has no rights whatsoever over the foetus (*C* v *S* (1987)).

It has long been thought that no offence could be committed against an unborn child which later caused death because it was not legally recognised as a 'person in being'. However, in *Attorney-General's Reference* (*No. 3 of 1994*) (1995) D stabbed his pregnant girlfriend, wounding the child in the womb. The stabbing caused the woman to give birth and the child died four months later. The Court of Appeal held that D could have been charged with murder or manslaughter of the child, once born alive. D's guilty intent could be transferred from the mother to the child, once born alive. The court emphasised that D's conduct must be unlawful. A doctor performing an abortion within the terms of the Abortion Act 1967 would not be guilty if the child initially survived but then died because he would have been acting lawfully.

The moment of death

Legal rights and duties cease at the moment of death. The person no longer has legal personality and is therefore not recognised in law. It is, therefore, very important to define the 'moment of death'. For many years, it was accepted as the moment when the heart ceased to beat. With developments in medicine and technology, it has become possible to keep patients alive with the use of a life-support machine. In *R* v *Malcherek* (1981) it was clearly stated that the moment of death was when a person was diagnosed as 'brain dead'.

3.4.3 STATUS

Legal personality establishes whether or not the law will recognise a 'thing' as having any rights or duties which may be protected or enforced by law. The status of a particular person denotes the extent of these rights and duties as a result of belonging to a particular class, group or category. The law classifies people. Rights may depend upon race, gender, age, nationality, occupation etc. Our status can vary according to the circumstances. The following examples illustrate this further:

❶ **Transsexuals:** Different rights and duties attach according to one's gender. Perhaps the most important of these is the right to marry. Modern science and technology has made sex change operations possible but English law does not allow people who have undergone such operations to change their birth certificates. In *Corbett* v *Corbett* (1971) a case involving the validity of a marriage ceremony between a man and a person who had been born a man, but who had undergone a sex-change operation in order to become female, the court decided that the person in question, despite the operation, was male. Therefore the marriage ceremony had not resulted in a valid marriage. The right to marry was an issue raised in *Cossey* v *UK* (1990). The applicant, a transsexual, argued that her right to privacy and right to marry under Articles 8 and 12 of the European Convention on Human Rights had been infringed by UK law. She lost her case on the grounds that those Articles imposed no positive obligations on the UK in relation to acknowledgement of change of sex so that she was not entitled to insist on an alteration to the birth certificate. Therefore the law remains unchanged on this issue.

❷ **Race and gender:** There are no general disabilities in law resulting from race, ethnicity or gender. The law has also taken some positive steps to ensure that there is no discrimination, for example, the Sex Discrimination Acts 1975 and 1986 and the Race Relations Act 1976.

3 **Age:** A minor's legal rights are different from an adult's. For example, a minor's capacity to make contracts is significantly reduced (Minors' Contracts Act 1987); the law does not recognise that a minor under 10 years old can commit criminal offences and special rules apply in relation to those between 10 and 13 years old. Minors are not able to marry until 16 years old, and those who marry at age 16 or 17 must have permission to do so.

4 **Persistant vegetative state:** In *Airedale NHS Trust* v *Bland* (1993) the patient, Anthony Bland, injured in the Hillsborough disaster in 1989, was still alive in legal terms. Bland's brainstem was alive and functioning. Bland was diagnosed as being in a persistent vegetative state (PVS) and having no chance of recovery. Bland's cerebral cortex (the centre of consciousness and all higher functions in the brain) had been effectively destroyed. The issue for the House of Lords was whether doctors could withdraw life-sustaining treatment. They held that although the fundamental principle is sanctity of life, the principle is not absolute. In all the circumstances it was not in Bland's best interests to continue treatment and therefore the doctors were under no duty to continue life-sustaining treatment. He had no right to life-sustaining treatment. His rights were affected by his medical condition.

3.4.4 ARTIFICIAL PERSONS

The significant artificial personality is the *company*. In English law, as in most legal systems, companies are held to have separate legal personalities from their members. The company has rights and duties in its own right, as if it were a 'being'. A company can commit criminal offences, including manslaughter. Although the *company* cannot be sent to jail if convicted of a serious crime, the *directors* may be (*R* v *OLL Ltd* (1995)). A company can breach a contract and can commit torts. Companies sue each other, sue individuals, and can be sued.

The 'corporate veil'

The company is distinct from the people who comprise it. In *Salomon* v *Salomon and Co Ltd* (1897) S lent money to his company, taking a charge on the assets of the company as security. Other creditors lent the company money but did not secure their loans. The company failed and the unsecured creditors claimed that S could not owe money to himself and they should be paid their money first. The House of Lords held that *'once a company is incorporated, it must be treated like any other independent person and is, in law, different altogether from its members'*. Thus S was entitled to keep £6,000 in part payment of his loan to the company. Therefore the law draws a veil between the company and its members (the 'corporate veil').

Limited liability

This separation of the owners (shareholders) of the company and the company itself means that shareholders enjoy *limited liability*. The *shareholders* appoint *directors* to control and run the company. They are not concerned with the day-to-day control of the company. The shareholders' liability is limited in the following ways:

- They have limited liability in relation to the debts of the company. Their liability will be limited to the value of their shares.

- They are not liable for the wrongful acts (civil or criminal) of the company.

The creation of a company

In order to create a company, and therefore, a separate legal entity, it must be *registered* under the provisions of the Companies Acts. The following documents must be registered:

- The Memorandum of Association (this is a statement to the world about the nature of the company and its objects).

- The Articles of Association (this is a statement to the company members about the internal running of the company, how shares are transferred, dates of meetings etc.).

- A declaration that the requirements of the Companies Acts will be met.
- The address of the registered office of the company.
- A statement of the directors and secretary.

Once these documents have been satisfactorily registered, the company is issued with a Certificate of Incorporation and it exists in its own right. It has legal personality.

Partnerships

Partnerships are governed by the Partnership Act 1890. Section 1 defines the partnership as '*a business carried on in common with a view to making a profit*'. The partnership does not have separate legal personality. The partners and the business are one and the same. Because the partners do not have separate legal identity, they do not have limited liability. This means they are personally liable for any debts of the business. A partnership is usually created by the partners drawing up a *deed of partnership* which sets out the relationship between the partners. This document is signed by all the partners and witnessed.

Significance of the corporate personality

The company is a very important form of business organisation. There has been rapid growth in the number and size of companies during the twentieth century. Because companies have separate legal personality, they enjoy a number of advantages over other forms of business organisation:

- since liability is limited, it is easier to attract investment;
- since ownership is separated from management, those who invest do not have to be involved in the day-to-day running of the business, and are, therefore, free to pursue other employment and interests;
- transfer of ownership, by transferring shares (privately or on the stock market), is easier than in other forms of business organisation;
- a company does not 'die' with the owner, as in other forms of business organisation.

However, some concerns about companies have been raised:

- The sheer size of some companies today makes it extremely difficult for shareholders to exercise control of the company. Directors are only obliged to call one meeting per year and voting is by simple majority.
- Society also experiences difficulty in controlling companies. For example, there have been few successful prosecutions of companies for manslaughter.
- Multi-national companies can become so large and command such enormous resources that it is difficult to call them to account and indeed, they may affect autonomy of individual states.

Illustrative questions

1 Consider whether there is any necessary connection between law and morality, illustrating your answer with examples. (25)
(*London*)

Tutorial note
This essay question requires a critical assessment of the relationship between law and morality. This analysis must be illustrated with area(s) of law, chosen from any aspect of the A Level course. It is essential that useful examples are selected and analysed when studying and revising this topic, rather than during the examination.

Suggested answer
Whilst the relationship between law and morality is complex, it is generally agreed

that the law cannot be morally neutral. There must be *necessarily* a connection between law and morality. The extent of this connection must be considered. In answering this question, law and morality should be defined, and, using any examples, the differences between them explained. This should focus on the creation and continued existence of each. The effect of breaching a law and a moral rule could be compared. It may be useful to provide examples of laws which have no moral basis (e.g. a parking offence), and morals which have no legal basis (e.g. adultery). In order to assess the connection between law and morality, the key theories on their relationship should be explored. This should include discussion of Mill's 'harm to others' principle, Professor Hart's 'paternalism' and Lord Devlin's 'legal moralism'. It is important not to just *describe* the theories, but to *critically evaluate* these theories. The theories should be illustrated with reference to relevant areas of law. For example, a discussion of *R v Brown* (1993) (see Unit 3.2) could be used to illustrate Lord Devlin's theory and a discussion of victimless crimes could neatly indicate the differences between Mill's and Hart's theories.

Alternatively, or in addition, an area of law (e.g. euthanasia, consent to medical treatment, abortion, animal rights etc.) could be explored. The legal rules should be described and their possible underlying moral basis revealed. In considering the connection between the two, opportunity should be taken to refer to the theories previously introduced. The conclusion should address whether there *is* necessarily any connection between law and morality and, if so, what the connection *should* be.

2 Legal personality attaches both to human beings and to corporations. Discuss its meaning and importance in connection with both. (25)

(*AEB*)

Tutorial note

The examiner reminds us that there are two types of legal personality. This essay requires both an explanation and a discussion of the importance of legal personality in relation to natural persons and corporations. It is therefore essential that *equal* amounts of time are devoted to *each* aspect.

Suggested answer

An introduction should define the concept of legal personality, emphasise the importance of rights and duties, and provide examples of correlative and absolute duties. A definition of natural persons should be given. The 'moment of birth' should be explored, emphasising the problems that have arisen in connection with the foetus. The 'moment of death' and its ensuing problems should be dealt with in a similar way. The relationship between personality and status must be considered by reference to one or two relevant categories, for example, minors, women, ethnic minorities, transsexuals, employees, etc.). A definition of artificial persons should be given, together with an explanation of the separation of companies from their owners and the consequences of this 'veil'. Limited liability should be emphasised. In order to fully explain the corporate personality, some comparison between companies and other forms of business organisation, e.g. partnerships, may be useful. Having described the meaning of both natural and artificial personality, the importance of each must be highlighted. The significance of being deemed a 'human being' can be shown by reference to cases and statutes concerning the rights of the foetus. The importance of varying status must be emphasised. Discussion of the significance of corporate personality should emphasise the prolific growth of the company as a form of business organisation during this century. This should be supported by examination of the consequent benefits to society and of problems to which the growth has given rise. The conclusion should briefly sum up the meaning and importance of natural and corporate personality.

Practice questions

1 Choosing any area(s) of law, discuss the extent to which the relevant rules and/or institutions represent evidence of the pursuit of 'justice'.   (25)
                                                                                        (AEB)

Pitfalls

This question requires an analysis of the meaning of justice, identification of appropriate legal rules and/or institutions and a consideration of whether they demonstrate justice. A danger in answering this question would be to omit any reference to the meaning of justice and simply to give examples of legal rules and institutions, asserting that they do or do not provide evidence of justice. Even worse, would be to use this as an opportunity merely to describe an area of law or a legal institution.

Key points

❶ Definition of justice: formal and substantial; distributive and corrective.

❷ Explanation and consideration of theories of justice.

❸ Selection of appropriate legal rules and institutions.

❹ Demonstration of how the operation of the rules and institutions may be viewed as fulfilling criteria of distributive and corrective, formal and substantial justice.

❺ Examination of possible examples of injustice in the operation of the rules and institutions.

❻ Some evaluative comments on whether the chosen rules of law or institutions represent the pursuit of justice.

2 With reference to the role of law in modern society, consider whether there are any circumstances in which civil disobedience may be justified.   (25)
                                                                                        (London)

Pitfalls

This is a difficult essay question to answer without prior thought. A key danger would be to omit discussion of the role of law in modern society and/or any reference to theories of why law is or should be obeyed. Another error would be to simply give a list of examples of instances of civil disobedience. Even where both the role of law and examples of civil disobedience are considered, a further danger would be to treat them as two separate 'mini-essays', with little or no correlation between the two.

Key points

❶ A discussion of the role of law in modern society, for example, preserving social control, establishing social order, regulating and facilitating private and commercial relationships.

❷ Explanation of the meaning of civil disobedience.

❸ Explanation of approaches to understanding the nature of law and the obligation of obedience, for instance, positivist and naturalist explanations and discussion of whether all laws must be obeyed according to the theories.

❹ Consideration of disadvantages of disobedience, for example, loss of respect for law and potential resulting disorder.

❺ Consideration of possible advantages of disobedience, for instance, exposing issues to public scrutiny, effecting a change in the law.

❻ Discussion of some areas of law which have provoked civil disobedience, for example, abortion, animal rights, poll tax, road building, trade union rights.

❼ An assessment of whether there are any circumstances where civil disobedience can be justified.

SANCTIONS AND REMEDIES

Units in this chapter

Chapter objectives

This chapter considers the consequences of successful legal action. In criminal law, a person who is found guilty will be sentenced. This chapter considers the available sentences and the aims pursued in sentencing.

A successful plaintiff in a civil action will usually be awarded damages, perhaps with some other remedy. This chapter explains the available remedies and considers the purpose of each.

Finally, there can be no remedy if the court will not hear a case. It is important that civil actions are brought within the time allowed and the rules governing those time limits are explained.

4.1 POWERS OF SENTENCING

4.1.1 SENTENCING OPTIONS

Adult offenders

The Criminal Justice Act 1991 (as amended) makes a distinction between four different kinds of sentences graded according to the severity of their consequences to the offender.

Discharges
There are two types of discharge:

- **absolute discharge**: no further action is taken.

- **conditional discharge**: no further action is taken unless the offender commits another offence within a specified period (up to three years). The offender may be sentenced for original offence if he or she does commit a crime within this period.

Fines
The **fine** is the penalty imposed for the vast majority of summary offences, and also remains the most frequently imposed penalty for indictable offences. The maximum fine for most offences tried in the Crown Court is unlimited, but magistrates' courts are limited to a maximum fine of £5,000. When setting the amount of a fine, the court is obliged to consider both the seriousness of the offence and the offender's financial circumstances. The courts have the power to imprison an offender who wilfully defaults on payment.

Community sentences
These sentences were restructured by the Criminal Justice Act 1991 (CJA 1991) in order to encourage their use. All **community sentences** restrict the offender's liberty in some way. Community sentences require the co-operation of the offender, and, therefore he or she must consent to the order. There are four adult community sentences:

- A **probation order**: the offender is placed under the supervision of a probation officer for a specified period of between six months and three years. Conditions may be imposed on the probation order. The court must be satisfied that supervision is desirable in the interests of rehabilitation, the prevention of the commission of further offences or public safety.

- A **community service order**: the order requires the offender to perform, over a period of twelve months, a specified number of hours of unpaid word for the benefit of the community; the number of hours must be between 40 and 240.

- A **curfew order**: the court may order that, within a six-month period, the offender should remain in a specified place for a period of between two and twelve hours in any one day.

- A **combination order**: this is a combination of between one and three years' probation combined with between 40 and 100 hours' community service.

Custodial sentences
Imprisonment is the most severe sanction which a court can impose. Life imprisonment is the mandatory sentence for murder, and is the maximum sentence for several serious crimes, including manslaughter, attempted murder, s. 18 OAPA 1861, robbery and rape. Offenders rarely serve their full sentence. The CJA 1991 introduced the concept of early release. Offenders serving sentences of up to four years' imprisonment will automatically be released after half the sentence has been served. Those serving more than four years' imprisonment may be released at a point somewhere between one half and two thirds of the sentence. Where a court passes a sentence of up to two years' imprisonment, it may order that the sentence will not take effect unless the offender commits another imprisonable offence during a fixed period of between one and two years. This is known as a **suspended sentence**.

Youth offenders

Youth offenders are all those under the age of 21. The primary aim in sentencing young people is rehabilitation. Offenders under 18 years old are normally dealt with in the Youth Court and the welfare of the child is an important principle. Those aged between 18–20 are dealt with in the ordinary adult courts but under different sentencing provisions. Some of the main youth sentences are:

- youth offenders' institutions (15–20 years old) or secure units (12–14 years old);
- community penalties (as for adults plus attendance centre order and supervision order);
- fines (the maximum for 10–13 year olds is £250 and for 14–17 year olds, £1,000).

4.1.2 SENTENCING PROCEDURE

This CJA 1991 intended to produce substantial changes in sentencing and, for the first time, the government stated relatively clearly its sentencing philosophy. Retribution or just deserts, concentrating on the seriousness of the offence, is the primary aim of sentencing.

The procedure the court follows when sentencing an offender can be summarised as shown in Figure 4.1 below:

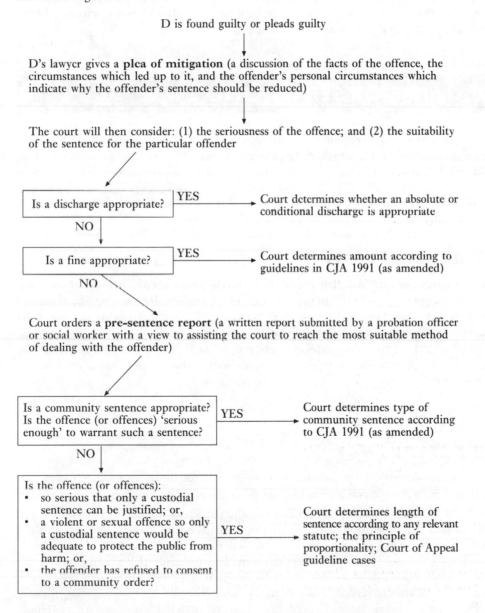

Figure 4.1 Sentencing procedure under the CJA 1991 (as amended)

Proportionality

This is the leading criterion for the length of sentences. Custodial sentences should not be longer than is proportionate, either for reasons of deterrence or for reasons of treatment of the offender. Therefore, retribution is the current aim of sentencing. There is only one group of cases in which courts are permitted to sentence above the level which is proportionate to the seriousness of the offence(s) committed: those convicted of violent or sexual offences may require longer sentences in order to protect the public from serious harm.

Court of Appeal guideline judgments

The Court of Appeal (usually presided over by the Lord Chief Justice) often takes the opportunity in a particular case to set out sentencing levels for various manifestations of an offence. For example, *R v Aramah* (1982) sets out guidelines on sentencing for drug offences and *R v Billam* (1986) sets out guidelines on sentencing for rape. People with similar backgrounds who commit similar offences in similar circumstances should receive similar sentences. The starting point is the Court of Appeal guideline. The sentence may then be lowered by mitigating factors. Reasons why the offender should be punished less severely include youth or old age, previous good character, provocation and domestic or financial problems. The sentence may also be raised by aggravating factors, for example, violence and brutality, where the victim is elderly, where the offender is a ringleader, where the offence is planned and where a weapon is used.

4.2 AIMS OF SENTENCING

Ultimately, the purpose of sentencing is to reduce crime. However, there are different theories on how this may be achieved. On the one hand, there is the aim of retribution which essentially involves punishing the offender for the crime committed. On the other hand, there are the utilitarian theories, including deterrence, rehabilitation and incapacitation, which embody the concept that punishment must serve a useful purpose, either for the offender or for society as a whole.

4.2.1 RETRIBUTION

Retribution is based on the idea that the offender needs punishing for his or her conduct. Society needs to 'get its own back' on the offender. He or she has done wrong and therefore deserves to be punished: an 'eye for an eye' mentality. A retributive sentence would be proportionate to the seriousness of the offence, because that is what the offender deserves. Under the CJA 1991 (as amended) retribution or proportionality is the leading aim. Harsher sentences based on deterrence are ruled out. Rehabilitation should be pursued only within the confines of proportionate sentences. Such an aim appears to be just and fair. However, factors other than the offence often intervene, such as the offender's personal circumstances and mitigating factors.

4.2.2 DETERRENCE

Deterrence is concerned with preventing the commission of future crimes. A distinction must be drawn between general and individual deterrence:

- **Individual deterrence** is aimed at deterring the particular offender from committing further crimes. Presumably, a sentencing strategy based on individual deterrence would require courts to pass increasingly severe sentences on offenders if they repeat their offendings, in the hope that eventually the sentences persuade the offender not to re-offend. In practice, this does not seem to happen. Statistics show that most first offenders (71%) are not reconvicted within six years, whereas the vast majority of those with five or more previous convictions (87%) are reconvicted within six years (Home Office Statistics).

- **General deterrence** is aimed at deterring potential law-breakers from committing crimes. Exemplary sentences are often passed under this aim. The court punishes an offender in order to show to the public generally what is likely to happen when people behave as the defendant did. Two issues need considering here. First, it is argued that it is not right to punish one person more severely in the hope that this sentence will deter others, and, secondly, it is doubtful whether the sentence will succeed in deterring others. It is argued that the key factor in deterrence is the risk of detection, rather than the risk of a high sentence. This aim also presupposes that potential offenders stop and think about the consequences of their conduct, which is debatable.

4.2.3 REHABILITATION

Rehabilitation or reform of the offender is another possible aim of the system. The idea here is to use sentencing to reform the offender, so that he or she is less likely to commit offences in the future, by education, training and other help. This aim was particularly popular during the 1960s. The CJA 1991 does not allow the courts to impose a custodial sentence or lengthen a custodial sentence specifically in the hope of rehabilitating the offender. However, it does suggest that the courts take rehabilitation into account when deciding which of the community sentences is most suitable for the offender (although proportionality is paramount). In extreme cases of rehabilitative sentences, the dignity and privacy of offenders can be inexcusably interfered with, such as compulsory electro-convulsive therapy. Rehabilitative sentences can also be controversial since it may appear that the offender is being 'rewarded' for committing crimes (such as 'holidays' for youth offenders). This can cause a great deal of outrage in society. Such sentences are also expensive and require investment of a great deal of resources. It is also debatable as to whether it is justifiable for the state to change the way people think, rather than just punish them for their wrongful conduct.

4.2.4 PROTECTION OF SOCIETY/INCAPACITATION

The present sentencing system provides a degree of public protection by placing some offenders in custody, and therefore preventing them from committing further offences. This is an aim already pursued in relation to certain convicted murderers. It is argued that an incapacitative sentencing policy ought to be pursued in respect of other high-risk offenders (for example, convicted paedophiles). It has its merits where highly dangerous offenders are concerned but it is very expensive way to deal with crime prevention, and since rates of recidivism are high, it may not ultimately achieve its aim.

4.3 AIMS OF REMEDIES

4.3.1 DAMAGES

The major remedy available through the courts is **damages**. The object of damages in *contract* is to put the injured party in the position he or she would have been in if the contract had been properly performed. As the measure is the plaintiff's loss, rather than the defendant's gain, it will be irrelevant that the defendant has gained overall by being in breach of contract. This is, indeed, the basis of many commercial decisions knowingly to break a contractual obligation.

In *Surrey C C & Mole DC v Bredero Homes* (1993) two councils sold land to a developer who covenanted to use a particular development scheme. The scheme was later changed, in breach of covenant, so that the developer made more profit. The plaintiffs claimed damages calculated on the basis of the extra profit made by the defendant. The Court of Appeal held that the councils had suffered no loss and thus were entitled only to nominal damages for the breach of covenant. The purpose of common law damages is to compensate the victim for loss.

The compensatory principle was also discussed in *Ruxley Electronics & Construction Ltd v Forsyth* (1996). F had a swimming pool built. It was not as deep as specified but the evidence was that it was deep enough to be safe for diving. The question was: was F entitled to damages for the cost of rebuilding to his specification or only to damages reflecting modest reduction in value of the pool? The trial judge awarded £2,500 general damages for loss of amenity and held, on the basis of expert evidence, that there was no difference in value between the pool contracted for and the pool as built.

The Court of Appeal held F to be entitled to the cost of rebuilding (£21,560), regardless of whether F chose to rebuild, even though this might be regarded as a windfall, putting F in a better position than he would have been in had the contract been properly performed. Staughton LJ stated: *'It is unreasonable of a plaintiff to claim an expensive remedy if there is some cheaper alternative which would make good his loss. Thus he cannot claim the cost of reinstatement if the difference in value would make good his loss by enabling him to purchase the building or chattel that he requires elsewhere. But if there is no alternative course which will provide what he requires, or none which will cost less, he is entitled to the cost of repair or reinstatement even if that is very expensive.'*

The House of Lords allowed the builders' appeal, reinstating the damages awarded by the trial judge. The normal measure of damages in building cases is the cost of reinstatement but if the court decides that it would be unreasonable for the plaintiff to insist on reinstatement then the measure of damages is the difference in value between what was contracted for and what the plaintiff received. Lord Lloyd stated: *'... the principle that a plaintiff cannot always insist on being placed in the same physical position as if the contract had been performed, where to do so would be unreasonable, is not confined to building cases.'*

This gives rise to the problem that the plaintiff has not obtained what he contracted for but is not compensated for his loss because it is not quantifiable: potentially, an invitation to contracting parties to break their obligations with impunity.

The purpose of damages in *tort* is to compensate the plaintiff by putting him or her in the position he or she would have been in if the tort had not been committed. Damages are therefore usually **compensatory** but in exceptional circumstances may be:

❶ **Contemptuous**: if the court wishes to demonstrate its disapproval of the plaintiff's conduct even though he or she is legally in the right. In *Pamplin* v *Express Newspapers* (1985) P had been described as a 'slippery, unscrupulous spiv' and won an action for defamation but was awarded one half-penny damages.

❷ **Nominal** damages will be awarded if no loss has been sustained. If A contracts with B for C's benefit and B does not perform, it is arguable that A can recover only nominal damages because A has suffered no financial loss. Similarly, in tort, nominal damages may be awarded if the plaintiff has suffered no loss as a result of the interference with his or her legal rights: such as if the defendant has trespassed on the plaintiff's land but done no damage.

❸ **Punitive** or **exemplary** damages are not awarded in contract and will be very rarely awarded in tort, because the primary purpose of the civil law is to compensate the plaintiff, not to punish the defendant. In *AB and others* v *South West Water Services* (1992) it was said that exemplary damages could be appropriate where a water authority continued to supply water which they knew to be contaminated and had assured consumers that the water supply was safe.

4.3.2 INJUNCTIONS

An injunction is a court order. It may be **prohibitory**, ordering a person not to do something, or **mandatory**, ordering them to do something. Failure to comply with an injunction amounts to contempt of court, for which a person may be fined or imprisoned.

An **interlocutory** injunction is granted if the plaintiff wishes to prevent the defendant doing something before a case is heard, such as, perhaps, demolishing a building that the plaintiff claims should not be demolished. There are two special kinds of interlocutory injunction:

- a *Mareva* **injunction** prohibits the defendant removing assets from the jurisdiction;
- an *Anton Piller* **order** permits the plaintiff to search the defendant's premises and remove evidence.

They are obtained by application to a judge, without the knowledge of the defendant. The secrecy involved is necessary, since both are needed to prevent a defendant taking action that would thwart the plaintiff but, because of the secrecy, there are rules to protect the defendant's interests.

An injunction issued after a case has been heard is called a **perpetual** injunction.

An injunction is an equitable remedy and, therefore, **discretionary**, which means a plaintiff is not entitled to the injunction, as he would be to damages, if he won the case. There is a body of precedent governing how the discretion is used. Injunctions are not granted if money is adequate to compensate the plaintiff and there is no need to control the defendant's behaviour.

4.3.3 SPECIFIC PERFORMANCE

An order of specific performance compels a party to a contract to perform his or her promise. Like an injunction, it is an equitable remedy, granted at the discretion of the court when it would be just and equitable to make such an order and in accordance with the principles established in past cases (see Unit 4.4).

4.4   REMEDIES FOR BREACH OF CONTRACT

4.4.1 DAMAGES

Damages are awarded to put the plaintiff in the position he or she would have been in had the contract been performed (see Unit 4.3.1). They are also awarded for loss incurred in reliance on the contract. In *Anglia Television* v *Reed* (1972) R, an actor, broke his contract to star in a television play. It was held that A could recover the cost already incurred in reliance on R's performing his contract.

Damages are recoverable for a loss which is foreseeable. The basic rule comes from *Hadley* v *Baxendale* (1854). P was a miller at Gloucester. The drive shaft of the mill being broken, P contracted with a carrier to take it to the makers at Greenwich so that they could use it for a pattern in making a new one. D delayed delivery of the shaft beyond a reasonable time, so that the mill was idle for much longer than should have been necessary. P sued in respect of loss of profits during the period of additional delay. It was held that the damage was too **remote**. In order to succeed, P would have to prove: (i) that in the usual course of events the work of the mill would cease altogether for want of the shaft; or (ii) that the special circumstances had been fully explained, so that D was made aware of the possible loss.

In *Victoria Laundry* v *Newman Industries* (1949) D agreed to deliver a new boiler to P by a certain date but failed to do so with the result that P lost: (i) normal business profits during the period of delay; and (ii) profits from dyeing contracts which were offered during that period. It was held that the normal business profits were recoverable but the additional profits were not as they were neither foreseeable nor within the contemplation of the parties.

To be foreseeable, a consequence has to be a serious possibility. In *Parsons* v *Uttley Ingham* (1978) D sold a hopper for storage of pig food to P and erected it. A ventilator was left closed and as a result food became mouldy and pigs died. D was held to be liable. The death of the pigs was not too remote.

Lord Denning stated: *'The test of remoteness ... is similar to that in tort. The contractor is liable for all such loss or expense as could reasonably have been foreseen, at the time of the breach, as a possible consequence of it. Applied to this case, it means that the makers of the hopper are liable for the death of the pigs. They ought reasonably to have foreseen that, if mouldy pig nuts were fed to the pigs, there was a possibility that they might become ill.'*

As long as the *type* of consequence is foreseeable, the loss will be recoverable.

The amount, or **quantum**, of damages payable will be determined by:

❶ The **market rule**: the difference between the agreed price and the market price. In *Thompson* v *Robinson* (1955) R agreed to buy a Standard Vanguard car from T. The next day R refused to take delivery. T sued for damages for breach of contract. It was held that T was entitled to recover the profit which would have been made on the sale. The decision depends to a large extent on the fact that in Yorkshire, at the time the contract was made, the supply of Standard Vanguards exceeded the demand; the market price was thus lower than the contract price.

❷ The **incidence of taxation**. If tax would have been payable on any profit, damages will be limited to the net sum the plaintiff would have received. In *British Transport Commissioner* v *Gourley* (1955), a case concerning damages in tort, it was held that the fact that P would have paid tax on his earnings must be taken into account so as to reduce the damages awarded in regard to lost earnings. As damages are awarded to compensate loss, it is not acceptable for P to receive the gross sum for lost earnings as he then makes a profit. This rule is the same with regard to damages in contract, but will not affect damages paid to a trader, since he or she will pay tax on damages as on any other form of income.

❸ The **duty to mitigate**. The injured party has a duty to **mitigate**, or reduce, his or her loss as far as possible. In *Bruce* v *Calder* (1895) D, a partnership consisting of four members, agreed to employ P as manager of a branch of the business for two years. Five months later the partnership was dissolved by the retirement of two of the partners and the business was transferred to the other two who offered to employ P on the same terms as before. He refused the offer and sought damages for wrongful dismissal. It was held he had been wrongly dismissed but would be entitled to only nominal damages, having acted unreasonably in refusing the offer of employment.

The plaintiff is required only to take reasonable steps to mitigate his loss. In *Pilkington* v *Wood* (1953) D, a solicitor, was sued for breach of contract, having advised P that the title to a house he was buying was good. He argued that P should have mitigated his loss by suing the vendor of the house for conveying a defective title. The court did not agree. The duty to mitigate does not extend beyond doing what is reasonable. It would not be reasonable to expect P to enter into litigation merely to protect D from the results of his negligence.

❹ Provision in the contract for **liquidated damages**. Parties may agree what damages are to be paid in the event of a breach occurring. A liquidated damages clause will be enforced; a **penalty clause** will not. A clause is likely to be held to be a penalty clause and unenforceable if:

- the sum stipulated for is extravagantly greater than the damage which could conceivably follow from the breach;

- where the breach consists only in failure to pay a sum of money, the sum stipulated is greater than the sum which ought to have been paid;

- a single sum is stipulated for the occurrence of one or more or all of several events, some of which may be serious and some trivial.

The fact that the payment is described in the contract as 'a penalty' or as 'liquidated damages' is relevant, but not decisive. If pre-estimation of the damages is nearly impossible, this does not stop the clause being a liquidated damages clause. In *Dunlop* v *New Garage & Motor Co* (1915) a resale price agreement between the parties stipulated a sum of £5 per tyre payable in the event of breach of the agreement. It was held to be enforceable. There is a presumption that where a single sum is payable on the occurrence of one or more or all of several events then the sum stipulated is a penalty because it is unlikely that all the events can attract the same loss. The contract in this case listed five events on the occurrence of which the sum of £5 was payable. Even so, the House of Lords held that the presumption need not always apply and that it did not apply in this case. Where precise estimation is difficult, as it was here, then any contractual provision is likely to represent the parties' honest attempt to provide for breach and the court will follow it.

4.4.2 SPECIFIC PERFORMANCE

An order of specific performance is an order by the court to the defendant requiring him to perform his promise. An equitable remedy and therefore discretionary, it is granted when it would be just and equitable to do so and in accordance with the principles established in past cases.

Specific performance will not be granted:

1 If damages would be a sufficient remedy, e.g. in contracts for the sale of goods, unless the particular item is very rare. In *Behnke* v *Bede Shipping* (1927) an order of specific performance was made in respect of a ship. It had been proved that there was only one other ship of similar specifications. Generally, specific performance will not be granted in a contract for the sale of goods.

2 In a contract for personal services. The two leading cases here relate to applications for injunctions, rather than specific performance, but the principle is the same: an order for specific performance would require a person to perform a contract, an injunction prevents him making a contract with someone else, or otherwise doing something to put himself in breach of contract.

In *Page One Records* v *Britton* (1967) P acted as managers for the Troggs. The group intended to repudiate the contract although P were not in breach and P sought an interlocutory injunction, restraining the group from repudiating the contract until the matter could be fully heard in court. An injunction was refused, since its effect would be to compel performance of a contract for personal services.

Compare this with *Warner Brothers* v *Nelson* (1937) where N, an actress, had entered into a contract in which she agreed to act exclusively for P for 12 months. She was anxious to obtain more money and so left America and entered into a contract with a person in England. An injunction was granted, restraining N from carrying out the English contract. The injunction was confined to work on stage or screen in England and Wales. This case was distinguished in *Page One Records* v *Britton* because:

- The Troggs were not capable of finding alternative employment, whereas the actress had been.
- The nature of the contract of management meant that it would be very difficult to perform it properly if there was not a good relationship between the parties. The only obligation on the part of Warner Brothers had been to pay money to N.

3 If constant supervision is required. In *Ryan* v *Mutual Tontine Westminster Chambers Association* (1893) R leased from M a flat with the services of a resident porter. These services were not supplied and R sought an order of specific performance. It was held that the appropriate remedy was damages. Specific performance would not be granted because supervision would be required to ensure that the order was complied with.

4 If there is absence of mutuality: specific performance is not granted to minors as it would not be granted against them.

The case of *Co-operative Insurance Society Ltd* v *Argyll Stores (Holdings) Ltd* (1997) demonstrates the discretionary nature of specific performance and that senior judges may differ in their opinions as to whether an order is appropriate. The Court of Appeal had ordered specific performance against Argyll Stores, obliging them to keep a supermarket open as they had promised to in the lease, emphasising the unreasonable conduct of Argyll and the absence of a need for supervision by the court. The House of Lords refused the order because it would oblige the defendants to carry on with a loss-making business, reversing the decision of the Court of Appeal and upholding the decision of the trial judge.

4.4.3 *QUANTUM MERUIT* (AS MUCH AS HE DESERVES)

This is a payment made to a party who has not fulfilled the contract but who has given value: for example, if partial performance is tendered and has been accepted by the other party.

4.4.4 RECTIFICATION

If a written contract does not accurately reflect the intentions of the parties, the court may order that it be amended.

4.4.5 RESCISSION

The effect of this order is to put the parties in the position they would have been in if the contract had never been made. It will be ordered if a contract is voidable, but not where:

1 The contract has been affirmed by the party seeking rescission. For example, if there has been a misrepresentation but the innocent party decided to carry on with the contract after learning the truth.

2 There has been a considerable lapse of time. In *Leaf* v *International Galleries* (1950) a painting was sold, both parties believing it to be by Constable. Five years later, an insurance valuation revealed that the painting was by a different artist with the same name and was, therefore, much less valuable than the parties had believed. This innocent misrepresentation by the seller would have given the buyer a right to rescission, but the court held that the right had been lost by delay.

3 Restitution is no longer possible: the parties cannot be returned to their original positions.

4 A third party has acquired rights in the property.

If recission takes the form of a money payment, it is called an **indemnity**. In *Whittington* v *Seal-Hayne* (1900) there was an innocent misrepresentation in the sale of a poultry farm. P was held to be entitled to an indemnity in respect of rent, rates and repairs but not to any payment for loss of profit and medical expenses, as this would amount to the payment of damages.

4.5   REMEDIES IN TORT

4.5.1 DAMAGES

General damages are calculated by the court and are awarded for things not precisely quantifiable, such as loss of reputation or pain and suffering. **Special damages** are claimed by the plaintiff as specific amounts for particular types of damage that *can* be easily quantified, such as loss of earnings between an accident and the court hearing or possessions which have been damaged or destroyed.

Damages in tort are recoverable for loss that is foreseeable by the reasonable person at the time the tort was committed. This rule was settled for the tort of negligence by *The Wagon Mound (No. 1)* (1961) and also applies to actions in nuisance and *Rylands* v *Fletcher*.

The kind of damage must be foreseeable, though not the precise sequence of events that led to the damage. In *Hughes* v *Lord Advocate* (1963) the House of Lords held that as injury through burns was a foreseeable consequence of leaving a manhole and paraffin lamps unattended, it was not relevant that it was an explosion, which was not foreseeable, that led to burns.

Contemptuous, exemplary and nominal damages may all be awarded in tort, as in contract (see Unit 4.3). The amount of damages in defamation and false imprisonment cases is determined by a jury. This has caused problems, the Court of Appeal reducing what were seen as excessive amounts for exemplary damages. In *Thompson* v *Commissioner of Police* (1997) the Court of Appeal set a maximum of £50,000 for exemplary damages in actions against the police. It should be remembered that this sum is in addition to compensatory damages.

The plaintiff has a duty to **mitigate** his or her loss, that is, to take reasonable steps to prevent financial loss being greater than necessary. In *Leisbosch Dredger* v *Edison SS* (1933) P's loss was greater than it might have been because P could not afford to replace the dredger which was damaged by D. The extra loss was held to be irrecoverable. This decision has been criticised because it runs counter to the eggshell skull rule (that you take your victim as you find him) and it penalises the poor plaintiff.

Damages for personal injuries

Damages are awarded for pain and suffering, loss of amenity (the things one can no longer do), loss of earnings to the time of trial and medical expenses.

Future loss of earnings is calculated by taking a figure for net annual earnings and multiplying it by a number which represents the years of working life left *minus* a factor to account for the normal contingencies of life such as illness, redundancy or early death.

The effect of these rules is that plaintiffs in personal injury cases tend to be under-compensated, particularly for more serious injuries. It has been suggested that exemplary damages might be introduced in cases in which the defendant's behaviour has been reckless; this would help to improve safety standards as well as increasing the sum paid to the plaintiff.

The defendant is obliged to repay to the DSS any amount which has been paid to the plaintiff as social security benefits, the balance is then paid to the plaintiff.

Money received from the plaintiff's own insurance or from charity is disregarded.

The court may make a provisional award of damages and the plaintiff may apply for increased damages at a later date if his condition deteriorates. This is particularly useful because it may be years before the full effect of an incident on the plaintiff's health is known.

The Pearson Commission (1978) recommended that damages for pain and suffering and loss of amenity (known as non-pecuniary damages) should be payable only for the first three months, that private medical fees should be recoverable only if it was reasonable on medical grounds to incur them and that damages should be paid in periodic payments, rather than a lump sum.

Damages are usually paid in a lump sum but a plaintiff can choose to have a **structured settlement**, under which damages are paid over a period of time by using the lump sum to buy an annuity.

Damages for death

At common law, death extinguished rights of action.

Under the Fatal Accidents Act 1975 a dependant may sue in respect of financial loss provided that he or she falls within one of the particular relationships covered. These include people living as husband and wife for at least the previous two years but not, apparently, gay relationships. The tort must have been actionable by the deceased and contributory negligence applies — so damages will be reduced if the deceased was to some extent responsible for his or her death. The amount recoverable is governed by the deceased's income, reasonable prospects of income and the extent of the dependency.

The Law Reform (Miscellaneous Provisions) Act 1934 provides that the deceased's right of action passes to his or her estate. Defamation is the only tort which does not survive the deceased. The claim is for loss of earnings until death, pain and suffering and loss of amenity. If the deceased died instantaneously nothing would be recoverable. There is now no claim in respect of loss of expectation of life.

The Administration of Justice Act 1982 allows close relations (spouse or the parents of an unmarried minor) to claim up to £7,000 for bereavement.

Funeral expenses may be claimed under either the 1934 or the 1982 Act.

4.5.2 INJUNCTIONS

Injunctions are especially useful in actions in trespass and defamation. See Unit 4.3.2.

4.5.3 SELF-HELP

It is permissible for a victim of tort to take steps to remedy the situation without recourse to the courts. For example, trespassers may be ejected or goods reclaimed with the use of reasonable force. A nuisance may be abated by the person whose enjoyment of land is being interfered with taking steps to stop the nuisance. Any person using self-help would be expected to have requested the return of property or cessation of the nuisance first, and should be very careful to stay within what the law considers reasonable. Given that tempers are likely to flare in the sort of situations considered here, self-help is a potentially difficult course of action and it may be that the use of a mediator (see Unit 1.6) would be wise.

4.6 LIMITATION OF ACTIONS

The Limitation Act 1980 lays down the time limits within which actions must be brought:
- oral or written contract: six years from the breach of contract
- contract made by deed: twelve years from the breach
- tort action: six years of the cause from action arising
- personal injury action: three years from the cause of action.

If there has been a fraud or mistake, time begins to run only when the plaintiff has, or ought to have, discovered the fraud or mistake. Time does not run against a minor, so time begins to run on the minor's eighteenth birthday. If written acknowledgement is made of a debt, time begins to run again.

In personal injury actions, the court has a wide discretion to set the time limit aside.

The Latent Damage Act 1986 deals with damage that is unknown to the plaintiff and could not reasonably be discovered. Time begins to run when the plaintiff knows or should have known of the damage. The limitation period is then three years. In addition, there is an overall limit of 15 years from the time that the tort was committed.

Illustrative questions

1 The main remedy for loss resulting from commission of a tort or from a breach of contract is damages.

(a) Examine the remedy, considering how satisfactory it is. (13)

(b) Critically assess the remedies which may be awarded in addition, or as alternatives, to damages. (12)

(AEB)

Tutorial note
Part (a) requires explanation and evaluation of the remedy of damages, part (b) identification, description and critical assessment of alternatives. It is necessary to be able to write on both parts of the question: a common failing of candidates is to produce a strong answer to one part of the question and a very weak answer to the other. It is impossible to cover in the time available in an examination all the issues that could be raised in answering such a wide question. It is not necessary to do so: just write enough to convince the examiner that you understand the principles involved and the problems that arise.

Suggested answer

Part (a)
Damages is a payment of money, designed primarily to compensate the injured party who has suffered a breach of contract or against whom a tort has been committed.

Damages in contract are calculated in such a way as to place the plaintiff in the position he would have been in had the contract been correctly performed. This means that, for example, if he has to buy goods to replace those which the defendant fails to deliver, he will be able to recover as damages any amount he has to pay for the goods which is more than he was to have paid to the defendant. This is known as the market rule. A court may decide that the expense of putting the plaintiff in precisely the same position he would have occupied had the contract been properly performed is not justifiable. In *Ruxley Electronics* v *Forsyth* (1994), the plaintiffs sued the defendant for payment in respect of a swimming pool and the defendant counterclaimed for damages for breach of contract in building the pool slightly shallower than was specified. The House of Lords held that it would not be reasonable in the circumstances to award the cost of rebuilding the pool, as the pool built was substantially the same as the pool contracted for.

The parties to a contract may agree, in advance, what the damages are to be in the event of a breach. This is known as a liquidated damages clause and will be enforced by the court, even if the amount of damages payable exceeds the loss sustained. If the parties have included a penalty clause in the contract, it will not be enforced. The distinction between the two is that a liquidated damages clause is an honest attempt at pre-estimate of likely loss, whereas a penalty clause is an attempt to coerce a party to perform the contract by the threat of disproportionate damages being payable for breach.

Damages in tort are designed to put the plaintiff in the position he would have been in had the tort not been committed. Sums for non-pecuniary loss, such as pain and suffering or loss of reputation, are notoriously difficult to assess. In most cases, they will be calculated by judges, using awards in similar cases as a guideline. In defamation and other cases heard by juries there have been problems of disproportionate awards.

In both tort and contract, damages are recoverable only if the loss was reasonably foreseeable. In contract, this rule comes from the case of *Hadley* v *Baxendale* (1854) in which the plaintiff was unable to recover damages for loss of profits because the loss was neither foreseeable by the reasonable man nor known to both parties as likely to occur. If the mill owner had told the carrier that this was the only millshaft and that the mill could not operate without it, then damages for the delay would have been payable.

The rule in tort is very similar: damages are payable only for a loss which is reasonably foreseeable. The rule comes from a Privy Council case, *The Wagon Mound* (1961), but has since been applied throughout the English court system. The defendant's action is judged on the state of knowledge at the time of the incident, so a plaintiff can be left without compensation merely because he suffered injury due to a risk that was not widely recognised when the accident occurred.

In both contract and tort, the plaintiff has a duty to mitigate his loss. That is, he cannot allow his losses to accumulate but must take reasonable steps to prevent further loss. Any loss caused by the plaintiff's failure to mitigate is not recoverable from the defendant. In *Bruce* v *Calder* (1895) failure to accept an offer of employment was held to be a failure to mitigate the loss caused by unfair dismissal.

Part (b)

In circumstances in which payment of money alone will not compensate the plaintiff, the court has a discretion to award one or more equitable remedies. Because these remedies are equitable, the plaintiff's behaviour is a factor to be taken into account in deciding whether an order should be made.

An injunction is an order of the court. A defendant may be ordered not to publish material, or to keep off the plaintiff's property, for example. If he breaches an injunction, a defendant is in contempt of court and may be fined or imprisoned. An order of specific performance is similar, in that it orders a defendant to fulfil his contractual obligations. These orders are made only where damages would not suffice so, for example, an order of specific performance will not be made if it would be necessary for the court to supervise the order, as in *Ryan* v *Mutual Tontine* (1893), where failure to provide a resident porter was compensated for by damages because this was a continuing obligation and the court would have to check whether an order of specific performance was being complied with.

Neither an injunction nor specific performance may be used to enforce a contract for personal services, so damages remain the only remedy available. An injunction will be granted, however, to prevent a person already under contract to one person forming a contract with another person. This was the case in *Warner Brothers* v *Nelson* (1937), but the court is careful to ensure that the effect of the injunction will not be to prevent the defendant earning a living. This was why an injunction was refused in *Page One Records* v *Britton* (1967) in which the defendants would have been compelled to work for the plaintiffs if an injunction was granted.

The courts have developed powerful forms of injunction. A *Mareva* injunction prevents a potential defendant moving assets out of the jurisdiction; an *Anton Piller* order allows a plaintiff to search for evidence on the defendant's premises. Both are obtained by the plaintiff applying to the court without the knowledge of the defendant. Whilst this is necessary to prevent the defendant disposing of assets or evidence, it is carefully controlled by the courts as it is a major infringement on the defendant's rights.

The court may order rectification of documents which do not reflect the intention of the parties, rescission of contracts obtained through innocent misrepresentation and payments on a *quantum meruit* basis. This means that the courts have at their disposal a wide range of remedies from which they can choose the most appropriate combination for the particular circumstances.

2 Discuss the aims pursued in the sentencing of criminal offenders. (10)
(AEB)

Tutorial note
The word to note here is 'discuss', which requires more than a description. This is just part of a full exam question, so precisely what to include is determined to some extent by whatever the examiner asks in the other part of the question. You may find this coupled with something on sentencing powers, or on the aims that may be pursued by the use of particular sentences, or it could be asked in conjunction with a specific case study in which you are asked to suggest a suitable sentence.

Suggested answer
The major aims pursued in sentencing criminal offenders are retribution, reform, deterrence and protection of the public.

Retribution means punishment. The object here is to make the offender suffer as the victim has suffered. It also carries a message about social attitudes to criminal behaviour as being unacceptable and likely to lead to unpleasant consequences. Conveying this message is also the aim of deterrence: sentences are set at a level thought to deter potential offenders. Deterrence may be individual, aiming to prevent an offender re-offending, or general, aiming to prevent people from becoming offenders. General deterrence is sometimes used as a reason for giving an apparently harsh sentence, out of proportion with the harm caused by an offender's actions.

Reform is designed to prevent an individual re-offending by changing him in some way. Protection of the public is the aim pursued when dangerous or repetitive offenders are imprisoned: they cannot offend whilst in prison and the public is thus protected from them.

The aims are not necessarily compatible with each other. A dangerous offender may be imprisoned for 20 years. This will protect the public and is retributive. It may act as a general deterrent but there is no guarantee that it will deter the offender himself and, without some attempt at reforming him as an individual, it does not deal with the long-term problem of what he is likely to do on his release.

The aims of retribution and deterrence are the easiest to explain to the public and tend, therefore, to be the aims promoted by politicians; whereas reform is sometimes seen as a 'soft option' for offenders because it is largely recognised that non-custodial sentences give a better chance of achieving reform. There is, therefore, constant conflict as to the aims to be pursued.

The conflict is heightened when Parliament passes laws that restrict the discretion of judges in sentencing individuals, as is the case with the Crime (Sentencing) Act 1997. Usually, Parliament lays down a maximum sentence but this Act lays down minima in certain circumstances. The aim of the Act is to deter repeat offending, the fear is that it could give rise to injustice in individual cases. This could be seen as the entire debate on the proper aim of sentencing in a nutshell: should judges be concerned with the best sentence to pass on the individual offender, or should they be pursuing policy aims?

Practice questions

1 Bernard, aged 16, is convicted by the Midshire Youth Court of causing criminal damage.

(a) What sentencing powers does the court have in respect of him?   (25)

(b) Why are there differences in the sentences available for young offenders and adult offenders?   (25)

(UODLE)

Pitfalls

Take careful note of the age given. Be sure to answer the question why in part (b), rather than simply stating what the differences are.

Key points

(a) Detention in a young offender institution, probation order, community service order, combination order, supervision order, attendance centre order, fine, discharge. Explain each of these briefly.

(b) Outline the *differences*: between prison and young offender institutions, for example. Explain *why* those differences exist: largely because of the recognition of the possibility of reforming and rehabilitating young offenders.

2 'In order to make the contract breaker liable under *Hadley* v *Baxendale* it is not necessary that he should have actually asked himself what loss is liable to result from a breach. It suffices that, if he had considered the question, he would as a reasonable man have concluded that the loss in question was liable to result.' (Asquith LJ, *Victoria Laundry (Windsor) Ltd* v *Newman Industries Limited* [1949] 2 KB 528 at page 540.)

Discuss the ways in which the courts have approached the problem of remoteness of damage in the light of Asquith LJ's statement.   (25)

(NEAB)

Pitfalls

Candidates do not make good use of quotations, which is a shame as they are introduced by examiners to be helpful. The art is to look at what the examiner wants you to discuss — here it is remoteness of damage — and then look at the quotation to see what aspect the examiner expects to see emphasised. The question comes from a contract law paper, but it could, on a different paper, invite a discussion of remoteness in tort as well as contract.

Key points

Defendant responsible for foreseeable losses: explain rule in *Hadley* v *Baxendale* (reasonably foreseeable or within the contemplation of the parties). Illustrate with respect to the facts in *Victoria Laundry*: what loss was foreseeable, what was within the contemplation of the parties? Is this one rule or two? Refer to the quotation: what would the reasonable man have concluded in these circumstances? Point out that it does not matter what the defendant 'actually asked himself'.

CRIMINAL LAW

Units in this chapter

Chapter objectives

This chapter aims to provide an outline of criminal law. The meaning and functions of criminal law are considered briefly. The basic elements which must be proved to establish criminal liability are guilty conduct (*actus reus*), guilty mind (*mens rea*) and absence of a defence. Each of these elements is explored. Some offences, known as strict liability offences, do not require proof of *mens rea*. The scope of strict liability, together with vicarious and corporate liability is considered. You should also refer to Chapter 9 on this topic. An individual may participate in a crime as a principal, or as a secondary party. Aiding, abetting, counselling and procuring are examined. Incitement, conspiracy and attempt are inchoate (incomplete) offences and their necessary elements are analysed. The chapter then goes on to examine various crimes: homicide, non-fatal offences against the person, rape and indecent assault, and key offences against property are all explored. Most A Level Law syllabuses also require knowledge of sentencing, and it makes sense to revise crime and sentencing together. You should refer to Chapter 4 for an outline of sentencing.

5.1   MEANING AND FUNCTIONS

5.1.1 DEFINITION

There is no really satisfactory definition of a crime. However, a working definition is '*a wrong which is committed against the state*'. The criminal law is a series of prohibitions (or requirements to act) backed up with the threat of punishment and society's ideas about what kinds of behaviour should be prohibited by the criminal law change over time. The range of conduct which is subjected to the criminal law is enormous and criminal law regulates almost every area of our lives. Offences range from serious crimes, such as murder, manslaughter, rape, burglary and robbery through to the less serious regulatory offences such as minor traffic offences.

There is much overlap between what is regarded as criminal and what is immoral, but the relationship is not a perfect one (see Unit 3.2). Whereas most people would generally agree that murder is an act of extreme immorality, it is equally true that many would also argue that genuine cases of mercy-killing ought not to be regarded in the same way. In addition, not all crimes would be regarded as immoral: e.g., failure to display a tax disc on the correct part of the windscreen is a criminal offence, but it is hardly an immoral act! Conversely, immorality does not necessarily make conduct criminal or illegal in any way (e.g., adultery).

5.1.2 FUNCTIONS OF CRIMINAL LAW

Conduct which is regarded as a criminal offence may also give rise to some other form of legal action in civil law. For example, injuring another person through careless driving could give rise to both a criminal law prosecution and an action in the tort of negligence. The distinction between crime and tort is not in the conduct itself, but in the legal proceedings which follow, and the purpose of those proceedings. A person may be both prosecuted by the state and sued by the victim (plaintiff). The fundamental aim of criminal law is to reduce certain kinds of conduct by measures which include punishment, deterrence, and rehabilitation, whereas the fundamental aim of tort is to compensate the victim.

5.1.3 SOURCES OF CRIMINAL LAW

The boundary between acceptable and unacceptable behaviour is determined by both Parliament, through statutes, and the courts, through the common law. Few crimes are now defined purely by the common law. Almost all are derived from statutes and the courts have generally renounced claims to be entitled to develop the common law so as to create new offences and defences. Such development, it is believed, should be undertaken by a democratically-elected Parliament, rather than unelected judges. However, judges must respond to situations which arise in cases before them, and there are still examples to be found of judicial development, although principally through the process of statutory interpretation.

5.2   ELEMENTS OF A CRIME: *ACTUS REUS* AND *MENS REA*

5.2.1 GENERAL REQUIREMENTS OF LIABILITY

Three basic elements must be proved to establish criminal liability:
- guilty conduct (*actus reus*);

- a guilty mind (*mens rea*);
- the absence of any defence.

The precise forms of these requirements may vary from offence to offence. The general meanings of *actus reus* and *mens rea* are explored here, whilst defences are considered in Unit 5.3.

5.2.2 ACTUS REUS

Types of *actus reus*

Actus reus refers to the external elements of a crime and includes all those parts of an offence except those which relate to the defendant's (D's) state of mind. The types of *actus reus* can be conveniently classified into three categories:

❶ Result crimes: D's behaviour must produce a particular result, for example, murder, where D's conduct must cause the death of a human being.

❷ Conduct crimes: Some crimes do not require proof of any consequence, for example, dangerous driving or bigamy.

❸ State of affairs crimes: Exceptionally, there are some crimes which do not even seem to require proof of any conduct by D, but merely that a state of affairs existed, see e.g., *R* v *Larsonneur* (1933).

Omissions

Inevitably, criminal conduct usually takes the form of some *act* although sometimes liability may be based on an *omission* to act. There are three requirements:

❶ It must be possible in law to commit the crime by omission, for example, homicide could be committed by, say, deliberately starving a child to death (failing to feed). It may not be possible to commit an attempt by an omission because s. 1 Criminal Attempts Act 1981 requires 'an *act* more than merely preparatory' (see Unit 5.6). Doubts exist as to whether the offences of assault and battery may be committed by an omission (see Unit 5.8).

❷ In a result crime, the omission must 'cause' the result, in the sense that the result might not have occurred if D had acted.

❸ There must be a duty to act. There is no general duty to act. However, the law imposes a duty to act in a number of situations:

- **A contractual duty**: for example, *R* v *Pittwood* (1902).

- **A parental, family or equivalent relationship**: for example, *R* v *Gibbins & Proctor* (1918). It is unclear how far the courts might go in developing obligations in other relationships (for instance, between friends or those who share accommodation and so on).

- **A statute**: many statutes make it an offence to fail to do something, creating a duty to act. For example, s. 170 Road Traffic Act 1988.

- **A public office**: for example, *R* v *Dytham* (1979).

- **A voluntary assumption of responsibility**: for example, *R* v *Stone & Dobinson* (1977).

- **The creation of a dangerous situation, whether deliberately or accidentally**: for example, *R* v *Miller* (1983).

Voluntariness

There can be no criminal liability in any offence requiring proof of conduct unless D's conduct was voluntary. D's claim to have acted involuntarily is a plea of automatism (see Unit 5.3). However, since state of affairs offences do not overtly require proof of conduct by D, the courts appear to have rejected any requirement for voluntariness in such offences.

Causation

In all crimes where a result must be proved, D's conduct must be shown to have caused that result. This requires proof that D's conduct was both a cause in fact and a sufficient cause in law.

Factual causation: the 'but for' test
To be a cause in fact, D's conduct must satisfy the 'but for' test: that the consequence would not have occurred 'but for' D's conduct. For example, in *R v Pagett* (1983), though police bullets had killed D's hostage, V, this would never have happened if D had not taken V hostage, fired at the policemen pursuing him and held V in front of himself as a shield. However, in *R v White* (1910), though D sought to kill his mother by poisoning her and she did in fact die during the night, the death resulted from a heart attack. The poison was not a 'but for' cause.

Legal causation: the 'significant contribution' test
To be a cause in law, D's conduct need not be the sole cause but must make a significant contribution to the result. This means that two or more persons, acting independently, and each of whose conduct makes a significant contribution to the result, can all be said to cause the result.

Potential breaks in the chain of causation
When analysing whether a chain of causation exists in a particular case, the enquiry often becomes one about whether the chain of causation has been broken by intervening events. The most commonly discussed are:

- **Refusal of treatment by victim (V)**: This will not usually break the chain. The courts will not enquire into the reasonableness of the refusal (see *R v Holland* (1841) and *R v Blaue* (1975)).

- **The especially susceptible victim (the 'thin skull' victim)**: The general rule is that D must 'take his victim as he finds him or her'. This means that if, because of some special weakness in V, D causes greater injury to V than would normally have been expected, for example, an attack which brings on death through heart failure on account of V's heart condition, D will nevertheless be held to have caused the greater injuries (*R v Hayward* (1908) and *R v Dawson* (1985)). This applies to mental as well as physical weakness (*R v Blaue*).

- **Injuries resulting from attempted escape**: V's attempt to escape from D's attack does not break the chain if V's conduct and resulting injuries were reasonably foreseeable, for example, *R v Roberts* (1971).

- **Negligent, poor or inappropriate medical treatment**: Negligent or inappropriate medical treatment is unlikely to break the chain. To do so it would have to be such as to make the original injury merely part of the history, so that it no longer makes a significant contribution to the result (*R v Jordan* (1956)). However, in *R v Smith* (1959) the court held that the original wound was still an operating and substantial cause of death, whether or not any other cause (poor medical treatment) additionally operated, and D was convicted. In *R v Cheshire* (1991), although there was strong evidence that the original wound no longer threatened V's life at the time of his death, D was convicted. The court argued that the allegedly negligent treatment would only break the chain of causation if it were '*so independent of D's acts, and in itself so potent in causing death*' that the contribution made by D's acts in causing death was insignificant.

5.2.3 *MENS REA*

Mens rea means the state of mind of the person committing the crime. The required *mens rea* varies from crime to crime. *Mens rea* means intention or recklessness. In general, the common law does not recognise negligence as a ground of liability (a significant exception being gross negligence manslaughter).

Intention

Intention is the most blameworthy state of mind. Most offences do not require proof of intention or knowledge (recklessness will suffice), but for some offences, such as murder and theft, it must be proved.

Direct intention

Defining intention is not easy. The general approach of the courts is that it is unnecessary for a judge to seek to define intention, since it can usually be left to the good sense of the jury to recognise. Therefore, no clear definition of intention emerges through the cases, though it would generally be agreed that *aim or purpose* to bring about a consequence would be enough. An aim or purpose in this sense is often called 'direct' intention.

Oblique intention

The difficult cases where guidance may need to be given to the jury arise where D, without aim or purpose, foresees that a consequence is virtually certain, very likely, or highly probable, and yet, despite this knowledge, continues with his conduct. As subsequently interpreted, *R v Moloney* (1985) and *R v Hancock & Shankland* (1986) suggest that foresight of consequences (of whatever degree) is not, in itself, intention. Foresight is merely evidence from which the jury *may* (but not *must*) infer intention. In *R v Nedrick* (1986) the Court of Appeal held, as a matter of law, that the jury were only entitled to infer intention when satisfied that D foresaw the consequences as *certain* or *virtually certain*. However, the Court of Appeal in *R v Walker & Hayles* (1989) reluctantly accepted '*very highly probable*' as an alternative expression and further confused the issue in *R v Woollin* (1997). Foresight without aim or purpose is sometimes called 'oblique' intention.

Recklessness

Proof of recklessness is sufficient to establish the *mens rea* for most criminal offences. There are two types of recklessness in law: subjective recklessness and objective recklessness.

	SUBJECTIVE RECKLESSNESS	OBJECTIVE RECKLESSNESS
Also known as:	*Cunningham* **recklessness**, after the case of *R v Cunningham* (1957) concerning the offence of 'maliciously administering a noxious thing so as to endanger life' under s. 23 Offences Against the Person Act 1861.	*Caldwell* **recklessness** after the case of *Metropolitan Police Commissioner v Caldwell* (1981) concerning criminal damage under s. 1(1) and (2) Criminal Damage Act 1971.
Meaning	This is the conscious taking of an unjustifiable risk. D will have given thought to, and will have recognised the risk, but gone on to take it.	Lord Diplock's 'model direction' in *Caldwell* was that D will be reckless where: '(1) he does an act which in fact creates an obvious risk [of a particular consequence] and (2) when he does the act he either has not given any thought to the possibility of there being any such risk or has recognised that there was some risk involved and has nonetheless gone on to do it'.
Key offences adopting each test	• assault • battery • wounding • infliction of GBH • rape • deception • secondary participation	• criminal damage

Figure 5.1 The distinction between subjective and objective recklessness

The Caldwell 'lacuna'

The *Caldwell* recklessness test is purely objective. As long as the reasonable person would have recognised the risk and would not have taken it, D will be liable even if, because of age, lack of knowledge or inherent lack of reasoning capacity, D would not have recognised the risk had he applied his mind to it (*Elliot* v *C* (1983)). However, a state of mind where D thinks about the situation and decides that there is no risk is not recklessness. In *R* v *Reid* (1992), D tried to overtake a car on the inside lane just where that lane narrowed to accommodate a taxi-driver's hut. D's car hit the hut and as a result of the collision, his passenger was killed and D was charged with the old offence of causing death by reckless driving. D contended that he made a decision about whether he could get past the car and saw no risk in the way he was driving. However, on the facts, the House of Lords concluded that D gave no thought to the risk, and was therefore reckless. Their Lordships also decided (*obiter*) that the lacuna (gap) exists because Lord Diplock did not include it in his model direction.

However, where D recognises a risk and takes steps to reduce it, he will still be liable if, after taking precautions, the risk that he recognises as remaining is not so negligible that he would be entitled to ignore it (*Chief Constable of Avon & Somerset* v *Shimmen* (1986)). Similarly, it was held in *R* v *Merrick* (1996) that, where D creates a risk in the belief that subsequent precautions will immediately eliminate it, he does not fall within the lacuna, since he recognises the risk and carries on regardless.

Evolution of subjective and objective recklessness

For many years the importance of the distinction received little attention. However, it has become very significant in recent years. The stages in the evolution of the tests applied since 1957 include:

- *R* v *Cunningham* (1957), the word '*malicious*' in the Offences Against the Person Act 1861 was held to require proof that D was aware of the risk.

- Increasing use of the subjective test culminating in its application to criminal damage in *R* v *Stephenson* (1979).

- Re-emergence of the objective test in the House of Lords' decisions in *Caldwell* (1981) (criminal damage) and *R* v *Lawrence* (1981) (reckless driving).

- Application of *Caldwell* recklessness to involuntary manslaughter by Lord Roskill in *R* v *Seymour* (1983), and his further suggestion that the *Caldwell* meaning should apply throughout criminal law.

- Renewed emphasis on the subjective test. Many offences have been held to impose a subjective test of recklessness (see Figure 5.1). The revival of the concept of gross negligence manslaughter in *R* v *Adomako* (1994) firmly rejected the application of *Caldwell* recklessness to manslaughter. Criminal damage now seems to be the only significant offence in which the objective test of recklessness continues to be imposed.

Negligence

Negligence is the failure to achieve the standard of conduct to be expected of the reasonable person. It is not usually the basis of criminal liability, though involuntary manslaughter can be committed by gross negligence, and statutory offences such as driving without due care and attention involve proof of a small degree of negligence. D will be negligent, whether or not he is aware of the risk of his failure to achieve the standard of the reasonable person. Objective recklessness is very close in meaning to negligence, perhaps only distinguished by the *lacuna* notion. Negligently concluding that there is no risk, having given thought to the matter, would not be recklessness but would be negligence.

The doctrine of transferred malice

Where D intends a consequence, say serious injury, in relation to victim X but, when trying to achieve it, causes that consequence to victim V, D's intention or recklessness can be transferred to the *actus reus* in relation to victim V. This is known as the doctrine of transferred intent. In *R* v *Latimer* (1886) D aimed a blow with his belt at X, but in fact actually struck and severely injured V. D was taken to have the necessary *mens rea* for the wounding of V. However, D's *mens rea* cannot be transferred to the *actus reus* of a different crime (*R* v *Pembliton* (1874)).

Contemporaneity of *actus reus* and *mens rea*

The *actus reus* and *mens rea* must be present together at some point, though not necessarily from the outset, if D is to be found guilty. In *Fagan* v *MPC* (1968) D accidentally drove his car onto the foot of V, a policeman, and when he realised what he had done, D refused to move the car. His conviction for assaulting a police constable in the execution of his duty was upheld, because though he did not initially have *mens rea*, the *actus reus* continued during the time that the car remained on V's foot, and the subsequent presence of *mens rea* was sufficient. Further applications of this principle can be found in *R* v *Thabo Meli* (1954), *R* v *Church* (1965) and *R* v *Le Brun* (1991).

5.3 GENERAL DEFENCES

General defences in criminal law set out the circumstances in which conduct, which would otherwise be a crime, is justified or excused. General defences are defences to all crimes, including murder.

5.3.1 INFANCY

In law, infants are persons under 18 years of age. For the purposes of this defence, infants are divided into three categories:

Under 10

Under s. 50 Children and Young Persons Act 1933 (as amended) a child under 10 years old is entirely exempt from criminal responsibility in all circumstances.

10 but under 14

A child aged at least 10 but less than 14 years is also presumed to be incapable of distinguishing right from wrong but the presumption is rebuttable. The prosecution must prove that D had a *'mischievous discretion'*, i.e., the child knew that what he or she did was *'seriously wrong'* (*R* v *Gorrie* (1918)). The continued existence of the presumption was affirmed in *C* v *DPP* (1995), where the House of Lords said that it must be proved that D knew it was *'a wrong act as distinct from an act of mere naughtiness or childish mischief'*.

14 years and over

Persons aged 14 years or more are presumed to be responsible for their actions. There is no possible defence of infancy.

5.3.2 INSANITY

D's sanity may be raised at either of two stages before trial.

Fitness to be tried

If D has been committed in custody awaiting trial, the Home Secretary may order him to be detained in a hospital because of his mental state, until fit to be tried (ss. 47 and 48 Mental Health Act 1983). When D is brought up for trial, the judge (or the jury, if the judge has doubts) has the power to decide that D is unfit to plead. A determination of whether D *'did the act or omission'* is still to be made so that, even if unfit, D will be completely acquitted if he has not done so. If D is found to have done the act or omission the judge has powers under the Criminal Procedure (Insanity) Act 1964 (as amended by the Criminal Procedure (Insanity and Unfitness to Plead) Act 1991) to make a hospital order, guardianship order, supervision and treatment order or an absolute discharge.

Insanity at the time of the commission of the alleged offence

This is governed by the *M'Naghten Rules* (1843). Unless the prosecution argues for insanity (in denial, say, of diminished responsibility or non-insane automatism), then D must prove on a balance of probabilities that, at the time of the commission of the offence, he was suffering from *'a defect of reason, from disease of the mind, as not to know the nature and quality of the act he was doing, or if he did know it, that he did not know that he was doing what was wrong'*.

If successful, D will be found 'not guilty by reason of insanity' and will be subject to any of the orders specified above in the examination of unfitness to plead. The *M'Naghten* Rules can be broken down into three elements:

1. **Defect of reason** means D was incapable of exercising powers of reasoning. Mere failure to exercise such powers, for example, through temporary absent-mindedness, is not enough (*R* v *Clarke* (1972)).

2. **Disease of the mind** meaning disorders of brain function affecting powers of reason, memory and understanding. As Lord Diplock expressed it in *R* v *Sullivan* (1984): '*It matters not whether the aetiology of the impairment is organic, as in epilepsy, or functional, or whether the impairment itself is permanent or transient and intermittent, provided that it subsisted at the time of commission of the act*' unless it is temporary impairment which '*results from some external physical factor such as a blow on the head causing concussion or the administration of an anaesthetic for therapeutic purposes*'. Thus, it includes epilepsy (*R* v *Sullivan* (1984)), arterio-sclerosis (*R* v *Kemp* (1957)), diabetes (*R* v *Hennessy* (1989)) and, clinical depression and schizophrenia. It extends also to 'night terrors' and sleepwalking (*R* v *Burgess* (1991)). Disorders attributable to the temporary effect of drugs will not be disease of the mind (*R* v *Lipman* (1969)).

3. **Nature and quality of act/not knowing it was wrong**. Nature and quality of act refers to the physical nature of the act, not its moral or legal nature, for example, D thinks he is chopping wood when he is in fact chopping someone's head off. '*Not knowing it was wrong*' requires D not to know that what he was doing was legally wrong (*R* v *Windle* (1952)), although the Australian High Court in *R* v *Stapleton* (1952) thought it meant morally wrong, so that the defence would succeed even if D knew his act to be legally wrong, if he believed it to be morally acceptable.

5.3.3 AUTOMATISM

As stated in Unit 5.2, generally the prosecution must prove that D's conduct was voluntary. D's claim to have been acting involuntarily is called a plea of automatism. For example, a person who, without fault, slips on ice and knocks another person over, clearly does not intend injury (no *mens rea*) but, more fundamentally, has no control over his movements and does not commit an *actus reus*. He was an *automaton*.

Fundamental loss of control

To raise this defence, D must prove a fundamental loss of control not merely some partial loss as might occur when a person's movements are poorly co-ordinated through tiredness or illness (*Broome* v *Perkins* (1987)). The loss of control is usually related to brain malfunction but there may be some instances, such as reflex actions or being pushed, where D remains conscious throughout but is simply unable to prevent movement of limbs. In *Hill* v *Baxter* (1958) a *hypothetical* example was given. The judge asserted that it would be automatism if D were to be attacked by a swarm of bees whilst driving and be unable to control the movements of his limbs because of bee stings.

The distinction between insanity and non-insane automatism

This is an important, and sometimes tricky, distinction.

Insanity (insane automatism)	Automatism (non-insane automatism)
The source of the impairment is from a disease of the mind (which has a broad scope, as interpreted by *R* v *Sullivan* (1984))	The source of impairment is from an external factor or a temporary disturbance which cannot be related to any notion of disease, e.g., hypoglycaemia (low blood sugar brought on by insulin injection) (*R* v *Quick* (1973), *R* v *Bailey* (1983))

Self-induced automatism

If D was in some way at fault in becoming an automaton, then he may still be liable. A person who is an automaton through drink or drugs will be subject to the rules on intoxication (see Unit 5.3.4).

A person who is at fault in some way **not** involving intoxication, for example, failing to follow the correct diet after taking prescribed insulin for diabetes, will be able to plead automatism to any offences. Even so, D may still be liable if, when he allowed himself to become an automaton, he knew he might commit an offence of the kind in issue. In *R* v *Bailey* (1983), D, a diabetic who had caused severe injury to V, contended that he had attacked V whilst suffering a hypoglycaemic attack. On the evidence this was held not to be credible and he was convicted. Nevertheless, it was accepted that if D had truly been suffering such an attack, then he would not have been guilty of the offence under s. 20 Offences Against the Person Act (OAPA) 1861 (see Unit 5.8) unless he was aware of the risk of causing such harm if he allowed himself to become an automaton. This would have been recklessness and recklessness was what had to be proved.

5.3.4 INTOXICATION

The rules on intoxication apply notably to drink but also to drugs taken other than under medical direction. The rules apply only to substances commonly perceived as having effects normally associated with intoxicants. Ordinary rules of criminal liability apply to those who become intoxicated on account of substances outside the special rules (*R* v *Hardie* (1984)). The rules on intoxication are summarised in Figure 5.2 below:

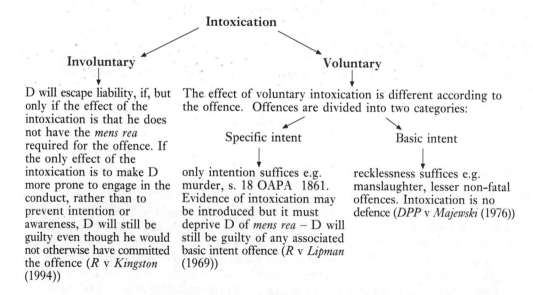

Figure 5.2 The legal effect of intoxication

In the highly unlikely event that D got drunk to acquire courage to commit an offence and then committed it whilst so drunk as to lack *mens rea*, he should be treated as still having the *mens rea* he possessed prior to the intoxication (*A-G for Northern Ireland* v *Gallagher* (1963)).

Remember the relevance of intoxication in insanity (excessive drinking may cause a disease of the mind) and diminished responsibility (see Unit 5.7).

5.3.5 MISTAKE

This defence is concerned with mistake of fact, not of law. Mistake is relevant in two situations.

Mistake as to *mens rea*

D denies *mens rea*, asserting that he made a mistake as to some element in the *actus reus*, for example, if D finds a pen on the floor and keeps it, mistakenly believing that it is the pen he lost the other day, he may not be guilty of theft because he believes it is his, and he is not acting dishonestly. The House of Lords held in *DPP* v *Morgan* (1975) that such mistakes do not have to be reasonable, merely genuine (although a reasonable belief is more likely to be accepted as a genuinely held belief). Obviously, if the offence requires proof merely of objective recklessness, or negligence, then any mistake must be reasonable.

Mistake which raises a defence

D admits *mens rea* but asserts a defence. However, he made a mistake and will not have the defence on the true facts. In *R* v *Gladstone Williams* (1983) M witnessed a youth snatching a woman's handbag, chased after him, caught him and knocked him to the ground. D, who then came on the scene, was told by M that he (M) was arresting the youth and that he was a police officer (which he was not). D asked M to produce his warrant card, but of course he could not do so. A struggle then ensued during which D punched M. Quashing his conviction for assault occasioning actual bodily harm, the Court of Appeal held that D would lack necessary *mens rea* if, on the facts as he mistakenly believed them to be, he was entitled to use reasonable force either in self-defence or in the prevention of crime.

5.3.6 NECESSITY, DURESS AND DURESS OF CIRCUMSTANCES

In all these defences, D claims that when he committed the alleged offence, he had to make a choice between two courses of action, to commit the offence or to allow some other harmful consequence to occur. It is advisable to revise these defences as a package and to be aware of the close relationship between them and the defences of self-defence/prevention of crime.

Necessity

In *R* v *Dudley and Stephens* (1884) the House of Lords held that the defence of necessity could not be pleaded to a charge of murder. However, the defence has succeeded in certain cases and has been incorporated into statutory provisions, for example *R* v *Bourne* (1939) and the Abortion Act 1967 (as amended); s. 5 Criminal Damage Act 1971; s. 87 Road Traffic Regulation Act 1984. These instances could be explained as limited to specific crimes and not as recognising any general defence of necessity. Since 1987, the courts have recognised the defence of duress of circumstances. This is very close to recognition of a general defence of necessity, although it is subject to the same restrictions as those applied in the defence of duress.

Duress

Duress has long been recognised as excusing D completely from liability. The force or threat of force is employed specifically for the purpose of compelling D to commit a criminal offence.

The elements

- Duress cannot be raised as a defence to murder or attempted murder (*R* v *Howe* (1987), *R* v *Gotts* (1992)). It can be raised as a defence to all other charges.

- Duress cannot be raised where D has voluntarily associated himself with those who have imposed the duress in circumstances where he knew that he might be subjected to such duress. For example, in *R* v *Ali* (1995), D was unable to use duress as a defence to a robbery at a building society. D was a drug user who had agreed to sell drugs on for his dealer, X, and was in no doubt that X would behave violently if D did not hand over the proceeds of sale. When D failed to do so, X gave him a gun and told him to get the money by robbing a bank or building society.

- Use, or threat of use, of extreme force (death or serious injury). In *R* v *Valderrama-Vega* (1985) a threat to disclose D's homosexuality was held to be of insufficient gravity.

- Against D, D's family but also against third parties.

- So as to be the overwhelming, though not necessarily the sole, reason for D's conduct.

- In circumstances where D *reasonably* believed that there was no other course of action open, e.g., no obvious means of escape. However, this was not interpreted by the courts quite as might have been expected in *R* v *Hudson and Taylor* (1971).

- A sober person of reasonable firmness would have responded as D did (*R* v *Graham* (1982)). This is the objective element. The reasonable person is of D's age and sex and possesses any other of D's characteristics which identify D as being in a category of people who might be less able to resist pressure, for example, serious physical disability, recognised mental illness or psychiatric condition, but not characteristics such as mere pliability, vulnerability, timidity, and the like, which are inconsistent with the notion of reasonable firmness.

Duress of circumstances

This has recently been developed by the courts in a series of cases all of which, initially, involved driving offences committed while under some external threat (*R* v *Willer* (1986), *R* v *Conway* (1989), *R* v *Martin* (1989), *DPP* v *Bell* (1992)). Here, unlike duress, the threat (whether from circumstances or other people) is not designed to compel D to commit an offence but it forces the choice upon him. However, the elements of the defence are otherwise exactly as noted above for duress. The decision in *R* v *Pommell* (1995) (a firearms offence case) makes it clear that the defence is not limited to driving offences but is of general application. Recent cases have stressed the importance of the objective test (*DPP* v *Davis* (1994)).

5.3.7 SELF-DEFENCE/PREVENTION OF CRIME

A distinction should be drawn between self-defence and defence of others on the one hand and prevention of crime on the other. Self-defence and defence of others is governed by common law. Prevention of crime is governed by statute. Section 3 Criminal Law Act 1967 states '*a person may use such force as is reasonable in the circumstances*' and this is the test employed by common law too. So, although there may be two defences, their rules are essentially the same and the use of force will be reasonable if two conditions are satisfied:

❶ **Necessary force:** that the use of some force is necessary on the actual facts, or in relation to the facts as D genuinely believed them to be, even if he was mistaken (see *R* v *Gladstone Williams* (1983) and Unit 5.3.5);

❷ **Justifiable force:** that the level of force actually used is justifiable as it would be viewed by a reasonable person. In *R* v *Owino* (1995) the Court of Appeal re-affirmed that the test is objective, and probably ended doubts on the issue raised by the decision in *R* v *Scarlett* (1993). Regard will be had to:

  - The proportion between the force and the danger.

  - Acknowledgement that D may have little time to measure his response (*R* v *Palmer* (1971)).

  - Extreme, even deadly, force will be justifiable to counter a threat of death or serious injury but not of damage to property. Yet some force will be justifiable in protection of property.

- Use of excessive force deprives D of the defence. Thus, on a charge of murder, D will either be acquitted or convicted of murder. There is no reduced liability by way of manslaughter (*R* v *Clegg* (1995)).

- Any restrictive rules which previously existed have now been removed. So, D is not obliged to retreat before using force. Indeed, D may strike first (*R* v *Bird* (1985)). Nor must D refrain from going to places where D may lawfully go but where D knows that danger may await (*R* v *Field* (1972)). Nevertheless, evidence of either may reduce the credibility of D's claim to have been acting in self-defence or in the prevention of a crime.

5.4 STRICT LIABILITY, VICARIOUS LIABILITY AND CORPORATE LIABILITY

5.4.1 STRICT LIABILITY

An offence is said to be one of strict liability where it is not necessary for the prosecution to prove *mens rea*.

The common law presumption in favour of a requirement to prove *mens rea*

There is a strong common law presumption in favour of *mens rea*. This is clearly illustrated by the case of *Sweet* v *Parsley* (1969).

Rebuttal of the presumption

In *Gammon* v *A-G of Hong Kong* (1985) Lord Scarman set out a useful framework for determining whether the presumption in favour of *mens rea* is displaced in any particular crime:

1 The presumption is particularly strong where the offence is 'truly criminal'. This is not altogether easy to apply. In *R* v *Blake* (1996) an offence of broadcasting without a licence was held to be 'truly criminal' because it carried a sentence of imprisonment.

2 It applies to statutory crimes and can be displaced only if this is clearly or by necessary implication the effect of the statute. Clearly, the words of the statute will be very important. Some words import *mens rea*, such as '*knowingly*'. Other words may do so, such as '*permits*', '*suffers*', '*wilfully*'; but '*causes*' generally does not. Absence of *mens rea* words in the section in question, but their presence in other sections suggests strict liability.

3 The statute must deal with an issue of social concern, some examples include:
- inflation (*St Margaret's Trust Ltd* (1958));
- drugs (*Warner* v *MPC* (1969), *R* v *Martindale* (1986));
- pollution (*Alphacell Ltd* v *Woodward* (1972));
- public safety (*Gammon* v *A-G of Hong Kong* (1985));
- public entertainment;
- trade descriptions;
- dangerous dogs (owning or being in charge of a dog dangerously out of control in a public place contrary to s. 3(1) Dangerous Dogs Act 1991, *R* v *Bezzina* (1994)).

4 Even so, strict liability must be effective to promote the objects of the statute by encouraging greater vigilance not to commit the prohibited act. Imposition of strict liability may raise standards all round. More pragmatic reasons might be that it makes it easier to obtain convictions and reduces the length of trials, so reducing the burden on the courts.

Evaluation of strict liability in criminal law can be found in Unit 9.2.

5.4.2 VICARIOUS LIABILITY

Vicarious liability means that one person may be legally responsible for actions of another and, in civil law, is applied to the employer/employee relationship (see Unit 7.10). The traditional common law view has been that a person should only be criminally responsible for those things which he personally does. Today, vicarious liability for criminal offences can arise in one of two ways:

Cases of 'extensive construction'

Sometimes the law will simply deem the actions of an employee to be those of the employer. This is the result of an extended construction of certain verbs that appear in criminal statutes, such as the word 'sell'. For example, in *Coppen* v *Moore (No. 2)* (1898), D, who owned a number of shops, was convicted of selling goods bearing false trade descriptions. Contrary to his instructions, one of the assistants had sold an American ham as a 'Scotch' ham. Under this principle, only the employee's *act* can be imputed to the employer. The employer can only be vicariously liable for the *actus reus* of his or her employee. Thus the employer can only be criminally liable if he or she has *mens rea*, or where it is a strict liability offence. The employee may also be liable.

The principle of delegation

Sometimes, where D delegates his responsibilities to another, he may render himself liable for what the other does in exercise of those responsibilities. Under the Licensing Acts, if a licensee delegates his responsibilities as a licensee to another, he may be liable for the criminal offences of the delegatee. In *Allen* v *Whitehead* (1930) a refreshment house licensee handed over control of it to an employee who, contrary to the licensee's instructions and in his absence, permitted prostitutes to enter the premises. The employer was convicted of an offence under s. 44 Metropolitan Police Act 1839. His employee's *acts* and *state of mind* were imputed to him.

5.4.3 CRIMINAL LIABILITY OF CORPORATIONS

A corporation (or company) is a separate person in law. Recall from Unit 3.4 that it is an individual in its own right, quite distinct from those persons who act on its behalf. A company can be liable for criminal offences in exactly the same way as an individual: personally and vicariously.

A company may be personally liable, but only through the acts and *mens rea* of those who *are* the corporation, i.e., '*those who represent the directing mind and will of the company and control what it does*' (*H L Bolton (Engineering) Ltd* v *T J Graham* (1957)). In *Tesco Supermakets Ltd* v *Nattrass* (1971) the House of Lords stated that crimes committed by those persons who control the company (the 'brains') could be attributed to the company; whereas the offences committed by mere servants of the company (the 'hands') could not (except, of course, by the vicarious liability rules). There are obvious limits on corporate liability under the criminal law. For example, a company cannot commit crimes such as rape and bigamy because these offences can only be committed by certain human beings. Neither can a company commit a crime which is punishable only by imprisonment, such as murder. However, a company may be guilty of manslaughter. This was confirmed in *R* v *P & O European Ferries Ltd* (1990), although the prosecution resulting from the Zeebrugge disaster failed on the evidence. However, in *R* v *OLL Ltd* (1994), D Ltd and its managing director, X, were convicted of manslaughter.

5.5 PARTICIPATION IN CRIME

5.5.1 PRINCIPALS AND ACCOMPLICES

There a number of ways in which a person may participate in crime:

- as a **perpetrator (principal)**, that is, as a person who actually commits the *actus reus* with the appropriate *mens rea* (if any is required);
- as a **secondary party (accomplice)**, that is, as a person who in some way assists, encourages, or acts to bring about the commission of the offence by the perpetrator(s) without actually committing the *actus reus* of the crime itself. Generally, there can be no liability as an accomplice if no offence is committed by a perpetrator. However, the person may be guilty of either incitement or conspiracy. Additionally, if the perpetrator gets to the stage of committing an attempt, the other person can be guilty as a secondary party to that attempt (see Unit 5.5).

It is necessary to make the distinction between perpetrators and secondary parties because:

- secondary participation in an offence requires proof of *actus reus* and *mens rea* elements which are different from those required for proof as a perpetrator of the offence;
- even in strict liability offences the secondary party must have *mens rea*;
- a person cannot be vicariously liable for secondary participation.

5.5.2 THE ACCESSORIES AND ABETTORS ACT 1861

Section 8 Accessories and Abettors Act 1861 provides: *'Whosoever shall aid, abet, counsel or procure the commission of any indictable offence ... shall be liable to be tried, indicted and punished as a principal offender'*. Section 44 Magistrates' Courts Act 1980 extends liability as an accomplice to summary offences.

5.5.3 THE *ACTUS REUS* OF SECONDARY PARTICIPATION

In *A-G's Reference (No. 1 of 1975)* (1975) Lord Widgery CJ insisted that the words aid, abet, counsel and procure represent distinct ways in which a person may be an accomplice, so that it should be possible to determine a separate meaning for each one.

Figure 5.3 sets out the key differences between each:

Type	Activity	Time of secondary participation	Does the perpetrator need to know of the secondary party's conduct?	Does it need to cause the perpetrator to commit the crime?	Cases
Aid	Assistance	Before/during the commission of the offence	No	No	*DPP for Northern Ireland* v *Lynch* (1975); *R* v *Bainbridge* (1959)
Abet	Encouragement, advice	At the time of commission of the offence	Yes	No	*Wilcox* v *Jeffery* (1951)
Counsel	Encouragement, advice	Prior to the commission of the offence	Yes	No	*R* v *Calhaem* (1985)
Procure	To bring about the commission of the offence	Prior to or during the commission of the offence	No	Yes	*R* v *Millward* (1994); *AG's Reference (No. 1 of 1975)* (1975)

Figure 5.3 Meaning of accomplice

Can D be liable when he is present at the commission of the crime but does nothing?

- Certainly, if his presence is part of a plan between himself and the principal.
- Possibly, even in the absence of any such plan, if his presence in any way renders

assistance or is an encouragement to the principal and D knows this. In *R v Clarkson* (1971) D was not guilty of aiding or abetting a rape when he stumbled across the offence and stayed to witness it. In *Clarkson*, D *could* have been guilty if, as is quite likely, his mere presence assisted the perpetrator (e.g., by causing V to believe that there was no point in resisting) and he was *aware* that this was so.

- Though he does nothing, D can be guilty as an accomplice if he has some right which enables him to stop the commission of the crime. In *Tuck v Robson* (1970), a public house licensee was convicted of aiding and abetting the consumption of alcohol out of hours when he made no effort to make his customers leave after closing time. D had a right of control and deliberately failed to exercise that right to prevent another from committing a crime.

5.5.4 THE *MENS REA* OF SECONDARY PARTICIPATION

The *mens rea* of secondary participation is complex and still evolving. It is important to recognise that the *mens rea* of secondary participation is distinct from that of the perpetrator.

Knowledge of effect of conduct

D must intend to engage in the conduct which amounts to aiding, abetting, counselling or procuring but he does not have to intend that the perpetrator should commit the crime. It is enough that D knows that his conduct will aid, encourage or bring about the commission of the crime (*NCB v Gamble* (1958), *DPP for Northern Ireland v Lynch* (1975)). In the case of a joint enterprise (see below) involving homicide, the House of Lords in *R v Powell & Daniels* (1997) has confirmed the earlier Court of Appeal decisions that the secondary party can be guilty of murder if he foresees a real risk that the perpetrator will kill with malice aforethought. Thus, unlike the perpetrator, the secondary party need not intend death or serious injury.

Knowledge of the crime

When giving assistance, encouragement and so on to the perpetrator, D must know:
- **either** the facts which would make the perpetrator guilty of a particular offence; **or**
- the facts which would make him guilty of one or more of a limited range of offences.

Though D may well have some particular offence in mind, so that he could specify precise details of the date, time, location and victim, such detailed knowledge is not required (for instance, the particular bank which is to be robbed (*R v Bainbridge* (1959) or the precise location of a bombing or shooting attack (*DPP for NI v Maxwell* (1978)). Knowledge that the crime is to be robbery or that a bombing or shooting is planned will suffice.

Joint enterprise or common purpose

- A secondary party who has entered into an **express or implied agreement** with the perpetrator is usually said to be engaged in a *joint enterprise* for a *common purpose*.
- In this situation, the **liability of the secondary party extends further**. It was held by the Privy Council in *R v Chan Wing-Siu* (1984) that where D engages in a joint enterprise, he will be liable not only for any crime committed by the perpetrator to which he expressly or impliedly agreed but also for any crime committed by the perpetrator in the course of conduct whilst carrying out the agreed enterprise, provided only that D recognised 'a real risk' that the perpetrator might engage in that conduct. D need not expressly or impliedly agree to this further conduct. He may even try to forbid it. As now confirmed by the House of Lords in *R v Powell & Daniels* (1997), his liability arises because he **foresees** it as a real risk and nevertheless participates. In *R v Hyde and Others* (1990) V had died from a vicious kick to the head. It was impossible to establish which of the three accused had delivered it but all were held to be guilty of murder because, at the least, each knew when taking part that the intention of the others

was to cause serious injury. As the Court of Appeal put it, they '*had in those circumstances lent themselves to the enterprise and by so doing they had given assistance and encouragement to (the principal)*'. This applies whether or not D is present at the commission of the offence (*R v Rook* (1993)).

- If the secondary party neither agreed (expressly or impliedly) to the perpetrator's conduct nor foresaw a real risk that the perpetrator might engage in that conduct in carrying out the joint enterprise, then the secondary party will not be liable for any offence resulting from that conduct (*R v Anderson & Morris* (1966)). This approach was confirmed by the House of Lords in *R v English* (1997), impliedly casting doubt on decisions in cases such as *R v Betty* (1963) and *R v Schofield* (1995) that D could be convicted of a lesser offence than the perpetrator (for example, of manslaughter rather than murder).

- It is possible for a **potential secondary party to withdraw from the enterprise** and so to avoid liability if this is done in a sufficiently unequivocal manner (though there would still remain the possibility of liability for inchoate offences such as incitement and attempt). Inevitably, the further advanced the execution of the crime, the more extreme the action required to withdraw. Thus in *R v Whitefield* (1984) it was enough for D to tell X that he was no longer prepared to allow X to gain access to an unoccupied flat via his own flat. But in *R v Becerra* (1975) D's shout of 'let's go', followed by his actual flight, was not enough when X stabbed and killed a person who had disturbed them in the midst of a violent burglary. Here, withdrawal would have needed, at the least, some warning to the victim, or even, some attempt by D physically to protect the victim.

5.6 INCHOATE (OR INCOMPLETE) OFFENCES

5.6.1 INCITEMENT

Incitement remains an offence at common law, triable in the same way as the offence incited.

Actus reus

Incitement means encouraging others to do something which would amount to a crime. For example, in *Race Relations Board* v *Applin and Another* (1973) the Ds were charged with inciting foster parents to discriminate in favour of white children. D cannot be guilty if what he incites the other to do is not a crime. In *R v Whitehouse* (1977) it was held that D could not be guilty of inciting his 15-year-old daughter to have incestuous sexual intercourse with him, since by s. 11 Sexual Offences Act 1956, it is impossible for a girl under 16 to be guilty of incest. D had effectively been charged with inciting his daughter to commit a crime which she could not commit.

Mens rea

The prosecution must show that D knew of, or was wilfully blind (subjectively reckless) to, the circumstances of the act incited which constitutes the crime, including *mens rea* on the part of the other (*R v Curr* (1968)).

5.6.2 CONSPIRACY

Kinds of conspiracy

The main form of conspiracy is statutory conspiracy which, under s. 1 Criminal Law Act 1977, consists of an agreement that one or more of the parties to the agreement will commit a criminal offence. All common law conspiracies were abolished by s. 5 Criminal Law Act

1977 except for:

- conspiracy to defraud;
- conspiracy to corrupt public morals;
- conspiracy to outrage public decency.

Under s. 12 Criminal Justice Act 1987, an agreement to engage in conduct which would be both a criminal offence and fraud can be charged as either statutory conspiracy or common law conspiracy to defraud.

Agreement in conspiracy

Agreement between two or more persons must be proved no matter what the kind of conspiracy. Agreement must often be deduced from all the evidence, but may occur when:

- all the conspirators are in contact with each other; or
- the conspirators communicate through a central conspirator, the 'hub' (sometimes called a wheel conspiracy); or
- conspirator A communicates with B who communicates with C and so on (sometimes called a chain conspiracy); or
- some combination of the above.

There is no conspiracy where the *only other* party to the conspiracy is D's spouse or a person under the age of criminal responsibility; or an intended victim of the offence.

Statutory conspiracy

According to s. 1(1) Criminal Law Act 1977, statutory conspiracy is committed when D:

> *agrees with any other person(s) that a course of conduct shall be pursued which, if the agreement is carried out in accordance with their intentions, either:*
> *(a) will necessarily amount to or involve the commission of any offence(s) by one or more of the parties to the agreement, or*
> *(b) would do so but for the existence of facts which render the commission of the offence(s) impossible.*

This would seem to mean that D must intend that the agreement be carried out by himself and/or at least one other party to the agreement. Yet in *R v Anderson* (1985) the House of Lords considered that the making of the agreement was enough, even if D, as in this case, never intended that it should be carried out and believed that it could not be carried out without his participation (he intended to take the money and not do the job). They also suggested, in this case, that D could not be guilty of conspiracy unless, in addition to being party to the agreement, he intended to participate in its execution. However, the Court of Appeal in *R v Siracusa* (1989) simply denied that the House of Lords meant what it had said and stated that D's agreement is all that is necessary.

D and at least one other party to the conspiracy must have intention or knowledge in relation to any consequences or circumstances required for proof of the substantive offence. Thus, even if the offence itself can be committed recklessly or without *mens rea*, conspiring to commit it requires intention or knowledge.

Common law conspiracies

Conspiracy to defraud

There are two reasons why conspiracy to defraud may be a useful charge:

- First, the conspirators may have agreed to conduct which does not amount to a criminal offence (and cannot therefore be charged as statutory conspiracy) but which does satisfy the very broad definition of 'defrauding' expressed in *Scott v MPC* (1974) to include '*by dishonesty to deprive a person of something which is his or to which he is or would be or might be entitled ... and by dishonesty to injure some proprietary right of his...*'.
- Secondly, even though the conduct agreed may result in the commission of criminal offences, those offences will not reveal the true scale and gravity of the criminal

enterprise, for example, where apparently minor acts of theft are merely part of a systematic attempt to deprive the victim of a large amount of property.

Conspiracy to corrupt public morals or outrage public decency
The House of Lords in *Shaw* v *DPP* (1961), where D published a 'Ladies directory' containing the names and addresses of prostitutes and the sorts of sexual activities they performed, convicted D of conspiracy to corrupt public morals. In *Knuller* v *DPP* (1972), it was held that an agreement to publish advertisements which would assist in the commission of homosexual acts between adult males in private was also a conspiracy to corrupt public morals. Two of the Law Lords felt that this was also a conspiracy to outrage public decency.

5.6.3 ATTEMPT

It is a statutory offence to attempt to commit an indictable offence or an offence triable either way under s. 1 Criminal Attempts Act 1981. However, there can be no attempt to commit a summary offence.

Actus reus

D must do '*an act more than merely preparatory to the commission of the offence*'. The statute tries to 'draw the line' between attempts and earlier stages by use of the term 'more than merely preparatory':

*   There is no clear formula for satisfying this requirement and pre-existing common law decisions are not to be regarded as authorities (*R* v *Jones* (1990), *R* v *Campbell* (1991)).
*   Whether an act is 'more than merely' preparatory must be a question of degree in all the circumstances. Cases provide examples of the way this has been interpreted. For example, in *R* v *Ilyas* (1983) D pretended that his car had been stolen, reported the theft to the insurer and obtained a claim form but did not fill it in. He *had not yet done sufficient* and his conviction was quashed. However, in *R* v *Boyle and Boyle* (1986), D intended to commit burglary and had got as far as damaging a door as part of the process of entering the house to be burgled. This was held to be sufficient.
*   D need not have reached the stage of the 'last act' which it is necessary and possible for him to do, but if he *has* reached this stage then he *must* have done an act more than merely preparatory.
*   The judge rules on whether there is evidence fit to go to the jury of an act more than merely preparatory. If any such evidence exists, the judge must leave it to the jury.

Mens rea

D must intend the commission of the offence. This means that he must intend any consequence required for the commission of the full offence (*R* v *Whybrow* (1951)). However, in the case of circumstances (such as V's lack of consent in rape) it is sufficient to prove recklessness if recklessness suffices for the completed offence (*R* v *Khan* (1990)).

5.6.4 IMPOSSIBILITY IN INCHOATE OFFENCES

Meaning of impossibility

Impossibility means that, unknown to D, it was impossible to commit the offence which was the subject of incitement, conspiracy or attempt. There are two kinds of impossibility:

*   physical impossibility, for example, D puts his hand into V's pocket to steal its contents but discovers that there is nothing there;
*   legal impossibility, for example, D has sexual intercourse with a girl whom he believes to be under the age of 16, but she turns out to be aged 17.

Effect of impossibility

Impossibility in statutory conspiracy and attempt is governed by statute. According to the Acts, impossibility is no barrier to conviction. D's liability should be determined on the facts as he thought them to be when he conspired or attempted. For example, in *R* v *Shivpuri* (1986) D was guilty of attempting to knowingly be concerned in dealing with a prohibited drug even though the substance in the suitcase, which he thought to be heroin, was actually a vegetable material (and not a prohibited drug). This case overruled the decision in *Anderton* v *Ryan* (1985).

Impossibility in incitement and common law conspiracy is governed by the common law and can prevent liability.

5.7 UNLAWFUL HOMICIDE

5.7.1 INTRODUCTION

Unlawful homicide usually encompasses murder, manslaughter, infanticide, and causing death by dangerous driving. When revising this part of your criminal law syllabus, you should refer back to rules previously encountered in analysing *actus reus* and *mens rea*.

5.7.2 THE *ACTUS REUS* OF MURDER AND MANSLAUGHTER

Murder and manslaughter are common law offences which share a common *actus reus*. The *actus reus* requires proof that D:

1 Causes the victim's death: This is a question for the jury. The rules on causation were discussed in Unit 5.2, to which reference would be made. Recall that the prosecution must prove causation in fact and in law. The Law Reform (Year and a Day Rule) Act 1996 has abolished the requirement for death to occur within a year and a day although consent of the Attorney-General is required in order to prosecute D where death occurs three years or more after the injury was caused.

2 The death must be of a human being within the Queen's peace: To be a potential victim of homicide, a child must be born alive. Preventing a child being born alive is not homicide. Injuring an unborn baby or pregnant woman so that, though born alive, the child later dies from the injuries can be homicide (*A-G's Reference (No. 3 of 1994)* (1995) (see Unit 3.4). A comatose victim properly diagnosed as 'brain dead' is no longer a human being. Withdrawal of treatment by doctors cannot break any pre-existing chain of causation nor can it render the doctors liable for any offence (*R* v *Malcherek* (1981)). The human being must have been within the Queen's peace. In practice, this would include everyone apart from enemy aliens killed in the heat of battle.

5.7.3 THE *MENS REA* OF MURDER

The prosecution must prove that, at the time he committed the fatal act, D intended to kill or cause grievous bodily harm. The meaning of intention is considered in 5.2. Grievous bodily harm extends to all kinds of serious injury, even that which no one would expect to be life-threatening in the ordinary run of things. So, if D intended to break V's leg and V died on account of some unexpected medical complications, this could be murder.

5.7.4 VOLUNTARY MANSLAUGHTER

Voluntary manslaughter covers those killings where D has the *mens rea* for murder but the law regards the killing as partly excused by provocation, diminished responsibility, or a suicide pact. These are partial defences available only to a charge of murder, and reduce the crime from murder to manslaughter, enabling the judge to pass a discretionary sentence, instead of mandatory life sentence.

Provocation

Provocation is a common law defence modified by s. 3 Homicide Act 1957. The essence of this defence is that D must be *prima facie* guilty of murder before provocation is relevant. If so, then if any evidence of provocation appears (whether expressly raised by D or not), the defence must be left to the jury and the onus will be on the Crown to disprove it beyond reasonable doubt (*R* v *Cambridge* (1994)).

In order to rely on the defence, the following elements must be established:

❶ *There must be some provocation*

- This can be words or conduct and can come from anyone, not just the victim (*R* v *Davies* (1975)).

- The provocative words/conduct do not have to be directed at D and need not consist of unlawful conduct. The case of *R* v *Doughty* (1986), where the crying of a small baby was held to be capable of being provocation, illustrates both these points.

- The provocation may be trivial in itself, if set within the context of a history of provocative conduct (*R* v *Humphreys* (1995)).

- It is not prevented from being provocation simply because it results from D's own provocative behaviour. For example, in *R* v *Johnson* (1989) D had stabbed V after being assaulted and threatened with a glass by V. In turn, V's actions had been in response to unpleasant behaviour and violent threats from D.

❷ *The subjective test – D must have lost self-control on account of the provocation*

- There must be a loss of self-control not merely of self-restraint (*R* v *Cocker* (1989)).

- The loss of self-control and the killing must be clearly related to the provocation. There is no rule that the killing must follow immediately (*R* v *Ahluwalia* (1992)), yet a response which does not follow immediately or within a short time may suggest that self-control was never lost or has been regained. In *R* v *Thornton (No. 1)* (1992) D was unable to rely on the defence of provocation since there was evidence that, although she had suffered threats of violence a relatively short time before, she had regained self-control by the time she killed her husband (a subsequent appeal on other aspects of provocation succeeded). However, in *R* v *Baillie* (1995) it was accepted that D may not only have lost self-control immediately on being provoked but may also have remained out of control for some considerable time, during which the killing was committed.

❸ *The objective test – would a reasonable person have done as D did?*

- This is entirely for the jury to determine.

- The test exists to deny the defence to those who are generally perceived as too quick to lose temper, the unusually excitable, or those with a pugnacious or irascible personality, by requiring D to display the self-control to be expected of an ordinary sober person, though not a person using powers of reason (*R* v *Morhall* (1995)).

- In considering the response of the reasonable person, the jury must envisage him as being placed in the same situation as D found himself and must consider 'the entire factual situation' which would affect the gravity of the provocation (its 'provocativeness'). This would include experience of the background to the loss of self-control as well as the actual provocation itself. The reasonable person is of the same sex and age (where relevant) as D (*R* v *Camplin* (1978)) and possesses any other of D's characteristics, whether permanent or otherwise, which are the specific target of the provocation, for example addiction to glue-sniffing (*R* v *Morhall* (1995)), attention-seeking traits (*Humphreys* (1995)) and obsessiveness and eccentricity (*R* v *Dryden* (1995)).

- Factors and characteristics which have no bearing on the 'provocativeness' of the words or conduct (such as short-temper, irritability, and the like) must be disregarded since they will be relevant, if at all, only to D's 'provocability', that is, to D's inherent capacity for self-control. Thus, in *R* v *Luc Thiet Thuan* (1996) the Privy Council held that organic brain disorder which impaired D's powers of self-control should not be taken into account when applying the reasonable person test. This decision casts doubt on the relevance of battered woman syndrome to the objective test (*R* v *Ahluwalia*, *R* v *Thornton (No. 2)* (1995)) and on the decision in *Dryden*. Yet the Court of Appeal refused to follow *Luc Thiet Thuan* in *R* v *Parker* (1997).

Diminished responsibility

Diminished responsibility was introduced by s. 2 Homicide Act 1957 and has no prior common law foundation. The burden of proof lies on D, on a balance of probabilities, unless the prosecution seeks to show that D was suffering from diminished responsibility, for example, where D's state of mind is put in issue by a plea of insanity or automatism. If D does not raise the issue but it emerges through the evidence, the judge has no duty other than to point it out to D's counsel.

There are three requirements:

1 D must have been suffering from an 'abnormality of the mind': In *R* v *Byrne* (1960) D, described as a sexual psychopath who suffered from perverted sexual desires, strangled a young woman and mutilated her body. In this case, the court defined 'abnormality of the mind' as 'a state of mind so different from that of ordinary human beings that the reasonable man would term it abnormal'.

2 The abnormality of the mind must come from a specified source: The abnormality must arise from a condition of:

- arrested or retarded development of mind; or
- inherent causes; or
- be induced by disease or injury.

Simple temporary abnormalities due to (for example) hate or jealousy are excluded. Abnormality due *only* to intoxication is excluded. In *R* v *Gittens* (1984) D killed his wife and step-daughter. At the time, he was suffering from depression for which he was being medically treated, and he had taken alcohol and other drugs. The jury were told that they should ignore his intoxication, and consider the effect of the depression only. However, abnormality due to disease or injury caused by the effects of drink or due to intoxication where the drinking is involuntary (irresistible) is admissible (*R* v *Tandy* (1988)).

3 D's mental responsibility must have been substantially impaired by the abnormality: D's difficulty in controlling his impulse must merely be substantially greater than that experienced by an ordinary person. The impairment need not be total, but it must be more than trivial or minimal.

Suicide pact

Under s. 4 Homicide Act 1957, D will be guilty of manslaughter where he kills P in pursuance of a suicide pact. A suicide pact is '*a common agreement between two or more persons which has its object the death of all parties to it*'. D's actions are not in pursuance of the pact unless done '*while he had the settled intention of dying in pursuance of the pact*'. The survivor of such an agreement is liable to be convicted of manslaughter. Where D is charged with murder, the burden of proving that he was acting in pursuance of a suicide pact is on D.

5.7.5 INVOLUNTARY MANSLAUGHTER

There are two categories of involuntary manslaughter. In both cases, D does not possess intention to kill.

Gross negligence manslaughter

This has only recently been revived by the case of *R* v *Adomako* (1994) (see Unit 5.2). The essence of this kind of manslaughter is that D causes death by conduct which amounts to a breach of duty and which displays gross negligence which the jury consider justifies a criminal conviction. Since it has only just been revived, there are doubts about the precise elements of this form of manslaughter. However, they may be expressed as:

① **Conduct**: The conduct does not have to be unlawful in itself and it may be either an act or an omission. In fact, it will very often be an omission.

② **D may need to be under a duty**: This aspect was strongly emphasised, though not explained, in *R v Prentice and Others* (1993). It was re-stated in *R v Adomako* (1994) but given little prominence. Duties arising out of professions, trades and work in general would qualify, as would those required to be provided for liability for an omission.

③ **The conduct must have created an obvious risk of death, or, perhaps, of serious injury.**

④ **The conduct must, in the eyes of the jury, justify a criminal conviction**: In *Adomako*, Lord Mackay stressed that, '*the essence of the matter, which is supremely a jury question, is whether, having regard to the risk of death involved, the conduct of the defendant was so bad in all the circumstances as to amount in their judgment to a criminal act or omission...*'.

Unlawful act/constructive manslaughter

The essence of this form of manslaghter is that D caused V's death whilst engaged in an act which was both a crime and which posed a threat of some personal injury. The elements are:

① **There must be an unlawful act**

- This really means a crime. Other kinds of wrongdoing, e.g. a tort, are not enough.

- All the elements of the crime must be proved, both *actus reus* and *mens rea* (*R v Lamb* (1967)).

- The crime must involve an act. An omission will not suffice (*R v Lowe* (1973)).

② **The unlawful act must be of a dangerous kind**

- According to the Court of Appeal in *R v Church* (1965), this means that the act must be '*such as all sober and reasonable people would inevitably recognise must subject the other person to, at least, the risk of some harm resulting therefrom*'.

- This is easy to prove where the crime alleged is actually an offence against the person such as assault (*R v Larkin* (1943)).

- Other crimes (e.g., crimes against property) can create a risk of personal injury and so be 'dangerous'. In *DPP v Newbury & Jones* (1976) D1 and D2 threw a half paving stone from a bridge into the path of an approaching train, killing the guard. The court held that any reasonable person would have realised there was a risk of injury to people on the train.

- In assessing whether the reasonable person would recognise the risk, he or she must be taken to possess the knowledge that D had and should have had at the time of the commission of the offence, including any knowledge which D acquired or should have acquired during the commission of the offence. In *R v Watson* (1989) D could clearly see that V, whose house he was burgling, was a frail old man who was reacting very badly to the experience. To the reasonable person, armed with the knowledge acquired by D during the burglary, there would have been no doubt that the burglary created a risk of personal injury to V.

5.7.6 SUMMARY OF MURDER AND MANSLAUGHTER

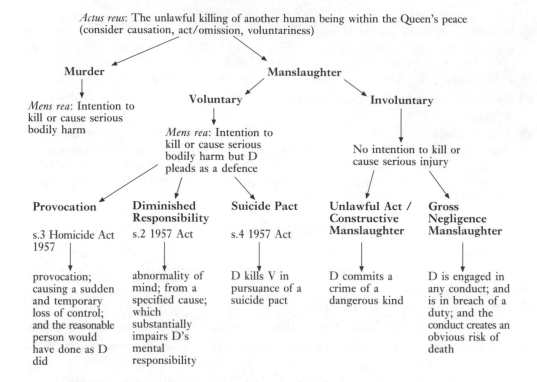

Actus reus: The unlawful killing of another human being within the Queen's peace (consider causation, act/omission, voluntariness)

Murder

Mens rea: Intention to kill or cause serious bodily harm

Manslaughter

Voluntary

Mens rea: Intention to kill or cause serious bodily harm but D pleads as a defence

Involuntary

No intention to kill or cause serious injury

Provocation

s.3 Homicide Act 1957

provocation; causing a sudden and temporary loss of control; and the reasonable person would have done as D did

Diminished Responsibility

s.2 1957 Act

abnormality of mind; from a specified cause; which substantially impairs D's mental responsibility

Suicide Pact

s.4 1957 Act

D kills V in pursuance of a suicide pact

Unlawful Act / Constructive Manslaughter

D commits a crime of a dangerous kind

Gross Negligence Manslaughter

D is engaged in any conduct; and is in breach of a duty; and the conduct creates an obvious risk of death

5.7.7 CAUSING DEATH BY DANGEROUS DRIVING

This offence replaces that of causing death by reckless driving (s. 1 Road Traffic Act 1988, as amended by the Road Traffic Act 1991). The statute defines 'driving dangerously' by reference to what would be expected of a competent and careful driver and to the state of the vehicle. The danger must be of personal injury or of serious damage to property. The maximum sentence on conviction is 10 years' imprisonment.

5.7.8 INFANTICIDE

Under s. 1(1) Infanticide Act 1938 a woman who kills her child within 12 months of giving birth will be guilty of infanticide and not murder, if the balance of her mind was disturbed through not having fully recovered from giving birth or because of the effects of lactation. The effect is that D is treated as if found guilty of manslaughter.

5.8 NON-FATAL OFFENCES AGAINST THE PERSON

There are close relationships between these offences. The facts of one problem may raise the possibility that a number of offences have been committed. The offences are distinguished by the increasing seriousness of consequence (touching, actual bodily harm, wounding or grievous bodily harm), except for s. 18 Offences Against the Person Act 1861 (OAPA 1861), which differs from s. 20 by virtue principally of *mens rea*.

5.8.1 ASSAULT AND BATTERY

The offences of assault and battery were always thought to be common law offences, but are now considered to be statutory under s. 39 Criminal Justice Act 1988 as interpreted in *DPP v Little* (1992). Although 'assault' is often used to mean 'battery' the two offences are distinct.

Actus reus of assault

The *actus reus* of assault is that D causes V to apprehend immediate unlawful personal violence, as by raising a fist or a weapon, aiming a kick, throwing a stone or making some other menacing gesture. V must be aware of it, so that, for example, striking from behind is not an assault nor is throwing a brick which is badly aimed and of which the intended victim is unaware. Key points to note include:

- Fear of application of *physical force* is the essence of assault. The House of Lords in *R v Ireland* (1997) affirmed this when upholding D's conviction for assault occasioning actual bodily harm by causing V psychological injury by making silent telephone calls. Causing psychological injury could not be a battery and the silent telephone calls were only an assault because V could have feared that D might come to her house and attack her immediately after the telephone call ended.

- 'Immediate' is interpreted generously, so that D was convicted of assault in *Smith v Superintendent of Woking Police Station* (1983) when he looked through the window of a house and frightened a woman in her dressing gown, even though it was unclear how quickly he would have been able to gain entry to the house. In *R v Constanza* (1997), it was held that it was enough for the Crown to prove a fear of violence *'at some time not excluding the immediate future'* (i.e. it might be very soon, though it could be later).

- Traditionally, it was doubted whether an assault could be committed by words alone, without accompanying threatening gestures (*R v Mead and Belt* (1823)). However, in *R v Ireland* (1997), it was held that assault could be committed by the making of silent telephone calls and the Court of Appeal in *Constanza* specifically asserted that words alone are sufficient. Conversely, words can help to make it clear that an otherwise threatening gesture is not intended to lead to the immediate infliction of violence, as in *Tuberville v Savage* (1669) where D put his hand on his sword and said 'If it were not Assize time, I would not take such language from you'.

- An act may be necessary (rather than an omission to act): *Fagan v Metropolitan Police Commissioner* (1968) supports this view (see Unit 5.2). However, in *DPP v K* (1990) the court appears to have upheld a conviction for assault occasioning actual bodily harm on the basis of D's failure to clear acid from a drying machine in a toilet, in consequence of which V suffered facial injuries when operating the machine.

The *actus reus* of battery

The *actus reus* of battery requires infliction of unlawful personal violence. 'Violence' means nothing more than some touching, including of the clothes where the blow is felt and possibly even where it is not. In *R v Thomas* (1985) there were *obiter* suggestions that D would have been guilty of a battery in touching a girl's skirt and rubbing it. Points to note include:

- It must be unlawful: there is no battery where P expressly or impliedly consents to the touching (as in crowds). However, the touching need not be 'hostile'; for example it could be constituted by unwelcome amorous advances!

- It can be by direct contact between D and V or through the medium of a weapon and even, perhaps, in less direct ways, such as in *DPP v K* (above).

- An act may be required (see above under '*Actus reus* of assault').

The *mens rea* of assault and battery

The *mens rea* is intention or recklessness in relation to causing apprehension of or the actual infliction of, unlawful personal violence. The recklessness required to be proved is subjective. This was confirmed in *R v Spratt* (1991).

5.8.2 ASSAULT OCCASIONING ACTUAL BODILY HARM

This is defined in s. 47 OAPA 1861 and carries up to five years' imprisonment. Its elements are entirely as for assault or battery (it is either an assault occasioning actual bodily harm or a battery occasioning actual bodily harm) but with the addition that actual bodily harm must result.

Actual bodily harm

This is difficult to define precisely. The Court of Appeal analysed the requirements in *R v Chan-Fook* (1994) as follows:

- 'harm' requires hurt or injury;
- 'actual' requires that it is not so trivial as to be wholly insignificant;
- 'bodily' is not limited to 'skin, flesh, bones' since the body includes organs, the nervous system, and the brain, thus it extends to psychological injury, but is not satisfied by mere fear or apprehension.

Mens rea

It is now clearly settled that the *mens rea* is that of assault or battery only. In *R v Savage* (1991) D intentionally threw a glass of beer over V. However, she asserted that the glass accidentally slipped out of her hand, resulting in V being cut by broken glass. The question was whether D could be guilty if she did not intend or foresee (i.e., was reckless as to) actual bodily harm (the cut). The House of Lords held that her *mens rea* for the battery (intending to soak V with the beer) was sufficient. The only other requirement was that the battery caused the actual bodily harm.

5.8.3 WOUNDING/GRIEVOUS BODILY HARM

These are two different sets of offences:

- The less serious set is unlawful and malicious wounding or infliction of grievous bodily harm (s. 20 OAPA 1861).
- The second set is unlawful and malicious wounding or causing grievous bodily harm with intent (s. 18 OAPA 1861).

Actus reus

The term '*wound*' requires all the layers of the skin to be broken. In *C (A Minor)* v *Eisenhower* (1984) D fired an air pistol and a pellet hit a young man in the area of his left eye. The court held that even though internal blood vessels may have been ruptured by the blow, there had been no wound, because there had been no breaking of the skin.

'*Grievous bodily harm*' means any really serious injury. A wound may or may not be serious injury and vice versa.

Section 18 refers to '*causing*' grievous bodily harm whereas s. 20 refers to '*inflicting*' grievous bodily harm. For many years the courts distinguished between these. '*Cause*' has always been viewed as a broad term so that it covers serious injury brought about in any way, including not only by the use of force but also poisoning or the transmission of diseases. '*Inflict*' was at first thought to require proof of a battery and more recently of some conduct which, though not necessarily a direct application of force itself, nevertheless resulted in some direct application of force, for example, tampering with car brakes resulting in direct injury to the victim in a crash. However, since the decision of the House of Lords in *R v Burstow* (1997), a case of severe psychological trauma caused to V by a 'stalking' campaign carried out by D without using force or the threat of force, the law no longer distinguishes between 'cause' and 'inflict'. Thus, any way of bringing about serious injury can be regarded as an infliction, whether or not force is used.

Mens rea

Section 18 OAPA 1861: D must intend grievous bodily harm. In *R v Belfon* (1976) where D seriously injured another man by attacking him with a razor, the Court of Appeal quashed the conviction under s. 18, and substituted a conviction under s. 20, because the trial judge had wrongly directed the jury that it would suffice if D had *thought it likely* that his actions would cause grievous bodily harm (i.e., was reckless).

Section 20 OAPA 1861: the House of Lords decision in *R v Parmenter* (1991) confirmed that D must intend or be subjectively reckless as to some injury, but not necessarily serious injury. In *Flack v Hunt* (1979) it was held that an intention merely to frighten is insufficient. At the very least, D must also foresee the possibility of some injury.

5.8.4 DEFENCES

Consent

Consent must be genuine. Fraud, as to identity or the nature of the act, lack of capacity to understand, and duress may all destroy this.

A distinction is drawn between simple battery and injury which amounts to actual bodily harm or worse. V can consent to suffer a battery but cannot consent to suffer the infliction or risk of infliction of injury amounting to actual bodily harm or worse, except:

*   surgical operations (even if for purely cosmetic purposes);
*   tattooing (unless under 18) and other forms of 'body adornment' (*R v Wilson* (1996));
*   boxing and wrestling;
*   other sports involving a risk of physical contact (most obviously football, rugby, hockey and the like);
*   rough and undisciplined play of young persons, and, by analogy, adults (in *R v Jones* (1987) rough horseplay was regarded as a defence to quite serious physical assaults causing injuries to schoolboys who had been tossed in the air);
*   dangerous displays and entertainments.

In *R v Brown and Others* (1993) the House of Lords held that consent is no defence where the injury is inflicted for the sexual gratification of D and/or V. They decided this on the basis of policy and public interest. However, in *R v Wilson* (1996) D was acquitted of assault occasioning actual bodily harm in having burnt his initials into his wife's buttocks with a hot knife at her express request. The decision is explicable on the narrow ground that the injury was entirely analogous with that inflicted in the course of 'body adornment' such as tattooing and body piercing and so could be the subject of valid consent, but it may have a wider significance, indicating that the courts may not be prepared to interpret *Brown* as applying with equal rigour to such activity in more conventional relationships.

Lawful correction

Parents and those in *loco parentis* may inflict moderate and reasonable chastisement. If the punishment inflicted is of unreasonable severity, the defence will fail (*R v Smith* (1985)).

Self-defence and prevention of crime

See Unit 5.3.

5.8.5 SUMMARY OF NON-FATAL OFFENCES AGAINST THE PERSON

Crime	*Actus reus*	*Mens rea*	Maximum sentence
Assault	Causing V to apprehend immediate unlawful physical violence	Intention or subjective recklessness in relation to causing apprehension of unlawful physical violence	6 months' imprisonment
Battery	Infliction of unlawful personal violence	Intention or subjective recklessness as to the infliction of unlawful physical violence	6 months' imprisonment
Section 47	An assault or a battery causing actual bodily harm	Intention or subjective recklessness as to the assault or battery	5 years' imprisonment
Section 20	Wounding (all layers of skin must be broken) or inflicting grievous bodily harm (serious injury)	Intention or subjective recklessness as to some injury, but not necessarily serious injury	5 years' imprisonment
Section 18	Wounding or causing grievous bodily harm	Intention to cause grievous bodily harm	Life

5.9 SEXUAL OFFENCES

5.9.1 RAPE

Section 1 Sexual Offences Act 1956, as amended by s. 142 Criminal Justice and Public Order Act 1994 provides that it is an offence for a man to rape a woman or another man.

Actus reus

The *actus reus* is sexual intercourse (any degree of vaginal or anal penetration) without consent. Penetration can be regarded as a continuing act, so that where it is initially consensual, or believed to be consensual, it can become rape when consent is withdrawn or D becomes aware that V is not consenting (*R* v *Kaitamaki* (1985)).

There will be no rape if V gave genuine consent, but there is no consent where V submits out of fear, whether or not threatened with violence (*R* v *Olugboja* (1981)). Nor is there consent where V is fundamentally deceived as to the nature of the act. In *R* v *Williams* (1922) D was found guilty of rape where he deceived V into believing that sexual intercourse was a method of improving breathing control and would assist her singing. Equally, there is no consent where V is unconscious (*R* v *Mayers* (1872)) or deceived as to the identity of D (*R* v *Elbekkay* (1995)).

Mens rea

D must intend to have sexual intercourse but may be guilty if he knows or is reckless as to the fact that V does not consent. *R* v *Satnam and Kewel* (1983) confirmed that the test is subjective but, of course, a reasonable belief in consent is more likely to persuade a jury of genuineness of belief. Section 1(2) Sexual Offences (Amendment) Act 1976 directs the jury to have regard to the presence or absence of reasonable grounds together with 'other relevant matters' in deciding whether D believed that V was consenting. In *R* v *McFall* (1994) D's claim to have been fooled by V's faking of orgasm into believing that she was consenting had to be weighed against the facts that he had kidnapped her at gunpoint, taken her on a 60 mile journey and had kept the gun with him at all times (the 'other relevant matters').

Marital rape

A husband no longer has an immunity from a charge of raping his wife, whether he lives with her or not. The immunity was originally founded on the presumption of a general consent given by the woman to her husband when she entered into the marriage; and it was believed to be expressed in the law by the statutory requirement that the sexual intercourse must be 'unlawful'. Changing social circumstances began a process of change culminating in the decision of the House of Lords in *R* v *R* (1991) to abandon the immunity entirely. The amendments made by the Criminal Justice and Public Order Act 1994 include the abolition of the requirement for the sexual intercourse to be unlawful.

5.9.2 INDECENT ASSAULT

The Sexual Offences Act 1956 makes it an offence for a person to make an indecent assault on a woman (s. 14) and on a man (s. 15). As well as by men, these offences can be committed by women on men and women on women.

Assault or battery

The offences require an assault or a battery (see Unit 5.8). If an assault, V must apprehend both the immediate touching and its indecency. If a battery, V need not know of the touching or the indecency (as when unconscious or asleep, or under the influence of drink or drugs). The requirement for 'hostility' evident in earlier cases now seems to have been abandoned. In *Faulkner* v *Talbot* (1981) D was guilty despite the fact that sexual intercourse and other acts that she performed with V (a boy under 16) were with his consent and so not 'hostile'.

'In circumstances of indecency'

The House of Lords held in *R* v *Court* (1988) that the question for the jury is whether *'right minded persons would consider the conduct indecent or not'*. Where the circumstances are incapable of being regarded as indecent, D's secret intentions cannot make them so, for example, in *R* v *George* (1956) D got sexual gratification merely from removing a shoe from a girl's foot.

Mens rea

The *mens rea* consists of:

- an intention to assault or batter, either in a manner which (objectively) is indecent or, alternatively, which could be indecent and is intended to be so (*R* v *Court* (1988)); and

- knowledge or subjective recklessness as to lack of consent, if lack of consent is required. A female or male under 16 cannot give consent, and D's reasonable belief that V is 16 or over is no defence (*R* v *Prince* (1875)). Neither can a female or male defective give consent but D must, at least, have had reason to suspect that D was a defective.

5.10 OFFENCES AGAINST PROPERTY

There are a wide variety of offences against property. Many are to be found in the Theft Acts 1968 and 1978. It is important to note that a number of the offences are defined so that proof of the elements of one offence (especially theft) may be necessary in establishing another. For instance, theft must be established in proving robbery and in some forms of burglary. The ability to recognise and distinguish between the different offences is vital when considering problems.

5.10.1 THEFT

The offence may seem complicated because of the number of elements, extent of statutory definition, and amount of case interpretation, but these are reducible to a number of fairly simple propositions. Theft is defined in s. 1(1) Theft Act 1968 as '... *dishonestly appropriates property belonging to another with the intention of permanently depriving the other of it...*'.

There are five elements, three of *actus reus* and two of *mens rea*:
* appropriation (s. 3);
* property (s. 4);   } *actus reus*
* belonging to another (s. 5);
* dishonesty (s. 2);   } *mens rea*
* intention of permanent deprivation (s. 6)

Appropriation

By s. 3(1) appropriation is '*any assumption of the rights of an owner*'. Theft is much wider than simply physically removing property. The rights of an owner include possession, use, change, disposal and destruction.

Appropriation and authorisation of the owner
The courts have struggled for many years with the issue of whether D can appropriate property when he appears to be 'authorised' to deal with it by the owner (has the owner's 'consent'). Despite the decision of the House of Lords in *R* v *Lawrence* (1971) that authorisation or consent was irrelevant (so that D, a taxi-driver, was convicted of theft for helping himself to an excessive fare from V's wallet, with V's permission but without his knowledge of the deceit), almost all the cases asserted that D could not be guilty of theft if he had authorisation/consent unless he went beyond the scope of that authorisation. Thus, in *R* v *Morris* (1983), the House of Lords held D to be guilty of theft of goods in a supermarket by engaging in the unauthorised act of swapping price labels on them but asserted, *obiter*, that he would not have been guilty, however dishonest his intentions, merely by doing something authorised (such as placing items in a supermarket basket).

However, the issue now appears to be resolved in favour of the *Lawrence* interpretation by the House of Lords' decision in *R* v *Gomez* (1993). D was the assistant manager of a shop, who persuaded the manager to sell goods worth £17,000 to D's accomplice. The goods were paid for with cheques which D and the accomplice knew were worthless. Following the decision in *Lawrence*, D was held to have appropriated the goods, even though he had the owner's authority to take possession. Yet doubts persist about the true scope of the decision in *Gomez*. Thus, the case of *R* v *Mazo* (1996) hints at a restrictive interpretation, namely that any dealing with the property which is expressly or impliedly authorised (consented to) can only be an appropriation if the authorisation (consent) is obtained by '*fraud, deception or false representation*'.

Other points to note include:
* appropriation can be an assumption of *any* of the rights (it does not have to be of *all* the rights) (*Morris* (1983));
* preliminary acts without touching the property could be appropriation, for example, arranging to sell (*Pitham* v *Hehl* (1976)) or issuing instructions for disposal of money in a bank account (*R* v *Governor of Pentonville Prison, ex parte Osman* (1989));
* a person who buys property in good faith but subsequently discovers that he or she has not got good title to the property is protected from theft charges by s. 3(2).

Property

Section 4(1) defines property as '*money and all other property, real or personal, including things in action and other intangible property*'. Though very broad, this definition does not include electricity (the subject of a separate offence) or trade secrets/confidential information (*Oxford* v *Moss* (1978)). Moreover, not all 'property' can be stolen. So, land can be stolen by first being severed (taking tiles from a roof or bricks from a building for instance) unless it is wild mushrooms or flowers, fruit or foliage picked from a plant growing wild (even here, it is theft if done for 'reward or for sale or other commercial purpose').

Important examples of things in action include a credit balance in a bank account (the customer's right to demand money from the bank), an agreed right to overdraw on a bank account and a right to other forms of credit (for example, by the use of a credit card). All are property and can be stolen. For example, if D forges the customer's signature on a cheque, enabling him to draw on the bank account and so cause the credit balance to diminish (*R v Kohn* (1979)).

Belonging to another

The basic definition of '*belonging to another*' in s. 5(1) is '*...possession or control or...any proprietary right or interest...*'. This indicates that:

- theft can be from owner, possessor, controller or anyone with some other 'proprietary right or interest' (*R v Woodman* (1974));

- an owner can steal his own property. In *R v Turner (No. 2)* (1971) D was convicted of theft of his own car when he dishonestly drove it away from a garage without paying for repairs and without informing the garage, which was in possession of it (and actually held the right to keep the car until paid for the repairs (a 'proprietary right')).

The basic definition is extended by s. 5(3) and 5(4). Section 5(3) ensures that property obtained 'from or on account of V' belongs to V for the purposes of theft (even if not in civil law) if D is 'under an obligation to retain and deal with the property or its proceeds in a particular way'. Thus, a travel agent did not steal money paid to him to book holidays which he never booked because he became owner of the money when it was paid to him and he was not required to keep each client's money separate and use it only to book that particular holiday (*R v Hall* (1973)). But money given to D by an acquaintance, V, to buy a car for V continued to belong to V, and so could be stolen from him, because D was obliged to use it only for that purpose (*R v Dubar* (1995)).

Section 5(4) provides that where D gets property by another's mistake, the property continues to belong to the other for the purposes of theft if D is 'under an obligation to make restoration of the property, proceeds or the value ...'. Thus, if a shop assistant gives excess change to a customer by mistake, the excess continues to belong to the shop because the customer is under an obligation to repay. However, the customer will only be liable for theft if he spends the money only after he discovers the mistake or there are 'proceeds' of the money still in his ownership when he learns of the mistake.

Dishonesty

The statute partly defines dishonesty. The definition in s. 2(1) asserts that D is *not* dishonest if he appropriates genuinely believing:

- he has the legal right to the property (*R v Robinson* (1977)); or

- he believes he has or would have the owner's consent;

- the owner cannot be discovered by taking reasonable steps. In *R v Small* (1987) D was found not guilty of theft of a car which he believed had been abandoned. He had kept watch for two weeks on a car parked in the street before removing it. The keys were in the ignition, the petrol tank was empty, a tyre was flat and the wipers did not work.

The general test
More generally, D's conduct will only be regarded as dishonest if it satisfies the test in *Ghosh* (1982). In this case it was held that two questions must be asked:

- Was D's conduct dishonest according to the standards of ordinary reasonable people? If not, D must be acquitted. If it was, then

- Was D aware that his conduct would be regarded as dishonest by ordinary reasonable people? Only if the answer to this second question is affirmative may he be treated as having acted dishonestly.

The more general issue of dishonesty will always arise if the prosecution can disprove any argument by D that he was not dishonest within s. 2(1).

Intention permanently to deprive

The basic proposition is that D must intend that V will not get his property back (whether in fact V does so or not). Intention to temporarily deprive is not enough (*R v Warner* (1970)). D must have made up his mind to steal (permanently deprive) (*R v Easom* (1971)).

Section 6(1) attempts to deal with certain cases where the existence of the intention might be thought doubtful:

- The **ransom** case where V must pay to recover property.
- **Borrowing**. In *R v Lloyd* (1985) the Court of Appeal held that there would be a sufficient intent to deprive if D's intention was to return the property in an essentially different state, so that all its 'goodness and virtue' had gone (as where a season ticket is taken with the intention of returning it intact but after its expiry date).
- The **pawning** case. If D pawns V's goods with no intention of ever redeeming them, he is guilty of theft. If D does intend to redeem them, he is still guilty if he knows that he may not be able to do so (s. 6(2)).

More recently, the courts appear to have moved away from the restrictive interpretation of s. 6 in *Lloyd* which would confine it to the above instances. So, in *Chan Man-Sin v A-G of Hong Kong* (1988), D was held to have intended permanent deprivation by treating V's property as his own to dispose of even though his actions could not have caused V to lose any of his property.

5.10.2 ROBBERY

Robbery is an aggravated form of theft requiring force or threat of force in order to steal. Section 8 states '*a person is guilty of robbery if he steals, and immediately before or at the time of doing so, and in order to do so, he uses force on any person or puts or seeks to put any person in fear of being then and there subjected to force.*' Key points to note include:

- The elements of theft must be proved (*R v Robinson* (1977)).
- Minimal force suffices but it must be on a person. Problems have arisen in identifying the precise boundary between robbery and theft. Only a very minimal degree of force need be used. In *R v Dawson* (1976) it was held that nudging a person so as make him lose his balance and thereby facilitate the theft might amount to robbery. It was a question of fact for the jury. In *R v Coulden* (1987) the Court of Appeal held that snatching a shopping bag out of a woman's grasp and running off with it could also be sufficient force for robbery.
- The force/threat of force must be used in order to steal and before or at the time of stealing. Thus, using/threatening force in order to escape, after the theft has been completed, will not constitute robbery. However, if D is still removing the goods when he uses/threatens force, he can be guilty of robbery. In *R v Hale* (1978) D took jewellery from V's bedroom and then tied her up on his way out. The Court of Appeal upheld the conviction for robbery even though the jewellery box may have been appropriated before any force was used against V. The theft was a continuing event and the jury could conclude that it was still in progress when V was being tied up.

5.10.3 BURGLARY

There are two different kinds of burglary defined in s. 9(1)(a) and (b) Theft Act 1968:

- Section 9(1)(a) provides that a person is guilty of burglary if he enters any building or part of a building as a trespasser with intent to commit theft, inflict grievous bodily harm, rape or cause criminal damage.
- Section 9(1)(b) provides that a person is guilty of burglary if having entered any building or part of a building as a trespasser he steals or attempts to steal anything therein or inflicts or attempts to inflict any grievous bodily harm therein.

	s. 9(1)(a)	s. 9(1)(b)
Actus reus	**Entry** The entry need be neither 'substantial' nor 'effective'; insertion of any part of D's body (other than for the purpose of gaining entry) suffices (*R* v *Brown* (1985), *R* v *Ryan* (1996)) **as a trespasser** Entry without express or implied consent will be trespass. Entry for a purpose beyond the scope of any express or implied consent will also be trespass (*R* v *Jones & Smith* (1976)) **of any (part of) a building** A building must have some degree of permanence. A 'part of building' may include, for instance, an area in a room which has been marked out such as the area inside or behind the counter in a shop (*R* v *Walkington* (1979))	
		In addition, D must commit: • the *actus reus* of theft; or • of attempted theft • the *actus reus* of infliction of grievous bodily harm; or • of attempted infliction of grievous bodily harm
Mens rea	knowledge or awareness of risk *at the time of entry* of the existence of facts which in law amount to entry, as trespasser of a (part of) a building and intention to commit the offence of: • theft; or • infliction of grievous bodily harm; or • rape; or • criminal damage D can be guilty without actually committing any of them – he only needs to intend to commit any of them.	knowledge or awareness of risk as opposite (*but at any time not later than completion of (attempted) theft or (attempted) grievous bodily harm* and • the *mens rea* of theft, or of attempted theft, or • of infliction of grievous bodily harm, or of attempted infliction of grievous bodily harm.

Figure 5.4 Similarities and differences between s. 9(1)(a) and s. 9(1)(b).

5.10.4   DECEPTION OFFENCES

The Theft Acts 1968 and 1978 contain various crimes concerned with obtaining something by deception. These include:

- Obtaining property by deception: s. 15 Theft Act 1968.
- Obtaining a pecuniary advantage by deception: s. 16 Theft Act 1968.
- Obtaining services by deception: s. 1 Theft Act 1978.
- Evasion of liability by deception: s. 2 Theft Act 1978.

Common elements

There are three common elements:

A deception
This is defined in s. 15(4) Theft Act 1968 (which applies to all the deception offences) as '*(whether deliberate or reckless) by words or conduct as to fact or as to law, including a deception as to ... present intentions*'. This definition can be further analysed:

- **Deliberate or reckless**: D knows the representation is false or is aware that it may be.
- **Words or conduct**: there must be words or some sort of conduct. Doing nothing cannot *per se* amount to deception. Deception may be by implied statement. Thus, when D goes into a restaurant and orders a meal, he impliedly represents that he intends to pay for it before he leaves (*DPP* v *Ray* (1973)). Similarly, when D tenders a cheque as payment there is an implied representation that D believes at that moment that the cheque will be honoured on presentation. According to *MPC* v *Charles* (1976), when a person uses

a cheque card in support of a cheque, *'he is impliedly representing to the payee that he has the issuing bank's permission to use it in relation to that particular transaction and thereby creates a legally-binding contract'*. A credit card operates on a similar basis (*R* v *Lambie* (1981)).

- **Fact or law**: statements of opinion are not in themselves capable of giving rise to a deception, but such statements often imply an underlying basis of fact which, if false, can amount to a deception.

Obtaining

It must be proved that there is a causal link between the exercise of deception and the obtaining. In *R* v *Laverty* (1970) D sold a stolen car after he had changed the registration plates. It was alleged that he had deceived the buyer into believing that the car was the one which originally bore those plates, but the conviction was quashed because it had not been proved that the alleged deception had had any operative effect on the mind of the buyer. It follows from this that the deception must precede the obtaining.

Dishonesty

The test in *Ghosh* applies.

Summary of the deception offences

When trying to differentiate between the deception offences in answering a problem, some key points that you should remember are:

- The obtaining etc. must come *after*, and *be caused by*, the deception. Be clear what the deception is and when it takes place.

- Whenever some kind of property (whether money, goods, land or less tangible property) is obtained, it is likely to be s. 15 Theft Act 1968 (obtaining property).

- The decision in *Gomez* means that most cases of obtaining property by deception will also be cases of theft.

- If no property appears to be obtained, look for evidence of other kinds of advantage such as services (s. 1 Theft Act 1978) or being able to avoid or delay payment or full payment (s. 2 Theft Act 1978).

- Be very careful about 'pecuniary advantage' (s. 16 Theft Act 1968). It is very narrowly defined by the statute itself and has no other meaning.

- On any set of facts, more than one of the offences may have been committed.

Obtaining by Deception

Is there a deception? Is there a causal link between the deception and the obtaining, and is there dishonesty?

PROPERTY	PECUNIARY ADVANTAGE	SERVICES	EVASION OF LIABILITY
s. 15 Theft Act 1968	s. 16 Theft Act 1968	s. 1 Theft Act 1978	s. 2 Theft Act 1978
Property is defined as in theft (and includes things in action).	The offence concerns only three kinds of advantage: • getting an overdraft (not personal loan), policy of insurance, or annuity contract, or better terms for any of them (*R v Waites* (1982)); • getting the opportunity to earn remuneration or greater remuneration in employment/self-employment (e.g., D gets a job by claiming qualifications which he does not possess); • getting the opportunity to win money by betting.	Service is defined very broadly (*R v Widdowson* (1985)) and includes not only when V does an act for D but also when he gets someone else to do an act or permits D to do an act (e.g. to fill his tank with petrol). However, the service must confer a benefit (*R v Halai* (1983)) and be provided on the understanding that it has been or will be paid for (not restricted to payment in money, but includes payment in other forms e.g., reciprocal services).	There are three different forms: • s. 2(1)(a): securing remission of whole or part of a liability – D persuades the creditor to give up the right to the debt or part of it or to look to someone else for payment (*R v Jackson* (1983)); • s. 2(1)(b): inducing the creditor to wait for or forgo payment – the creditor is led to wait for, or to stop asking for (but not to give up the right to) payment (*R v Sibartie* (1983)); • s. 2(1)(c): D obtains an exemption from or abatement of a liability – D pays nothing, or less than would have been required (*R v Firth* (1990)).
Mens rea: • intention or recklessness in making the deception; • dishonesty; • intention to permanently deprive.	*Mens rea:* • intention or recklessness in making the deception; • dishonesty.	*Mens rea:* • intention or recklessness in making the deception; • dishonesty.	*Mens rea:* • intention or recklessness in making the deception; • dishonesty; • in (b) there must be an intent not to repay.

5.10.5 MAKING OFF WITHOUT PAYMENT

This offence is contained in s. 3 Theft Act 1978. It deals with the classic cases such as where D walks out of a restaurant without paying or drives off from a petrol station without paying, and enables conviction even if no deception before receiving the food or the petrol can be proved. The offence requires proof that:

- Goods were supplied or a service done.
- Payment on the spot was required or expected.
- D made off from the spot in any way, such as openly, by stealth, with force, or by fraud from any point where payment is required. In *R* v *Brooks and Brooks* (1982) it was suggested that the offence was completed by D 'passing the spot where payment is required' which implies that the spot is the cash point/desk rather than the restaurant door.
- As to the *mens rea*, D must act dishonestly. He must also know that payment on the spot is required or expected and there must be an intent to avoid payment permanently. An intent to delay or defer payment is not enough. In *R* v *Allen* (1985) D had left a hotel without paying the bill, but he always said that he intended to pay it. The House of Lords quashed his conviction.

5.10.6 CRIMINAL DAMAGE

Under the Criminal Damage Act 1971, there are three offences:

- intentionally or recklessly destroying or damaging property belonging to another (s. 1(1));
- intentionally or recklessly destroying or damaging property, intending or being reckless as to the endangering of life by that damage (s. 1(2));
- doing either of the above by fire – the offence of arson (s. 1(3)).

Section 1(2) differs from s. 1(1) in two ways:

- for s. 1(2) there must be *mens rea* as to endangering life;
- for s. 1(2) the damage can be to D's own property in which no one else has any right or interest, as well as to that of anyone else.

Destroy or damage

The destruction/damage need not be permanent, so that graffiti on a wall is capable of amounting to damage. In *Hardman* v *Chief Constable of Somerset & Avon Constabulary* (1986) painting silhouettes on the pavement using water-soluble pain amounted to damage, for the local authority would have to pay to have them removed. Physical damage as such is not required if it can be shown that there is impairment (whether temporary or permanent) of value or usefulness. Thus, a machine may be damaged by having parts removed so that it will not work, even though the parts removed are themselves undamaged. Food and drink can be damaged by being adulterated.

Property belonging to another

Property is defined essentially as for theft except that it includes land but excludes intangible property. '*Belonging to another*' means that property belongs to the person who has custody or control of it, or who has a proprietary right or interest in it (such as a lessee or bailee) so that the owner could be guilty of damaging his own property in which V has such a right or interest.

Without lawful excuse

All three offences require that the destruction or damage be without lawful excuse. For the basic offence (s. 1(1)), this is further defined in s. 5(2) to include a belief in the owner's consent (as in *R* v *Denton* (1982) where D was held to be not guilty of damaging his employer's mill because of his belief that he had been encouraged by his employer to do this so that his employer could make a fraudulent insurance claim) and a belief that the damage was necessary for the immediate protection of his own or another's property and that the protective steps were reasonable. There is no further definition of 'lawful excuse' for the aggravated offence.

Mens rea

The *mens rea* requires intention or recklessness as to destroying or damaging property belonging to another. Thus, D has a defence to s. 1(1) if he mistakenly thought he was destroying/damaging his own property (*R* v *Smith* (1974)). As to the meaning of recklessness, *MPC* v *Caldwell* (1981) applies; objective recklessness is sufficient *mens rea*.

Under s. 1(2) there must be intention or (objective) recklessness as to the endangering of life by the destruction or damage alleged. It is not enough that D causes damage in the course of other conduct which endangers life. In *R* v *Steer* (1987) D fired an automatic rifle at the door and bedroom window of the bungalow of his former business partner who was in the bedroom at the time. There could be no conviction under s. 1(2) because the danger to life was caused by the shot from the rifle and not by the damage to the window.

Illustrative questions

1   O found a ring in the street one day when he was walking to work. He decided to keep it and had just picked it up and was about to put it in his pocket when R ran past and snatched it from him. O was so angry about this that he went up to the next person he saw, who happened to be S, and shouted very loudly in her ear, causing her to jump backwards, trip and twist her ankle. This left her with a painful bruise. He then went to a coffee bar where he ordered a cup of coffee and a piece of cake. After he had been served, he realised that he had not brought any money out with him. When he had finished the coffee and cake, he ordered more coffee and told the cashier that he was just going to buy a newspaper from the shop next door and would return immediately. As soon as he was outside, he walked away rapidly. Having borrowed some money from a colleague at lunch time, he went to a bar and drank four pints of beer in fifteen minutes. When he left the bar, he took a briefcase which looked very much like his own, forgetting that his own was at work, and kissed a customer who violently objected but whom he was convinced was an old friend.

   Are O and R guilty of any offences? Would O be able successfully to plead any defences?   (25)

(*London*)

Tutorial note
This question raises a large number of legal issues. It is not necessary to deal with all of them in detail to achieve good marks, but it would be advisable to identify as many as possible and ensure that some of them are analysed in detail. The best way to structure this question is to analyse it as three separate incidents, namely, possible theft of the ring by O and R and assault of S; possible deception and making off without payment offences in respect of the cafe; and possible theft and battery offences in the bar.

Suggested answer
The first possible offence to consider is O's theft of the ring. You should define theft, as set out in s. 1 Theft Act 1968 and consider whether the necessary elements are present. Consider whether O has committed the *actus reus* of theft. O has certainly appropriated the ring (s. 3), and it is clearly property belonging to another. Whether O has the necessary *mens rea* of theft will depend, firstly, on whether he believed it had been abandoned or lost. If he believed it had been abandoned, then he has no intention to permanently deprive anyone of it and nor is he dishonest (s. 2(1), *R* v *Small*). If he believed it was lost, then he does have intention to permanently deprive

and his liability will turn on whether he genuinely believed that there were no reasonable steps he could take to find the true owner (s. 2(1)). When considering what steps O could have taken to discover the rightful owner, you should consider the nature of the ring, where and when it was found and how long it might have been there. It is likely that O has committed theft. However, whether or not O stole it, R certainly stole it from O, who was in possession and control of it at the very least (s. 5(1)).

When O shouted loudly in S's ear, he may well have assaulted her (s. 39 Criminal Justice Act 1988). It seems established that assault can be committed by words alone (*R v Constanza*). It would need to be shown that S feared immediate personal injury and that O intended her to do so, or was (subjectively) reckless as to her doing so (*R v Spratt*). If there was an assault, then since her response was such as might have been expected, the assault has caused her actual bodily harm (*R v Roberts*), and it is possible that O could be convicted under s. 47 Offences Against the Person Act 1861.

When O goes to the coffee bar and orders a cup of coffee and a piece of cake, he is honest and does not commit any offence. However, he realises that he does not have any money after he has been served, and it is possible that he commits theft when he consumes them. He certainly has the *mens rea* of theft, but it is arguable that he does not have the *actus reus*. This would depend on whether the cake and coffee were 'property belonging to another', or whether they belonged to him at that time. In any case, he obtained services by deception in asking for more coffee whilst having no intention to pay for it (s. 1 Theft Act 1978, *DPP v Ray*). He also evaded liability to pay for the original coffee and cake by deception (s. 2 1978 Act), since O would have been expected to pay for it before leaving the coffee bar if he had not deceived the cashier into believing that he would be back shortly. Thus, his deception induced the creditor to delay payment s. 2(1)(b), *R v Sibartie*). He also made off without payment (s. 3 Theft Act 1978).

In relation to O taking the briefcase, O may be guilty of theft. The argument against theft is that he was not dishonest, since he believed in his right to the property (s. 2(1) Theft Act 1968, *R v Robinson*) and that he had no intention to permanently deprive anyone else of the property. When O kissed the customer, he could be guilty of battery (*R v Thomas*). However, he believed he had consent (which is a defence to a simple battery). Of course, he was mistaken about the facts in both instances, and this was probably because of intoxication. Voluntary intoxication is available only to an offence of specific intent and may not be used to support a mistake in connection with a defence. Theft is an offence of specific intent, in relation to the intention to permanently deprive element, and O may be able to avoid liability. However, the chances of avoiding liability for the battery are significantly less, since this is an offence of basic intent (*DPP v Majewski*).

2 Consider whether or not the defence of provocation is in need of reform.   (50)
                                                                              (*UODLE*)

Tutorial note
This essay should comprise of an explanation of the elements of the defence of provocation, selecting aspects which raise difficulty and/or controversy. It is advisable, if you conclude that the defence is in need of reform, to try to make some suggestions of what form any changes might take, however tentative your suggestions.

Suggested answer
You should begin this essay question with some background information on the defence of provocation. You should state that this is only a defence to a charge of murder, and, if successfully pleaded, will reduce the crime from murder to (voluntary) manslaughter, enabling the judge to pass a discretionary sentence, instead of a mandatory life sentence. State that provocation is essentially a common law defence which has been modified by s. 3 Homicide Act 1957.

It would then be appropriate to describe the defence. Concentrate on the three elements: provocation, loss of self-control and the reasonable person test. When describing the various elements, you should refer to cases to clarify your discussion.

Since this an area of criminal law which has undergone clarification and development in recent years, it is important to select cases which illustrate this such as *Ahluwalia*, *Baillie*, *Morhall*, *Humphreys*, and *Luc Thiet Thuan*.

When considering the problems with the defence of provocation, you should have regard to the elements. You could consider what can be provocation, and whether this is too broadly defined. It does not have to be directed at anyone and it can come from someone other than the victim. It has been held that something as innocent as the crying of a baby could, in principle, be sufficient provocation. In relation to the second element, the requirement that D must kill on account of the provocation is raising difficulties for those who do not kill immediately, e.g., battered women. Many argue that women do not, in general, experience a sudden loss of control. Instead, they endure until they reach breaking point which may or may not be triggered by a precipitating event. There has also been much discussion of the objective test, and the current view seems to be that the reasonable person must be regarded as having been subjected to all those factors (including possessing relevant characteristics of D) which have a bearing on the provocativeness of what is said or done (*R v Morhall*). On the other hand, those factors, including characteristics, which bear only on D's provocability must be disregarded (*R v Luc Thiet Thuan*). Yet cases such as *Alhuwalia*, *Thornton (No. 2)* and *Humphreys* are difficult to fit within this framework. Once again the relevance of battered-woman syndrome is particularly difficult to assess.

Finally, when considering reform of the defence, you should make sensible suggestions which link with your criticisms. For example, you may believe that the mandatory life sentence for murder should be abolished, therefore removing the need for the defence. Evidence of provocation would merely be a mitigating factor (as in other crimes) to be considered when determining sentence. On the other hand, you may argue for smaller scale reform, which could, perhaps, involve codification of the current law.

Practice questions

1 During the five years of their marriage Donald has on several occasions assaulted his wife Helen in order to force her to submit to sexual intercourse. Last Friday he returned home late in the evening very much the worse for drink. He told her that if she would not sleep with him he would throw her and the two children out of the house. Helen feared that he might attack her or that his shouting would wake the children if she did not submit. After they had had intercourse, and whilst Donald was asleep, Helen took the children and went to stay with her mother, who persuaded her to report the matter immediately to the police.

Consider and comment on the issues relating to both the possible criminal liability of Donald on a charge of rape and the determination of an appropriate sentence if he were found guilty.

(30)

(*NEAB*)

Pitfalls

This problem question clearly asks you to consider the offence of rape and sentencing in relation to this crime. It would be pointless discussing any other issues. If you have a good knowledge of rape or sentencing, but could not answer both parts adequately, you should not attempt this question. This indicates the need to read questions fully, before beginning your answer. You must be able to offer some critical discussion of the rules of law and sentencing. It is important to be able to evaluate the recognition of marital rape, but do not focus on this solely. There are many other issues you could address. Sentencing is dealt with in Units 4.1 and 4.2 and you should refer back to these sections for further information.

Key points

❶ Definition of rape (s.1 Sexual Offences Act 1956).

❷ Marital rape (*R* v *R* , Criminal Justice and Public Order Act 1994).

❸ Explanation of the *actus reus* of rape and the issue of consent and an application of this to the problem (*R* v *Olugboja*);

❹ Explanation of the *mens rea* of rape, with particular reference to recklessness (*R* v *Satnam and Kewel*) and an application of this to the problem.

❺ Consideration of the possible defence of intoxication, and how voluntary intoxication is no defence to a crime of basic intent (such as rape).

❻ Explanation of sentencing procedure under Criminal Justice Act 1991 (as amended); Court of Appeal guidelines in *R* v *Billam*; experience of sentencing in marital rape since *R* v *R*.

❼ Critical discussion of the issues raised in relation to the elements of rape, marital rape and sentencing.

2 Whilst having a drink in a pub with his wife, Nin.a, Mark was subjected to a lot of rude comments from a very noisy and drunken group of women sitting nearby. Jane was particularly persistent in making sexual suggestions and, eventually, Nina went across to the group and threw a pint of beer over Jane. Mark and Nina then left.

Later that evening, Nina found herself in the toilets of a nightclub at the same time as Jane and called her a 'squint-eyed slut'. (Jane was, in fact, rather sensitive about the appearance of her eyes.) She immediately produced a small knife from her bag and stabbed Nina twice. One of the stab wounds pierced Nina's lung and she died a few days later.

Nina's death brought about a significant personality change in Mark. He found it difficult to concentrate, drank heavily and was treated for depression by his doctor. He worked in the service department of a garage and had been responsible for carrying out repairs on a car which had subsequently crashed into a bus shelter, resulting in injuries to a number of people in the queue and the death of a passer-by, Ian, from a heart attack. When examined, the car's steering was found to be seriously defective but, though the fault must have been present before the service, the service made no mention of it.

When questioned, Mark was able only to say that he had felt 'very down' when he serviced the car, did not really know what he was doing at the time and had no recollection of it now.

(a) Discuss Jane's liability for the murder of Nina. (15)

(b) Discuss Mark's liability for the manslaughter of Ian. (15)

(*AEB*)

[Please note: parts (c) and (d) have been omitted.]

Pitfalls

As with all multiple-part questions it is essential that you divide your answer as the examiner has requested. In part (a), the defence of intoxication must be considered and it is common to see confused explanations of crimes of specific and basic intent in this respect. In part (b), it is clear that Mark's liability depended upon an omission. Therefore a lengthy discussion of unlawful act manslaughter would not be appropriate. Another pitfall would be to fail to discuss any defence, or, perhaps, to only identify one of the three possible defences.

Key points

Part (a)

❶ Explanation and application of the *actus reus* of murder.

❷ Explanation and application of the *mens rea* of murder, explaining the meaning of intention with reference to major cases such as *R* v *Moloney*, *R* v *Hancock*, *R* v *Nedrick* etc.

3 Explanation of the legal effect of intoxication in relation to crimes of specific intent (*R* v *Lipman*); application to the problem.

4 Explanation and application of the defence of provocation.

5 A conclusion which states whether Jane is likely to be liable for the murder of Nina, or whether she is more likely to be found guilty of manslaughter (by pleading provocation or intoxication).

Part (b)

1 Identification that this clearly raises involuntary manslaughter (since there is no intention to kill).

2 Identification of the two types of involuntary manslaughter.

3 Discussion of causation and application to the problem, with particular emphasis on the thin-skull rule.

4 Discussion of omission as the *actus reus* and whether Mark was under a duty to act (arising from his contract of employment, *R* v *Pittwood*).

5 Explanation and application of the elements of unlawful act/constructive manslaughter, with particular emphasis on the need for there to be an act rather than an omission.

6 Explanation and application of the elements of gross negligence manslaughter.

7 Explanation and application of relevant defences — insanity, automatism and, possibly, intoxication (which is no defence to a crime of basic intent) — being careful to state the effect of each of these defences.

8 A conclusion which states whether Mark is likely to be convicted of the manslaughter of Ian. State whether he committed the *actus reus* of homicide, and which type he is most likely to be convicted of (probably gross negligence), or whether you think he could successfully plead automatism or insanity.

CHAPTER 6

CONTRACT

Units in this chapter

Chapter objectives

This chapter explains how contracts are made and the essential ingredients of all contracts. It explores the things that can go wrong in the making of a contract and the consequences that follow from each kind of defect. The different ways in which terms enter a contract are discussed and the legal rules concerning a particular kind of term, one that tries to exclude or limit liability for breach of contract, are explained. Parliament has made special rules for contracts of employment and consumer contracts: these rules are described and explained. Finally, the chapter considers the different ways in which a contract may come to an end.

6.1 MEANING AND FUNCTIONS OF THE LAW OF CONTRACT

A contract may be defined as: '*an agreement between two or more parties which is intended to be legally binding*'.

Verbal contracts are usually legally binding, although it is always sensible to put commercial contracts in writing so that it is clear exactly what has been agreed. Contracts which *must* be in writing are:

- contracts of marine insurance
- transfer of shares in a registered company
- bills of exchange, cheques and promissory notes
- regulated consumer credit agreements
- contracts for the sale of land.

Contracts of guarantee have to be evidenced in writing.

Some contracts have to be made by deed: for example, a lease of land for more than three years. Any agreement which is not a contract but which the parties intend should be enforced must also be by deed.

The law of contract is characterised by a body of common law principles which apply to all contracts and sets of statutory rules which apply to particular types of contracts, such as those involving sales to consumers and contracts of employment considered below in Unit 6.6.

Much of our present law of contract consists of rules made in the second half of the nineteenth century. The Victorians saw contract as a relationship between two individuals who had equal bargaining power and were best left to negotiate their own terms. Effectively, the parties made their own 'law of the situation'. So, in 1875, Sir George Jessel said in the course of giving judgment: '*if there is one thing which more than any other public policy requires it is that men of full age and competent understanding shall have the utmost liberty of contracting, and that their contracts when entered into freely and voluntarily shall be held sacred and shall be enforced by Courts of Justice.* '

This philosophy is known as **laissez-faire**, which is defined in the *Shorter Oxford English Dictionary* as 'let people do as they think best' and described as 'a phrase expressive of the principle of non-interference by government with the actions of individuals ...' . A good example of this is the rule that consideration must be valuable but need not be adequate; the court is not interested in whether the parties got a fair deal: see Unit 6.2. Similarly, the basic principle of *caveat emptor*, which governs the law of mistake, puts responsibility for ascertaining what is being bought with the buyer: see Unit 6.3.5.

After the Second World War the notion of the proper role of government changed. The welfare state and the national health service both rest on the idea that it is not acceptable to say 'each person for himself or herself'. During the next few decades this philosophy seeped into contract law, through legislation and through decisions of the courts. It was seen that the notion of 'freedom of contract' is acceptable only if the parties have equal bargaining power. The laissez-faire approach is still evident in cases involving businesses dealing with other businesses (see *Williams* v *Roffey Brothers* (1990) at Unit 6.2.4).

6.2 FORMATION OF A CONTRACT

The first concern in any situation involving the law of contract is to determine whether a contract has come into existence. To create a binding contract there must be:

- an offer
- acceptance

- consideration
- an intention to create legal relations.

6.2.1 OFFER

An offer is a proposition which has only to be accepted for a contract to come into existence. It must be distinguished from **an invitation to treat**, which is a stage in negotiation and cannot be 'accepted'.

In *Pharmaceutical Society of Great Britain* v *Boots Cash Chemists* (1953) the Society had responsibility for enforcement of the Poisons Act 1933. D opened a self-service store and displayed drugs which had, under the terms of the Act, to be sold under the supervision of a pharmacist even though no prescription was required for them. Customers were able to select goods from the shelves and place them in a wire basket. A pharmacist was on duty at the cash desk and had authority to refuse to sell to a particular customer if he thought fit. The Society argued that the display of goods was an offer, which was accepted by the customer removing the goods from the shelves and that a sale therefore took place without supervision. The Court of Appeal held that the display of goods in this way did not constitute an offer. The contract of sale was not made when a customer selected goods from the shelves, but *when the cashier accepted the offer to buy what had been chosen*. There was, therefore, supervision in the sense required by the Act at the appropriate moment.

It has been held that display of goods in a shop window is also an invitation to treat (*Fisher* v *Bell* (1961)), as is an advertisement in a newspaper (*Partridge* v *Crittenden* (1968)).

It is possible for an advertisement to contain an offer if it is an **offer to the world at large**. This is possible if the contract is a **unilateral contract**, requiring the other party to do something which amounts to both **acceptance** and **performance** of their part of the contract.

In *Carlill* v *Carbolic Smokeball Co* (1893) D advertised 'The Carbolic Smokeball' in several newspapers. They claimed that anyone using it would be cured of a variety of illnesses and, in particular, would not catch 'flu. The company said that anyone catching 'flu would be paid £100 and that they had deposited £1,000 with the Alliance Bank, Regent Street, 'to show our sincerity in the matter'. P used the smokeball and caught 'flu. She sued for £100. The Court of Appeal decided that there was a binding contract: the advertisement was an offer to the world at large and P had accepted by using the smokeball.

Sometimes an advertiser invites people to submit **tenders**. The submission of a tender is an offer and the advertiser chooses one, so accepting an offer and making a contract.

At an **auction** the bidder makes the offer, which is accepted by the auctioneer. Advertising an auction amounts to an invitation to treat. In *Harrison* v *Nickerson* (1873) D, an auctioneer, advertised in London newspapers that a sale of office furniture would be held at Bury St. Edmunds. A broker with a commission to buy furniture came from London to attend the sale. Several conditions were set out in the advertisement, one being: 'the highest bidder to be the buyer'. The lots described as office furniture were not put up for sale but were withdrawn, though the auction itself was held. The broker sued for loss of time in attending the sale. It was held that he had no contract with the auctioneer because the lots were never put up for sale and the advertisement was simply an invitation to treat.

Merely providing information does not constitute an offer. In *Harvey* v *Facey* (1893) P sent the following telegram to D: 'Will you sell us Bumper Hall Pen? Telegraph lowest cash price.' D telegraphed in reply: 'Lowest price for Bumper Hall Penn £900.' P then telegraphed: 'We agree to buy Bumper Hall Pen for £900 asked by you. Please send us your title deeds in order that we may get early possession.' D made no reply. It was held that there was no contract. The second telegram was not an offer, but was an invitation to treat. The third telegram could not, therefore, be an acceptance.

6.2.2 TERMINATION OF OFFER

An offer comes to an end:

❶ If it is **revoked** (withdrawn) before it is accepted. In *Byrne* v *Van Tienhoven* (1880) on 1 October D in Cardiff posted a letter to P in New York offering to sell tin plate. On 8

October D wrote revoking the offer. On 11 October P received D's offer and immediately telegraphed their acceptance. On 15 October P confirmed their acceptance by letter. On 20 October D's letter of revocation reached P who had by this time entered into a contract to resell the tin plate. It was held that the revocation was not effective until it was received, so a contract came into being on 11 October.

Revocation can be effectively communicated by a third party: *Dickinson* v *Dodds* (1876).

❷ If it is **rejected**. A counter-offer acts as a rejection. In *Hyde* v *Wrench* (1840) D offered to sell his farm for £1,000. P's agent made an offer of £950 and D asked for a few days to think about it. D then wrote saying he could not accept the offer of £950. P then wrote purporting to accept the offer of £1,000. D did not consider himself bound to sell and P sued for specific performance. It was held that P could not enforce this 'acceptance' because his counter-offer of £950 was an implied rejection of the original offer to sell at £1,000 and the original offer was therefore no longer in existence.

❸ On the **lapse of any set time**, or, if no time is set, after a reasonable time. In *Ramsgate Victoria Hotel* v *Montefiore* (1866) D offered by letter dated 8 June 1864 to take shares in a company. No reply was made by the company but on 23 November 1864 they allotted shares to D and demanded payment of the balance due on them. D refused to take the shares and the court held that the refusal was justified. His offer had lapsed through the company's delay in notifying their acceptance.

❹ On failure of a **condition precedent** (something which must happen if the contract is to be effective). In *Financings* v *Stimpson* (1962) an offer to take a car on hire purchase lapsed when the car was involved in an accident. It was held to be a condition precedent of the contract that the car should be in good condition.

If the offeror dies before acceptance, it appears that acceptance by the offeree will make a valid contract provided that:

- she or he did not know of the death; and
- the contract does not involve personal services.

6.2.3 ACCEPTANCE

A contract comes into being at the moment acceptance of the offer is **communicated** to the offeror. It is necessary to identify the separate elements of offer and acceptance. In *Gibson* v *Manchester City Council* (1979) G was in the process of buying his council house from the Council when a Labour government came into power and instructed all local authorities to complete sales to which they were committed but to undertake no new sales. There was no written contract as such between G and the Council but there was correspondence between the parties from which it was possible to determine what was being sold and the price which had been agreed. The Court of Appeal held that there was a binding contract, even though one could not identify an offer and an acceptance. In the House of Lords the judges were not prepared to take this view and held that there was no contract.

Acceptance may be **inferred from conduct**. In *Brogden* v *Metropolitan Railway Co* (1877) the parties had been negotiating a new contract for the supply of coal. Even though no written acceptance of the new terms was made, the buyers continued to order coal and it was held that they were bound by the new terms, which they must be taken to have accepted because of their conduct in continuing to order coal.

Acceptance must be **unconditional**. Any 'ifs' or 'buts' make a **counter-offer**: *Hyde* v *Wrench* (above). In practice, it is common in business for both the seller and buyer to have a set of pre-printed forms containing their terms of business. These **standard form contracts** are likely to contain different terms. If there is a disagreement, the court has to decide which terms apply to the contract in question. It is usual, though not automatic, to hold that the last form sent contains the contractual terms. In *Butler Machine Tool Co Ltd* v *Ex-Cell-O Corp* (1979) the sellers made an offer and the buyers made a counter-offer, each on their own standard terms. The sellers then returned a tear-off slip from the buyer's form and the Court of Appeal held that this amounted to an acceptance of the buyer's terms.

Acceptance must be communicated, except in a unilateral contract where performance amounts to acceptance: *Carlill* v *Carbolic Smokeball Co* (above). If performance is continuing, the offeror has to wait to see whether performance is completed: the offer cannot be withdrawn during performance. In *Errington* v *Errington* (1952) a father made a gift of a house to his son and daughter-in-law on condition that they continued to pay the mortgage. This was held to be a unilateral contract. They became entitled to the house once the whole mortgage had been paid off. If they ceased to pay the mortgage at any time, the house reverted to the ownership of the father or his estate.

The need for communication means that the *offeror cannot 'bind the offeree by silence'*. In *Felthouse* v *Bindley* (1862) an uncle and nephew were negotiating over the sale of a horse. The uncle wrote to the nephew, naming a price and saying 'If I hear no more from you I shall consider the mare to be mine'. The nephew intended the uncle to have the horse and told the auctioneer to withdraw the horse from a sale of his possessions. The auctioneer sold the horse at auction and the uncle sued the auctioneer in conversion (an old tort which was the civil equivalent of theft). It was held that there was no contract between the uncle and the nephew because the nephew had not communicated acceptance. The horse thus remained the property of the nephew up to the time of the sale by the auctioneer and the auctioneer therefore had not committed the tort of conversion as against the uncle.

Acceptance is generally communicated at the *moment it is received*. In *Entores* v *Miles Far Eastern Corporation* (1955) an acceptance sent by telex from Holland to England was held to be effective upon receipt, so that the contract was governed by English law as the contract was made in England.

Acceptance sent by post is governed by a special rule: it is effective as soon as it is *posted*. This well-established rule was laid down in *Adams* v *Lindsell* (1818) and affirmed in *Byrne* v *Van Tienhoven* (1880) (above), but an offeror can exclude this rule by stipulating that acceptance must be communicated to him or her. The offeror did this in *Holwell Securities* v *Hughes* (1974). The acceptance was sent to Hughes' solicitor, who sent a copy to Hughes. The copy was never received by Hughes and the Court of Appeal held that, as the offer expressly required communication of the acceptance to Hughes, there was no contract. In *Brinkibon* (1983) the House of Lords said that the problem was solved by reference to the intention of the parties, sound business practice and a judgment as to where the risk should lie.

Acceptance must be made by the offeree or his or her agent. In *Powell* v *Lee* (1908) a person was told after an interview that he was to be given a job. No formal offer was made and it was held that the employer was not bound because the person who had spoken to the candidate was not authorised to speak for the employer.

If an act is done without knowledge of the offer, there is probably no contract; but the offer need not be the motive for the action which amounts to acceptance. In *Williams* v *Carwardine* (1833) a woman gave information about a wanted criminal. She had not been motivated by the reward that had been offered but, as she knew of it, she was entitled to claim the reward.

If two people make identical offers there is probably not a contract between them. This point has never been decided, although it was discussed in *Tinn* v *Hoffman* (1873), in which the majority took the view that there would not be a contract because there could not be said to be agreement between the parties.

6.2.4 CONSIDERATION

Simple contracts, that is, those not made by deed, require consideration. Consideration is the element of **bargain** in a contract. It has been defined as being *some benefit accruing to one party or some detriment suffered by the other*. Pollock's explanation of consideration is: *'The act or forbearance of one party, or the promise thereof, is the price for which the promise of the other is given and the promise thus given for value is enforceable.'* It is useful to think of consideration as the **price** for an act or a promise. An example to illustrate what 'consideration' means is: if I sell you my car, the money you pay me is the consideration provided by you; the car is the consideration provided by me.

There are several rules about consideration:

1. **Consideration need not be adequate, though it must be of value (or *sufficient*):** In *Thomas* v *Thomas* (1842) the Court held a payment of £1 a year to be good consideration, whilst in *White* v *Bluett* (1853) a son's promise to stop complaining was held not to be good consideration. From these two cases it would be reasonable to say that consideration must have some monetary value, but the case of *Chappell & Co Ltd* v *Nestle Ltd* (1960) makes it clear that the position is not quite so simple. P owned the copyright in a song. D ran a promotion, offering a free record of the song in exchange for three chocolate wrappers and a small payment. A question arose as to how royalties payable to P were to be calculated and it was necessary to decide whether the chocolate wrappers were part of the consideration. It was decided that they were. Lord Somervell said: '*A contracting party can stipulate for what consideration he chooses. A peppercorn does not cease to be good consideration if it is established that the promisee does not like pepper and will throw away the corn.*'

This is logical if you remember the definition of consideration being a detriment to one party. Even though the chocolate wrappers were of no benefit to the company, who threw them away, collecting and posting them was a detriment to the customer.

Promising not to sue (a *forbearance* in terms of Pollock's explanation) is good consideration if the promisor has a good case, but it will not be good consideration if he has no real claim.

2. **Consideration must move from the promisee:** In order to sue on a contract, the plaintiff must have provided consideration. In *Tweddle* v *Atkinson* (1861) the fathers of a couple who were about to marry promised each other that each would pay to the groom a sum of £100. The bride's father failed to pay and the son-in-law sued the father's executor. It was held that, as the son-in-law had not provided any consideration, he was not a party to the contract and could not, therefore, sue on it.

The converse of this rule is that a person who has provided consideration can sometimes claim to be a party to a contract which appears to be between other parties: see *New Zealand Shipping* v *Satterthwaite* (1975) below.

The Law Commission has recommended (in July 1996) that a third party in this kind of situation should be able to enforce the contract if the parties intended it should be enforceable by him or her.

3. **Consideration must not be past:** Past consideration is consideration performed *before* the promise is made. In *Re McArdle* (1951) a woman lived with her mother-in-law. She made improvements to the house and her husband's family, who would inherit the house on their mother's death, promised to pay for those improvements when the estate was distributed. They refused to pay and it was held that they were not obliged to do so because the work had been completed before the promise to pay was made.

If, however, an act is performed *at the request of another party and there is an assumption that payment will be made*, a promise to pay will be enforced even though it is made after the act is performed. In *Lampleigh* v *Braithwaite* (1615) D was in prison and asked P to obtain for him a pardon from the King. P went to expense to do so, and when the pardon had been obtained, D promised to reimburse P. He failed to do so and the Court held that he was obliged to pay because the work was undertaken at his request.

4. **Consideration must not be something the promisor is already bound to do.** There are three possible situations:
   - **A duty imposed by law:** In *Collins* v *Godefroy* (1931) P was promised money for appearing as a witness but he was subpoenaed to attend (a court order was issued, obliging him to give evidence). It was held that he was not entitled as he was obliged by law to attend and give evidence. He had thus not provided any consideration: he was doing something he was legally bound to do.

     If, however, the *performance exceeds the duty imposed by law*, it will constitute consideration. In *Glasbrook Brothers* v *Glamorgan County Council* (1925) provision of extra police to protect property during a miners' strike was held to amount to performance over and above the police force's duty to protect property and keep the peace. The colliery owners were therefore liable to pay for that extra policing. In *Ward* v *Byham* (1956) two judges in the Court of Appeal held that a promise to keep a child happy went beyond the mother's legal obligation to care for the child and so could support a promise from the father to pay money for the child's care. Denning LJ went further and said: *'I have always thought that a promise to perform an existing duty, or the performance of it, should be regarded as good consideration, because it is a benefit to the person to whom it is given.'*

- **A duty imposed by a contract between plaintiff and defendant:** The law was long thought to be settled by the decisions in two old cases. In *Stilk* v *Myrick* (1809) sailors left a ship during a voyage and the captain promised to split their wages between the remaining crew at the end of the trip. He refused to do so and it was held that the sailors were entitled to no more than their originally contracted wage as they had done no more than they were obliged under their contracts to do. In *Hartley* v *Ponsonby* (1857) a similar situation arose but the crew were held to be entitled to the extra payment promised because the ship was rendered unseaworthy by their being too few left to sail her safely. They had thus done more than they were contractually obliged to do.

  In *Williams* v *Roffey Brothers* (1990), however, the Court of Appeal held that a promise to make further payment to a person to encourage them to do what they were already bound to do could be good consideration. The decision was based on Lord Scarman's judgment in *Pao On* v *Lau Yiu* (1979) during which he said: *'Justice requires that men, who have negotiated at arm's length, be held to their bargains unless it can be shown that their consent was vitiated by fraud, mistake or duress.'* The situation in *Williams* v *Roffey Brothers* was that P, a carpenter, had contracted to complete work on some flats. It became apparent that he had quoted too low a price and would not be able to complete the work. The parties renegotiated and it was agreed that a further sum would be paid to the carpenter. Further work was done but D refused to pay the additional sum, alleging that the agreement to do so was unenforceable because it was unsupported by consideration. It was held that the carpenter was entitled to more money because the promise to pay more had been freely made and it was to D's advantage that the work be completed. It was stressed that there was no suggestion that D had been subject to economic duress at the time they agreed to the additional payment.

  The Court of Appeal had the opportunity to consider the point again in *Re Selectmove Ltd* (1994) and restricted the scope of the decision in *Williams* v *Roffey Brothers*. A company fell into arrears with its income tax and national insurance contribution payments to the Inland Revenue. Eventually, the Inland Revenue petitioned to wind up the company. The company claimed that the Revenue had agreed to accept payment of arrears by instalment, so petitioning for winding up amounted to breach of contract. In any event, the company had not kept to the allegedly agreed terms of payment but the issue as to whether the alleged contract would have been enforceable in the apparent absence of consideration was discussed. It was held that payment of a debt by instalments was not good consideration. This decision followed the authority of *Foakes* v *Beer* (1884), which concerned payment of a judgment debt by instalment, in preference to *Williams* v *Roffey Brothers*, which was distinguished on the basis that it was concerned with a contract for goods and services.

- **A duty to do something for A that one is already under a duty to do for B:** In *Scotson* v *Pegg* (1861) S agreed to deliver coal to X or to the order of X. X sold the coal to P and then told S to deliver the coal to P. P then made a contract with S to unload the coal at a given rate. The consideration for the contract between P and S was said to be the delivery of the coal. It was held that this amounted to good consideration, even though S was already bound to deliver the coal under his contract with X.

  The same view was taken by the Privy Council in *New Zealand Shipping* v *Satterthwaite* (1975). Here, stevedores dropped a piece of equipment whilst unloading it. In order to escape liability they needed to show that they were covered by an exclusion clause in a contract between the owner of the equipment and the shipper. To do that they had to demonstrate that they had provided consideration. It was held that unloading the equipment was good consideration, even though they were already obliged to unload the ship under a contract between themselves and the shipper.

6.2.5 PAYMENT OF A LESSER SUM

If A promises B that he will accept only partial performance of a contract, such as £500 instead of the full £1,000 he is owed, the common law rule is that A will not be bound by that promise because B had provided no consideration for it. This is the rule in *Pinnel's Case* (1602). Early payment or payment in a different way (such as, my diamond ring instead of the £1,000) are consideration, provided A has agreed to the change.

Pinnel's Case was followed by the House of Lords in *Foakes* v *Beer* (1884); but in *Jordan* v *Money* (1854) and *Hughes* v *Metropolitan Railway Co* (1877) the House of Lords held that *if a promise to forgo a legal right had been relied upon, the legal right could not be enforced at a later date.* These cases were followed in *Central London Property Trust* v *High Trees House Ltd* (1947) where Denning J said: *'The courts have not gone so far as to give a cause of action in damages for the breach of such a promise, but they have refused to allow the party making it to act inconsistently with it. It is in that sense ... that the promise gives rise to an estoppel ... The logical consequence, no doubt, is that a promise to accept a smaller sum in discharge of a larger sum, if acted upon, is binding notwithstanding the absence of consideration.'*

In *Alan* v *El Nasr* (1972) Lord Denning said D must have acted upon the promise, but not necessarily to his detriment. In *Brikom Investments Ltd* v *Carr* (1979) he said reliance was the key issue. D does not necessarily have to have acted on the promise in the sense of doing something he or she would otherwise not necessarily have done. Roskill LJ commented in the *Brikom* case that it would be wrong to extend the doctrine of promissory estoppel *'whatever its precise limits at the present day'* to the extent of abolishing *'in this backhanded way'* the doctrine of consideration.

The doctrine of promissory estoppel can be pleaded only as a defence. It is *'a shield, not a sword'* (*Combe* v *Combe* (1951)). Thus, P cannot sue on a promise unless he can show that he has given consideration; but D can claim that he is not obliged to pay because P promised to forgo the debt.

The duty to pay the whole may apparently be revived by the creditor giving notice of his intention to resume his full rights. In *Alan* v *El Nasr* (1972) Lord Denning said: *'(the creditor's) strict rights are at any rate suspended ... He may on occasion be able to revert to his strict legal rights for the future by giving notice. But there are cases where no withdrawal is possible. It may be too late to withdraw, or it cannot be done without injustice to the other party.'*

6.2.6 INTENTION TO CREATE LEGAL RELATIONS

There is a *presumption* that business contracts are intended to be legally binding (*Edwards* v *Skyways* (1964)) and that social and domestic arrangements are not (*Jones* v *Padavatton* (1969)). A presumption is something that a court will assume, unless there is evidence to prove the contrary.

In *Rose & Frank Co* v *Crompton* (1925) the presumption that a business contract is intended to be legally binding was rebutted. There was an 'Honourable Pledge Clause' within the contract, stating that it was not a legal agreement but 'a definite expression and record of the purpose and intention of the three parties concerned'. A common example of an agreement which is stated not to be legally binding is a football pool coupon. Anyone submitting a winning coupon cannot sue if the pools company refuses to pay them (*Appleson* v *Littlewoods Pools* (1939)).

The presumption against social and domestic arrangements being legally binding was rebutted in *Parker* v *Clark* (1960). A couple gave up their house to move into a house with some relations. When there was disagreement, it was held that the owners of the house could not eject the relations. Devlin J said: *'The question must, of course, depend on the intention of the parties, to be inferred from the language they use and from the circumstances in which they use it.'*

6.3 VITIATING FACTORS

There are various defects that affect the validity of a contract. Some defects will make a contract **void**, of no effect at all; some will make it **voidable**, effective until the innocent party decides he or she wishes to avoid it; a few defects make a contract **unenforceable**, i.e., valid but not one which the courts will enforce.

The vitiating factors that will be considered in this section are:

* incapacity
* duress and undue influence
* illegality
* mistake
* misrepresentation.

6.3.1 INCAPACITY

Minors, corporations, drunks and persons of unsound mind have limited contractual capacity; that is, not every contract they make may be binding.

Minors

The law was simplified by the Minors Contracts Act 1987. There is a general rule that contracts made by minors (those under 18) are not binding *but*:

❶ A minor is bound to pay a reasonable price for **necessaries**: s. 3(2) Sale of Goods Act 1979. A **necessary** is something suitable to the minor's 'station in life' and his requirements at the time of sale. In *Nash* v *Inman* (1908) a minor ordered 20 fancy waistcoats from his tailor and failed to pay for them. His father gave evidence that he was already well supplied with clothes. The minor was not, therefore, liable to pay for the waistcoats as they were not necessary to his needs at the time of sale.

❷ A minor is bound by a contract of employment or apprenticeship or training if it is, taken as a whole, substantially for his benefit. In *De Francesco* v *Barnum* (1890) a contract between some dancers who were minors and a theatrical entrepreneur was held to be not binding because, taking the contract as a whole, it was not beneficial to the minors. For example, they were not allowed to work for anyone else but were not entitled to be paid if there was no work available for them and the employer was under no obligation to provide work.

There are some contracts that are *voidable* by the minor, but *enforceable by the minor* against the other party: purchases of shares, partnership agreements.

If a minor borrows money, the contract is not enforceable against him or her but if an adult guarantees payment the guarantee is enforceable: s. 2 Minors Contracts Act 1987.

Corporations

Section 35 Companies Act 1985 (as amended) states that '*The validity of an act done by a company shall not be called into question on the ground of lack of capacity by reason of the fact that it is beyond the objects of the company stated in the memorandum of association.*' This provision means that all contracts made by a company are binding on the company. If a company's employees or directors make a contract that is outside the objects clause, it is a matter for the shareholders to deal with as it amounts to a fraud on them, their money having been used for an unauthorised purpose.

Drunks and those of unsound mind

These people can make contracts for necessaries: s. 3(2) Sale of Goods Act 1979. Other contracts are voidable at their option, provided that at the time the contract was made the other party knew or ought to have known of their impaired capacity.

6.3.2 DURESS AND UNDUE INFLUENCE

The presence of duress or undue influence at the time the contract is made makes the contract voidable at the option of the oppressed party.

Duress is *any threat that coerces the will and vitiates consent*. The threat may be of violence or of economic damage, provided its effect is that entry into the contract was not voluntary.

Undue influence is an equitable doctrine which recognises that the pressure inducing a person to contract may be very subtle. In *BCCI* v *Aboody* (1988) the Court of Appeal formulated a classification of the circumstances in which there may be undue influence:

Class 1   Actual undue influence; burden of proof lies on the party alleging undue influence.

Class 2A   Undue influence presumed; for example, in a solicitor/client, parent/child, doctor/patient, trustee/beneficiary relationship. The burden of proof is on the person claiming the contract was freely entered into.

Class 2B   A *de facto* relationship of trust and confidence. Once the existence of this relationship is established, the burden of proof is on the person claiming the contract was freely entered into.

In Class 2A and 2B relationships the presumption of undue influence would normally be rebutted by showing that the oppressed party has had independent advice on the transaction: *Barclays Bank* v *O'Brien* (1993).

In the absence of a special relationship (Class 1 situations) the party seeking to avoid the transaction must prove that pressure was applied. The court will look at the circumstances of the transaction. In *National Westminster Bank* v *Morgan* (1985) the matrimonial home was mortgaged to a building society, payments were in arrears and the building society applied for possession of the house. Mrs Morgan signed a charge on the matrimonial home in favour of the National Westminster Bank, who provided a loan to pay off the building society, and later claimed that it had been obtained through undue influence. She had not had independent legal advice but the House of Lords decided it was not necessary as she had achieved her objective of saving the house from repossession by the building society. In *Credit Lyonnais Bank Nederland NV* v *Burch* (1997) a junior employee, B, mortgaged her flat to provide security for her employer's business borrowing. B was advised to take independent legal advice but decided not to do so. When the business was unable to pay its debt to the Bank, the Bank sought possession of the flat and B claimed the mortgage should be set aside for undue influence exercised over her by her employer. The Court of Appeal held that the mortgage should be set aside. Millett LJ said: '...*where the transaction is so extravagantly improvident that it is virtually inexplicable on any other basis, the inference* [of undue influence] *will be readily drawn'.* B had nothing to gain from this transaction and no competent solicitor would have advised her to enter into it.

Undue influence is an **equitable doctrine**. The right to have the transaction set aside will, therefore, be lost in the event of delay, affirmation after any special fiduciary relationship has ceased or if third parties acting in good faith have acquired rights for value.

6.3.3 ILLEGALITY

Some contracts are void at common law for illegality:

❶ **Contracts in restraint of trade:** These are void unless they protect a valid interest of one party and are reasonable, both as between the parties and in the public interest. If the contract is for the sale of a business or a contract of employment, a restriction on a person's future employment will be enforceable only if: the person to whom the promise is made had an interest to protect (*Faccenda Chicken* v *Fowler* (1986)); and the restraint is reasonable as regards geographical area (*Mason* v *Provident Clothing & Supply Co* (1913)); duration (*M & S Drapers* v *Reynolds* (1957)); and the activities covered (*Attwood* v *Lamont* (1920)).

Similar rules are applied to agreements designed to prevent a party from trading with anyone he or she chooses (*Esso Petroleum* v *Harper's Garage (Stourport) Ltd* (1968)).

There is also statutory control through the:

- Restrictive Trade Practices Act 1976
- Resale Prices Act 1976
- Article 85 of the Treaty of Rome.

❷ Contracts to oust the jurisdiction of the court except provision for arbitration: **Arbitration Act 1996**.

❸ Agreements prejudicial to the married state.

Some contracts are void because a statute makes them illegal (*Re Mahmoud and Ispahani* (1921)) or makes the manner of their performance illegal (*Anderson* v *Daniel* (1924)).

Some contracts are illegal at common law on grounds of **public policy**:

❶ A contract to commit a crime or a tort: *Everet* v *Williams* (1725) agreement between highwaymen.

❷ A contract with an alien enemy.

❸ A contract damaging to foreign relations: *Regazzoni* v *Sethia* (1944) agreement to circumvent sanctions.

❹ A contract tending to promote corruption in public life: *Parkinson* v *College of Ambulance* (1925) agreement for the sale of honours.

❺ A contract promoting sexual immorality: *Pearce* v *Brooks* (1866) agreement to sell a carriage to a prostitute.

❻ A contract to defraud the Revenue.

Generally, the court will not assist a party to an illegal contract but if parties are not equally guilty the court may assist the less blameworthy of the two. If it is possible to sever the illegal from the legal part of the contract, the legal part may be enforced; but the whole contract must not have been tainted by illegality.

If a contract is illegal in its performance, the modern trend is for the court to look at the consequences for the parties and to decide the case in such a way as to advance Parliament's purpose (*Shaw* v *Groom* (1970)) or to decide whether there is 'an affront to public conscience'. In *Euro-Diam Ltd* v *Bathurst* (1988) and *Howard* v *Shirlstar Container Transport Ltd* (1990), illegalities committed in the performance of contracts were held not to vitiate the contracts as they were not regarded as such an 'affront'.

6.3.4 MISREPRESENTATION

If one party has been induced to enter into a contract by a factual statement which turns out to be untrue he will have a remedy even though the statement has not become a term of the contract. If a statement is a *term* and turns out to be untrue, there is a breach of contract. If the statement is a *representation*, the available remedy will depend on whether the statement was made fraudulently, negligently or innocently.

The statement must be of **fact**, not **law**: *Solle* v *Butcher* (1950) see Unit 6.3.5.

Nor must the statement be **opinion**. In *Smith* v *Land and House Property Corporation* (1884) a hotel was advertised for sale and the tenant was described as 'a most desirable tenant'. The tenant became bankrupt before the sale and the defendant company refused to complete their purchase of the hotel, claiming the contract to buy was voidable because there had been a misrepresentation about the tenant. The Court held this was a representation of fact, rather than opinion, and that the contract was therefore voidable. The distinction between fact and opinion was explained by Bowen LJ: '*In a case where the facts are equally well known to both parties what one of them says to the other is frequently nothing but an expression of opinion ... but if the facts are not equally well known to both sides, then a statement of opinion by one who knows the facts best makes very often a statement of material fact, for he impliedly states that he knows facts which justify his opinion.*'

Note that the Property Misdescriptions Act 1991 makes it a criminal offence for an estate agent to make a 'false or misleading statement' in the course of business.

Nor must the statement be **intention**. In *Edgington* v *Fitzmaurice* (1885) directors stated that they intended to use money for expanding the business, in fact, they intended to use it to pay off debts. Their conduct was held to be fraudulent, as the statement was not about mere future intention but was a statement of fact. Bowen LJ said: *'The state of a man's mind is as much a fact as the state of his digestion. It is true that it is very difficult to prove what the state of a man's mind at a particular time is, but, if it can be ascertained, it is as much a fact as anything else.'*

Silence will not usually amount to a misrepresentation. The rule generally is **caveat emptor**: let the buyer beware. But there are exceptions:

* Contracts of the **utmost good faith**, e.g. insurance contracts, where there is a duty to disclose all material facts.

* Failure to disclose a **change of circumstances**: *With* v *O'Flanagan* (1936) a falling-off in the value of a doctor's practice.

* Failure to disclose the **complete truth**, once a statement is made: *Dimmock* v *Hallett* (1866) that all the tenants of farms had been given notice to quit.

The representation must be **made to a party to the contract**. In *Peek* v *Gurney* (1873) P had bought shares from a third party, relying on statements made in the prospectus issued when shares were sold by the company. It was held that he could not rely on the statements, which turned out to be untrue, because the prospectus was addressed only to the original purchasers of shares sold by the company.

The statement must **induce the representee to enter into the contract**. In *Attwood* v *Small* (1838) the vendors of a mine exaggerated claims as to its capacity in order to sell it but the purchasers appointed their own surveyors to check the accuracy of the statements. They reported, quite wrongly, that the claims were correct and, relying on this, the purchasers bought the property. If it was held that they were bound by the contract as they had not relied on the vendors' statement.

Misrepresentations may be **fraudulent**, **negligent** or **innocent**. A **fraudulent** representation is *a false statement made*:

* *knowingly*,

* *without belief in its truth*, or,

* *recklessly, careless whether it be true or false.*

The plaintiff may claim **rescission** and **damages**. The damages are for the **tort of deceit**, so the measure of damages is to put the plaintiff in the position he would have been in had the statement not been made.

An untrue statement will be **negligent** unless the person making the statement can prove that he had reasonable grounds to believe and did believe up to the time the contract was made that the statement was true: s. 2(1) Misrepresentation Act 1967. If a party to a contract tries to exclude liability for negligent misrepresentation he can do so only if to do so is reasonable, having regard to the circumstances which were or ought reasonably to have been known to or in the contemplation of the parties when the contract was made: s. 3 Misrepresentation Act 1967 and s. 11(1) Unfair Contract Terms Act 1977. The remedy for negligent misrepresentation is damages and/or rescission.

If the untrue statement is **innocent**, that is, the party making it believed it to be true and that belief was reasonable, the misrepresentee can claim rescission or damages in lieu of rescission: s. 2(2) Misrepresentation Act 1967.

6.3.5 MISTAKE

The general rule is that a mistake made by the parties to a contract does not affect the validity of the contract. It will be **operative** only if it is so vital that it can be said to have robbed the contract of any element of agreement between the parties. An operative mistake makes a contract void: that is, of no effect at all.

Mistake as to person

If a party to a contract believed he or she was dealing with X and he or she is, in fact, dealing with Y, the contract will be void only if the identity of the other party is of crucial importance.

Compare *Cundy* v *Lindsay* (1878) in which a person pretended to be a particular company and the defendant had intended to deal with that company, with *Kings Norton Metal* v *Edridge* (1897) in which the plaintiffs had taken no steps to discover who they were really dealing with. In the first case the contract was void for mistake, in the second it was valid.

If the parties are face-to-face it becomes more difficult to show that a mistake as to identity has been made: see *Phillips* v *Brooks* (1919) involving purchase of jewellery and *Lewis* v *Averay* (1972) involving purchase of a car. Though the seller in each case was mistaken as to the buyer's identity, the court held the sellers had intended to deal with the person in front of them and the contract was, therefore, valid.

Mistake as to subject-matter

If there has been no *consensus ad idem*, if the parties really have not been thinking about the same thing, there will be no contract. In *Scriven* v *Hindley* (1913) H bought tow at an auction, thinking he was buying hemp. The circumstances were such that this error was not due to his negligence. The contract was held to be void for mistake. Similarly, in *Raffles* v *Wichelhaus* (1864) the parties contracted to sell and buy a cargo of cotton 'ex Peerless from Bombay'. There were, in fact, two ships of that name arriving with cargoes of cotton. The purchasers believed they were buying the earlier cargo, the sellers believed they were selling the later cargo. There was held to be no contract.

The court will not, however, give relief to a party merely because he has made a bad bargain. In *Tamplin* v *James* (1880) J bought a public house, believing that he was buying a plot of land adjoining in addition to the public house. When he discovered his mistake, which arose because the landlord of the pub had rented the land and J had not checked the plans of the property at the sale, J refused to go ahead with the purchase. It was held that he was obliged to buy the property because, by his conduct, J had suggested that he was well aware of exactly what he was buying. Mistakes by solicitors which resulted in their clients making disadvantageous contracts were held in *Centrovincial Estates* v *Merchant Investors Assurance* (1983) and *OT Africa Line Ltd* v *Vickers plc* (1996) to be inoperative. The contracts were upheld by the courts in both cases. It is relevant in these cases whether the other party realises a mistake has been made. In none of these cases was that so; if it is the case, the court is likely to set the contract aside as being inequitable.

A **mistake as to quality** is not an operative mistake. Again, the court will not put right what was merely a bad bargain. In *Bell* v *Lever Brothers* (1932) a company paid employees compensation for loss of office and then discovered it could have sacked them for misconduct and paid no compensation. This was held to be a mistake as to quality and therefore irrelevant. However, in *Sybron Corporation* v *Rochem* (1983) in similar circumstances, although the contract was not void it was **voidable** for misrepresentation, as the employee had kept silent about misconduct of other employees when he had a duty to report it to the company.

Mistake as to the existence of subject-matter

If the contract concerns subject-matter which, unknown to both parties, has ceased to exist, the contract is void: see *Couturier* v *Hastie* (1852) where a deteriorating cargo was sold by the ship's captain before C and H made their contract.

Under s. 6 Sale of Goods Act 1979, where there is a contract for the sale of specific goods and the goods, without the knowledge of the seller, have perished at the time when the contract is made, the contract is void.

Non est factum

A document will be void if the person who signed it can claim 'it is not my deed'. This defence is rarely available to a person of full capacity who signs a document appearing to have legal effect without reading it. In *Saunders* v *Anglia Building Society* (1971) Mrs Gallie signed documents without reading them because she had lost her glasses. She was bound by the documents.

Equity and mistake

Even if both parties to a contract make the **same** mistake about the quality of the subject-matter, the contract will be valid at common law. Equity, however, takes the view that such a contract is voidable. In *Solle* v *Butcher* (1950) B agreed to lease a flat to S for £250 p.a., the lease to run for seven years. Both parties acted on the assumption that the flat, which had been substantially reconstructed as a new flat, was no longer controlled by the rent restriction legislation then in force. If it had been controlled, the maximum rent would have been £140 p.a. Nevertheless, B would have been entitled to increase the rent to about £250 by charging S 8% of the cost of repairs and improvements, if he had served a statutory notice on S before the new lease was executed. After two years, S realised the mistake and sought to recover the rent he had overpaid and to continue as tenant for the balance of the seven years at £140. B counter-claimed for rescission of the lease in equity. It was held that the lease was valid at common law as the mistake was as to quality. In equity, however, B was entitled to rescission. S was offered an option: to surrender the lease entirely or to remain in possession as a mere licensee until a new lease could be drawn up after B had had time to serve the statutory notice which would allow him to add the sum for repairs to the £140 rent, so as to bring the lawful rent up to £250 p.a.

In *Grist* v *Bailey* (1967) a house was sold for £850. It was occupied by a tenant who both parties believed to be protected from eviction. The tenant left the property and the vendor then refused to complete the sale, saying the house with vacant possession was worth £2,250. The contract was held to be **voidable**. It was set aside, provided the defendant gave the plaintiff 'first refusal' to buy the house at £2,250.

The court may also grant **rescission** or **rectification** (see Unit 4.4).

As this is an equitable doctrine, the right to equitable relief will be lost:

- if there is **delay**;
- if the party seeking relief has **acted inequitably**;
- if the party seeking relief has **affirmed the contract**;
- if a **third party has acquired rights**.

6.4   TERMS IN A CONTRACT

Terms may be either express or implied.

6.4.1 EXPRESS TERMS

These are terms spoken or written by the parties. If the contract is written the court will generally not accept any evidence to suggest that the terms are otherwise than those contained in the contract. This is called the **parole evidence rule**. Sometimes, courts will find that there are two contracts, the one written and the other a **collateral contract**, the terms of which may conflict with the written contract. In *City & Westminster Properties* v *Mudd* (1958) the defendant signed a lease which forbad him to live on the business premises. The landlords knew he lived there and told him before he signed that it was acceptable for him to continue to do so. They then sued, alleging he was in breach of covenant by living on the premises. The Court held that there was a collateral contract: the defendant had agreed to sign the lease in return for a promise that he could continue to live on the premises.

Incorporation of terms

A term becomes part of a contract if adequate notice of it is given to the other party. In *Chapelton* v *Barry UDC* (1940) C was injured by a deck-chair he had hired from D. They alleged that they were not liable because a clause on the back of the receipt issued to C excluded liability. It was held that printing a clause on a mere receipt did not constitute adequate notice.

Notice may be inferred from a previous course of dealing (*Hillas* v *Arcos* (1932)) or from a trade practice (*British Crane Hire Corporation* v *Ipswich Plant Hire Ltd* (1975)).

Notice of the term must be given **before** the contract is made. In *Olley* v *Marlborough Court* (1949) a couple checked into a hotel. On the wall in the bedroom was a notice saying that responsibility would not be accepted for valuables unless they were left with the manager for safe keeping. A fur coat was stolen from the room. The hotel denied liability, relying on the notice. It was held that the contract had been made in reception, before the customers saw the notice. It was not, therefore, a term of the contract between the guests and the hotel, and the hotel was liable.

A term or a representation?

It used to be very important to know whether a statement was a term of the contract or a representation, because if it was a 'mere' representation the only remedy was for misrepresentation and, prior to the Misrepresentation Act 1967 (see Unit 6.3.4), damages were available only if the plaintiff could prove fraud. Now that the 1967 Act obliges a person who makes a misrepresentation to prove that he or she was *not* negligent and provides for the payment of damages in respect of negligent misrepresentation, this distinction is not so vital but it is still necessary to know whether a statement is a representation or a term. The distinction will depend on:

1. The strength of the statement: *Schawel* v *Reade* (1913) telling a purchaser about to examine a horse, 'You need not look for anything: the horse is perfectly sound' is a strong statement and thus a **term**.

2. The importance of the matter to the parties: *Bannerman* v *White* (1861) the purchaser made it clear he was not interested in even knowing the price of hops if sulphur had been used in producing them. The statement that no sulphur had been used was held to be a **term**.

3. The relative expertise of the parties: compare the cases of *Oscar Chess* v *Williams* (1957) in which a statement made by a **customer** selling a car in part exchange about the age of the vehicle was held to be a **representation** and *Dick Bentley Productions* v *Harold Smith (Motors) Ltd* (1965) in which the same kind of statement made by a **garage** was held to be a **term**.

4. The time at which the statement was made: a statement made near to the time at which the contract is made is more likely to be a term than a statement made before the contract is made. In *Routledge* v *McKay* (1954) a statement about the age of a motorbike made a week before the sale was held to be a **representation**.

In considering any given set of facts it is necessary to look at the situation as a whole and to consider the probable intentions of the parties.

6.4.2 IMPLIED TERMS

Terms may be implied into a contract by **custom or business practice**. The parties are presumed to intend that such terms shall be part of the contract, so if there is a written contract which is contrary to the customary rule, the written term prevails. In *Les Affreteurs Reunis Societe Anonyme* v *Walford* (1919) a written term as to when commission became payable was held to override the custom as to time of payment. The role of custom and practice is thus to clarify the terms of a contract, not to override the wishes of the parties.

Many terms are implied into contract by **statute**. Parliament provides that contracts of a certain type will include certain terms and, often, the parties are not allowed to exclude those terms. Examples are: contracts for the sale of goods, contracts for consumer credit and contracts of employment (see Unit 6.6).

Finally, a term may be implied into a contract to give it **business efficacy**. The term must be obvious and necessary. If, while the parties were making their bargain, someone had said to them: 'What will happen if ...' their response would have been 'Of course, this will happen ...', then the Court will imply a term to that effect into the contract. The principle was first explained in *The Moorcock* (1889) in which the obvious term was that a ship would be safe on a mooring.

6.4.3 DIFFERENT TYPES OF TERM

A **condition** is a really important term. Failure to perform a condition gives the innocent party:

- a right to regard the contract as repudiated, freeing that party from all obligations under the contract;

- a right to damages.

A **warranty** is a relatively minor term, breach of which gives right to damages only.

These expressions were first used in a technical sense in the Sale of Goods Act 1893. The use of the word 'condition' or 'warranty' by the parties is not conclusive as to the nature of the term. In *Schuler AG* v *Wickman Machine Tool Sales Ltd* (1973) a term requiring representatives of the defendant company to make a certain number of calls was described as a condition. There was breach of the term and the plaintiff claimed the right to treat the contract as repudiated. The Court held that this term was, in fact, a warranty since so minor a breach could not have been intended by the parties to have such serious consequences.

An **innominate** or **intermediate term** is a term the nature of which is unclear until a breach occurs. The court then looks at the consequences of the breach to decide on the appropriate remedy. In *Hong Kong Fir Shipping Co Ltd* v *Kawasaki Kisen Kaisha Ltd* (1962) Lord Diplock said: '*The correct approach was to look at what had happened as a result of the breach and then decide if the charterers had been deprived of substantially the whole benefit which it was the intention of the parties they should have.*'

This approach was applied by the Court of Appeal in *The Hansa Nord* (1975) when a cargo that had been rejected because part of it was in poor condition was sold to a third party who then sold it to the original purchaser, who used it for the original purpose. The price paid by the third party and the purchaser was very much lower than the original contractual price. The Court held that there had been no right to reject the cargo; there should merely have been a small reduction in price.

The court looks at the contract after breach and says: 'How serious were the consequences to the injured party?' instead of looking at the contract before performance and saying 'What sort of term is this?' The difficulty is that in commercial agreements it is important that the parties should know what the effects of any breach are likely to be before performance is due, rather than having to wait to see what view a court will take of the particular term.

The case law has been incorporated into the Sale of Goods Act 1979 by the Sale and Supply of Goods Act 1994 which inserted a new s. 15A:

(1) Where in the case of a contract of sale —

    (a) the buyer would, apart from this subsection, have the right to reject goods by reason of a breach on the part of the seller of a term implied by section 13, 14 or 15 above, but

    (b) the breach is so slight that it would be unreasonable for him to reject them, then, if the buyer does not deal as consumer, the breach is not to be treated as a breach of condition but may be treated as a breach of warranty.

The section applies unless the parties exclude it and it is up to the seller to show that the breach is so slight that it would be unreasonable for the buyer to reject the goods.

6.5 EXCLUSION AND LIMITATION CLAUSES

In the course of making a contract, agreeing to supply goods or a service, a contracting party will often include a term that aims to deny liability for a defect in the goods or service. For many years, the courts have recognised this as a potential problem. Purchasers, often in a weaker bargaining position, may be denied the very thing they thought they were buying because the seller has said, in effect, 'My obligation is to supply this, but if I fail to do so

I will have no obligation.' A limitation clause says: 'My obligation is to supply this, but if I fail to do so I will be liable to pay you a limited amount.'

6.5.1 THE COMMON LAW APPROACH

Exclusion and limitation clauses are subject to all the rules applied to other terms (see Unit 6.4), so they must be incorporated into the contract: the clauses in *Chapelton* v *Barry UDC* and *Olley* v *Marlborough Court Hotel* (see Unit 6.4.1) were both exclusion clauses. Only a party to the contract can claim the benefit of an exclusion clause. In *Adler* v *Dickson* (1955) a clause excluding a company from liability for the negligence of its employees was held not to prevent the plaintiff successfully suing the employee in person. As he was not a party to the contract between the plaintiff and the company, the employee could not use the exclusion clause in that contract to exclude his liability in tort. Note, however, *New Zealand Shipping Co* v *Satterthwaite* (see Unit 6.2.4) in which, by demonstrating that they had provided consideration, the stevedores became parties to the contract and were thus protected by the exclusion clause within the contract.

Consistent with the principles governing formation of contract and mistake, a person who signs a contract that contains an exclusion clause cannot say: 'I didn't read the contract and so I shouldn't be bound by its terms'. In *L'Estrange* v *Graucob* (1934) a woman who bought a cigarette machine was held to be bound by the terms of the contract she had signed, including an exclusion clause, even though she had not read the contract.

If an exclusion clause is ambiguous, it will be interpreted in the way most favourable to the person whose rights are being excluded or limited. This is called the *contra proferentem* rule. In *Hollier* v *Rambler Motors* (1972) the plaintiff's car was damaged by a fire whilst it was being repaired at the defendant's garage. Their standard terms included a clause: 'The company is not responsible for damage caused by fire to customers' cars on the premises'. This clause was held to be ambiguous and therefore not to cover a fire caused by negligence.

For a long time, the courts were fighting a battle to protect weaker parties to contracts. In the course of this battle they developed the concept of a **fundamental breach**: a breach that deprived the party to the contract of everything he might reasonably expect from performance. The courts held that no exclusion clause could cover a fundamental breach.

Finally, Parliament began to legislate to protect weaker parties and in *Photo Production Ltd* v *Securicor* (1980) the House of Lords, in recognition that Parliament had now provided (through the Unfair Contract Terms Act 1977) protection for weaker parties, held that the common law should allow parties with **equal bargaining power** to make their own rules. Securicor had provided a security service to Photo Production. An employee of Securicor called at the premises and checked them several times during the course of each night. In the course of doing this job he started a fire that caused extensive damage. The contract contained an exclusion clause by which Securicor would be responsible for this employee's conduct only if they had been negligent in employing him. They had not been negligent but Photo Production's case was that there had been a fundamental breach of contract (the very person who was supposed to protect the factory had caused substantial damage) and that the exclusion clause was, therefore, invalid. The House of Lords held that Securicor were not liable and that the clause was effective. Lord Diplock said: '*A basic principle of the common law of contract, to which there are no exceptions that are relevant in the instant case, is that parties to a contract are free to determine for themselves what primary obligations they will accept.*'

6.5.2 THE STATUTORY APPROACH

The Unfair Contract Terms Act 1977 (UCTA 1977) provides that a **business** can never exclude liability for death or personal injury in contract or in tort (s. 2(1)); note the exception in the Occupiers' Liability Act 1984.

In respect of most other contractual obligations, a business may exclude itself from liability only if the term is **reasonable**. Section 11 provides the term '*shall have been a fair and reasonable one to be included having regard to the circumstances which were or ought reasonably to have been known to or in the contemplation of the parties when the contract was made*'.

In contracts for the sale of goods, schedule 2 of the Act provides guidelines for deciding what is reasonable. In practice, these guidelines are also used to gauge reasonableness in other types of contract:

- the strength of the bargaining position of the parties;
- the availability of other supplies;
- the existence of any inducement to agree to inclusion of the clause;
- the buyer's knowledge of the clause;
- trade custom and previous dealings;
- if goods are made or adapted to the customer's specification it may be reasonable for the supplier to exclude liability.

In *George Mitchell (Chesterhall) Ltd* v *Finney Lock Seeds Ltd* (1983) M sold winter cabbage seed to F. Their standard conditions limited liability to replacing defective seeds or refunding the price. The seeds were, in fact, autumn cabbage and the crop was worthless. The House of Lords held the clause to be unreasonable and therefore void.

In *Smith* v *Eric S Bush* (1990) a surveyor valued a house which later was found to have serious defects. His report to the building society, which was paid for by the purchasers of the house, said that the house was good security for the amount of the loan. The defects caused the house to be worth much less than the purchase price. The House of Lords held that the surveyor could not rely on a limitation clause. Lord Griffiths said: *'I would not ... wish it to be thought that I would consider it unreasonable for professional men in all circumstances to seek to exclude or limit their liability for negligence. Sometimes breathtaking sums of money may turn on professional advice against which it would be impossible for the adviser to obtain adequate insurance cover and which could ruin him if he were to be held personally liable. In these circumstances it may indeed be reasonable to give the advice on the basis of no liability or possibility of liability limited to the extent of the adviser's insurance cover.'* As Lord Templeman pointed out, however, *'The public are exhorted to purchase their homes ... it is not fair and reasonable for building societies and valuers to agree together to impose on purchasers the risk of loss arising as a result of incompetence or carelessness on the part of valuers.'*

Lord Griffiths said that the factors to be taken into account when deciding whether an exclusion clause is reasonable are:

1 Were the parties of equal bargaining power?

2 Would it be reasonably practicable to obtain advice elsewhere, having regard to cost and time?

3 How difficult is the task? The more difficult, the more reasonable it becomes to exclude liability.

4 What are the practical consequences of the decision? For example, is one party insured?

Note that the question of insurance is not relevant to **exclusion** clauses, but s. 11(4) provides that the court should have regard to the availability of insurance when considering **limitation** clauses.

If a customer **deals as consumer** terms implied by statute into a contract for the supply of goods or services cannot be excluded: ss. 6 and 7 UCTA 1977. This affects, most notably, the provisions of the Sale of Goods Act 1979.

Section 12(1) UCTA 1977 provides that a party deals as consumer if:

- he neither makes the contract in the course of business nor holds himself out as doing so; and
- the other party does make the contract in the course of business; and
- the goods passing under or in pursuance of the contract are of a type ordinarily supplied for private use or consumption.

It has been held that a business may deal as consumer if the transaction could not be regarded as an integral part of the business: *R & B Customs Brokers* v *United Dominions Trust* (1988). In that case the purchase of a car by a company was held to be only incidental to the carrying on of its business. The contract was thus regarded as falling within s. 12(1)(a) and it was therefore not possible for the seller to exclude s. 14 of the Sale of Goods Act 1979 (the provision that goods shall be of merchantable (now satisfactory) quality).

A 'consumer' who buys, for example, a commercial freezer, rather than a domestic one, may find that the seller is able to exclude the provisions of the Sale of Goods Act 1979 because the contract does not fall within s. 12(1)(c).

If a contract **between two businesses** is a **standard form contract** (one in which the terms are pre-set by one party and there is no negotiation on those terms) any exclusion or limitation clause must be **reasonable**: s. 3 UCTA 1977.

In addition, s. 13(1) prevents:

'*(a) making the liability or its enforcement subject to restrictive or onerous conditions;*
(b) excluding or restricting any right or remedy in respect of the liability, or subjecting a person to any prejudice in consequence of his pursuing any such right or remedy.'

In *Stewart Gill* v *Horatio Myer & Co Ltd* (1992) P supplied and fitted an overhead conveyor system for D. P's standard terms contained a clause stating that customers could not withhold payment for any reason. Payment was by stages: D withheld the final 10% because of defects in the work and claimed the clause was unreasonable and so void. The Court of Appeal held that this was not an exclusion or limitation clause, so s. 3 did not apply, but that s. 13 did apply. The clause was held to be unreasonable because it was very wide. Stuart-Smith LJ said: '*There can be no possible justification for preventing a payment or credit to be set off against the price claimed and the width of the concluding words* 'or for any other reason whatsoever which the Customer may allege excuses him from performing his obligation' *is unlimited and would extend, for example, to a defence based on fraud.'*

The Unfair Contract Terms Act 1977 does **not** apply to:

1 Contracts in which **neither** party is acting in the course of a business.

2 Contracts on terms **negotiated** between **businesses**.

3 Contracts of insurance.

4 Contracts for the sale of land.

For the Unfair Terms in Consumer Contracts Regulations 1994, see Unit 6.6.

6.6 SPECIFIC CONTRACTS: CONTRACTS OF EMPLOYMENT AND CONSUMER CONTRACTS

As we have already seen, there are areas of contract law in which Parliament makes the rules. Two good examples of this are contracts of employment and consumer contracts.

6.6.1 CONTRACTS OF EMPLOYMENT

The relationship between an employer and an employee is fundamentally contractual: the employer buys the employee's time and talents and the employee sells that time and those talents for a wage. A contract of employment can exist by virtue of an oral agreement or from the behaviour of the parties and the common law implies certain terms into that contract.

The employer has an obligation to:

- pay wages
- take reasonable care for the employee's safety
- reimburse expenses incurred by the employee in the course of employment.

The employee must:

- obey reasonable orders
- keep the employer's secrets
- not compete with the employer's business

- take reasonable care and skill in performing his or her duties
- take reasonable care of the employer's property.

Statutory provisions and the contract of employment

Since the early 1960s there has been legislation, laying down additional terms that are part of every contract of employment. It is generally not possible to contract out of these provisions. The current legislation is the Employment Rights Act 1996, a consolidating Act that replaced the Employment Protection (Consolidation) Act 1978, the Employment Acts of 1980, 1982, 1989 and 1990 and part of the Wages Act 1986 and the Trade Union Reform and Employment Rights Act 1993.

It is necessary to have a two year period of continuous employment in order to acquire most of the statutory employee rights. Part-time staff have to work for a minimum number of hours each week to acquire certain rights but the House of Lords decision in *R v Secretary of State for Employment, ex parte Equal Opportunities Commission* (1994) means that there is no minimum number of hours necessary for part-time staff to qualify for redundancy payments and the right not to be unfairly dismissed.

The more important statutory provisions are:

1 An employee is entitled to **written particulars** of employment not later than two months after beginning work. Those particulars are:

- names of the employer and employee
- date the employment began
- date on which the period of continuous employment began
- scale or rate of remuneration, or the method of calculating remuneration
- hours of work
- holiday entitlement
- sick pay
- pension arrangements
- notice required to terminate employment
- job title, or brief description of work
- period for which work will continue, if not permanent; or the date on which a fixed term will end
- place(s) of work
- particulars of collective agreements affecting the terms and conditions.

An employer who employs 20 people or more must also supply details of:

- disciplinary rules
- grievance procedure.

Any change in the information must be notified to the employee within one month of its occurrence.

2 Each employee is entitled to an **itemised pay statement**.

3 An employee is entitled to **guaranteed payments**.

4 An employee has a right *not to be subjected to any* **detriment** by any act or failure to act of the employer on the ground that he *carries out his duties* as a *health and safety representative or officer*. Similarly, there is protection for an employee who reports risks to his employer if there was no representative or officer or it was not reasonably practicable to report through them and for an employee who *in circumstances of serious and imminent danger* took or proposed to take appropriate steps to *protect himself or other persons* from the danger.

5 An employee has a right to time off work for:

- public duties
- ante-natal care
- trade union duties and

- looking for work or training following notice of redundancy.

6 An employee has a right, regardless of the length of time for which she has been employed, to **maternity leave**. This is a period of 14 weeks from no sooner than 11 weeks before the baby is due (unless the employee is off work sick on account of the pregnancy on any day within the six weeks before the baby is due) in which case the maternity leave begins then.

An employee who has been *continuously employed for two years* has a right to return to work between the end of the maternity leave and 29 weeks after the beginning of the week in which the child was born. The right is to return to *the same job or an alternative on the same contract of employment and terms and conditions which are no less favourable.* There is no right to return if the employer employs fewer than six people.

To obtain the right to return to work the employee must:

- inform the employer of the date on which she intends maternity leave to begin not less than *21 days* before that date and that she intends to return to work

- reply in writing within 14 days to any written request from the employer, made no sooner than three weeks before the end of the 14 week maternity period, confirming the intention to return to work

- give *21 days* written notice of intention to return to work.

7 Employees of a business that is sold or otherwise transferred to a different employer, have a right to keep their jobs on the same terms and conditions. The terms cannot be changed *because* there has been a transfer: so a new employer who changes terms and conditions must demonstrate that there is a different reason for the change.

8 All employees have a right to belong to a trade union, or to choose not to belong to a trade union. Employees have a right not to be dismissed, or have action short of dismissal taken against them or to be chosen for redundancy, because of union membership or participation in activities.

There is no obligation on an employer to recognise a trade union or to negotiate with it. Many employers do, however, have recognition agreements, setting out which union or unions they will negotiate with. The fruits of these negotiations are called **collective agreements**. Each employee's contract of employment contains a term that it is subject to collective agreements and individual employees' terms and conditions of employment can then be changed as a result of the agreement made between the employer and the union, without agreement from the individual employee.

An employee who goes on **strike** is in breach of his or her contract of employment and may be **dismissed**. Employers are, however, not allowed to dismiss only some employees for going on strike, as this would be unfair. An employer would have to dismiss *all* employees who went on strike, or *none*.

A union intending to call a strike must give the employer seven days' notice of intention to hold a ballot and seven days' notice of strike action. There has to be a secret postal ballot before a strike may be held.

Health and safety

There is a considerable amount of detailed legislation regarding employees health and safety. The parent Act is the Health and Safety at Work etc. Act 1974 and there are other provisions in respect of different occupations and places of work.

The Working Time Directive 93/104 provides that no employee (with significant exceptions such as junior doctors, transport workers and seamen) can be obliged to work more than 48 hours per week. If employees do work longer, employers must keep records which will be inspected by the Health and Safety Executive. The Directive also provides for annual leave and a minimum daily rest period of 11 consecutive hours.

Termination of the contract of employment

A contract of employment may come to an end because:

- it was for a fixed term, which has expired

- it was for a specific task, which has been completed
- it has been frustrated (see Unit 6.7 for an explanation of the doctrine of frustration)
- the employee reaches retirement age

or the employee may bring the contract to an end by giving the appropriate notice. The notice required will be that stated in the contract, or, if there is no provision in the contract, the **statutory minimum** of one week.

If the employer gives notice, the employee may be entitled to a longer period of notice, dependent upon the length of service:

less than one month	no notice
one month to two years	one week
two to three years	two weeks
three to four years	three weeks
four years to five years	four weeks

and so on, up to a maximum period of twelve weeks' notice for a person who has worked for twelve years or more.

Notice given by either party is binding and can only be withdrawn on the agreement of both parties. An employer may choose to give **pay in lieu of notice**, provided that this is a term of the contract of employment.

If the employer is a company and the company becomes **insolvent**, employment may continue under the **receiver** or the business may be transferred to a different employer. If the business ceases, employees are **preferential creditors** and are entitled to arrears of wages, holiday pay, guarantee payments and redundancy pay. If the company does not have enough money to pay these amounts, application can be made by the employee to the Department of Employment, which will pay limited sums.

Dismissal

An employee may be dismissed:

- for being in **breach of contract** (such as going on strike, failing to keep the employer's secrets, competing with the employer's business)
- because the job has ceased to exist (this is **redundancy**)
- because it is no longer legal for the employee to do the job (for example, if a person whose job involves a lot of driving loses their driving licence).

In each case, it is for the employer to show that **appropriate procedures** were followed. The company should have a disciplinary procedure that provides for **warnings, verbal** then **written**, to be given to employees who commit relatively minor breaches of their obligations, such as a refusal to carry out reasonable instructions, poor timekeeping, absence from work. If the reason for dismissal is **incapacity** to do the job, the employer will have to demonstrate that steps have been taken to improve the employee's performance, such as training, or to offer a different job.

A dismissal is automatically unfair if it is:

- on grounds of race, gender or pregnancy
- for asserting a statutory right
- because of a business transfer
- for trade union membership or participation in union activities (or for non-membership).

A person who is placed in a position in which they feel they have no alternative but to resign may claim **constructive dismissal**.

An employer may also dismiss for **some other substantial reason**, such as:

- business reorganisation resulting in new terms and conditions which an employee refuses to accept
- a clash of interests, such as an employee having a close personal relationship with a competitor
- expiry of a fixed-term contract.

Immediate dismissal may be valid if the employee is guilty of **gross misconduct**. The employer must still follow fair procedures (such as hearing both sides of the story) but is not obliged to issue any warning and may dismiss as a result of one incident. Examples of gross misconduct are:

- stealing from the employer or other employees
- deliberate damage to the employer's property
- serious breach of safety procedures
- sexual or racial harassment.

Redundancy occurs where the **job ceases to exist**: if an employer company goes into liquidation, if the employer ceases to engage in a particular activity or if fewer employees are required.

The employer must follow fair procedures in selecting employees for redundancy and, if the employer recognises a trade union, must consult with the union.

A redundant employee is entitled to receive:

- time off to search for work
- the period of notice to which they are contractually entitled
- redundancy pay, which may be an agreed amount or the statutory amount.

Statutory redundancy pay is calculated according to **age** and **length of service**:

- 0.5 week's pay for each year of service between the ages of 18 and 21
- 1 week's pay for each year of service between the ages of 22 and 40
- 1.5 week's pay for each year of service between the ages of 41 and 64

There is, however, a maximum statutory payment. Payments negotiated between employer and employee may well be larger and will be tax free up to £30,000.

Wrongful dismissal is a dismissal in breach of contract.

Discrimination

All aspects of employment (recruitment, training, promotion, dismissal) are governed by laws against discrimination on the grounds of **gender, race** and **disability**. The legislation is the Sex Discrimination Act 1975, the Equal Pay Act 1970, the Race Relations Act 1976 and the Disability Discrimination Act 1995.

Sex discrimination occurs when a woman is treated *less favourably* than a man (or a man less favourably than a woman). *Different* treatment is not illegal, only *less favourable* treatment. It is also discriminatory to treat a married person less favourably than a single person.

Discrimination may be direct: such as saying: 'We don't employ women in this kind of work', or having different retirement ages. It is *always* unfair to dismiss a woman for being pregnant. In *Webb* v *EMO* (1994) W was employed to cover for maternity leave of another employee, though not on a fixed-term contract. She became pregnant and was dismissed. It was held that she was unfairly dismissed as the reason for her dismissal was her pregnancy.

It is not discriminatory to have different dress codes for men and women, provided they are comparable: *Smith* v *Safeway Ltd* (1995).

Indirect discrimination occurs when an employer imposes a requirement on all employees but that requirement is such that a smaller proportion of women than men (or men than women) can comply with it and, as a result, an employee suffers a **detriment**.

Employees who are subject to **sexual harassment** suffer a detriment. The employer thus has a duty to make sure the working environment is acceptable.

Women are entitled to equal pay for work of equal value.

Race discrimination: It is unlawful to discriminate on grounds of **race, colour, nationality, ethnic** or **national origin**.

Both kinds of discrimination are subject to exceptions relating to employment in private households and 'authenticity', where being a member of a particular race or gender is a **genuine occupational qualification**.

The **Equal Opportunities Commission** and the **Commission for Racial Equality** have duties in monitoring the law, issuing Codes of Practice and advising employers. They may also bring cases to court.

Disability discrimination: It is illegal for an employer employing more than 20 people to treat a disabled person *less favourably* than others, unless the employer can show justification. Employers have a duty to make reasonable adjustments to the workplace and work practices to prevent **substantial disadvantage** to disabled people.

Codes of Practice are prepared by the **National Disability Council**.

Almost all claims in respect of employment law are heard by industrial tribunals, which are governed by the Industrial Tribunals Act 1996.

6.6.2 CONSUMER CONTRACTS

A consumer contract is, broadly, a contract in which the customer does not make the contract as part of a business but the seller does. The major protection for consumers of goods is found in a combination of the Sale of Goods Act 1979 and the Unfair Contract Terms Act 1977:

1 Section 12 of the Sales of Goods Act 1979 provides that the seller has the right to sell the goods that are the subject-matter of the contract.

2 Section 13 provides that in a **sale by description** the goods shall correspond with the description given to them.

3 Section 14 provides that **where the seller sells in the course of a business** the goods must be of **satisfactory quality**: that is, they meet the standard that a reasonable person would regard as satisfactory, taking account of:

- **any description of the goods,**
- **the price** (if relevant), and
- **all other relevant circumstances.**

Section 14(2B) provides that quality includes **state** and **condition** and the following are aspects of quality:

- fitness for all the purposes for which goods of the kind in question are commonly supplied
- appearance and finish
- freedom from minor defects
- safety
- durability.

Section 14(2C) provides that goods will not be regarded as unsatisfactory in respect of *any matter specifically drawn to the buyer's attention* before the contract is made.

Although s. 14 is described in the Sale of Goods Act 1979, as amended, as being a **term**, in consumer contracts it is a **condition**, as are ss. 12, 13 and 15. This means that any breach of these terms gives the buyer a *right to his or her money back*, as well as damages for any reasonably foreseeable loss flowing from the breach.

Section 15 provides that if a sale is made by sample the bulk must correspond with the sample. Section 35 says that the buyer must have a reasonable opportunity of comparing the bulk with the sample.

The Supply of Goods and Services Act 1982 applies standards to provision of services similar to those laid down for the sale of goods by the Sale of Goods Act 1979. Thus, s. 13 provides that '*in a contract for the supply of a service where the supplier is acting in the course of a business, there is an implied term that the supplier will carry out the service with reasonable care and skill*'. Section 14 provides that services must be provided **within a reasonable time** if no time is specified in the contract and s. 15 gives the supplier a right to charge a **reasonable amount**.

The Unfair Contract Terms Act 1977 defines 'consumer': see Unit 6.5.2 above. It provides that terms implied into a consumer contract by statute cannot be excluded.

An EC Directive (93/13), incorporated into UK law by the Unfair Terms in Consumer Contracts Regulations 1994, provides that when a seller of goods or supplier of services **acting in the course of a business** makes a contract with a consumer (any natural person buying goods or services other than for a business purpose) a term which is unfair will be invalid.

Note that the regulation applies to **terms**, not merely to exclusion or limitation clauses. A term may be unfair if:

* it has not been individually negotiated; and
* it unreasonably causes significant imbalance in the parties' rights and obligations to the detriment of the consumer.

Fairness is judged with reference to:

* the circumstances at the time the contract is made,
* strength of bargaining position and
* any inducement to enter into the contract.

The contract remains binding but the unfair term will not be binding on the consumer.

The following terms *cannot* be challenged:

* terms implied by statute
* terms regarding provisions of international conventions
* terms defining the main subject-matter of the contract and the price to be paid
* terms in insurance contracts defining the risks insured.

The Regulation gives examples of terms that may be regarded as unfair, for example, a term enabling the seller or supplier to alter the terms of the contract unilaterally without a valid reason which is specified in the contract. Consumer protection organisations may apply to the court for a declaration as to whether terms in sellers' contracts are unfair.

Many consumer sales are on credit. These are governed by the Consumer Credit Act 1974, which applies if the sum borrowed is not more than £15,000. The **APR** (annual percentage rate) must be shown on all advertisements and documents). The agreement will be **unenforceable** unless it is:

* in writing
* contains all the express terms, and
* is signed by the borrower and the lender or their representatives.

A copy of the agreement must be given to the borrower when the agreement is signed and, if it has to be sent away for signature by the lender, a *further copy* must be sent to him once the agreement has been signed.

If the borrower fails to make a repayment, the lender must issue a **default notice**, giving the borrower at least seven days to bring payments up to date. If the borrower fails to do so, the lender can:

* end the agreement,
* demand payment of the whole sum due,
* recover the property, and
* enforce any security.

Once one-third of the price has been paid, goods become **protected goods**. These can never be recovered by the lender unless a **court order** is obtained first.

A debtor may terminate a regulated hire-purchase agreement if he has paid at least *one half* of the sum due, plus any compensation payable to the lender in respect of damage to the goods.

If (i) the agreement was signed at *any place other than the place of business of the creditor* or his associates and (ii) in negotiations before the agreement was signed, *oral representations were made to the debtor* by a person acting as a negotiator, the debtor may *cancel the agreement*, provided he gives notice of his intention to do so *within five days* of receiving his copy of the agreement. This is known as the **cooling off period**.

The Act provides for a system of licensing of credit brokers, administered by the Office of Fair Trading.

If goods bought on credit are faulty, the buyer may sue the credit company instead of the seller if he or she wishes.

Finally, it should be noted that in addition to the contractual protection that the law gives to consumers, there is protection through the law of tort and through statutes creating criminal offences.

6.7 DISCHARGE OF CONTRACT

Discharge brings a contract to an end. A contract may be discharged by **performance**, **agreement**, **breach**, or **frustration**.

6.7.1 PERFORMANCE

A party will be discharged from his obligations if he *completely and precisely* performs his obligations. In *Cutter* v *Powell* (1795) C agreed to serve as second mate on a ship bound from Kingston, Jamaica to Liverpool for the sum of thirty guineas, 'provided he proceeds, continues and does his duty ... from hence to the port of Liverpool'. He died during the voyage and his widow claimed the part of his wage relating to the period before his death. It was held that she was not entitled to any money because he had not fulfilled the whole of his contractual obligation.

This is a strict rule but it is made less so by the existence of several exceptions:

❶ **The doctrine of substantial performance.** A person who has performed his or her obligations substantially is entitled to payment of the contract price, minus a deduction for the defect in performance: there is a breach of warranty, as opposed to a breach of condition.

In *Hoenig* v *Isaacs* (1952) D employed P to decorate and furnish a flat. There were minor defects in the work and D refused to pay £450 of the £750 owed. It was held that, subject to a deduction for the cost of putting the defects right, P was entitled to payment in full, because he had substantially performed his obligations.

In comparison, in the case of *Bolton* v *Mahadeva* (1972), P had installed a combined heating and domestic water system in D's house. It gave off fumes and did not heat adequately. P was held not to be entitled to payment, having failed to substantially perform his obligations.

See also s. 15A Sale of Goods Act 1979 at Unit 6.4.3.

❷ **Acceptance of performance.** If the other party chooses to accept partial performance, the contract is properly discharged: provided there was a real option to accept or refuse. In *Sumpter* v *Hedges* (1898) P was to erect some buildings for D. He did part of the work and was paid something for that part but he then said he was unable to continue and claimed full payment for the work he had done on a *quantum meruit*. D completed the building work. It was held that P was not entitled to payment because D had had no choice.

❸ **Incomplete performance due to the other party.** If one party prevents the other from completing the contract, that failure to complete cannot be a breach of contract and the innocent party is entitled to payment for partial performance.

In *Planche* v *Colburn* (1831) P agreed to write a book to be published by C as part of a series. When he had written part of the book, C abandoned the series. It was held that P was entitled to payment on a *quantum meruit*, having been prevented from completing performance by C.

❹ **Severable contracts.** If a contract consists not of one obligation but of several, performance of each obligation fulfils part of the whole contract and payment for it is due. For example, building contracts are often constructed in this way and stage payments become due as each stage of the building is completed.

The court will decide whether a contract is severable.

Performance by a third party is usually sufficient, except in the case of a contract for personal services.

The *time of performance* is crucial only if time is to be *of the essence of the contract*, when late performance will be a breach of condition. Otherwise, late performance is only a breach of warranty. This is illustrated by the case of *Charles Rickards Ltd* v *Oppenheim* (1950). D ordered a Rolls-Royce chassis from P. It was not delivered by the agreed date but D continued to press for delivery. Finally, he gave up and bought another car. When the body was complete P sued for payment. It was held that time had originally been of the essence, then it ceased to be so because D had pressed for delivery after the due date. He again made time of the essence by stipulating a final date after which he would not accept delivery. D was, therefore, entitled to reject delivery.

6.7.2 AGREEMENT

If the contract has not yet been performed by either party, they may each make a promise not to require performance from the other party.

If one party has performed and the other has not, either:

*   the agreement must be in a deed, so that no consideration is required; or
*   the obligation of the party who has not yet performed may be varied: this is known as **accord** and **satisfaction**. The **accord** is the agreement to accept modified performance, the **satisfaction** is the consideration which supports that promise.

6.7.3 BREACH

Breach by one party of a **condition** absolves the other party from his obligations. It does not actually bring the contract to an end. For example, a party may opt to treat a serious breach as a **breach of warranty**.

Anticipatory breach is a breach before the due date for performance. It occurs when one party informs the other that he does not intend to perform his obligations. Examples of anticipatory breach occurred in *White & Carter (Councils) Ltd* v *McGregor* (1961), when a company refused to accept cancellation of a contract made by an employee of the other party who had no authority to make the contract, the company was held to be entitled to payment; and in *Averay* v *Bowden* (1855) when it was held that telling the captain of a ship that there was no cargo for him amounted to anticipatory breach of the contract under which the defendant was obliged to provide a cargo. Interestingly, in that case the captain kept the ship at Odessa after the anticipatory breach and, before the period for performance was at an end, the Crimean War was declared and the contract became frustrated (see Unit 6.7.4).

6.7.4 FRUSTRATION

Frustration occurs when performance is rendered *impossible*. It *automatically* brings the contract to an end. It may occur through one of several different sets of circumstances.

Illegal contracts

If a contract was legal at the time it was made but *subsequently* becomes illegal, it will be frustrated. In *White & Carter* v *Carbis Bay Garage* (1941) a contract to display advertisements on a metal sign was frustrated when wartime regulations designed to conserve materials made such advertising illegal.

Death or incapacity

If a contract is for personal services, the death or incapacity of the person who is to provide the services will frustrate the contract:

*   *Robinson* v *Davison* (1871) a pianist was unable to perform through illness. It was held that there was no breach of contract; the contract had been frustrated.
*   *Morgan* v *Manser* (1948) the entertainer Charlie Chester's ten year contract with his agent made in 1938 was held to have been frustrated by his being called up for military service in 1940.

Destruction of the subject-matter

If the subject-matter of the contract is destroyed between the contract being made and the time for performance, the contract is frustrated. In *Taylor* v *Caldwell* (1863) C agreed to let a music hall to T for four concerts. Before the first concert was due to take place the building was destroyed by fire. The plaintiff sued for damages for breach of contract. It was held that the fire damage made performance of the contract impossible and the contract was thus frustrated.

Compare this with the position when the subject-matter was, without the knowledge of either party, destroyed before the contract was made. The contract is then void for mistake: see Unit 6.3.5.

Frustration or breach?

The change of circumstances must be such that performance becomes either *impossible* or, at least, *radically different* from what was undertaken by the parties. Two famous cases can be contrasted to illustrate this point:

- In *Krell* v *Henry* (1903) P owned a room overlooking the proposed route of the Coronation procession of Edward VII. He let it to D for the purpose of viewing the procession. The procession did not take place because of the King's illness. D refused to pay for the room. It was held that the cancellation of the procession discharged the parties from their obligations under the contract, as it was no longer possible to achieve the real purpose of the agreement.

- In *Herne Bay Steamboat Co* v *Hutton* (1903) P agreed to hire a steamboat to D for two days, in order that D might take paying passengers to see the naval review at Spithead on the occasion of Edward VII's Coronation. An official announcement was made cancelling the review (because of the King's illness) but the fleet was assembled and the boat might have been used for the intended cruise. This contract was held not to be discharged because the King's review of the fleet was not the foundation of the contract. D was, therefore, obliged to pay the agreed hire fee.

The frustrating event must not have been brought about by the party claiming frustration. In *Maritime National Fish Limited* v *Ocean Trawlers Ltd* (1935) M chartered a trawler from O but, as M had only three licences and five trawlers, he did not allocate one of his licences to the hired trawler. This meant it could not be used. It was held that he was still liable to pay the charter fee as it was his own conduct that made using the trawler impossible.

The doctrine of frustration may be applied to leases, but only if a substantial proportion of the purpose of the lease is affected. In *National Carriers* v *Panalpina Ltd* (1980) N leased a warehouse to the plaintiff for ten years. Access to the building was disrupted for 20 months. This was held to be an insufficient proportion of the ten years to frustrate the lease, but the court confirmed that the doctrine does apply to leases.

Consequences of frustration

The contract comes to an end *automatically*, at the date of the frustrating event. Compare this with:

- a void contract, which never exists
- a voidable contract, which exists until the injured party chooses to avoid it
- a breach of condition, which gives the injured party a choice as to whether to continue with the contract or not.

At common law, the loss *lay where it fell*. This was changed by the Law Reform (Frustrated Contracts) Act 1943 which provides that if a person has been paid in advance, the money is treated as if he held it as a trustee for the party who paid him and he can be ordered to make repayment, less expenses incurred if the judge deems a claim for expenses to be reasonable.

If a person has received some benefit under the contract, he has to pay the other party for that benefit.

The court ignores the effect of insurance, unless the contract or a statute imposed an obligation to insure.

Illustrative questions

Tutorial note
Both the questions are 'problem style'. As with all questions of this type, the first thing to decide is what points of law the examiner is expecting to see discussed. It is then necessary to explain what the law is, using cases and statutes as appropriate, before applying that law to the facts in order to advise Jim, or Mary, as the case may be.

1 Whilst out shopping for himself and his neighbour, Jim notices the following promotional campaign in the window of a shop called Wizelectrics, 'Any customer purchasing a model Super 99 video recorder will receive a Minilux portable television free of charge.'

Jim is tempted to treat himself to a video recorder under the promotion, but decides to go home to review his finances. On the way he delivers some shopping to his elderly next door neighbour, Mrs Earnest. She is grateful to Jim and promises him £15 for his recent kindness to her. However she does not pay him.

Later that week Jim, persuaded by the promotion, decides to buy a video recorder from Wizelectrics. He pays, and the shop assistant places the video recorder on the counter for him to take, apologizing that the last television has been given away that morning and that there are no more available at present.

Advise Jim regarding both the television and the money from Mrs Earnest. (50)
(*UODLE*)

Suggested answer
This problem is concerned with the rules on offer and acceptance and the doctrine of consideration.

An advertisement, or a display in a shop window, is usually regarded as an invitation to treat. In *Fisher* v *Bell* (1961) it was held that the display of a flick knife in a shop window was not an offer for sale, but an invitation to treat. The customer makes an offer to buy the goods and the shopkeeper may accept or refuse the offer. The exception to this principle arises if an advertisement is held to be an offer to the world at large, as was the case in *Carlill* v *Carbolic Smokeball Co* (1893). A newspaper advertisement stating that anyone who used the smokeball and caught 'flu would be paid £100 was held to constitute an offer, so that Mrs Carlill, who used the smokeball, was entitled to the £100 as she had accepted the offer by using the ball.

Alternatively, this problem could be viewed as involving a collateral contract. Here, there are two contracts. Entering into one contract is consideration for the second contract. In *City & Westminster Properties* v *Mudd* (1958) it was held that entering into a lease was consideration for a promise to allow the tenant to live on the premises.

If the notice in the shop window is an invitation to treat, Jim makes an offer to buy the video, into which, in the circumstances, might be implied a condition that he received a television. The shop is then not accepting his offer unconditionally and, although they are not obliged to give him a television, he is not obliged to buy the video and can have his money back. If the notice is an offer to the world at large, Jim accepts it by paying for a video and is entitled to a television.

If there are two contracts, one to buy a video which is conditional on a second contract to supply a television, then the condition has not been met and there is no contract to buy a video.

An agreement will be held to be binding only if there is consideration. The general rule is that a promise to pay for something that has already been done is not binding, as the consideration is past. In *Re McArdle* (1951) a promise to pay for decorating work that had already been done when the promise was made was held not to be legally enforceable. There is an exception to this rule if work is done at a person's request and there is an expectation that the work will be paid for. This exception comes from the case of *Lampleigh* v *Braithwaite* (1615) in which a promise to pay was upheld, even though it was made after services were provided.

It is unlikely that a court would regard getting shopping for an elderly neighbour to be a service for which payment is expected and, therefore, it is more likely that the rule in *Re McArdle* would be applied and Jim would not be entitled to the £15.

2 Mary regularly parks her car in the customers' 'pay and display' Car Park at Jones Ltd department store. Inside the car park at all exit points are large notices stating in bold lettering, 'Cars parked at owner's risk'. Underneath is displayed in smaller letters a series of terms and conditions. One of the terms states:

> The company, its employees and agents accept no responsibility for any damage to customers' vehicles whatsoever and howsoever caused. Any term, condition or warranty whether express, implied or statutory covering damage to customer vehicles is hereby specifically excluded.

The next occasion Mary uses the car park she fails to see a notice placed at the entrance and before the automatic ticket barrier which states:

> Jones Ltd regrets the inconvenience caused to customers during the refurbishing and modernisation work. Customers are strongly advised to seek alternative parking during this period but may still use areas of the car park facility not undergoing refurbishing on the clear and express understanding that they do so entirely at their own risk and that the company, its employees and agents accept no responsibility whatsoever for any losses or damage howsoever caused.

Mary takes her ticket from the automatic machine and enters the car park. She suffers facial injuries and damage to the car when a brick is dropped through the car windscreen.

Advise Mary whether she can recover damages for her own injuries and for the damage to the car. (25)

(*NEAB*)

Suggested answer
This problem is about the use of exclusion clauses to exclude liability for damage to property and for personal injury.

Any contractual term takes effect only if it is brought to the attention of the party affected by it before the contract is made. In *Thornton* v *Shoe Lane Parking* (1971) it was held that a person using a car park is affected only by terms displayed before the contract is made at the entrance barrier. A person who has used a car park previously will be bound by terms he or she could have read on an earlier occasion.

In interpreting exclusion clauses, the courts apply the contra proferentem rule, interpreting the clause in the way least favourable to the person trying to rely on it.

Section 2(1) Unfair Contract Terms Act 1977 states that a business can never exclude liability for personal injury or death. This means that a person who is injured would have to show that the defendant had been negligent or was in breach of their contractual obligations, but the defendant would not be able to exclude such liability.

The Supply of Goods and Services Act 1982 provides that in a contract for the supply of services there is an implied term that the service will be provided with reasonable care and skill. The Unfair Contract Terms Act 1977 prevents this term being excluded in a contract between a business and a consumer. The Unfair Terms in Consumer Contracts Regulations 1994 provide that unfair terms are invalid. A term will be unfair if it causes significant imbalance in the parties' rights and obligations to the detriment of the consumer.

Only a party to a contract may claim the benefit of an exclusion clause. If the brick was dropped by someone who was not a party to the contract, Mary can sue them in negligence without any reference to alleged exclusion terms. This course of action was successful in *Adler* v *Dickson* (1955) when a woman sued a company's employee rather than the company itself.

Mary enters into a contract with Jones Limited when she takes a ticket from the automatic barrier. Both notices are terms of that contract, but only to the extent that their contents have been made known to Mary before the contract was made and are allowed by law.

The first notice is a term of the contract because Mary had an opportunity to read it on the previous occasions she has used the car park. It would be effective to protect Jones Limited in respect of damage caused by a third party but they are under an obligation to provide the service of a car park with reasonable care and would be liable for any damage to a vehicle arising from their lack of reasonable care.

Mary will be bound by the second notice if it was placed in such a way that the reasonable person would have seen it. In the case of *L'Estrange* v *Graucob* (1934) it was held that a person who signs a contract without reading it is still bound by its terms. By analogy, a person who enters a car park without reading a prominent notice at the entrance would be bound by its contents. It has, however, been stated judicially that the existence of an exclusion clause must be made plain: it will not be effective if it is hidden in small print, or tucked away out of sight.

As Jones Limited are in a better position to appreciate the risks than Mary, a court would probably hold that they had failed in this obligation by allowing her to park in a dangerous area and that s. 2(1) Unfair Contract Terms Act 1977 prevents them denying liability for her injuries. Further, as s. 13 Supply of Goods and Services Act 1982 cannot be excluded in a contract between a business and a consumer, Jones Limited are likely to be held liable in respect of the damage to the car.

The 1994 Regulations would probably make the first notice invalid because it is not individually negotiated and it unreasonably creates a significant imbalance in rights and obligations between Mary and Jones Limited. Interestingly, because fairness is judged with regard to the circumstances at the time the contract is made, the second notice might be upheld under the Regulations.

Mary will be able to recover damages from Jones Limited in respect of both her injuries and the damage to her car.

Practice questions

1 Critically examine the ways in which an offer may be terminated. (50)
(*UODLE*)

Pitfalls
This kind of question gives very little information about what is required. Make sure you offer a critical evaluation, as well as an accurate description supported by cases.

Key points
An offer may be terminated by rejection, by counter-offer, by lapse of time, by revocation or by failure of a condition precedent. Explain what each of these means and illustrate each with an appropriate case. Then take each rule and evaluate it in terms of whether the rule is likely to give effect to the intention of the parties or may be regarded as a just means of dealing with a situation in which the parties may not necessarily have any particular intention.

2 *R* is a sewing machine operator. She is paid a wage which is average for such work on a national comparison. She believes that her skills and the responsibility attached to her job are similar to those of the cutting machine operators. The cutting machinists are all male and receive twenty per cent more in wages than the sewing machinists. *R* wishes to raise this issue with the management and wonders whether she should do so, and whether there might by any advantage in joining the national trade union, SEWNO, in this situation. She has received support from the shop steward, *S*, who, in pursuing the issue, has had to leave work to attend meetings with SEWNO national officials. The company have issued *S* with a summary dismissal notice.

How can the law help *R* and *S* in these matters? (25)

(*London*)

Pitfalls

Remember this is a problem question, so identify the issues and explain the law before attempting to answer the specific question: *how can the law help?*

Key points

The question is concerned with the law on the right to equal pay for work of equal value and the right not to be unfairly dismissed, with particular reference to protection for union officials. Notice that R is not a member of the union and consider how this affects S's position.

3 Henry drove into town to do some shopping and parked his car in a car park which he had used a few times before and which was operated by Safeparks. At the entrance to the car park was a notice which stated, 'For the sole use of customers of the shops in this precinct. Exit by token available from shops with any purchase.' As he walked towards one of the shops, Henry met an old friend who had acquired a token which he did not need and who now gave it to Henry. Henry decided that he no longer needed to buy anything from the precinct shops and, leaving his car in the car park, went off and ordered a dining room carpet from Comfyfloors. When he later tried to leave the car park, he was stopped by security staff doing a spot check on customers and it was discovered that he had not bought anything at the shops, despite having a token. The security staff pointed to a notice displayed at the exit barrier and to a notice at the entrance to the shops (some distance from the entrance to the car park) which stated that exit without a token would cost £25. Henry was told that he could not now go and make a purchase and he had to pay the £25 before the security staff would open the barrier.

Henry engaged Ken, a carpet fitter, to lay the carpet for him and, after a brief inspection of the completed work, signed a document to say that he was completely satisfied. When he was able to examine the carpet and the fitting more carefully, he discovered that there were variations in the colour and pattern and that Ken had cut it short in three or four places, so that it did not reach the wall. When he complained to Comfyfloors, he was reminded that the delivery note which he had signed informed him that no liability for any defects would be accepted once the carpet had been cut by anyone other than Comfyfloors employees or authorised agents. Additionally, Henry complained to Ken about the fitting, but Ken rejected the complaint by reminding Henry of the document that he had signed on completion of the work.

(a) Discuss the rights, duties and remedies between Safeparks and Henry arising out of the above incidents. (15)

(b) Discuss the rights, duties and remedies arising out of the incidents involving Henry and Comfyfloors **and** Henry and Ken. (15)

(c) Explain the mechanisms, both formal and less formal, which exist for the resolution of the disputes between the various parties. (10)

(d) Assess the contribution made by the judges to the development of the rules which you have explained and applied in answering parts (a) and (b) above. (10)

(*AEB*)

Pitfalls

This is the AEB's style of problem question. It is longer and carries more marks than those set by other Boards, it is more diverse and it asks rather more specific questions. Make sure you benefit from these differences! The major skills are to manage your time so that you do justice to all four parts of the question (notice the allocation of marks between the parts and allocate your time in the same proportions) and do exactly what each question asks. Read all the questions carefully before you begin answering, so that you do not cover in an answer to one part material that should be used in answer to another.

Question (c) is concerned with material you will have revised for the Paper 1 examination, so remember that you still need that material for Paper 2. Questions of the kind asked in (d) sometimes alarm candidates. They require the ability to think, under exam conditions, and to use the law you know to answer a question you might not have considered in quite this context. The best approach is to keep your answer simple and to use the law you have already explained, rather than to think up fresh examples.

Key points

1. Offer and acceptance, consideration, incorporation of terms, remedies for breach: describing appropriate cases. Apply the rules, giving attention to the question of where and when the contract was made, what was incorporated within it, what Henry's obligation was.

2. Relevant provisions of the Sale of Goods Act 1979 (as amended) and the Supply of Goods and Services Act 1982. Apply to the facts, being careful to deal with both contracts.

3. Explain the jurisdiction of the county courts and the High Court; small claims procedure, arbitration schemes run by trade organisations, mediation, negotiation.

4. Judges contributed to the rules discussed in (a) (give some examples); but not as much to those discussed in (b), which were created by Parliament. Judges contributed to the rules in (b) in terms of statutory interpretation, give an example. Then assess those contributions.

TORT

Units in this chapter

Chapter objectives

This chapter examines the law of tort. The law of tort is an important part of civil law. Its role is to provide a remedy to persons who have been harmed by the conduct of others. When a tort is committed, the law allows the victim to claim a remedy. The law of tort protects many different interests, including physical harm, a person's reputation or liberty, use and enjoyment of land, or even financial interests. It is therefore difficult to provide a general definition of tort. In this chapter the meaning and functions of the law of tort are outlined and various torts are explored.

Much of the chapter is devoted to the tort of negligence, since this is the most relevant tort in today's society. The development of the tort of negligence into areas such as psychiatric damage and economic loss illustrate the influence of policy considerations on the creation of legal rules and you may find it useful to refer back to the doctrine of precedent in Unit 2.2. Generally, the law of tort is fault-based (refer to Chapter 9), but there are instances of strict and vicarious liability requiring understanding, and these are dealt with. If you are studying this as your specialist topic, you should have a good understanding of all the torts you are required to know by working through this chapter. For other syllabuses you should refer to you syllabus checklist if you are unsure as to which torts you require knowledge of.

7.1 MEANING AND FUNCTIONS OF THE LAW LAW OF TORT

The law of tort covers a wide range of situations. The interests that the law of tort protects include physical harm, both to the person and property, a person's reputation, dignity or liberty, or use and enjoyment of land, or even his financial interests. It is therefore difficult to provide a definition of tort. In broad terms it is a breach of a duty fixed by civil law.

The principal function of the law of tort is to provide a remedy to persons who have been harmed by the conduct of others. The harmful conduct may be intentional, careless or even accidental. When a tort is committed, the law allows the victim to claim money, known as damages, to compensate for the commission of the tort. This is paid by the **tortfeasor** (person who has committed the tort). Other remedies may be available as well. However, it is not for every loss that the law will provide a remedy. The law of tort must strike a balance between competing claims and values. It must decide what types of loss are actionable. At one end of the scale, if the law does not impose liability for a loss, then the person who suffers the damage will bear the loss. At the other end of the scale, if strict liability in relation to a particular activity is imposed by law, the effect of imposing liability may restrict an activity to such an extent that it produces a net social loss. For example, strict rules on defamation may limit freedom of speech. It is the role of tort to decide what types of loss are actionable. Policy issues will often influence the law-makers in reaching this decision.

There is considerable overlap between tort and contract (both branches of the civil law). In contract a person voluntarily assumes duties and obligations whereas in tort, the obligations are imposed by law. In contract the duties are only owed to other parties to the contract. In tort the duties are owed to people in general. However, closer examination of these areas of law shows these distinctions blurring. Often duties in contract are fixed by law (by implied terms). Sometimes liability in tort depends upon agreement (for example, in relation to liability for negligent statements).

The distinction between tort and crime is not in the conduct itself. Many criminal offences are also torts. The difference lies in the consequences which follow. The aim of criminal law is to punish the offender and vindicate the public interest in the maintenance of law and order. The state prosecutes the individual. Criminal law focuses on the offender. The aim of tort is to compensate the victim of a private wrong. An individual sues the tortfeasor. The law of tort focuses on the victim. But these distinctions are also blurred. Sometimes a tortfeasor may be ordered to pay damages at a higher rate than the sum needed to compensate the victim in order to punish his or her behaviour and provide a deterrent to others. Similarly, the offender's punishment may involve compensating the victim of the crime, although this is still not a primary aim of criminal law, and the compensation is likely to be lower than would be ordered in a tort action.

7.2 THE TORT OF NEGLIGENCE

7.2.1 INTRODUCTION

The tort of negligence is committed when a person fails to live up to a standard of care expected of him, as a matter of law, and someone else is injured or suffers loss as a result. The tort of negligence was fully established in the famous case of *Donoghue* v *Stevenson* (1932). The case owes its chief importance to the fact that it contains an attempt by the House of Lords to provide a general formulation of liability in negligence. Before 1932 no generalised duty of care in negligence existed. The common law had recognised particular circumstances where a duty of care should be owed, for example, road accidents, but whether a duty existed in a new situation was decided on the facts of each case rather than on the basis of a general principle. In *Donoghue* v *Stevenson* P suffered gastric illness and shock as a result of drinking ginger beer which contained a decomposed snail. A friend had bought the ginger beer so she sued the manufacturers. The House of Lords held, by a majority of 3 to 2, that the manufacturer owed a duty of care to the ultimate consumer. The case also laid down a principle much wider than the facts of the case required. Lord Atkin's *obiter dicta* in the case attempted to formulate a general test of negligence. Lord Atkin created the '**neighbour principle**': *'You must take reasonable care to avoid acts or omissions which you can reasonably foresee would be likely to injure your neighbour. Who then, in law, is my neighbour? The answer seems to be persons who are so closely and directly affected by my act or omission that I ought reasonably have them in contemplation as being so affected when I am directing my mind to the acts or omissions which are called into question.'*

7.2.2 THE DUTY OF CARE

To succeed in an action for negligence, a plaintiff must show that a duty of care was owed by the defendant. The key issue for the courts is to decide when foreseeable damage is actionable. Policy considerations have influenced the courts in determining the scope of legal duty. The function of the duty of care is to define the limits of liability for negligence. *Dicta* from the appeal courts indicate that they are very much aware of the effect of their decisions on society as a whole. The general principle promoted in *Donoghue* v *Stevenson* potentially opened the 'floodgates' and in the following years there was a large increase in negligence claims. A duty of care was imposed in a wide variety of situations. This trend was gradually reversed during the 1980s. The current trend shows the 'floodgates' are closing. These key principles are discussed below. It is important to note that they are *principles* rather than *substantive rules of law*.

Reasonable foreseeability test (the neighbour test)

It emerged from Lord Atkin's speech that we owe a duty of care to our '*neighbour*', i.e. those whom we can reasonably foresee we may harm. Using this principle, lawyers could argue that there should be liability for negligently inflicting damage in *new* situations, not covered by previous law, *because* the damage was reasonably foreseeable.

The two-stage test

During the 1970s a broad approach was adopted to decide whether a legal duty of care existed. The House of Lords developed the '**two-stage test**' to determine whether a duty of care was owed. In *Anns* v *London Borough of Merton* (1977) Lord Wilberforce said there was no need to bring the facts of a novel situation within those of previous cases in which a duty of care has been held to exist. He formulated what is now referred to as the 'two stage test' to determine whether a duty exists in a particular case:

- Is there sufficient proximity between the two parties? (and, if so,)
- Are there any policy considerations for not imposing a duty of care?

The first part of the test corresponds with the neighbour principle. This case has come to be regarded as the '*high-water mark*' in terms of determining the scope of the duty of care.

The three-stage test

The House of Lords began to worry about the growth in liability in negligence. The 1980s saw rapid judicial retreat. A more restricted approach to determining duty of care was developed in *Peabody Donation Fund* v *Sir Lindsay Parkinson & Co Ltd* (1985), a case similar to *Anns*, in that the building owners were claiming against the local authority for economic loss suffered when the wrong drains were fitted to the properties. The House of Lords held that no duty of care existed. Lord Keith modified Lord Wilberforce's two-stage test. He developed what may be referred to as the '**three-stage test**':

- Is the damage reasonably foreseeable? (if so)
- Is there sufficient proximity between the two parties?

- Even where the above are satisfied, it must be 'just and reasonable' to impose such a duty.

The incremental approach

Recent cases have indicated that the House of Lords are now very reluctant to find new duty situations. The Wilberforce approach started from a *prima facie* presumption that if the defendant's carelessness caused reasonably foreseeable damage, a duty of care *would* exist *unless* there were policy considerations for *not* imposing such a duty. The courts now determine the duty issue on a case by case basis.

This incremental development of new duty situations now being adopted by the House of Lords means that bringing actions in negligence based on new situations is becoming increasingly more difficult. It would seem that a duty will be imposed in new situations where there are extremely good policy reasons *for* doing so, which is almost a reversal of the Wilberforce approach. This approach, referred to as the **incremental approach** or **development by analogy**, was expressed by Lord Bridge in *Caparo Industries plc* v *Dickman* (1990) (see Unit 7.2.5): *'Whilst recognising, of course, the importance of the underlying general principles common to the whole tort of negligence, I think the law has now moved in the direction of attaching greater significance to the more traditional categorisation of distinct and recognisable situations as guides to the existence, the scope and the limits of the varied duties of care which the law imposes.'*

7.2.3 BREACH OF DUTY

Standard of care: the reasonable person

Even if the plaintiff can prove that the defendant owed him a duty of care, the plaintiff may only sue for negligence if he can show that the defendant breached that duty of care. The standard of care required in law, generally, is the standard of the **reasonable person**. We do *not* have to act perfectly. In imposing a requirement on the defendant that he should have acted reasonably, the law is judging him by an objective standard. The standard by which the defendant's conduct is assessed is that of a reasonable person in the same situation as the defendant. In *Nettleship* v *Weston* (1971) the court held that a learner driver must show that standard of driving skill of a reasonably competent qualified driver. Although this seems to ignore the fault basis of negligence, unless the test is largely objective, liability in negligence would be hard to establish, to the detriment of the victim.

Factors in determining reasonable care

Factors are applied to the specific facts of the case. The courts are engaged in a balancing exercise to determine whether the risk of harm to others which the defendant's conduct created was justified. The law cannot insist upon absolute safety since most activities entail some degree of risk. Relevant factors are:

❶ **Probability of event happening:** The greater the probability of damage occurring, the more the law expects us to guard against it. A defendant is not negligent if the damage was not a foreseeable consequence of his conduct. In *Bolton* v *Stone* (1951) P, standing in the road, was struck by a cricket ball which had travelled 100 yards. Evidence established that balls had been hit out of the ground on five or six occasions in the preceding 30 years. The House of Lords held that D was not liable because in the circumstances it was reasonable to ignore such a small risk. However, in *Miller* v *Jackson* (1977) the probability of cricket balls being hit over P's garden fence and damaging brickwork and tiles was sufficiently high for the defendant to be in breach of duty.

❷ **Seriousness of risk:** If the defendant knows that the plaintiff has a particular disability, or is particularly sensitive in some area, then the defendant is under a stricter duty of care towards the plaintiff than he would be towards a normal person. The more serious the risk, the greater the precautions that should be taken, for example in *Paris* v *Stepney*

Borough Council (1951) the House of Lords held D liable when P, who had only one good eye, was rendered totally blind because he had not been issued with safety goggles for his job.

❸ Cost and practicability of averting risk: If a large reduction of risk could be obtained by a small expenditure, the defendant has acted unreasonably if he does not take the precautions. If great expense would only produce a very small reduction in risk it will be reasonable to do nothing. In *Latimer* v *AEC Ltd* (1953) the House of Lords decided that shutting D's factory because of the risk of slipping on the floor, due to heavy rain, was not necessary as the slippery patches were clearly visible. Such an onerous precaution would be out of proportion to the risk.

❹ Social utility of the defendant's activity: The social utility of the defendant's activity may justify taking greater risks than would otherwise be the case. In *Daborn* v *Bath Tramways Motor Co. Ltd* (1946) D was held not liable for an accident injuring P when using a left-hand-drive vehicle as an ambulance during wartime when there was a shortage of vehicles.

Professional care

A person who possesses a special skill will not be judged by the standard of the reasonable person, but by the standard of his or her peers. For example, the standard of care owed by doctors and other medical professionals is determined by general practice within the medical profession by those who carry on the same activity. The classic test of negligence in a situation which involves the use of some special skill or competence is found in *Bolam* v *Friern Barnet Hospital Management Committee* (1957) (the so-called '**Bolam** test'): '*The test is the standard of the ordinary skilled man exercising and professing to have that special skill. A man need not possess the highest expert skill at the risk of being found negligent ... it is sufficient if he exercises the ordinary skill of an ordinary competent man exercising that particular art.*'

Proving breach: *res ipsa loquitur*

The burden of proof rests with the plaintiff. Sometimes an accident may occur in circumstances in which accidents do not normally happen unless there has been negligence. In certain circumstances the court will draw an inference of breach of duty against the defendant. In such cases the plaintiff is allowed to plead the doctrine of *res ipsa loquitur* (the facts speak for themselves). The effect of the doctrine is to transfer the burden of proof to the defendant. The court will *presume* that the defendant *has* been negligent *unless* he or she can prove otherwise. An inference of negligence under the doctrine of *res ipsa loquitur* can be rebutted by the defendant. The doctrine of *res ipsa loquitur* is a *rule of evidence* and was applied in *Byrne* v *Boadle* (1863): P was walking past D's warehouse when a barrel of flour rolled out of a door of an upper floor of the warehouse injuring P. Common experience indicates that barrels of flour do not fall from warehouse windows into the street in the absence of negligence. There was no other reasonable explanation for P's injury other than D's negligence.

7.2.4 RESULTING DAMAGE

Factual causation

Before the plaintiff can succeed in an action in negligence, he or she must show that the injuries or damage complained of are a *direct result* of the defendant's act of negligence. The breach of duty must *cause* the damage *factually*. In order to determine this, the so-called '**but for**' test is used. If harm to the plaintiff would not have occurred '*but for*' the defendant's negligence then that negligence is a cause of the harm. The operation of the test can be seen in *Barnett* v *Chelsea and Kensington Hospital Management Committee* (1968). A patient, who had been sent away by a doctor in the casualty department without an examination or treatment, died from arsenic poisoning five hours later. The court held that breach of duty did not cause his death. There was evidence that even if he had been examined, it was too late for any treatment to save him, and therefore it could not be said that *but for* the hospital's negligence, he would not have died. The **chain of causation** must not be broken by an **intervening event** *(novus actus interveniens)*. If the defendant can prove that after his or her act of negligence, a third party negligently intervened causing even greater harm to the plaintiff, then the defendant will not be liable for this extra harm. The defendant will only be liable for such damage as occurred up to the intervening event.

Legal causation (remoteness of damage)

Even where it is obvious that the defendant's conduct 'caused' the harm, it may be said that the damage was too '**remote**' if it is not of the same type as would normally be anticipated in similar circumstances. This may be referred to as causation in *law*. The law cannot take account of everything that follows a wrongful act. The basic test is one of '**reasonable foreseeability**'. The type of damage must be reasonably foreseeable. This was created in the very important case of *The Wagon Mound (No 1)* (1961) where the House of Lords held it was reasonably foreseeable that *some* damage would be caused to the wharf from the spillage of oil by D, but it was unforeseeable that the wharf would be damaged by fire since oil needs to be raised to a high temperature before it will ignite on water.

The test can be harsh. It very much depends on how narrowly the court interprets the type of damage suffered in a particular case. In *Doughty* v *Turner Manufacturing* (1964) P was burnt by chemical eruption when an asbestos lid was negligently knocked into a cauldron of molten metal. The House of Lords conceded that burning by splashing was reasonably foreseeable but the particular chemical reaction was unknown at the time, so although the chemical reaction caused exactly the same kind of damage as the splashing, D was not liable. The House of Lords had asked '*was burning by eruption reasonably foreseeable?*'. However, in *Hughes* v *Lord Advocate* (1963) they had framed the question '*was burning foreseeable?*'. Consequently, P was successful in claiming for burns suffered when he knocked a lamp into an excavation causing a violent explosion. Evidence showed that the explosion was unforeseeable at the time, so, had the court asked '*was burning by explosion foreseeable?*', the result in *Hughes* would have been different.

The thin skull principle

Provided that the plaintiff can prove that his injuries are the direct result of the defendant's negligence, and the initial injury is reasonably foreseeable, he will be entitled to recover damages for the *full extent* of the injury suffered, even if the seriousness of the injury was not reasonably foreseeable. This principle is known as the '**thin skull**' or '**egg shell skull**' principle. The defendant cannot complain that the person he has injured would not have suffered such serious harm if he had been a 'normal' person. In *Smith* v *Leech Brain & Co* (1962) the burn suffered by P was a reasonably foreseeable consequence of D's negligence. Therefore D was liable for the P's death when it activated a malignant cancer.

7.2.5 CATEGORIES OF RESTRICTED LIABILITY

A victim may suffer many different types of loss as a result of a defendant's negligence. Certain types of loss are subject to a restricted duty of care. In particular, the courts have been wary of admitting claims for 'pure' economic loss and psychiatric injury. The courts have sought to impose rules of law which restrict the defendant's liability for such claims. The underlying reasons for this are based on policy considerations. The courts have been influenced by the '*floodgates*' policy. If liability for such loss was based on reasonable foreseeability of financial loss and psychiatric injury, the defendant's liability may be out of all proportion to his or her negligence. A flood of claims arising from the incident would overburden the courts. There would be a spiralling effect on the legal aid budget and insurance premiums. Economic and social policy considerations have led the courts to develop mechanisms to limit potential claims for certain types of loss.

	Primary victims	Secondary victims	Rescuers	Employees
Definition	P suffers psychiatric injury in addition to physical injury or because of fear of physical injury.	P suffers psychiatric injury as a result of fear for the safety of another.	P suffers psychiatric injury as a result of being involved in a rescue operation.	P suffers psychiatric injury whilst acting in the course of a duty.
Policy considerations	There are no policy reasons for restricting D's liability.	Since there could, in theory, be a large number of secondary victims, policy considerations require that such potentially wide liability be restricted.	Competing policy considerations operate. The law is keen to restrict wide liability, but public policy requires that those brave and unselfish enough to attempt rescues should be properly compensated. Rescuers are treated leniently.	There are no policy reasons for restricting D's liability.
Rule of law	If it is reasonably foreseeable that P will suffer some personal injury (physical or psychiatric), D will be liable for P's psychiatric injury (even if P has an 'egg-shell' personality).	Psychiatric injury must be reasonably foreseeable in a person of normal fortitude in P's position; and there must be sufficient proximity between P and D, i.e. P must be at the scene of the accident or come across the immediate aftermath; and have a 'close tie of love and affection' with the primary victim.	If P is of normal fortitude and is sufficiently involved in the rescue, D will be liable for P's psychiatric injury.	If it is reasonably foreseeable that P will suffer some personal injury (physical or psychiatric), D will be liable for P's psychiatric injury. A duty of care exists solely by reason of the master/servant relationship.
Key cases	*Page v Smith* (1995): D negligently caused a minor accident which caused P's myalgic encephalomyelitis to return. D was liable since some personal injury was reasonably foreseeable. *Dulieu v White* (1901): P feared for her safety when D's horses hurtled towards her. It was reasonably foreseeable that P may suffer shock as a result of fear for her personal safety.	*Alcock v Chief Constable of South Yorkshire Police* (1991): P's suffered psychiatric injury following the disaster at Hillsborough football ground, caused by D failing to cut off access to spectator pens from which there was no exit. The proximity test above was formulated, although when applied to the P's, none were successful. *McLoughlin v O'Brian* (1982): P suffered psychiatric injury from seeing her family (injured by D's negligent driving) at hospital, but untreated. D was held liable since coming across the immediate aftermath was equivalent to being at the scene of the accident.	*Chadwick v BRB* (1967): P helped in the aftermath of a rail disaster and suffered psychiatric injury. D was liable, even though P was not related to any victims of the crash. *McFarlane v EE Caledonia Ltd* (1994): P, who had a history of depression, suffered psychiatric shock when he witnessed the Piper Alpha disaster. D was not liable since he was not sufficiently involved in any rescue operation.	*Frost v Chief Constable of South Yorkshire Police* (1996): P, an on-duty police officer, not regarded as a rescuer, suffered psychiatric injury by reason of prolonged exposure to the disaster at Hillsborough. D, his employer, was liable since a duty of care arose from the employer/employee relationship.

Table 7.1 Liability for psychiatric injury

Psychiatric injury

Psychiatric injury is more commonly known as nervous shock. A medically recognised psychiatric illness must have developed as a result of the shock. Such illnesses include anxiety neurosis, clinical depression and post-traumatic stress disorder. This point was clearly stated by Lord Denning in *Hinz v Berry* (1970): '*In English law no damages are awarded for grief or sorrow caused by a person's death. No damages are given for the worry about the children, or for the financial strain or stress, or the difficulties of adjusting to a new life. Damages are, however, recoverable for nervous shock, or to put it in medical terms, for any recognised psychiatric illness caused by the breach of duty by the defendant.*'

Victims suffering psychiatric injury as a result of the defendant's negligence may be usefully classified into four groups (see Table 7.1 opposite). Different rules of law apply to each category of victim.

Negligent statements

Negligent statements causing physical damage: If a negligent statement leads to physical injury or damage to property, this will result in liability. Since this is likely to be rare, there are no policy reasons for restricting liability. In *Clay v A J Crump & Sons Ltd* (1963) D, an architect, negligently advised that a wall on a demolition site was safe. D was liable when the plaintiff was killed by the wall falling on her.

Negligent statements causing economic loss: Negligent statements are obviously more likely to cause pure economic loss than physical damage. Economic loss means financial loss which does not involve injury to the person or damage to property. The courts have been wary of imposing a duty of care in relation to negligent statements. The effects of words spread easily and a statement can be made casually so liability must, for policy reasons, be restricted. For a long time the law imposed no duty to take care when making statements (*Candler v Crane, Christmas & Co* (1951)). However, the House of Lords has now developed general principles of liability for negligent statements causing pure economic loss although it is difficult to state, in the abstract, a specific test for the existence of a duty of care in such cases. The courts seem wary of attempting to identify factors which can apply in all cases. The current approach is to decide each case on its particular facts, in the light of similar cases. This embodies the incremental approach to deciding new duty situations. However, the concept of **special relationship** is paramount. Various criteria for determining whether a special relationship exists between the parties can be derived from the cases, which can be adapted to the particular circumstances of each case. These are:

- D possesses a special skill or knowledge;
- P relies on D's skill and judgement;
- D knows that it is very likely that P will rely on the information, i.e., he knows the type of transaction and that the information will go to P;
- D has voluntarily assumed responsibility towards P;
- reliance by P is reasonable in the circumstances.

These criteria for determining the existence of a *special relationship* were developed in certain key cases. The first case which held that a defendant can owe a duty of care was *Hedley Byrne & Co Ltd v Heller & Partners Ltd* (1964) where P, advertising agents, lost £17,000 when a client went into liquidation. They had offered credit, relying on a reference supplied by D. The House of Lords held that D did owe a duty of care to P (although P lost the case because a disclaimer meant that on the actual facts of the case D was not liable). The House of Lords stated that for a duty of care to exist in relation to statements, there must be a *special relationship of reliance* between the parties. In determining whether reliance is reasonable, a distinction has been made between merely passing on information when it would be less reasonable to rely on it and actually giving advice when it would be more reasonable to rely on it. If advice is given in the course of a business, or in a professional relationship, which the plaintiff relies on, this will usually give rise to a duty of care. As a general rule it will not be reasonable to rely on advice given on a social occasion although *Chaudhry v Prabhaker* (1989) is an exception. However, this case has been heavily criticised and it is arguable that it does not form the basis of any general duty in relation to gratuitous advice but should be viewed as particular to its facts.

In *Caparo Industries plc* v *Dickman* (1990) the House of Lords, holding that it was not reasonable to impose a duty of care since there was no relationship of proximity between the auditors and a member of the public or individual shareholders since this would give rise to unlimited liability on the part of the auditor, restated the requirements for a special relationship. The defendant must know the type of transaction; that the information will go to the plaintiff (directly or indirectly); and it is very likely that the plaintiff will rely on the information. This requirement of actual knowledge rather than mere foresight, clearly limits the situations in which a duty of care will arise.

In *Henderson* v *Merrett Syndicates Ltd* (1994) the House of Lords held that sub-agents acting on behalf of Lloyd's 'names' owed a duty of care to the 'names' because they had assumed such a responsibility, despite the fact that they were not, and had chosen not to be, in a contractual relationship. The relationship, for the purposes of tort, depended on one party having *assumed or undertaken a responsibility* towards the other. Lord Goff said that D had assumed responsibility for P's economic welfare.

Negligent acts causing economic loss

In *Hedley Byrne & Co Ltd* v *Heller & Partners* the House of Lords distinguished between negligent words and negligent acts causing economic loss. It was felt that the tort of negligence was developed to compensate for personal injury or damage to property, so compensation for pure economic loss should be made in contract rather than tort. However, a plaintiff can claim for economic loss arising from a negligent act in limited circumstances. These are:

❶ Where economic loss is consequent upon physical damage: The law has accepted that a person can claim for *economic loss* if they have also suffered physical damage. The distinction between pure economic loss and economic loss consequent upon physical damage is illustrated by *Spartan Steel & Alloys Ltd* v *Martin & Co* (1973). D negligently damaged an electric cable leading to P's factory, cutting off power to the factory. The Court of Appeal held that P could recover for the damage to property and consequential economic loss but the loss of profits on the additional melts was not sufficiently connected with the physical damage and therefore no duty of care was owed by D in respect of it.

This distinction between pure economic loss and economic loss consequential on damage to property or person has caused difficulty. It has been argued that it is an artificial distinction which is not always appropriate in complex cases, for example, in connection with defective buildings. In *Anns* v *London Borough of Merton* (1978) P had not suffered personal injury or damage to other property as a result of his flat having been built on inadequate foundations, and arguably therefore, he was claiming for pure economic loss. However, the court held that since there was physical damage to the building, it was not just pure economic loss. This controversial decision was overruled by the House of Lords in *Murphy* v *Brentwood District Council* (1990) which stated that the loss in *Anns* was purely economic. It was said that where there was a latent defect in a building and this was discovered before any personal injury or damage to other property was caused, then any expense in putting right the defects was pure economic loss. This could not be recovered in the tort of negligence.

❷ Where there is a special relationship between the parties: Claims for *pure economic loss* have been allowed. In *Junior Books* v *Veitchi Ltd* (1984) P claimed for the cost of relaying the floor, negligently laid by D, and the loss of profits from closing while the floor was being relaid. D denied that he owed a duty of care in respect of the pure economic loss. The House of Lords held by a majority decision that D was liable for the full claim, including pure economic loss. The House stressed it was deciding the case strictly on its particular facts. The relationship between the parties was '*almost as close a commercial relationship ... as it is possible to envisage short of privity of contract*' (per Lord Roskill). The *Hedley Byrne* principle of *special relationship* was applied. There was no question of indeterminate liability because it was plainly foreseeable that P was likely to be affected by D's negligence.

Whilst *Junior Books* could have been treated as a springboard for the extension of liability for pure economic loss, instead, in subsequent cases, it was treated as laying down a narrow exception to the general principle. In *Simaan* v *Pilkington* (1988) the Court of Appeal stated that a claim for pure economic loss would only succeed if P could show a special relationship with D, which was such that P relied on D. A special relationship existed in *Ross* v *Caunters* (1980) where P was unable to claim a gift in a will because D, the solicitors, had negligently allowed her to witness the will. The court held that D was liable for the pure economic loss since there was close proximity between D and P, who was a beneficiary. This made it foreseeable that P would suffer loss if D was negligent. Also, the duty owed to P was to an individual not an unlimited group.

The House of Lords have now extended the *Ross* v *Caunters* principle to negligent *omissions* causing pure economic loss. In the controversial case of *White* v *Jones* (1993) the testator's solicitors failed to change his will according to his instructions. The testator died suddenly and his daughters did not receive their planned inheritance. They sued the solicitors for negligence and their claim was allowed by the House of Lords, despite the fact that their loss was purely economic and resulted from a *failure to act*. The decision was based on *Ross* v *Caunters*. The House said that it was foreseeable that the beneficiaries would suffer financial loss; there was a sufficient proximity between D and the beneficiaries; and it was fair, just and reasonable that liability should be imposed on D who was in breach of his professional duty, when there was no effective remedy in contract. It remains to be seen whether the principle that economic loss resulting from a negligent *omission* is recoverable, will be extended to other areas of law. *White* v *Jones* may be interpreted narrowly in future cases, or could be interpreted much more widely to cover all professionals who provide a service, regardless of whether the potential plaintiffs are personally identifiable.

7.3 OCCUPIERS' LIABILITY ACTS 1957 AND 1984: LIABILITY FOR DEFECTIVE PREMISES

7.3.1 INTRODUCTION

Liability of occupiers of premises to persons suffering injury whilst on the premises may be regarded as a further aspect of negligence. The liability of occupiers is divided into liability to *lawful visitors* which is governed by the Occupiers' Liability Act 1957 and liability to *trespassers* which is governed by the Occupiers' Liability Act 1984. Occasionally non-occupiers may be liable to entrants. The Defective Premises Act 1972 creates a statutory form of negligence in respect of landlords, builders and architects.

7.3.2 LIABILITY OF OCCUPIERS TO VISITORS

The key elements of the Occupiers' Liability Act 1957 are summarised in Fig.7.1. It should be noted that an exclusion notice or clause may be used to impose a lesser duty of care or even none at all. The existence of an exclusion notice or clause may be used as a defence *if* it complies with the law. Therefore it is important to examine the rules of law governing the use of such clauses. Different rules apply to private occupiers and business occupiers. The private occupier is more able to exclude/limit liability. The law may be summarised as in Table 7.2.

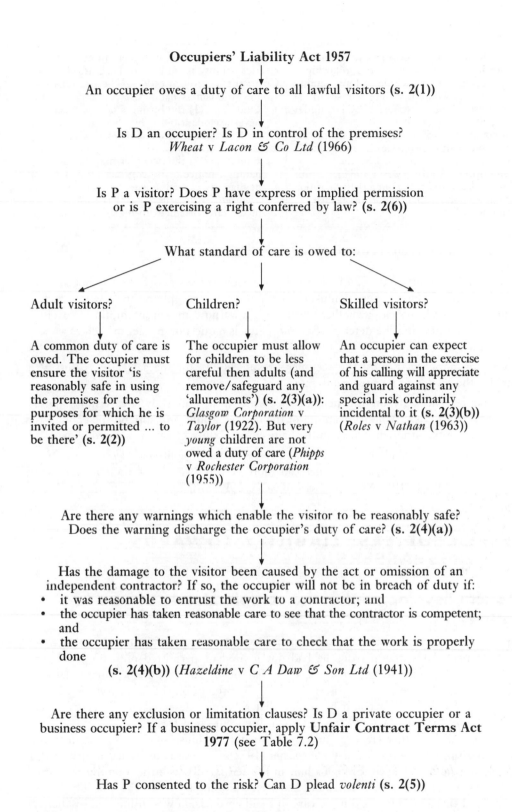

Occupiers' Liability Act 1957

An occupier owes a duty of care to all lawful visitors (s. 2(1))

Is D an occupier? Is D in control of the premises?
Wheat v *Lacon & Co Ltd* (1966)

Is P a visitor? Does P have express or implied permission
or is P exercising a right conferred by law? (s. 2(6))

What standard of care is owed to:

Adult visitors?

A common duty of care is owed. The occupier must ensure the visitor 'is reasonably safe in using the premises for the purposes for which he is invited or permitted ... to be there' (s. 2(2))

Children?

The occupier must allow for children to be less careful then adults (and remove/safeguard any 'allurements') (s. 2(3)(a)): *Glasgow Corporation* v *Taylor* (1922). But very *young* children are not owed a duty of care (*Phipps* v *Rochester Corporation* (1955))

Skilled visitors?

An occupier can expect that a person in the exercise of his calling will appreciate and guard against any special risk ordinarily incidental to it (s. 2(3)(b)) (*Roles* v *Nathan* (1963))

Are there any warnings which enable the visitor to be reasonably safe? Does the warning discharge the occupier's duty of care? (s. 2(4)(a))

Has the damage to the visitor been caused by the act or omission of an independent contractor? If so, the occupier will not be in breach of duty if:
- it was reasonable to entrust the work to a contractor; and
- the occupier has taken reasonable care to see that the contractor is competent; and
- the occupier has taken reasonable care to check that the work is properly done

(s. 2(4)(b)) (*Hazeldine* v *C A Daw & Son Ltd* (1941))

Are there any exclusion or limitation clauses? Is D a private occupier or a business occupier? If a business occupier, apply **Unfair Contract Terms Act 1977** (see Table 7.2)

Has P consented to the risk? Can D plead *volenti* (s. 2(5))

Figure 7.1 Liability of occupiers to visitors

PRIVATE OCCUPIERS	BUSINESS OCCUPIERS
The right of private occupiers to exclude or restrict liability is subject to the following: • he or she cannot exclude or limit liability to persons who enter the premises in exercise of rights conferred by law under s. 2(6); • it could be sensibly argued that the private occupier cannot exclude the minimum standard of care imposed by the **Occupiers' Liability Act 1984** since this would leave trespassers in a better position than visitors, which would be against public policy.	The right of business occupiers to exclude or restrict liability is subject to the **Unfair Contract Terms Act 1977**. The Act only applies to business liability. • Under s. 2(1) the business occupier can never exclude liability, by notice or contract term, for negligently caused *death or personal injury to a visitor*. • Under s. 2(2) the occupier may exclude liability, notice or by contract term, for negligently caused *damage to property or financial loss to a visitor if* it is *reasonable* in the circumstances to do so.

Table 7.2 Power of occupiers to exclude or limit liability

The occupier's liability and use of warnings, exclusion notices and *volenti* is not an easy area of law and is liable to cause confusion, particularly when applying the law to a factual situation. It is not always clear whether D is issuing a warning and/or attempting to exclude liability and/or is raising the defence of *volenti*. This is a question of fact in each case. Key points to note are as follows:

- a warning notice *may* fulfil the occupier's responsibility for the safety of visitors *if* it enables the visitor to be reasonably safe;

- an occupier *may* rely on the defence of *volenti* if he can show the visitor *actively consented* to the risk. A notice warning of the danger would probably not be enough for *volenti* to apply, although it may fulfil the occupier's duty of care (as stated above);

- an occupier *may* exclude or limit his liability by notice or contract *subject to restrictions imposed by law*. The private occupier can more readily exclude or limit liability than business occupiers. Business occupiers must comply with the Unfair Contract Terms Act 1977.

7.3.3 OCCUPIERS' LIABILITY TOWARDS TRESPASSERS

Historical development of the occupiers' duty of care to trespassers

At one time the common law took a very harsh view of the degree of protection an occupier could be expected to offer persons he had not invited or permitted onto his land. The occupier owed no duty to trespassers except that he or she could not intentionally or recklessly inflict damage on a trespasser known to be present on the land (*Robert Addie & Sons* v *Dumbreck* (1929)). It could be argued that a burglar deserved no better treatment but it was more difficult to apply this law to an innocent child trespasser.

The harshness of this law was mitigated when the House of Lords overruled this decision in *British Railways Board* v *Herrington* (1972). The case concerned injury to P, a child aged 6, who had strayed through a hole in D's fence and was burned on the electrified line. D knew of the hole in their fence and had seen children playing on the line. The House of Lords held that D did owe a duty of care to P. Their decision was influenced by the fact that, although P was a trespasser, the known danger and the known presence of children should have prompted D to repair the fence. However, the House of Lords stated, that since the trespasser forces himself into a relationship of proximity with the occupier, a lower standard of care should apply. They stated that the standard of care should be one of '*common humanity*'. This could be interpreted as a duty to take reasonable steps to enable the trespasser to avoid the danger. Such a duty would be owed when '*a reasonable man knowing the physical facts which the occupier actually knew, would appreciate that a trespasser's presence at the point and time of danger was so likely that in all the circumstances it would be inhumane not to give an effective warning of the danger'*. This test was vague and criticised from the outset as difficult to apply. It was also questioned as to whether the duty of care, *if* owed, should be lower.

Following a Law Commission Report in 1976, *British Railways Board* v *Herrington* has now been replaced by the Occupiers' Liability Act 1984 (OLA 1984). The Act is based very much on *Herrington*, and for that reason, it is still a very important case.

The Occupiers' Liability Act 1984

The key elements of the OLA 1984 are summarised in the Fig 7.2. Section 1(3)(a) and (b) are *subjective*: they are concerned with what the occupier knew or should have foreseen. Section 1(3)(c) is *objective*. Whether the risk is one against which the occupier may reasonably be expected to offer some protection will depend upon factors which are more usually taken into account when assessing the standard of care. In *White* v *St Albans City Council* (1990) P was injured when he fell down a 12 foot trench while he was taking a short cut across council land to a car park. Since there was no evidence that the land was used as a short-cut to the car park, the Court of Appeal held that D was not liable. The mere fact of D having taken measures to stop entry onto their land containing some danger did not necessarily mean that the *'reasonable grounds to believe'* element in s. 1(3) had been satisfied.

Section 1(4) is an objective negligence standard. What constitutes reasonable care will vary considerably with the circumstances. The occupier may discharge his or her duty of care by taking reasonable steps to give a warning of the danger concerned, or to discourage persons from incurring the risk. However, warning notices will often be inadequate for children, either because the child cannot read or because he or she is incapable of appreciating the danger. In that event the occupier may have to take additional steps such as erecting an obstacle, particularly if the danger is an allurement. However, a reasonable warning would be more successful with adults, although a 'keep out' sign would probably not be enough to discharge any duty of care. It would merely inform the entrant that he or she is about to become a trespasser. The Act does not state whether liability under the Act can be excluded or limited by notice or contract. This is contrary to the Law Commission's recommendations, and such an omission suggests that liability cannot be excluded. Indeed, it could be argued that the OLA 1984 creates a minimum obligation and, therefore, the occupier should not be permitted to exclude it.

7.3.4 LIABILITY OF NON-OCCUPIERS TO ENTRANTS

There are three broad categories of non-occupiers who may be liable to an entrant. These are independent contractors, landlords and builders/architects:

❶ Under the principles of common law negligence, a contractor owes a duty to take reasonable care to avoid harm to persons he or she could reasonably expect to be affected by his or her work.

❷ The Defective Premises Act 1972 states that a landlord is generally not the occupier, unless he or she has retained control of the common parts of the building. The Act goes on to create a statutory form of negligence. The landlord owes a duty of care by virtue of his or her obligation or right to repair premises (s. 4). For the duty to be breached, the landlord must know or ought reasonably know of the defect. The duty is owed in respect of both personal injury and damage to property.

❸ Section 1 Defective Premises Act 1972 creates a statutory duty to build dwellings properly: *'a person taking on work for or in connection with the provision of a dwelling owes a duty to see that the work is done in a workmanlike or professional manner, and with proper materials, so that as regards that work the dwelling will be fit for habitation when completed'*. The duty is, therefore, owed by builders, architects, engineers, surveyors and subcontractors and exists in connection with construction, conversion and enlargement. The duty is owed to persons who order the work and every person who subsequently acquires an interest in the dwelling. Under the rules of common law a builder can be liable in negligence. However, defects in the actual building are now regarded as pure economic loss which is not recoverable (*Murphy* v *Brentwood District Council* (1990)). Similarly, an architect could be liable in negligence, but not for defects in the actual building (pure economic loss). If the design is regarded as a statement rather than an act, and the plaintiff could prove a special relationship existed between himself and the architect, he may be able to sue under the principles of *Hedley Byrne & Co Ltd* v *Heller & Partners* (1964). However, it is unusual for a special relationship to exist between architects and those living in a defective dwelling.

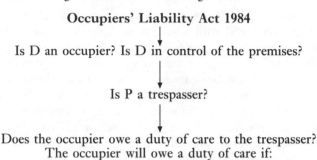

Occupiers' Liability Act 1984

Is D an occupier? Is D in control of the premises?

Is P a trespasser?

Does the occupier owe a duty of care to the trespasser?
The occupier will owe a duty of care if:

- he is aware of the danger or has reasonable grounds to believe that it exists;
- he knows or has reasonable grounds to believe that the trespasser is in the vicinity of the danger concerned or that the trespasser may come into the vicinity of the danger; and
- the risk is one against which, in all the circumstances of the case he may reasonably be expected to offer protection.

(s. 1(3) OLA 1984; *White* v *St Albans City Council* (1990); *Herrington* v *BRB* (1972))

Is the occupier in breach of his duty of care?

Has the occupier taken such care as is reasonable in all the circumstances of the case to see that the trespasser does not suffer injury on the premises by reason of the danger concerned? Essentially this is a matter of fact in the particular case. Relevant circumstances will include:

- gravity and likelihood of the probable injury;
- foreseeability of entrant;
- nature of trespass (e.g. with malice, carelessness, for a criminal purpose etc);
- age of trespasser
- nature of the premises and danger on the premises;
- extent of the risk;
- cost of precautions;
- presence of allurements.

(s. 1(4) OLA 1984)

Are there any warnings that enable the trespasser to be reasonably safe?
(s. 1(5) OLA 1984)

Has the trespasser consented to the risk?
(s. 1(6) OLA 1984)

Figure 7.2 Liability of occupiers to trespassers

7.4.1 INTRODUCTION

There are two torts of nuisance: private nuisance and public nuisance. Although the two actions are different, sometimes the same facts result in liability in both. Private nuisance is unreasonable interference with the plaintiff's use and enjoyment of land. Public nuisance is a crime which protects certain public rights. Its place in the law of tort depends upon the fact that the plaintiff can prove that he or she has suffered special damage from the defendant's commission of the common law crime of public nuisance. Nuisance is a 'semi' strict liability tort. The defendant will be liable regardless of whether the creation of the nuisance involved negligence. However, the damage suffered by the plaintiff as a result of the nuisance must be reasonably foreseeable (*The Wagon Mound (No 2)* (1967); *Cambridge Water Co* v *Eastern Counties Leather plc* (1994)) (see Unit 7.5).

7.4.2 PRIVATE NUISANCE

Private nuisance is the unlawful indirect interference with a person's use and enjoyment of his or her land.

Indirect interference

An indirect interference is essentially the type of interference where no direct physical force is used. Direct interference, such as entering another's land, will be trespass. The interference may be caused by a variety of different types of invasion, for example, vibrations, flooding, electricity, fire, smell, noise, dust, sewage, invading tree roots and even falling earth. Obstruction of a view is not recognised as an indirect interference. Similarly, in *Hunter* v *Canary Wharf Ltd and Docklands Development Corporation* (1995) residents who sued for the interference caused to their television reception by the presence of D's building were unsuccessful. The Court of Appeal held that this was similar to obstruction of a person's view.

Damage

The interference must have caused damage. This may be actual damage to land or property or interference with use and enjoyment of such land not accompanied by any actual damage (intangible damage), or a combination of both. Usually a plaintiff is claiming interference with use and enjoyment of his land. In such cases, this is a matter of degree. The interference must be sufficiently serious. The courts must balance the conflicting interests of the defendant's use and the effect on the plaintiff. However, an occupier is entitled to expect protection from physical damage. In *St Helens Smelting Co* v *Tipping* (1865) D's copper smelting works damaged P's trees. The court differentiated between physical damage and intangible damage. They are not engaged in a balancing exercise where damage to land is complained of, suggesting that almost any amount of physical damage will be actionable in nuisance.

Unlawful interference

This essentially means the interference must be unreasonable and without lawful authority. In balancing the conflicting interests, the courts will take into account all the circumstances of the case. Although it is a question of fact and degree in each case, the court will take into account certain factors:

❶ Locality: In *Sturges* v *Bridgman* (1879) Thesiger LJ stated '*what would be a nuisance in Belgrave Square would not necessarily be so in Bermondsey*'. Essentially this means that people living in an industrial area are expected to tolerate a higher level of noise, vibrations and smells than people living in rural areas. If the interference substantially exceeds the prevailing standards of the locality, there may be liability in nuisance. In

Halsey v *Esso Petroleum* (1961) P successfully sued in nuisance for the noise, vibrations and acid smuts caused by D's boiler, despite the locality being predominantly industrial

2 **Time:** The time of day is especially important when considering noise interference. What is an acceptable level of noise at midday may be totally unacceptable at 2 am when people are trying to sleep.

3 **Sensitivity of the plaintiff:** If the plaintiff or his property are abnormally sensitive, he cannot complain about interference which affects him. In *Robinson* v *Kilvert* (1889) D was not liable for the damage to P's sensitive brown paper caused by heat from his boiler, since the heat was not excessive and would not have affected persons or property generally. However, if the defendant's activity would have interfered with an ordinary use of land in any event, he will be liable, notwithstanding the delicate nature of the plaintiff's operations (*McKinnon Industries* v *Walker* (1951)).

4 **Malice on the part of the defendant:** Where the defendant's conduct is motivated by malice this may convert acts which would not otherwise amount to a nuisance into an actionable nuisance. In *Christie* v *Davey* (1893) D, who was annoyed by P's music lessons, retaliated by banging on the party wall, beating trays and shouting. North J granted an injunction against D, indicating that he would have taken a different view of the case if D's acts had been 'innocent'.

5 **Duration:** The existence of a nuisance is usually associated with a 'continuing' state of affairs rather than a single act of the defendant, although in *British Celanese Ltd* v *A.H. Hunt Ltd* (1969) it was held that an isolated happening by itself can create an actionable nuisance. Duration must be measured against the gravity of the interference.

6 **Any public benefit derived from the defendant's use:** Generally the courts have looked with disfavour on an argument based on the public interest. There is no reason why the public in general should be entitled to draw benefit from an activity which damages one or more private persons (unless Parliament expressly provides for it). However, in *Miller* v *Jackson* (1977) the Court of Appeal refused to grant an injunction to prevent D from playing cricket even though it affected P's use and enjoyment of his land because it felt that the usefulness of the club outweighed P's interest.

Who can sue and who is liable?

Who can sue?	Who is liable?
Plaintiffs have to have an interest in the land affected by the private nuisance in order to sue. In *Malone* v *Laskey* (1907) P was held not to have a claim in private nuisance because she had no interest in the land. This was confirmed by the House of Lords in *Hunter* v *Canary Wharf Ltd and London Docklands Development Corporation* (1996) which overruled the Court of Appeal's ruling in *Khorasandijan* v *Bush* (1994).	• The *creator* of the nuisance by some act (rather than an omission) can be sued regardless of any interest in the land. • *Occupiers* are liable for nuisance caused by themselves and their employees. If the nuisance was created by someone other than the occupier or his employee, then it must be proved that the defendant knew of the situation and its possible consequences. The occupier may even be liable for nuisance created by trespassers or previous occupiers, where the occupier is or should be aware of the presence of the nuisance on the premises (*Sedleigh-Denfield* v *O'Callaghan* (1940)). • *Owners* who lease land to tenants are not usually liable for nuisances created by tenants. However, if the nuisance already existed before the letting, or the landowner authorised the nuisance, he will be liable (*Tetley* v *Chitty* (1986)).

Table 7.3

Specific defences

1 Prescription: The continuation of a private nuisance for 20 years will, in theory, entitle the defendant to claim a prescriptive right to commit the nuisance, but, in practice, this plea has rarely succeeded. The defendant must prove that the interference amounted to an actionable nuisance throughout the 20-year period rather than proving that he has carried on the activity for 20 years (*Sturges* v *Bridgman* (1879)).

2 Statutory authority: If a statute authorises the defendant's activity, the defendant will not be liable for interferences that are an inevitable result of the activity, i.e. could not have been avoided by the exercise of reasonable care. This was a successful defence in *Allen* v *Gulf Oil Refining* (1981) where the alleged nuisance was an inevitable consequence of the operation of the oil refinery which had been authorised by statute.

Remedies

There are three possible remedies available to to the victim of a nuisance:

1 Damages: An award of damages in the case of physical damage to property is calculated on the same basis as other torts. It is more difficult to calculate damages to compensate for personal discomfort and inconvenience. Nor is it always an appropriate remedy.

2 Injunction: An injunction aims to make the defendant stop the activity which is causing the nuisance completely or at certain times. Since it is an equitable remedy, it is discretionary. However, in practice, where the nuisance is continuing, the plaintiff is usually granted an injunction.

3 Abatement: This remedy, a type of self-help, allows the plaintiff to take steps to end the nuisance. If this requires the plaintiff to enter the defendant's land, notice must be given, otherwise the plaintiff will be become a trespasser.

7.4.3 PUBLIC NUISANCE

Public nuisance was defined by Romer LJ in *Attorney-General* v *PYA Quarries Ltd* (1957) as '*any nuisance which materially affects the reasonable comfort and convenience of life of a class of Her Majesty's subject ...*'. Historically, the crime of public nuisance covered four broad categories: public decency, public health, convenience and public safety. The first two are now largely regulated by statute. The latter two are mainly concerned with nuisance on the highway. There are two key elements in the tort of public nuisance.

A class of Her Majesty's subjects

An action in the tort of public nuisance only arises if the nuisance is such as to affect a section of the public, and not just one person. Whether the number of people affected amounts to a class of people is a question of fact. If the defendant's nuisance affects a number of people, he may have committed the crime of public nuisance. The Attorney-General has the power to prosecute.

Special damage

In order to succeed in the tort of public nuisance, the plaintiff must prove special damage arising from the nuisance. The plaintiff must show he has suffered greater damage than that suffered by the public in general. This is because the infringement of public rights could lead to extensive damage and numerous claims, which it might be unreasonable to expect the defendant to meet. The requirement of special damage acts as a control factor. Examples of special damage include:

* personal injury (*Castle* v *St Augustine's Links Ltd* (1922));
* physical damage to property (*Halsey* v *Esso Petroleum Co Ltd* (1961));
* economic loss (*Tate & Lyle Industries Ltd* v *GLC* (1983).

7.4.4 THE DISTINCTION BETWEEN PRIVATE AND PUBLIC NUISANCE

Although the same conduct can amount to both a private and public nuisance, as was the case in *Halsey* v *Esso Petroleum Co Ltd*, the two actions have different foundations. The key differences are:

Private Nuisance	Public Nuisance
Protects a person's use and enjoyment of land	Protects public rights. It is not necessarily connected with an interference with the use of land
Tort only	Primarily a crime. A plaintiff must suffer 'particular damage' over and above the damage sustained by the public generally before he can bring an action in tort
May only affect one person	Must affect a number of people
Plaintiff probably cannot recover for personal injury	Plaintiff can recover for personal injury
Defendant may be able to rely on the defence of prescription	Prescription does not apply because no one can acquire the right to commit a crime

Table 7.4

7.5 THE RULE IN *RYLANDS* v *FLETCHER*

7.5.1 *RYLANDS* v *FLETCHER*

This tort derives from the decision in the case of *Rylands* v *Fletcher* (1868) where D, a millowner, employed independent contractors to build a reservoir on his land for the purpose of supplying water to his mill. In the course of making excavations upon D's land, the contractors came upon some disused mine-shafts which, unknown to them, connected with mines underneath adjoining land. P had taken a lease of this land in order to work the mines. The contractors negligently failed to seal up these shafts and when the reservoir was filled with water, the mines were flooded. The House of Lords held D to be personally liable. Blackburn J gave judgment in the High Court and this contains the celebrated statement of the law: '*We think that the true rule of law is, that the person who for his own purposes brings on his lands and collects and keeps there anything likely to do mischief if it escapes, must keep it in at his peril, and, if he does not do so, is prima facie answerable for all the damage which is the natural consequence of its escape.*'

In the House of Lords, a qualification was made upon this statement of the rule byBlackburn J by Lord Cairns. The '*defendant was only liable if he brought the thing on his land in the course of non-natural use of the land*'. This qualification has been accepted by later cases as an essential part of the rule.

7.5.2 THE ELEMENTS

The defendant must bring and collect the thing on his land for his own purpose/use

The defendant need not *own* the land on to which he has brought the thing. Generally the *occupier* will be liable. Neither does the requirement that the things must be brought on the land for the purposes of the defendant mean that it must benefit the defendant.

Where the thing is naturally present on land, the defendant cannot be liable for its escape under *Rylands* v *Fletcher*. The escape of such things as weeds, vermin, rocks and flood water is thus normally outside the rule. In *Giles* v *Walker* (1890) D was not liable for thistle seeds which were blown in large quantities from D's land onto the P's land since '*thistles were a natural growth of the soil*'.

The defendant must be using the land for a non-natural purpose

Non-natural use was further clarified in *Rickards* v *Lothian* (1913) as '*... some special use bringing with it increased danger to others and must not merely be the ordinary use or such a use as is proper for the general benefit of the community*'. Most domestic or agricultural uses are natural uses. Whether industrial use is non-natural is debatable. In *Read* v *Lyons* (1947), the House of Lords hinted that a munitions factory would be regarded as a natural use. However, in the more recent case of *Cambridge Water Co* v *Eastern Counties Leather plc* (1994) Lord Goff held that storage of substantial quantities of chemicals on industrial premises should be regarded as non-natural use.

The defendant knows or ought reasonably to have foreseen that the thing is likely to cause damage of the relevant kind if it escapes

Until recently it was not thought necessary that the defendant occupier should be able to foresee the type of damage that could be caused by the thing if it were to escape, in order to be liable. However, the case of *Cambridge Water Co* v *Eastern Counties Leather plc* (1994) seems to have added this requirement. D (ECL), an old established leather manufacturer, stored and made use of a chemical solvent (PCE) in its tanning process. This solvent was regularly spilled in the process and over the years it had seeped down though the factory floor into the soil below until it reached an impermeable strata from where it percolated through the aquifer to P's borehole some 1.3 miles away. The time taken for this seepage from tannery to borehole was about nine months. Because of EC regulations, P could not use the water from the contaminated borehole, and as a result, a new borehole was dug at a cost of over £1 million. P brought actions in negligence, private nuisance and *Rylands* v *Fletcher*.

It was held that for liability to exist in negligence, private nuisance and *Rylands* v *Fletcher*, the damage must be reasonably foreseeable. The only foreseeable damage from a spillage of PCE was that somebody might be overcome by fumes from a substantial spillage on the surface of the ground (which had not happened). Therefore P was unsuccessful in all three actions.

The thing does escape from the defendant's land

This requirement was emphasised in the important case of *Read* v *Lyons* (1946) where P was unsuccessful in her action under *Rylands* v *Fletcher* because the personal injury she suffered as a result of an exploding shell in D's munitions factory was caused on D's premises. The explosives had not escaped.

Damage is caused to the plaintiff

The first question arising here is who can sue. There remains doubt as to whether the plaintiff must have an interest in the land affected by escape. In *Weller* v *Foot & Mouth Disease Research Institute* (1966) P was held to have no action under *Rylands* v *Fletcher*, when the escape of a virus caused P, cattle auctioneers, to close their auction and suffer economic loss. However, in *Charing Cross Electricity Supply Co* v *Hydraulic Power Co* (1914), P was successful in recovering damages under *Rylands* v *Fletcher* even though they had no proprietary interest.

Neither is it clear whether the plaintiff can claim for personal injury. In *Hale* v *Jennings Brothers* (1938) P, a stallholder at a fair, suffered personal injuries when she was struck by D's chair-o-plane which had 'escaped'. It was held that she had a good claim under *Rylands* v *Fletcher*. The issue is more problematic in the case of personal injuries sustained by a non-occupier. In *Read* v *Lyons*, Lord MacMillan stated *obiter* '*the rule derives from a conception of mutual duties of neighbouring landowners and is therefore inapplicable to personal injuries*'. However, in *Perry* v *Kendricks Transport Ltd* (1956) in which a 10-year-old boy was injured when the petrol tank of a disused bus exploded, Parker LJ did not think it was open to the Court of Appeal '*to hold that the rule applies only to damage to adjoining land or to a proprietary interest in land and not to personal injury*'. This was in spite of the *dicta* in *Read* v *Lyons*.

Specific defences

There are a number of specific defences available to a defendant (general defences are discussed more fully in Unit 7.9). These may be identified as:

- **Act of a stranger and act of God**: D is not liable where the damage is caused by the act of a third party acting independently or the escape is caused purely by natural forces in circumstances which D could not have been expected to foresee or guard against (*Nichols* v *Marsland* (1876)). However, it could be argued that the defence of act of God has been subsumed by the requirement of foreseeability.

- **Statutory authority**: terms of a statute may authorise collection of dangerous things on D's property.

7.5.3 THE DISTINCTION BETWEEN THE RULE IN *RYLANDS* v *FLETCHER* AND OTHER TORTS

Nuisance	Negligence
Rylands v *Fletcher* is confined to the escape of physical objects whereas nuisance covers damage done by intangibles such as noise and smells.	Negligence requires D to be at fault. D must not have exercised reasonable care. Under *Rylands* v *Fletcher* the degree of care taken by D to avoid escape is irrelevant, since liability is strict.
Rylands v *Fletcher* protects against isolated escapes from land whereas, generally, private nuisance requires more frequent interference.	Negligence clearly does not relate to any proprietary interest in land, whereas *Rylands* v *Fletcher* is derived from mutual duties of neighbouring landowners. It remains unclear as to whether it depends on ownership or other proprietary interest in land.
Nuisance does not require land to be used for a non-natural use and accumulation and escape are not necessary.	Negligence does not require land to be used for a non-natural use and escape is not necessary.

Table 7.5

7.5.4 REFORM

The rule in *Rylands* v *Flecther* is often described as a redundant tort. It could be argued that Blackburn J, in his original judgment, was merely extending the tort of private nuisance. With a wide interpretation it could have been a mechanism for the imposition of strict liability on extra-hazardous activities. Subsequent interpretation of *Rylands* v *Fletcher* narrowed the rule. It did not develop into a general principle of liability for 'ultra-hazardous activities' such as that which exists in US law. For many years there were few cases under *Rylands* v *Fletcher*. Two reports (neither acted upon) recommended reform:

- Royal Commission on Civil Liability and Compensation for Personal Injury (Pearson Commission) (1978) recommended that it should be abolished and replaced with legislation empowering a minister to list, through issuing regulations, all dangerous activities incurring strict liability and providing for compensation for personal injuries caused by the listed activities.

- The Law Commission proposed in a report (Civil Liability for Dangerous Things and Activities, 1970) the concept of 'special danger' which would cover activities constituting an above-average risk of accidents or a risk of more than ordinary damage if accidents in fact occurred.

Some argue that the recent case of *Cambridge Water Co* v *Eastern Counties Leather plc* revives the rule in *Rylands* v *Fletcher* and broadens the meaning of non-natural use to include industrial activities. However, Lord Goff stated that it was inappropriate for the courts to develop the common law in respect of strict liability for the purposes of protecting the environment. He felt that this was the role of Parliament. Future uses and the importance of the rule in *Rylands* v *Fletcher* remains to be seen.

7.6 TRESPASS TO THE PERSON; TRESPASS TO LAND

7.6.1 INTRODUCTION

An action for trespass descends from the ancient writ of trespass, which was available for unlawful interference with the person, with goods or with the possession of land. The writ of trespass shared three important factors. First, they were (and still are) *actionable per se*, i.e., *without proof of damage;* secondly, trespass has to be a *direct result* of the defendant's act; and thirdly, the defendant must act *intentionally*. There are three torts of trespass: trespass to the person; trespass to land and; trespass to goods. A Level syllabuses require knowledge of the first *two* only.

There is a great deal of overlap between civil law and criminal law in this area. Most cases of assault and battery are also criminal offences. The Criminal Injuries Compensation Scheme and the power of criminal courts to grant compensation orders against defendants often remove the need for a civil action. In general, trespass to land is not a crime. However, statutes such as the *Criminal Law Act* 1977 and the *Criminal Justice and Public Order Act* 1994 have created certain limited circumstances when trespass will be a criminal offence as well as a tort.

7.6.2 TRESPASS TO THE PERSON

There are three forms of trespass to the person: false imprisonment, assault and battery. All of them aim to protect an individual's person and liberty.

False imprisonment

False imprisonment was also defined in *Collins* v *Wilcock* (1984) as '*the unlawful imposition of constraint on another's freedom of movement from a particular place*'.

➊ **Imprisonment:** The plaintiff must be completely deprived of his personal liberty for any length of time, no matter how short. Imprisonment in the sense of incarceration is not necessary. An unlawful arrest constitutes false imprisonment. False imprisonment could be achieved by words alone, for example, by pointing a gun and saying 'do not move'. If the plaintiff could leave, although not by the route he would prefer, there is no imprisonment. In *Bird* v *Jones* (1845) P could have gone back the way he had come so there was no false imprisonment because it was not a total restraint of his liberty. So, if there is a means of escape, then provided it is reasonable to expect the plaintiff to have taken it, there will be no false imprisonment. Any escape involving danger is probably unreasonable.

➋ **Knowledge of the detention is not necessary:** In *Meering* v *Grahame-White Aviation Co Ltd* (1920) Atkin LJ said that the plaintiff's lack of knowledge was irrelevant so a person could be falsely imprisoned while he was unconscious or insane or otherwise unaware of his position. In this case P was questioned at his employer's office about stealing paint. Unbeknown to him, two police officers remained outside the door during the questioning. D was held liable for false imprisonment even though P believed he was quite free to leave if he wanted to. The Court of Appeal held that P could not be said to be a free agent and knowledge of the detention was irrelevant to whether the tort had been committed. A person who is unaware that he has been falsely imprisoned and has suffered no harm will normally receive only nominal damages, but because of the importance attached to individual liberty the detention will be actionable.

Assault and battery

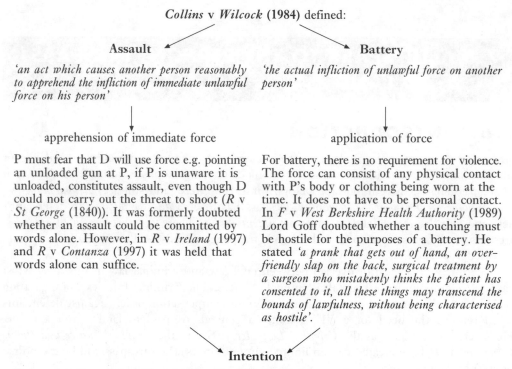

Collins v *Wilcock* (1984) defined:

Assault

'an act which causes another person reasonably to apprehend the infliction of immediate unlawful force on his person'

apprehension of immediate force

P must fear that D will use force e.g. pointing an unloaded gun at P, if P is unaware it is unloaded, constitutes assault, even though D could not carry out the threat to shoot (*R* v *St George* (1840)). It was formerly doubted whether an assault could be committed by words alone. However, in *R* v *Ireland* (1997) and *R* v *Contanza* (1997) it was held that words alone can suffice.

Battery

'the actual infliction of unlawful force on another person'

application of force

For battery, there is no requirement for violence. The force can consist of any physical contact with P's body or clothing being worn at the time. It does not have to be personal contact. In *F* v *West Berkshire Health Authority* (1989) Lord Goff doubted whether a touching must be hostile for the purposes of a battery. He stated '*a prank that gets out of hand, an over-friendly slap on the back, surgical treatment by a surgeon who mistakenly thinks the patient has consented to it, all these things may transcend the bounds of lawfulness, without being characterised as hostile*'.

Intention

For assault D must intend to frighten P, although D does not have to intend to actually use the violence. For battery D must have intended to commit the act that constitutes the trespass, but an intention to injure is not necessary (*Wilson* v *Pringle* (1986)).

Direct harm?

In *Wilkinson* v *Downton* (1897) P suffered nervous shock when D told her (untruthfully) that her husband had been seriously injured. The court held D liable for trespass, because he had wilfully done an act calculated to cause physical harm to P and had thereby caused physical harm even though it was not 'direct'. The rule in *Wilkinson* v *Downton* could be regarded as a category of trespass to the person or a possible interpretation is that trespass covers intentional conduct (direct or indirect) and the tort of negligence covers unintentional conduct. Authority for this view is found in *Letang* v *Cooper* (1965).

Figure 7.3

Defences

Defences which are particularly relevant to trespass to person are *volenti*, self-defence, and lawful authority which includes lawful arrest and parental authority.

❶ *Volenti non fit injuria* (**consent**): The normal rules on the defence of *volenti* apply (see Unit 7.9). There are many instances where conduct that would otherwise constitute trespass to the person is not actionable because of express or implied consent. Examples of consent include physical contacts that are reasonably necessary and an ordinary consequence of everyday life. Participants in a sport impliedly consent to contacts that occur within the rules of the game where physical contact is part and parcel of the game. A patient who agrees to a medical examination or operation by a doctor or dentist consents to trespass to person. Where a surgeon operates on an adult patient who needs emergency treatment but is unable to consent because he or she is unconscious, the defence of necessity may be relied upon.

② **Self-defence**: A person may use reasonable force to defend himself from attack or unlawful arrest. The force must be the minimum necessary and reasonable in the circumstances. The general principle in determining reasonableness, is that the degree of force must be balanced against the seriousness of the attack. The reasonableness requirement does not require a person to wait for the other to give the first blow, since it then might be too late.

③ **Lawful authority**: Lawful arrest is not false imprisonment, and in so far as the person carrying out the arrest is entitled to use reasonable force it will not be a battery either (see Unit 8.2). A sentence of imprisonment passed by a court also provides a complete defence to an action for false imprisonment. Parents may administer reasonable chastisement to their children and restrain their freedom of movement, but parental authority must be exercised for the welfare of the child (*Children and Young Persons Act 1933*).

7.6.3 TRESPASS TO LAND

Trespass to land consists of an unauthorised interference with a person's possession of land. It is one of the oldest actions known to the common law.

Interference

Interference must be direct and physical. Indirect interference is covered by nuisance. The usual type of trespass is entry by the defendant on to the plaintiff's land, but it can take other forms, such as placing objects on the land or even placing objects in contact with the property, such as planting a vine so that it grows up the plaintiff's wall, or leaning a bike against a shop window. A person who has permission to enter land but abuses the permission or right by acting outside the purpose for which it was granted, or remains on the land after it has expired, may commit trespass. A defendant who enters land by authority of law (as opposed to the plaintiff's authority) and abuses that authority becomes a *trespasser ab initio*. He is treated as a trespasser from the time he entered, no matter how innocent his conduct up to the time of abuse (*the Six Carpenters' Case* (1610)). Although this has been criticised, it has subsequently been applied to mini-cab drivers touting for business (*Cinnamond* v *British Airports Authority* (1980)). It provides some protection for the individual against abuses by public officials, such as the police.

Possession of land

The plaintiff need not own the land. The plaintiff must be in possession of the land. Land includes not only the soil itself, but things under it, any building that is fixed to the surface, and such airspace above as is needed for the normal use. In *Kelson* v *Imperial Tobacco Co Ltd* (1957) D was required by mandatory injunction to remove an advertising sign which projected eight inches above P's property. However, in *Bernstein* v *Skyviews & General Ltd* (1978) it was not trespass to fly an aircraft many hundreds of feet above the property, since this did not interfere with '*the ordinary use and enjoyment of the plaintiff's land and the structures on it*'.

Intention

Trespass to land is regarded as an intentional tort in the sense only that the defendant must voluntarily enter the plaintiff's land. Deliberate entry onto the plaintiff's land is sufficient. It is irrelevant that the defendant did not know that he was entering the plaintiff's land, or believed the entry was authorised, or even honestly and reasonably believed the land was his.

Remedies

The tort of trespass to land allows some specific remedies. A person who has been dispossessed may bring an *action for the recovery of land*, formerly known as **ejectment**. This is particularly relevant in relation to squatters, and a special summary procedure has been devised to assist the plaintiff. An action for *mesne profits*, unlike ejectment, allows the plaintiff to claim damages for his loss during the period that he has been dispossessed, for example, where a tenant stays on the land at the end of the lease, the plaintiff may claim for a reasonable rent for the use of the property. A person who has been wrongfully dispossessed may undertake a form of *self-help* known as **re-entry**. The plaintiff must use reasonable force to effect the eviction or expel the trespasser, provided he has first asked him to leave. In *Collins* v *Renison* (1754) the defendant found a trespasser up a ladder on his land. He claimed '*he gently shook the ladder and gently overturned it and gently threw the plaintiff from it upon the ground*'. The amount of force was found to be unreasonable.

7.7 DEFAMATION

7.7.1 INTRODUCTION

Defamation protects a person's reputation. It is a peculiar tort. It is one of the few civil actions that are still (generally) tried with juries. Though a county court *can* be given jurisdiction, generally an action will be brought in the High Court, and legal aid is not available. The Faulks Committee suggested that the purpose of the law of defamation is to preserve a balance between the individual's right to protect his reputation and the general right of free speech. It is arguable whether the balance is being achieved. In *Tolstoy Miloslavsky* v *UK* (1995) the European Court of Human Rights declared that libel damages of £1.5 million awarded against the defendant amounted to a violation of his right to freedom of expression under Article 10 of the European Convention on Human Rights.

Defamation can be either libel or slander. The key differences between these are summarised in Table 7.6:

Libel	Slander
Defamatory material in permanent form	Defamatory material in transitory form
Actionable *per se* (without proof of damage)	Actionable only on proof of damage, except for four categories which are imputation: • of an imprisonable crime; • of a contagious disease; • of unchastity or adultery; • designed to disparage P in any office, business, trade carried on by him
Libel may be a crime	Slander is only a tort

Table 7.6

Apart from these differences, the requirements are the same. The plaintiff must prove that the defendant published a defamatory statement which refers to him or her. Once this has been established the defendant may be able to prove a defence.

7.7.2 THE ELEMENTS

Defamatory statement

A statement is defamatory if it lowers the plaintiff's reputation in the minds of right-minded people (*Sim* v *Stretch* (1936)). Vulgar abuse or insults spoken in the heat of an argument are not defamatory since insults do not reflect on a person's reputation (*Parkins* v *Scott* (1862)). The test is objective. It is the function of the jury to decide whether words are defamatory, but the judge must first determine whether the words are capable of bearing a defamatory meaning in their natural or ordinary meaning or whether they are capable of bearing the innuendo that the plaintiff alleges. In *Liberace* v *Daily Mirror* (1959) D described P as '*this winking, mincing, sniggering, snuggling, ice-covered, fruit flavoured heap of mother love*' causing the audience to abuse him. This was held to have lowered his reputation. Statements which appear to be innocent may be defamatory innuendo if, given some special knowledge, the statement bears a different meaning. For example, in *Cosmos* v *BBC* (1976) the BBC showed a film of a Cosmos holiday camp whilst playing the music from 'Return to Colditz' This was held to be defamatory, the innuendo being that Cosmos Holiday camps were no better than prisoner of war camps. Similarly, in *Tolley* v *Fry* (1931) the House of Lords held that an advertisement, a cartoon depicting P, an amateur golfer, with D's chocolate in his pocket, was defamatory, since it implied that P had abused his amateur status. Words must be interpreted in their context. In *Charleston* v *News Groups Newspapers Ltd* (1995) D published photographs in which the heads of the plaintiffs, actors in '*Neighbours*' were superimposed on to two near-naked bodies engaged in sexual acts. However, the article did make it clear that the photographs had been reproduced from a computer game. The House of Lords dismissed their claim holding that the pictures could not be taken in isolation from the text.

Reference to the plaintiff

The defamatory statement must refer to the plaintiff, but the reference need not be express. The test is whether the ordinary sensible reader would understand the words as referring to the plaintiff. As a general rule, defamation of a class is not actionable, so a statement that '*all lawyers are thieves*' is not actionable by any particular lawyer (*Eastwood* v *Holmes* (1858)). However, if the reference is to a limited class or group, the words can be taken to refer to every member and they will all be able to sue (*Knupffer* v *London Express Newspapers Ltd* (1944)).

Publication

The defamatory statement must have been communicated to some person *other* than the plaintiff or the defendant's spouse. The tort protects the plaintiff's reputation in the eyes of others, not his personal feelings. A person will be liable for any publication which he or she intends or can reasonably anticipate, for example, leaving documents where they may be read or speaking so loudly that others are likely to overhear. Letters addressed to a particular person are presumed to be published to the addressee. In *Huth* v *Huth* (1915), a letter was sent in an unsealed envelope by D to P. The butler secretly read the letter without permission. This was not treated as publication, as D could not have anticipated the butler's behaviour. However, in some cases the sender should anticipate that it may be read by someone else, such as a secretary (although the sender can protect himself by marking the envelope 'private').

Where defamatory matter is contained in a book or a newspaper there will be a series of publications, for example, by the author to the publisher, by the author and publisher jointly to the printer, by the author, publisher and printer jointly to the distributor, and so on. Each repetition, if intended or authorised, may be a fresh publication creating a new cause of action. The common law drew a distinction between those who *produced* the libel (author, publisher and printer) and those who merely *disseminated* it. The Defamation Act 1996 modernises the common law principle. Section 1(1) states that a person who innocently disseminates matter in the ordinary course of business will not be held to have published the matter unless he or she has actual knowledge or reasonable foreseeability of a 'defamatory statement' contained in the matter. Section 1(1) applies to printers, distributors, sellers, broadcasters of live programmes, and the operators of a communications system by means of which a defamatory statement is communicated, for example, the Internet. It does not apply to the author, editor or publisher.

7.7.3 DEFENCES

Justification or truth	Fair comment	Absolute privilege	Qualified privilege	Unintentional defamation and innocent dissemination
• Defamation does not protect an individual's reputation damaged by *true* statements. It does not protect privacy. It is, therefore, a complete defence for D to prove that the defamatory statement is true, even where D was motivated by malice. • It is not necessary to prove the literal truth of a statement if the material facts are proved to be true in substance (*Alexander v North Eastern Railway Co* (1965)). • Where D repeats a defamatory statement made to him, he must prove that the statement was true. A person who circulates an unfounded rumour is as responsible as the person who started it. • In practice, justification is rarely pleaded, because if it fails, damages may be higher than they would otherwise have been, to mark the fact that D has persisted in the untruth.	• The defence of fair comment protects honest expressions of opinion on matters of public interest. It is an important element of freedom of speech and the courts are careful to preserve its broad scope. For the defence to apply it must be: • a comment on a matter of public interest. Whether a matter is of public interest is a question to be determined by the judge; • it must be a statement of opinion based on facts which are true. Section 6, Defamation Act 1952 states that not all the facts need to be proved to be true, only those facts on which the comment is based. • The comment must be 'fair'. Once D's comment is 'honest'. In this context, 'honest'. Once D's comment is considered fair by an objective test, it is presumed to be the honest expression of his view. • Comments motivated by malice will be unfair. As a general rule, if D does not believe the statement to be true he acts maliciously.	• D is protected on privileged occasions no matter how dishonest or malicious his motives. The defence is justified on the basis that the public interest in the statement being made outweighs any injury to P. Absolute privilege is confined to four broad categories: • Parliamentary proceedings, i.e. statements made during parliamentary proceedings (but not statements made by MPs outside Parliament) and anything published under the authority of Parliament, including statements in official Parliamentary papers, such as *Hansard*; • judicial proceedings, i.e. statements made in the course of judicial proceedings, any professional communications between solicitor and client in relation to judicial proceedings, and fair, accurate and contemporaneous reporting on radio, television and in newspapers of judicial proceedings; • official communications, i.e. any statement made by one officer of state to another, in the course of the officer's duty, although it is not clear how widely this privilege extends — possibly not to officials below the rank of Minister; any statement made by one spouse to another.	• Qualified privilege offers a defence for the same reason as absolute privilege. It does not provide absolute immunity. It is for the judge to determine whether the occasion was privileged. Qualified privilege can be considered under three heads: • statements in pursuance of a duty, i.e. statements made by someone who has a legal or moral duty to pass on the information and the person to whom the statement is made has a legal duty to receive it, e.g. giving a reference about an employee to a prospective employer or supplying information to the police in response to their questions about a criminal; • protection of an interest, i.e. statements made by D for the protection of a lawful interest, such as his own interest, a common interest or the public interest (*Adams v Wards* (1917)); • privileged reports: this includes fair and accurate reports of Parliamentary proceedings and judicial proceedings (not limited to contemporaneous or newspaper reports). The Defamation Act 1996 now contains a full list of reports subject to qualified privilege. Proof that D was motivated by malice defeats the defence (*Egger v Viscount Chelmsford* (1964)).	• The Defamation Act 1996 makes the defence of 'innocent' publication available to any person publishing material which he did not know referred to P, or did not know was false and defamatory of P. D must be willing to 'make amends', which, in addition to correction and apology, involves a payment of compensation. If no agreement is reached the level of compensation will be set by the court in the absence of a jury. Innocent dissemination was discussed under publication.

Table 7.7

7.7.4 PROCEDURE

Defamation is tried before judge and jury. Damages are awarded by the jury. The Defamation Act 1996 which mainly changes the conduct of defamation cases rather than making wholesale reform of the substantive law, introduces the summary disposal procedure. This enables the court *alone* (i.e., without a jury) to dispose summarily of those cases that are inordinately weak, and to provide *'summary relief'* in those cases that are inordinately strong. The rationale for this reform is to allow for swift correction and moderate compensation. Summary disposal reduces the role of the jury in defamation actions. However, awards made using this procedure can not exceed £10,000, so the practical impact of the procedure remains to be seen. The Defamation Act 1996 also reduces from three years to one year the time within which all defamation actions have to begin.

7.7.5 REMEDIES

Damages

Damages may simply compensate for the plaintiff's loss, or may be exemplary, designed to punish the publisher. In mitigation of damages the court may consider whether the defendant apologised as quickly as possible and whether the plaintiff already had a bad reputation. The role of the jury in assessing damages has attracted much criticism. Juries sometimes make awards of damages which far exceed the sums that would be awarded in cases of very serious personal injury. The Court of Appeal now has the power, where the damages awarded by the jury are excessive or inadequate, to determine the level of an award of damages (s. 8 Courts and Legal Services Act 1990). In *Rantzen* v *Mirror Group Newspapers* (1993) P's damages were reduced from £250,000 to £110,000. Similarly, in *Sutcliffe* v *Pressdram Ltd* (1990), the Court of Appeal, reducing P's damages from £600,000 to £60,000, commented that juries do not always distinguish between grave allegations and trivial comments. In *John* v *Mirror Group Newspapers* (1996) P was initially awarded £350,000 for claims that he was hooked on a bizarre diet and had an eating disorder. This was slashed to £75,000. The Court of Appeal stated that judges should refer the jury to what they consider to be an appropriate award. Juries should be directed to make comparisons with damages awarded for personal injury actions, the purpose being to provide a general check on the reasonableness of the proposed award.

Injunction

Damages may not always be an appropriate remedy since they cannot 'buy back a reputation'. Occasionally, an interim injunction may be granted, preventing allegedly defamatory material from being published. In order to obtain this, the plaintiff must act quickly and prove that publication will amount to immediate and irreparable injury.

7.8   PRODUCT LIABILITY

7.8.1 THE CONSUMER PROTECTION ACT 1987

A person injured, or whose property is damaged, by a defective product, may have both contractual and tortious rights. If the person injured was the *purchaser* of the product, he may be able to sue the retailer in the law of contract. However, privity of contract is essential. A consumer of *dangerously defective* goods who is *not* the purchaser must pursue a tort-based remedy. The *ultimate consumer* of the product may be able to sue the manufacturer in the tort of negligence. In addition to these rights, the injured person may have a right of action under the **Consumer Protection Act 1987** (CPA 1987). Part I of the 1987 Act seeks to implement the European Community Directive on Product Liability

(85/374/EEC). This Act imposes strict liability on producers of goods which prove to be defective and which cause damage to persons, or in some cases property. To date there have been no reported court decisions involving the Act. Little *apparent* use is being made of the Act. The National Consumer Council, in its Report (*Unsafe Products,* November 1995) suggests this may be due to delays in the legal process, ignorance of the availability of the provisions, or perhaps, it may be that producers are settling cases, by providing compensation, without consumers resorting to court action or even legal advice.

Some benefits of the implementation of the CPA 1987 can be identified as:

* it simplifies the plaintiff's task in establishing liability;
* fault no longer has to be proved to recover for dangerously defective goods;
* there are often several potential defendants to sue.

However, difficulties still exist:

* the allegation that a product is defective may be strongly contested with lengthy debate over the level of safety persons are entitled to expect;
* the plaintiff must prove that the damage is attributable to the defect and, when dealing with complex products, there can be great difficulty in proving causation;
* claims less than £275 are not allowed, leaving the consumer who has suffered less to rely on the tort of negligence;
* in cases of new products with unexpected defects, the availability of the development risks defence raises the whole issue of fault and may result in the new strict liability tort action being must less of a revolutionary development than expected;
* claims for pure economic loss are not allowed.

7.8.2 LIABILITY FOR DEFECTIVE PRODUCTS

	Contract	Tort	CPA 1987
Who is liable?	Seller	Manufacturer	Producer, own brander, importer into European Community
Who can claim?	Buyer only	Consumer	Consumer
Basis of liability?	Strict (no defences)	Fault	Strict (but subject to defences, including 'development risks' defence)
What must the plaintiff prove?	The product is not of satisfactory quality or is unfit for its purpose (Sale of Goods Act 1979, as amended)	The manufacturer has not exercised reasonable care and that the type of damage caused is reasonably foreseeable	There is a defect in the product which has caused damage
What damage is actionable?	Death, personal injury, damage to property including the defective product itself	Death, personal injury, damage to property but not including the defective property itself	Death, personal injury, damage to personal property exceeding £275 but not including the defective property itself
Exclusion and limitation of liability?	Prohibited if buyer deals as a consumer; prohibited if death or personal injury result from negligence, otherwise possible if 'reasonable' (UCTA 1977)	Prohibited if death or personal injury result, otherwise possible if 'reasonable' (UCTA 1977)	Prohibited in all cases

Table 7.8

7.9   GENERAL DEFENCES

7.9.1 INTRODUCTION

A plaintiff may succeed in proving the requirements of a particular tort but may still lose where the defendant can rely on a particular defence. As a general rule, the burden of proof in establishing a defence rests with the defendant. There are two types of defence in tort actions; those which apply only to a specific tort, and those which apply to a range of torts, known as general defences. Specific defences are discussed with the relevant tort.

7.9.2 CONTRIBUTORY NEGLIGENCE

This defence operates when the harm suffered by the plaintiff is partly attributable to the fault of the defendant and partly to the fault of the plaintiff. The plaintiff must contribute to his damage, not the tort. In such circumstances, apportionment of loss is allowed, and damages will be reduced reflecting the plaintiff's degree of fault for his injuries. This is provided for by s. 1(1) Law Reform (Contributory Negligence) Act 1945 which states: '*Where any person suffers damage as the result partly of his own fault and partly of the fault of any other person or persons ... the damages recoverable in respect thereof shall be reduced to such extent as the court thinks just and equitable having regard to the claimant's share in the responsibility for the damage.*'

The defence of contributory negligence clearly extends to actions in negligence. However, it is not restricted to this tort. It may be used as a defence to a claim in nuisance and *Rylands* v *Fletcher* and breach by occupiers of their statutory duties in relation to their land. It is not available in actions concerning trespass to the person or deceit.

Standard of care

A plaintiff must exercise reasonable care. Essentially, this is the same standard of care as that applied to defendants. The test is *objective*. Therefore, the failure to wear a seat belt in a motor vehicle will be regarded as unreasonable and therefore negligent, even though the plaintiff sincerely believes that he would be safer not to wear the belt because of the risk of becoming trapped in an accident (*Froom* v *Butcher* (1976)). When deciding what is reasonable care, allowance is made for children. The court will consider what may reasonably be expected of a child of the plaintiff's age. This is not an entirely subjective test, since the child plaintiff will be judged against a *reasonable child of his or her age*. In *Gough* v *Thorne* (1966) Lord Denning said: '*a judge should only find a child guilty of contributory negligence if he or she is of such an age as reasonably to be expected to take precautions for his or her own safety.*'

Reduction of damages

Where contributory negligence is proved by the defendant, the plaintiff's damages will be reduced. The 1945 Act leaves the exact calculations to the discretion of the court. They tend to treat it as a question of fact, although where a particular type of accident is common, they have developed guidelines for the appropriate deduction in order to produce consistency and certainty. In *Froom* v *Butcher* it was decided that where a plaintiff causes his own injuries by failing to wear a seatbelt, his damages should be reduced by 25%. If the injuries would have been the same even with the use of a belt there should be no reduction.

7.9.3 *VOLENTI NON FIT INJURIA*

Volenti non fit injuria literally means 'no injury can be done to a willing person'. The requirements for the defence are that the plaintiff *voluntarily agreed* to absolve the defendant from the legal consequences of his conduct, and the plaintiff had *full knowledge of both the nature and extent of the risk*. If satisfied, *volenti* is a total defence.

Agreement (express or implied)

The plaintiff must agree to waive legal rights that may arise from harm that is being risked. This is an *objective* test. Knowledge alone may be evidence of acceptance, but it is not conclusive proof. It is a question of fact whether consent has been given in each case. Agreement may be *express* (for example, where a person consents to an operation), or *implied* from the parties' conduct. For example, in *Morris* v *Murray* (1990), P was a passenger in a light aircraft piloted by D which crashed shortly after take-off, killing D and injuring P. Both P and D had been drinking heavily. P was held to have consented to the risk. There was implied agreement since D's drunkenness was so extreme and obvious that to participate in the flight was to engage in an intrinsically and obviously dangerous occupation. Such implied agreement depends on there being some sort of relationship between the parties. In deciding whether there is implied agreement, the courts are effectively making a policy decision about the types of conduct that should defeat a claim. A defendant may try to show the plaintiff agreed to the risk by including it in a contractual term or notice. This is now inextricably bound up with rules on exclusion and limitation of liability. It must comply with the Unfair Contract Terms Act 1977. For example, the plaintiff can not agree to waive any rights in relation to death or personal injury caused by the defendant's negligence (s. 2(1)). A notice or contractual term which purports to exclude liability for negligently causing damage to property or financial loss must be reasonable in the circumstances (s. 2(2)).

Knowledge of nature and extent of risk

Knowledge of the risk in itself is not sufficient. In order to establish the defence of *volenti*, the defendant must show that the plaintiff had full knowledge of the *nature* and *extent* of the risk. This is a subjective test. This was discussed in *Morris* v *Murray* (1990). In this particular case, the court concluded that the plaintiff was capable of appreciating the risk. Where a plaintiff does not appreciate the risk, but ought to, judged by the standard of the reasonable person, *volenti* will not be a defence. However, this could be relevant to contributory negligence.

Voluntariness

The plaintiff's agreement must be voluntary, meaning that he must have a genuine choice. Consent obtained by wrongful threats allows no defence. An employee who continues to work, knowing of a particular danger caused by poor safety precautions, is not deemed to be voluntarily consenting to that risk since employees cannot afford to give up a job, even though they are aware of a danger. It could be argued that rescuers voluntarily take a risk in order to rescue someone else. However, the defence of *volenti* will not usually apply. A rescuer is deemed to be acting instinctively and not exercising real freedom of choice. The rescuer must act reasonably and foreseeably. In *Haynes* v *Harwood* (1935) P, a police constable, tried to stop D's runaway horses from trampling on a woman and her children and was injured in the process. The Court of Appeal rejected the defence of *volenti*. A person who negligently caused danger to the life or safety of others was liable to a person who, acting reasonably, comes to the rescue. However, in *Cutler* v *United Dairies Ltd* (1933) it was held to be unreasonable to go to the assistance of a cart driver whose horse had bolted into a field and was endangering nobody. The principle that a rescuer acting foreseeably and reasonably does not consent to his injuries is based on public policy. This principle has been extended to professional rescuers. In *Ogwo* v *Taylor* (1987), the House of Lords held that a person who negligently started a fire was liable for any injury sustained by a fireman, even though a fireman undertook to bear the ordinary risks of his job.

7.9.4 ILLEGALITY

A person who is injured whilst in the act of committing a criminal offence may be barred from claiming in tort by the defence of illegality. This is usually expressed in the Latin maxim *ex turpi causa non oritur actio* (an action cannot be founded on a base cause), or more generally 'bad people get less'. The problem is to determine *when* the plaintiff's criminal conduct will defeat his claim, since the mere fact that the plaintiff's behaviour is wrongful will not be sufficient. The fact that the plaintiff's conduct is illegal does not place an automatic bar on his compensation claim. *Ex turpi causa* is based on judicial policy. Therefore there is an element of judicial discretion involved in each case. The court will take into account the 'public conscience' test, expressed by Kerr LJ in *Euro-Diam Ltd* v *Bathurst* (1988) as: '*The ex turpi causa defence ... applies if, in all the circumstances, it would be an affront to the public conscience to grant the relief which he seeks because the courts would thereby appear to assist or encourage the plaintiff in his illegal conduct or to encourage others in similar acts.*'

Exercise of judicial discretion can be seen in *Ashton* v *Turner* (1981) where P and D had participated in a burglary. P was injured by D's negligent driving of the getaway car. His action in negligence failed. The court stated that this was a case in which the law should not find a duty of care, since that duty would arise from the commission of a crime. However, in *Revill* v *Newbury* (1996), a case which attracted a great deal of media attention, D, a 76-year old man, was sleeping in his allotment shed and, on hearing P attempting to break in, poked his shotgun through a small hole in the door and fired, injuring P. The Court of Appeal held D could not rely on illegality as a defence since he had *used force out of all proportion to the plaintiff's conduct*. However, P's damages were reduced by two thirds for contributory negligence. Clearly for the defence to have any chance of success, the defendant's conduct must be in proportion to the occasion.

7.9.5 NECESSITY

This defence may justify an intentional interference with persons or property where it is necessary in order to prevent greater damage to the public, a third party or the defendant. This defence is sometimes referred to as the 'choice between two evils'. Since this defence sanctions the commission of a tort, policy reasons have led the court to be cautious in allowing it. In *Southwark London Borough Council* v *Williams* (1971), homeless squatters who occupied a vacant council house were denied the defence. A defendant raising this defence must have acted reasonably. In *Cope* v *Sharpe* (1912) D was held not liable for trespass when he entered P's land in order to prevent the spread of fire to his employer's land. He had acted reasonably, even though it transpired that the fire would not have damaged his employer's property.

When the defence is raised, the court has to make a value judgment as to whose interests are to be preferred. As a general principle, a defendant who damages property in order to protect the life or limb of another, will be able to use this defence. A surgeon who performs a life-saving operation without consent on an unconscious patient will probably be able to successfully rely on this defence. However, it would not be a defence in relation to a competent and conscious patient who refuses the same operation. In *Malette* v *Shulman* (1990) a doctor was held liable for battery in performing a possibly life-saving blood transfusion on an unconscious patient who was a Jehovah's witness carrying a card specifically refusing blood transfusions.

7.9.6 MISTAKE OF FACT

A mistake of law by the defendant is never a defence in law. A mistake of fact will not usually be a defence in any tort based on reasonableness, since the defendant's conduct is judged against that of a *reasonable* person, not the *honest but unreasonable* person, unless, of course, it is felt that the reasonable person could have made the same mistake. Where, however, the defendant's motive is a condition of liability, mistake may negative liability. So a person is not liable in deceit if he honestly believed in the truth of his statement.

7.10 STRICT AND VICARIOUS LIABILITY

7.10.1 STRICT LIABILITY TORTS

Most torts in English law require the tortfeasor to be at fault. **Strict liability** is a form of liability that does not depend upon proof of fault. An individual may be liable even though he has exercised all reasonable care in the circumstances. Strict liability is not a precise term. It can range from *absolute* liability where no defences are available, to torts where, although the plaintiff need not prove any fault, the defendant may plead specific defences. Generally, the courts do not favour no–fault liability. However, several strict liability torts have evolved:

Rylands v *Fletcher* and nuisance

The actual escape element of the rule in *Rylands* v *Fletcher* requires no fault on the part of the occupier. The courts are not interested in examining whether the occupier is to blame in any way. Similarly, nuisance (both public and private), requires no fault on the part of the occupier in relation to the indirect interference. However, in both torts, the occupier is only liable for damage which is reasonably foreseeable. There are also a number of specific defences available in each action, which also incorporate a fault requirement. Consequently, it can be concluded that the rule in *Rylands* v *Fletcher* and public and private nuisance can be classified as 'semi' strict liability torts. (See also Units 7.4 and 7.5.)

Product liability

Enactment of the Consumer Protection Act 1987 has created strict liability for producers of dangerously defective goods. However, the inclusion of certain defences, in particular the 'development risks' defence, does introduce a degree of fault resulting in a strict liability tort rather than absolute liability (see Unit 7.8).

7.10.2 VICARIOUS LIABILITY

Vicarious liability, which some class as a type of strict liability, is where one person is liable for the torts of another, irrespective of fault. Most usually, it is where the *employer* is responsible for damage caused by the torts of his *employees*. The employer is liable *in addition* to the employee who remains legally responsible for his tort. Vicarious liability makes employer and employee joint tortfeasors. Each are fully liable to the plaintiff. Hence an employer who is sued on the basis of vicarious liability is entitled to sue the employee in turn, and recover some or all of the damages paid for the employee's tort. This is called an **indemnity**. The employer's right to sue may derive either from the provisions of the Civil Liability (Contribution) Act 1978 or in common law. The essential requirements for an employer to be vicariously liable can be identified.

A tort committed by an employee

Obviously, a plaintiff must first establish that a tort has been committed by an employee, e.g., negligence. Employers are only liable for the torts of *employees*. They are not liable for torts committed by *independent contractors*. The distinction between employees and independent contractors is of vital importance. An employee is under a contract *of* service, whereas an independent contractor has a contract *for* services. In order to determine the relationship, the courts take into consideration a number of factors. These are:

❶ **Degree of control**. A traditional test of the employment relationship is the ability of the employer to control the work. An employee works under the supervision and direction of the employer who orders not only what is to be done but how it should be done.

② **Is the worker in business on his own account?** This is a test which has grown in popularity with the courts. Workers will be viewed as in business on their own account if, for example, they provide their own equipment, take financial risks (such as doing work on credit), hire helpers, have managerial and investment responsibilities, charge varying amounts for different jobs, send out invoices for their work, and have quite a few clients.

③ **Intention of the parties**. Any expression of intention of the parties as to the nature of their relationship is a relevant factor but again it is not conclusive. The test is an *objective* test. In *Ferguson* v *Dawson* (1976) a building labourer was held to be an employee for the purposes of health and safety law irrespective of a specific contractual term stating that he was self-employed.

A useful case which illustrates some of these factors and indicates how difficult the distinction can be in practice is *Ready Mixed Concrete (South East) Ltd* v *Minister of Pensions and National Insurance* (1968). In this case the company organised a scheme for the delivery of concrete through 'owner–drivers' who were paid a fixed mileage rate. The court held that the provisions of the contract were more consistent with a contract for service rather than a contract of service. In particular, the chance of profit and the risk of loss were the 'owner-driver's'. The ownership of the vehicle was the driver's and he had to make the vehicle available throughout the contract period, at his own expense. These factors were inconsistent with an employer-employee relationship.

Who was acting in the course of employment

In order for the employer to be vicariously liable, the tort must be committed in the course of the employee's employment. The employer must be '*engaged in his master's business, not on a frolic of his own*' (*Joel* v *Morison* (1834)). Whether an employee is acting in the course of his employment is a question of fact. The court will have regard to *what the employee is engaged to do*. There is no single test for deciding this. Often the result depends upon how widely the courts are prepared to define the precise *scope* of the employee's work. It is essential to understand this when examining the cases. If the employee is performing an authorised act, then usually he will be held to be acting in the course of his employment, ✓ even if he is performing that act in an improper manner. For example, in *Century Insurance* v *Northern Ireland Road Transport Board* (1942), a driver of a petrol lorry was held to be acting in the course of his employment even though he was smoking when delivering petrol to P's garage (causing an explosion and fire). He was performing an *authorised act in an unauthorised manner*.

If the employee is radically departing from what he is authorised to do, then he will be held to be '*on a frolic of his own*' and the employer will not be vicariously liable. For example, in *Beard* v *London General Omnibus Co* (1900) a bus conductor, who in the driver's absence, decided to turn the bus around for its return journey, causing damage, was held not to be acting in the course of his employment. Conductors were not employed to drive buses.

An act may be within the course of employment, even though it has been *expressly forbidden* by the employer, if the employee is performing an authorised act. Even though this seems unfair, if an express prohibition were always effective it would be easy for employers to avoid vicarious liability. In *Limpus* v *London General Omnibus Co* (1862) employees of D had express instructions not to 'race with, or obstruct other omnibuses of rival companies'. An employee disobeyed this instruction, causing a collision. The driver was acting in the course of his employment since he was employed '*to drive and promote his employer's business*' and what he was doing was merely *an authorised act in an unauthorised manner*.

The issue of prohibitions by the employer has given rise to particular difficulty where the employee has *given unauthorised lifts* in the employer's vehicle. Is the employer liable to the passenger for injuries caused by the driver's negligence? There are two apparently conflicting cases. In *Twine* v *Bean's Express Ltd* (1946) the Court of Appeal held that the employer was not vicariously liable when his employee gave a lift to a hitch-hiker contrary to express instructions, and negligently injured him. The giving of a lift constituted '*an act of a class which (the driver) was not employed to perform at all'*. However, in *Rose* v *Plenty* (1976) a milkman, who employed a boy aged 13 years to assist him on his milk round contrary to the employers' express instructions not to allow children to assist or to allow passengers (and negligently injured him), was held to be acting in the course of employment, perhaps because the engagement of P was meant to further the employer's business.

7.10.3 JUSTIFICATION

Strict and vicarious liability run against the fundamental idea of *'no liability without fault'* which is supposedly the very basis of tortious liability (see Unit 9). It might seem unjust to hold a person liable even though he is not at fault. However, once we appreciate the idea that strict and vicarious liability are founded upon notions quite distinct from that of fault, it is possible to explain and justify their existence in various ways. Arguments include:

1 **Loss distribution**. Loss is distributed more evenly when strict and vicarious liability operate. The cost of insurance against such liability is reflected in higher prices and consumers pay for the risks created by the business rather than innocent victims. Compensation through insurance payments is made to the injured person, not by one individual but by a sizeable section of the community. Losses are distributed amongst the community.

2 **Compensatory function of the law of tort**. A fundamental aim of the law of tort is to provide compensation to injured persons. The imposition of strict and vicarious liability is more likely to achieve this aim than fault liability.

3 **Accident prevention/hazardous activities**. Strict liability is often (but not always) imposed in relation to particularly hazardous activities. Those who engage in such activities should bear the burden of the greater risk of damage. Imposing strict liability in relation to hazardous activities may encourage a greater degree of care being exercised when carrying out those activities. Similarly, vicarious liability encourages accident prevention by giving an employer a financial interest in encouraging his employees to take care for the safety of others.

4 **Moral fairness**. An argument often used to justify the doctrine of *vicarious* liability is that the employer makes a profit from the activities of his employees, therefore, he should bear any losses that those activities cause.

Illustrative questions

1 In January 1994 George went to the Accident and Emergency department of the Hartsville Hospital complaining of a severe headache. Dr Brown, a junior doctor spoke to George but did not examine him. He told George to go home as there was nothing wrong. George went home but his pain got worse and he suffered a stroke later that day so that an ambulance was called to take him back to the hospital. On the journey, through no fault of the driver, the ambulance skidded and collided with a brick wall. George, who had not been strapped into the ambulance by the attendant, was thrown out of the rear doors on to the ground.

On arrival at the hospital, it was discovered that George had also fractured his spine when he fell from the ambulance. He has now left hospital but is brain-damaged and partially paralysed. It is not known whether the brain damage which was caused by the stroke, or the injury to his back, has caused the paralysis but George wishes to claim damages for the paralysis.

Advise George in relation to the possible liability of Dr Brown and the ambulance attendant.

(50)

(UODLE)

Tutorial note

This problem question requires you to demonstrate your knowledge of the tort of negligence. The key issues raised by the facts are the standard of care required of professionals and the requirements of causation and the concept of remoteness of damage. When tackling this sort of problem question, it is essential that you plan your answer carefully. Start by identifying the injuries suffered by George, and consider who he should sue for each. This is a difficult question to structure.

Suggested answer

You should start by providing a definition of negligence and identifying the three elements emerging from *Donoghue* v *Stevenson*, stating that this important case provided a general formulation of liability in negligence. Before tackling the paralysis and brain-damage, you are advised to examine the liability of Dr Brown and the ambulance attendant for his other injuries. It is appropriate to examine the liability of Dr Brown for George's stroke first. It is well-established in English law that doctors owe patients a duty of care. A key issue here is whether Dr Brown has breached his duty of care. In law a person who possesses a special skill will not be judged by the standard of the reasonable person, but by a professional standard, and you should explain and apply the '*Bolam* test'. Although Dr Brown is a junior doctor, it was held in *Wilsher* v *Essex AHA* that even junior doctors must exercise the care of a competent doctor. It is likely that Dr Brown's failure to conduct a medical examination of George is a breach of duty. However, George must prove that Dr Brown's breach caused the stroke factually. The 'but for' test must be applied. Applying the decision in *Barnett* v *Chelsea and Kensington Hospital Management Committee*, Dr Brown's liability for George's stroke would depend on whether a medical examination and treatment would have prevented the stroke. George must also show that his damage is not too remote from Dr Brown's breach. George's stroke must be a reasonably foreseeable consequence of his breach (*The Wagon Mound*). If these can be proved, it is very likely that Dr Brown will be liable for George's stroke.

The next thing to consider is the ambulance attendant's liability for George's fractured spine. Clearly the ambulance attendant owed George a duty of care. Whether he had breached this duty in failing to strap George into the ambulance would depend on whether it was common practice to do so (apply *Bolam* test once more). Assuming It Is, the ambulance attendant will be liable for George's fractured spine.

Ultimately, George has suffered brain damage and partial paralysis. However, it is not known whether this is due to the stroke or the back injury. The problem is determining *who* George should sue. This calls into question the factual chain of causation once more. George would not be able to prove that the stroke or the fractured spine caused the paralysis and brain damage (*Loveday* v *Renton*). He would also have difficulty in proving legal causation against either. Indeed the chain of causation between Dr Brown and George's paralysis has probably been broken. The accident in the ambulance, together with the failure of the ambulance attendant would be a *novus actus interveniens*, suggesting the ambulance attendant would be liable. However, are paralysis and brain damage a reasonably foreseeable consequence of failing to strap him in to the ambulance?

Finally, you should conclude on the respective liability of Dr Brown and the ambulance attendant for George's injuries.

2 Peter owned a large area of land which had formerly been surrounded by open country but which now, to his considerable annoyance, was bordered on two sides by a newly built housing estate. His great hobby was maintaining his collection of traction engines, which he moved closer to some of the houses. He worked on the engines and drove them about at all kinds of odd hours. The engines were noisy and created fumes and oily smuts.

Additionally, he built a brick store for fuels and cleaning chemicals. Though generally aware of the need to keep the materials apart and to prevent them from becoming damp, he was unaware of recent research work which showed that, in very damp conditions, some of these materials could combine explosively though separated by substantial distances.

In fact, his building skills were not as highly developed as he had supposed. The brick store became very damp and an explosion took place. In consequence, nearby houses were showered with dangerous chemicals and fumes, the area was closed off for three days and the local shop's takings were reduced by 50% for that week and Richard, a homeless man who had been in the habit of sleeping rough in Peter's field near to the brick store, was badly burned.

(a) Ignoring any possibility of an action in negligence, discuss the rights of the owners of the neighbouring houses in connection with any disturbance and damage suffered as a result of Peter's activities.　　　　　　　　　　　　　　　(10)

(b) Consider what rights in the tort of negligence, if any, may be available to the house owners and to the owner of the local shop.　　　　　　　　　(15)

(c) Discuss the possible liability of Peter for the injuries suffered by Richard.　(10)

[*Please note, parts (d) and (e) have been omitted.*]

(AEB)

Tutorial note

This is a structured question and it is essential that you divide your answer in the manner required by the examiner. Always read the questions carefully. Part (a) requires you to consider the liability of Peter broadly, and raises three possible torts. It is common to see students only identify and write about one possibility, and therefore lose marks. In Part (b), given the mark allocation, you should recognise that rather more is required than a simple outline of the three elements of negligence. It is important to differentiate between the physical damage suffered by the house owners and loss of profits suffered by the shop owner. In Part (c), the question does not provide sufficient information for a decision to be reached on whether Richard is a visitor or a trespasser. In this situation, you must consider both possibilities.

Suggested answer

Part (a)

The neighbours may be able to prove that the noise, and possibly fumes and oily smuts, generated by the traction engines interferes with their use and enjoyment of their land, and, therefore is a private nuisance. You should define private nuisance and apply the elements. Noise, oily smuts and fumes are an indirect interference. Noise and fumes are intangible damage, and this raises the issue of reasonable user, although the oily smuts would be considered to be physical damage, and would not be subject to this requirement (*St Helens Smelting Co* v *Tipping*). It is a question of fact and degree as to whether Peter's use of land is unlawful (i.e., unreasonable). The court would consider the changing locality (*Halsey* v *Esso Petroleum*) and Peter's possible malice (*Christie* v *Davey*). The fact that the owners had moved to the nuisance would not be a barrier to an action in private nuisance. Since Peter's activities affect a class of people, there is the possibility that he is committing the crime of public nuisance (*Attorney-General* v *PYA Quarries Ltd*). However, in order to succeed in the tort of public nuisance, one neighbour would have to prove special damage, and there is no suggestion in the facts that one neighbour is suffering more than the others.

The explosion and consequent dangerous effects suggest that Peter may be strictly liable in the tort in *Rylands* v *Fletcher*. You should define this tort and apply the elements. The neighbours would have to prove that the damage was foreseeable (*Cambridge Water* v *ECL*). However, we are told that recent research has shown that the explosion was reasonably foreseeable, so this element can probably be satisfied. There is a possibility that the neighbours would be able to sue in private nuisance for the explosion, since an isolated incident such as an explosion can be a private nuisance if it arises out of a continuing situation (*British Celanese Ltd* v *A H Hunt Ltd*).

In view of the different incidents, the remedies available to the neighbours include both damages and an injunction. Each should be briefly explained and applied, ensuring you explain the discretionary nature of the equitable remedy of injunction.

Part (b)

In relation to the house owners, you should provide a general explanation and application of the elements of the tort of negligence. It is fairly clear that Peter owes a duty of care to each of the house owners. When considering whether he has breached his duty of care, it is important to consider the standard of care he owes. The key issue here is what level of skill he is required to display and the degree of knowledge he is required to possess. If he is treated as a professional, he will be judged against similar professionals (*Bolam* test), and would be expected to have knowledge of the recent research on the explosive qualities of the materials he stored and used.

When considering the liability of Peter to the shopowner, you should speculate on whether this is pure economic loss or loss consequential on damage to property. If the shop was physically damaged, the owner would have a better chance of success (*Spartan Steel & Alloys Ltd* v *Martin & Co*). However, if this is a claim for pure economic loss, the shop owner would have to establish that there is sufficient proximity between him and Peter (*Junior Books* v *Veitchi, Simaan* v *Pilkington*). There is no suggestion that this is the case and a claim would probably fail.

In your conclusion, you should sum up the liability of Peter in the tort of negligence to the house owners and shop owner.

Part (c)

Peter may be liable to Richard under the Occupiers' Liability Act 1957 or 1984. It is crucial to consider whether Richard is a visitor or a trespasser, in order to determine whether Peter owed a duty of care to him. There are insufficient facts provided to judge this with any certainty. Therefore you should consider Peter's liability under both Acts.

If Richard is regarded as a trespasser, Peter will only owe him a duty of care if the requirements of s. 1(3) OLA of the 1984 Act are satisfied. We are told that Richard regularly sleeps on Peter's land, which suggests that Peter has reasonable grounds to believe that there is a trespasser in the vicinity of the danger, although ultimately this is a question of fact. The court would have to decide if this is a risk against which Peter could reasonably be expected to offer some protection.

Peter may owe a duty of care to Richard as a trespasser. If so, it is necessary to consider whether he has breached this duty under s. 1(4). You should consider whether Peter has taken reasonable care in the circumstances. Relevant circumstances include the gravity and likelihood of the probable injury, foreseeability of Richard's act of trespass and cost of precautions.

The fact that Richard is in the habit of sleeping in the field suggests that this may have been tacitly accepted by Peter, and Richard is a visitor. Therefore you should consider Peter's liability to Richard under the 1957 Act. Peter owes a common duty of care under s. 2(2) and you should consider whether this has been breached.

In conclusion you should sum up the liability of Peter to Richard, first if he is regarded as a trespasser, and secondly if he is regarded as a visitor.

Practice questions

1   Recently Reggie Ray, a man with a long criminal record for offences of violence, died whilst in police custody at the Headquarters of the Southside police force. An official enquiry cleared the police of all blame but Bill, a student activist, believes Reggie Ray was ill-treated by the police. He therefore drew up a poster which shows a large and conspicuous picture of a pig and which reads: 'Who killed Reggie Ray? Who are the guilty men?' (The word 'pig' is sometimes used as a term of abuse when describing the police.)

Bill hung the poster on the official notice board of the Department of Sociology of Westshire University, where he is a student. Greg, the Head of the Department, notices the poster which had been there for a fortnight, but he chose not to remove it. This matter was then drawn to the attention of Police Constable Brown, who had been in charge of Reggie Ray when he was in police custody.

Consider PC Brown's likelihood of success in an action for defamation.

(30 marks)
(*NEAB*)

Pitfalls

In answering this problem question involving the tort of defamation, it is essential to consider the liability of both Bill and the University. The questions gives you the opportunity to discuss both the elements of the tort and relevant defences. As with all problem questions, poor structuring of the answer is a common error. Another pitfall is poor use of cases, or worst still, no cases!

Key points

1. Definition of defamation.
2. The distinction between libel and slander with application of the elements of libel to the problem.
3. Is the statement defamatory: definition of defamatory (*Sim* v *Stretch*); defamation by innuendo (*Tolley* v *Fry*).
4. Does the statement refer to the plaintiff: defamation of a class not actionable; *Eastwood* v *Holmes*; *Knupffer* v *London Express Newspapers*.
5. Who should be sued: Bill and/or the university?
6. Has the statement been published?
7. Possible defences; unintentional defamation (Defamation Act 1996); fair comment and effect of malice.
8. Consideration of practical issues: cost, legal aid, procedure.

2. AB Chemicals Ltd has a factory on the outskirts of a small village. The factory produces various chemicals and AB Chemicals Ltd store some of the raw materials in large metal drums which are piled by the boundary fence. Unknown to AB Chemicals Ltd, some of the drums are not secure and the chemicals have leaked into a nearby stream. The leak has only been discovered when sheep kept by Giles on a neighbouring field became ill after drinking from the stream.

Giles has already made several complaints to AB Chemicals Ltd about the thick black smoke from the factory's chimneys which from time to time blows across the farm. This forces Giles to stay indoors with the windows closed to keep out the smuts and the smell.

Advise Giles whether or not there is any action he can take in tort against AB Chemicals Ltd to recover the cost of treating the sheep and to stop the factory creating the smoke.

(50)
(*UODLE*)

Pitfalls

This problem question raises three separate torts. A common error would be to omit discussion of one or more of them. When considering AB Chemicals' liability for the cost of treating the sheep, you should consider the effect of *Rylands* v *Fletcher* being strict liability and negligence being fault-based and link this with the fact that AB Chemicals are unaware of the leak. Once again, use cases sensibly and plan your answer carefully. Failure to do these two things are the most common pitfalls.

Key points

1. Possibility of an action in tort of *Rylands* v *Fletcher* in relation to Giles' damaged sheep; emphasis on the strict liability nature of this tort.
2. Explanation and application of elements of *Rylands* v *Fletcher*.
3. Possibility of an action in tort of negligence in relation to the damage to his sheep; emphasis that this is a fault based tort.
4. Explanation and application of elements of negligence.
5. Possibility of an action in tort of private nuisance in relation to the smoke.
6. Explanation and application of elements of private nuisance.
7. Conclusion which sums up the likely success of Giles suing AB Chemicals in the torts of *Rylands* v *Fletcher*, negligence and private nuisance.

3   'Tort has a significant role to play in the protection of civil liberties'. (Stanton, *The Modern Law of Tort.*)

In the light of the defences available, does the tort of trespass to the person play such a role?   (50)

(*UODLE*)

Pitfalls

This essay question requires you to critically examine the tort of trespass to person from the perspective of whether it usefully contributes to the protection of civil liberties. It is not just requiring you to describe each of the torts. Few marks would be obtained for this approach. It is essential that you use your material to answer the question set. You must be prepared to think in the examination when a difficult or unusual angle to a topic is examined.

Key points

1. Historical background to the tort of trespass to person.
2. Discussion of what might be meant by 'civil liberties' in this context.
3. Identification of the three forms of trespass to the person; discussion of their common features.
4. Critical discussion and illustration of assault and battery and whether these significantly protect civil liberties.
5. Critical discussion and illustration of false imprisonment and whether this significantly protects civil liberties.
6. Critical discussion and illustration of defences in relation to civil liberties.
7. Discussion of practical issues (cost, legal aid, burden of proof, time and stress).
8. Explanation that most cases of assault and battery are also criminal offences and a victim may be better protected by the criminal law and Criminal Injuries Compensation Scheme.
9. A conclusion which attempts to assess whether the tort of trespass to person significantly protects civil liberties.

CHAPTER 8

FREEDOM UNDER ENGLISH LAW

Units in this chapter

Chapter objectives

Protection of liberty is a fundamental function of any legal system. This chapter explores the way rights and freedoms are protected under English law. The differences between rights and freedoms are explained. Unlike many other countries, English law has a system of negative freedoms. We are able to do anything unless there is a law prohibiting it. Therefore, in order to assess our freedoms, it is necessary to explore the restrictions that exist. Particular freedoms are examined. Freedom of person and property, expression and assembly and association are considered. In any society, freedom must be balanced against public order and key restrictions and criminal offences associated with public order are outlined. The UK has been a signatory to the European Convention on Human Rights for many years. The content of the Convention and its status is examined. Other methods of protecting freedoms are also identified. Finally, the chapter considers reform of the current system for protecting liberty. In particular, the idea of a Bill of Rights is explored, with particular emphasis on its likely effect and advantages and disadvantages of such a reform. Please note that not all A Level Law syllabuses include this topic, and you should refer to the Syllabus Checklists if in any doubt.

8.1   INTRODUCTION

In modern democratic societies, freedom (or 'liberty') is highly valued (recall from Chapter 3 that Rawls made his first principle of justice 'the most extensive total system of equal basic liberties compatible with a similar system of liberty for all'). Freedom means freedom to do or not to do as one wishes. It is incompatible with obligation or compulsion, so that there is no freedom in relation to a particular activity where another has an enforceable right to demand that one should or should not engage in that activity.

Freedom can never be completely unconstrained. As Rawls's way of putting it makes clear, each person's freedom will inevitably be restricted to some extent by every other person's interests in freedom. But more than this, they will sometimes have to give way to what are perceived to be other legitimate interests.

Yet the danger is that particular freedoms (and so 'freedom') will constantly be reduced by legislative, judicial and administrative action founded on the protection of other claims. Freedoms must constantly be guarded if they are not to disappear.

8.2   RIGHTS OR FREEDOMS?

Broadly speaking, there are two ways in which freedoms can be dealt with in a state:

- a rights-based approach;
- a residual freedoms-based approach.

Using the position in the USA and in the UK as examples, Table 8.1 below compares the approaches, indicating usual characteristics and some advantages and disadvantages.

	rights-based	freedoms-based
example	United States	United Kingdom
characteristics	• recognition of a series of rights (human, civil – perhaps, even, political and social) • declared in and protected by the constitution • the rights are 'entrenched' (special procedure for repeal or amendment) • the rights are enforceable ultimately by reference to some special court • any legal rule or administrative practice which infringes a right can be declared invalid	• no *overriding* rights (though there are usually some *rights*) • 'freedoms' are defined in a negative way – whatever a person is compelled to do or not to do • freedoms are *residual* (what remains where there is no compulsion) • freedoms have no special protection in law
advantages	• rights and obligations are clearly established • promotes constant vigilance to ensure that the rights are not eroded	• flexible and responsive to change • tends to stress *obligations* to others rather than *rights* against others
disadvantages	• may tend to inhibit necessary change by making amendment or abolition very difficult to achieve • excessive power in the hands of the judiciary • depends heavily upon the integrity of those who administer the system (gross abuse of human rights is often evident in countries with impressive constitutions guaranteeing human rights)	• system of residues, so constantly subject to erosion • judicial commitment to the protection of freedom is at best half-hearted, at worst non-existent • judges are independent but relatively powerless against the dictates of the legislature

Table 8.1 Comparing the approaches

In view of the explanation in Table 8.1, it will be obvious that examination of the scope of any particular freedom requires analysis of the rules and practices which restrict the freedom.

8.3 PARTICULAR FREEDOMS

8.3.1 FREEDOM OF PERSON AND PROPERTY

Freedom of person includes freedom from arbitrary arrest and detention. Freedom of property is freedom from arbitrary interference with ownership, use and enjoyment of property. The scope of these freedoms is restricted by criminal and civil laws and associated legal and administrative practices. For example, there may be broad criminal and civil law constraints on the use and enjoyment of property on grounds of public safety or for the protection of the environment.

Police powers of stop and search, arrest, detention for questioning, and entry, search and seizure of property represent a very significant set of constraints on these freedoms. The *general* powers are largely, but by no means exclusively, contained within the **Police and Criminal Evidence Act 1984**, which is supplemented by Codes of Practice. (See Table 8.2 on the page following.)

8.3.2 FREEDOM OF EXPRESSION

Freedom of expression involves both:

- freedom to *communicate* facts, beliefs, opinions, ideas in any way;
- freedom of *access to information* on which the above can be based.

Thus, freedom of expression is constrained not only by rules and practices which prevent communication but also by those which prevent access (such as those concerned with state security and 'official' secrets).

This freedom is subject to a very large number of constraints. Some examples are:

- The tort of defamation: a person has a right to protect his reputation against damage by *untrue* statements (see Unit 7.7).

- The law of confidentiality: a person may prevent publication or other misuse of information imparted in circumstances of confidence, so long as it is not in the public interest for it to be known. This is an equitable doctrine with discretionary remedies but is sometimes based on contract, as in an employee's duty to his employer not to reveal or misuse confidential information and trade secrets acquired in the employment.

- The law concerning possession and publication of obscene and indecent materials: for example, under the Obscene Publications Act 1959.

- The law of contempt of court: generally, to preserve the integrity of the legal process by ensuring that there is no prejudging of issues, especially by television and newspapers.

- Laws designed to preserve public order: prohibition or control of activities likely to cause serious offence to others and lead to breach of the peace. They may relate to specific matters such as promotion of racial hatred or to more general activities such as abusive or insulting conduct (see below).

- Laws designed to preserve state secrecy and national security.

	Stop and Search	Arrest		Detention	Entry, Search and Seizure
Sections	ss. 1–3 and Code of Practice A	s. 24 (arrestable offences)	s. 25 (non-arrestable offences)	ss. 34–52	ss. 8–23
Main provisions	• a police constable must have reasonable grounds to suspect that he will find stolen articles, offensive weapons, 'blades' or articles to be used in connection with offences of theft, burglary, deception or taking conveyances without consent • the constable must inform the person of the reasons for the search and must subsequently make a written record which must be supplied to the person on request • the Code of Practice requires searches to be conducted with maximum co-operation and minimum embarrassment. Public searches must be superficial and of outer clothing only. More thorough searches must be out of public view and conducted only by, and in the presence of, constables of the same sex.	A police constable has very wide powers of arrest. He may arrest any person who • has committed, • is committing, or • is about to commit an arrestable offence.	A police constable may also arrest a person where he reasonably suspects that a non-arrestable offence has been or is being committed or attempted – but only where it appears that service of a summons will be impracticable or inappropriate because one or more 'general arrest conditions' are satisfied. These include: • the person's true name or address cannot be established; or where the police constable has reasonable grounds to believe that: • the person may cause harm to himself or others or suffer physical injury • the person may cause loss or damage • the person may be a threat to a child or other vulnerable person.	Responsibility for treatment whilst in detention is undertaken by the custody officer, who must ensure that the person: • is charged if there is sufficient evidence and is released on bail unless one or more conditions are satisfied • is released on bail or without bail if there is insufficient evidence to charge, unless continued detention without charge is justified to permit questioning for evidence while detained, is treated in accordance with the provisions of the Act (including the keeping of all relevant records, and the right to consult a solicitor privately at any time, as soon as practicable following a request.	This could be carried out with a warrant obtained from a magistrate, or, in the case of excluded material and special procedure material, a circuit judge. No warrant is available where the material is legally privileged. Entry and search (and seizure where appropriate) may take place without a warrant: • to effect an arrest • to save life or limb or prevent damage to property in relation to any premises occupied or controlled by a person under arrest for an arrestable offence, or where he was immediately before he was arrested, where the police constable has reasonable grounds for suspecting that there is evidence relating to the offence or to some other arrestable offence connected with or similar to that offence • to prevent a breach of the peace.

Table 8.2   Summary of police powers under Police and Criminal Evidence Act 1984

8.3.3 FREEDOM OF ASSEMBLY AND ASSOCIATION

Obviously, there is a close connection between freedom of expression and freedom of assembly and association. People may wish to come together for the purposes of expressing opinions and ideas. Thus, constraints on this freedom may also be constraints on freedom of expression.

There are few limits on association for political purposes, though both criminal and tortious conspiracy may be of general significance and there are various prohibitions on membership, and participation in the activities, of terrorist and para-military organisations.

The major general restrictions on assembly (meetings) and 'procession' (marches/demonstrations) are to be found in:

* obstruction of the highway (both a tort and a crime);
* the requirements of ss. 11–15 Public Order Act 1986 as to notice and control of processions and meetings;
* the constraints in the Criminal Justice and Public Order Act 1994;
* common law rules concerning breach of the peace.

8.4 BALANCING FREEDOM AGAINST PUBLIC ORDER

Some degree of order and control is necessary for freedom to be meaningful in any society, but a society characterised by excessive concern for order and control would stifle healthy debate and criticism, repress freedom and probably lack imagination and dynamism. Any attempt to encourage freedom carries dangers of lawlessness and disorder. Yet, ultimately, attempts to repress are also likely to end in protest and violence.

Many incidents which threaten or involve breaches of public order are associated with events and activities which have a serious purpose in society. For instance:

* protest about major social and political issues;
* concern with questions of employment;
* concern with the pursuit of alternative life-styles which do not easily fit in with the way in which communities are usually organised and run.

When public order is threatened by these kinds of events and activities rather than by ordinary acts of violence, disorder and vandalism, there is an important balancing task to be performed by the law and those who uphold it. It is to balance the need for the preservation of order against the need to preserve and support fundamental freedoms.

8.4.1 PREVENTIVE OR RESTRICTIVE POWERS AND PROVISIONS

The most effective way to maintain public order may be to prevent trouble arising in the first place by strictly controlling or even prohibiting relevant activities and events. Yet there is a danger that this may be seen as the easy way out of the problem, with the result that freedom of expression, assembly and association are effectively suppressed. The court resisted this temptation in *Beatty* v *Gillbanks* (1882) when holding that marchers behaving peacefully and lawfully should not be prohibited from marching merely because another group of marchers would oppose them and thus threaten the peace. Effectively, the authorities had to control the other group. Nevertheless, there are now many preventive powers which may be used to restrict otherwise lawful activity.

Control of processions and assemblies under the Public Order Act 1986

- **Section 11**: the police must be given six days' notice of a procession intended to show support for or opposition to the views or actions of a person or group, to publicise a cause or campaign, or to mark or commemorate an event (the aim is to target 'political' processions). This is not required if it is 'not practical' to give such notice; otherwise it is an offence to fail to give notice, or to deviate from the details (time, place, etc.) given in the notice.

- **Section 12**: the police are given power to impose conditions as to time or place of a procession if they think it might result in serious public disorder, damage to property, or serious disruption of the community, or that the procession is intended to intimidate people into doing things they do not want to do, or not doing things they want to do. It is an offence to break the conditions imposed.

- **Section 13**: on the application of the police, the local authority (with the Home Secretary's consent) can impose a 'blanket ban'.

- **Section 14**: the police are given power to impose conditions on static public assemblies, held wholly or partly in the open air, if more than 20 people are going to be present. As well as the power to impose conditions in advance, the section allows the police to impose conditions at the time of the assembly and then to arrest those who fail to comply with the direction.

- **Section 14A**: on the application of the police, s. 14A gives power to local authority (with the Home Secretary's consent) to prohibit the holding of all trespassory assemblies for a specified period of not more than four days in the whole or part of the district (but not exceeding an area represented by a circle with a five miles radius from a specified centre).

Breach of the peace

- At common law the police have the power to arrest without warrant if a breach of the peace has been committed, if there is reasonable belief that a breach of the peace will be committed, or if they think it will be repeated (widely used during the miners' strike of 1984/5 to prevent pickets from getting to the place they intended to picket). In *Moss v McLachlan* (1984), it was held that the police were justified in stopping miners some distance away from a colliery where there had been disturbances and preventing them from travelling there provided they honestly and reasonably believed that there was a real danger of a breach of the peace.

- The police have a general duty to disperse unlawful and riotous assemblies. If they think there will be a breach of the peace they may prevent a meeting from taking place or continuing.

- The police have the power to enter private premises if they believe that a breach of the peace is actually taking place there or if they believe that a breach of the peace is likely to occur unless they are present.

- Magistrates' courts have power to 'bind over' anyone to be of good behaviour or to keep the peace. This means asking the person to promise to forfeit a sum in the event of a failure to comply.

Criminal Justice and Public Order Act 1994 provisions

- **Section 61**: at the request of an occupier, the police have power to require trespassers to leave land on which they were intending to reside if they have damaged the land or used threatening abusive or insulting behaviour to the occupier, his family or employees/agents or have brought at least six vehicles on the land.

- **Section 63**: the police have power to break up or prevent open air gatherings of 100 or more people at which the playing of loud music is likely to cause serious distress to the inhabitants of the locality.

- **Section 69**: gives the police power to stop actual or anticipated offences of 'aggravated trespass'. Such offences are committed by trespass on land (or on adjoining land) in the open air and to intimidate, obstruct or disrupt lawful activity (as, for instance, hunt saboteurs).

8.4.2 CRIMINAL OFFENCES ASSOCIATED WITH BREACHES OF PUBLIC ORDER

Offences under the Public Order Act 1986

* **Section 1 (riot):** using unlawful violence for a common purpose in circumstances where 12 or more persons who are present together threaten or use unlawful violence for a common purpose and the conduct of them (taken together) would cause a person of reasonable firmness present at the scene to fear for his personal safety.

* **Section 2 (violent disorder):** using or threatening the use of unlawful violence in circumstances where three or more together do so and the conduct of them (taken together) is such as would cause a person of reasonable firmness to fear for his personal safety (though no such person need be present or be likely to be present).

* **Section 3 (affray):** using or threatening use of unlawful violence by one person towards another in such a way that it would cause a person of reasonable firmness present at the scene to fear for his personal safety.

* **Section 4 (fear or provocation of violence):** the accused either uses towards another threatening, abusive or insulting words or behaviour, or distributes or displays to another person any writing, sign or other visible representation which is threatening, abusive or insulting. There must be an intent to cause that person to believe that immediate unlawful violence will be used against him or another by any person, or to provoke the immediate use of unlawful violence by that person or another, or it must be so that that person is likely to believe that such violence will be used or it is likely that such violence will be provoked.

* **Section 4A (intentional harassment, alarm or distress):** this offence is identical to that currently found in s. 5 (see below) except that the accused must *intend* to cause harassment, alarm or distress and must actually *do* so. In addition, the maximum penalties are far higher than those in s. 5.

* **Section 5 (harassment, alarm or distress):** this offence deals with relatively minor acts of public disorder and is committed by any person who either uses threatening, abusive or insulting words or behaviour or disorderly behaviour, or displays any writing, sign or other visible representation which is threatening, abusive or insulting. It must be within the hearing or sight of a person likely to be caused harassment, alarm or distress.

8.5 THE EUROPEAN CONVENTION ON HUMAN RIGHTS

Though there is no major constitutional guarantee of human rights in the UK, nonetheless the UK is a signatory to the European Convention on Human Rights 1953, of which account must be taken in any analysis of the protection of freedom in the United Kingdom.

8.5.1 THE CONTENT OF THE CONVENTION

The Convention guarantees a number of fundamental rights and freedoms. For example:

* the right to life;
* the right to freedom from torture or inhuman or degrading treatment or punishment;
* the right to liberty and security of person;

- the right to respect for private and family life, home and correspondence;
- the right to freedom of expression;
- the right to freedom of assembly and association.

However, many are qualified by recognition of the need to balance other interests.

8.5.2 ENFORCING THE CONVENTION

Allegations that the law or practices of a particular state contravene provisions of the Convention may be made by individuals (who must first exhaust all domestic remedies) against states or by states against other states. This was originally done by presenting a petition to the European Commission on Human Rights but cases now go directly to the European Court of Human Rights.

8.5.3 THE STATUS OF THE CONVENTION IN THE UK

The convention has not been directly enforceable in UK courts. Thus, in *Malone* v *Commissioner of Police of the Metropolis (No. 2)* (1979), P was refused a declaration that interception of telephone communications was in breach of his fundamental rights under Article 8 of the Convention (guaranteeing the right to respect for private and family life, home and correspondence). His only means of redress in the case of such alleged breach was to exercise his right to petition the European Commission on Human Rights (which he subsequently successfully did).

However, there is a general presumption that, in interpreting uncertain or ambiguous law, courts in the UK will have regard to international obligations such as those imposed by the Convention. In reality, this has not proved to be a very significant influence on the approach adopted by the courts. They have found it all too easy to ignore the provisions of the Convention (see, for instance, *Brind* v *Secretary of State for the Home Department* (1991) and *R* v *Brown & Others* (1993)).

Even so, the Convention has proved to be of enormous significance in securing rights and freedoms in the UK because successive governments have not wished to defy rulings of the European Court of Human Rights that UK law was in breach of the Convention. Some examples of changes which have been brought about in this way include:

- Prisoners' rights: *Golder* v *UK* (1975) and *Silver* v *UK* (1983) led to changes in the prison regime.
- Contempt of court: *Sunday Times* v *UK* (1980) led to the Contempt of Court Act 1981.
- Telephone tapping: *Malone* v *UK* (1984) led to the Interception of Communications Act 1985.
- Homosexual acts: *Dudgeon* v *UK* (1981) led to changes in the law in Northern Ireland.
- Corporal punishment: *Campbell & Cosans* v *UK* (1982) led to the abolition of corporal punishment in most schools.

But the Convention has not always secured the rights that applicants may have hoped from it:

- Transsexuals have not succeeded in being formally recognised for the purpose of marriage etc.
- The UK may exercise the right to derogate from the Convention in specific instances (for example, public emergency threatening the life of the nation) and so avoid the consequences of an adverse decision of the European Court of Human Rights, as in *Brogan* v *UK* (1988), in which the UK avoided the consequences of the Court's decision that UK rules on detention of terrorists contravened the Convention.

Parliament is considering incorporating the Convention into English law. The Human Rights Bill, being read during the Spring and Summer of 1998, proposes that a person who is a victim of an act or omission by a public authority which is incompatible with the Convention will be able to challenge that act or omission in the courts. The court will be able to point out that there is an incompatibility and the appropriate Minister can then change the law by Order in Council, though he will have no obligation to do so. Parliament will still be able to pass Acts that are incompatible with the Convention, and will make a statement in the Bill that that is their intention.

8.6 MECHANISMS FOR ASSERTING FREEDOMS

Until the Human Rights Bill becomes law there are no special rights, or mechanisms for enforcing freedoms in the UK. The protection of freedoms depends simply on using any available ordinary rights and remedies. Amongst these we may include:

- Action in the civil courts: for example, for nuisance, trespass, defamation, false imprisonment.
- Action in the criminal courts: private prosecutions may be brought though they are often difficult and expensive and may be terminated by the Crown.
- An action for judicial review of administrative action: a way of controlling the activities of the government, local authorities and others exercising executive power.
- An action before a tribunal: some statutes have created rights which may be enforced before tribunals; for example, in connection with sex and race discrimination.
- Complaint to an ombudsman: most notably, the Parliamentary Commissioner for Administration, who has power to investigate complaints of injustice in consequence of maladministration by government departments and certain other public bodies.
- Taking a case to the European Court of Human Rights.

8.7 REFORM OF THE SYSTEM

8.7.1 PIECEMEAL REFORM

The protection of civil liberties in English law is piecemeal. Rights can be added to and eroded relatively easily, sometimes without major debate. One method of reform, which would not change the legal status of rights, would be to consolidate and/or codify current law. More positive rights could be created. Reforms which give individuals better access to the courts could be implemented. Rights and freedoms could be reformed on a piecemeal basis but this approach does not solve the fundamental problem that freedom has no legal protection.

8.7.2 A BILL OF RIGHTS?

Meaning

A far-reaching reform would be to enact a Bill of Rights. A Bill of Rights is, fundamentally, a list of rights which, by law, can be enjoyed by citizens of that country. It may form part of a written constitution or accompany the constitution. A Bill of Rights is normally entrenched. This means that it will be superior to ordinary law, in that it can only be changed by special procedure, such as by holding a referendum, or requiring that, for example, a two-thirds majority in Parliament is secured.

Content

Starting from scratch

It would be difficult to reach consensus as to what rights a Bill of Rights should contain. At one extreme, some argue that it should contain every conceivable right which should be protected in a civilised country, including environmental, economic and social rights. At the other extreme, others argue that it should simply cover areas not already protected by common law.

Incorporating the Convention

Because of the difficulties in determining potential content, many argue that the Convention should be incorporated as our Bill of Rights. Arguments which support this include:

- it has been in existence for many years, and has been ratified by all the main political parties;
- it has widespread acceptance and familiarity;
- there is a large body of case law already in existence, which could assist the judges.

Arguments against incorporation of the Convention include:

- it is over 30 years old and rights have not been added, for example, race discrimination has very limited protection;
- it does not protect environmental, economic and social rights;
- it is broadly drafted compared to domestic legislation. Those who are called to interpret it and apply it to individual cases, such as the judges, would have a great deal of discretion.

The proposals under the Human Rights Bill do not amount to a Bill of Rights because the government may refuse to remove incompatible legislation and may use its majority in the House of Commons to force through an incompatible Bill. This addresses some of the problems inherent in introducing a Bill of Rights but also removes most of the advantages.

Constitutional effect

If a Bill of Rights was adopted in the UK, there would be far-reaching consequences on English law and the UK constitution. Key issues include:

1. **Entrenchment and the doctrine of parliamentary sovereignty:** It is difficult to see how a Bill or Rights could be entrenched in English law, and therefore become higher law. Under the doctrine of parliamentary sovereignty, one Act of Parliament cannot bind a future Parliament, if the subsequent Parliament should wish to change the law (see Unit 2.1). Also, judges may not question or change Acts. If a subsequent Act is inconsistent with a previous one, the judge must give effect to the most recent. Therefore the Bill of Rights could not govern future legislation. Although strictly speaking a technical problem of constitutional law, nevertheless this is an issue which cannot be ignored or dismissed.

2. **Power of the executive:** All powers of government would be subject to a Bill of Rights. Therefore, it would curb executive power, since the courts could simply refuse to apply legislation which conflicted with it. This, in turn, would be a powerful incentive for government to avoid introducing conflicting legislation in the first place.

3. **The role of the judges:** An entrenched Bill of Rights would, effectively, pass sovereign power to judges. They would make the final political decision on major questions. However, the judges are appointed rather than elected, and therefore, they have no mandate to make such decisions and they are not accountable in any way for what they do with this enormous power. Most Bills of Rights are loosely drafted, giving judges a great deal of scope to determine whether a right has been infringed in a particular case. It is open to question whether ultimate political power should be entrusted to the judges.

Advantages and disadvantages

Both those in favour of a Bill of Rights and those against such a development have advanced arguments to support their view. Often their arguments contradict one another. The arguments must be carefully evaluated in order to reach a conclusion. The arguments for a Bill of Rights include:

- It would provide a comprehensive and easily accessible statement of rights and freedoms, as opposed to the current scattered and complex legislation and common law concerning civil liberties.
- It would give rights and freedoms legal status and provide a constitutional safeguard.
- It would prevent rights from being eroded by Parliament (when passing new legislation) or judges (through the common law).
- It would strengthen the citizen's hand against government and other public authorities.
- It would be an influential moral and educational force.
- It would bring the UK into line with most other western democracies.
- It makes no sense to have ratified the Convention yet not incorporated it.
- The procedure for enforcement of human rights under the Convention is too slow and costly.

Arguments against a Bill of Rights include:

- Human rights are adequately protected under the current law.
- It would give too much power to the judges.
- A Bill of Rights is only as good as those who interpret it, and our judges are not equipped for this task.
- A Bill of Rights would lack flexibility, requiring special procedures to be followed if it were to be amended.
- A Bill of Rights would need to be entrenched and would thereby restrict Parliament's freedom to legislate in the light of prevailing circumstances (for example, would it allow for emergency legislation?).
- Having a Bill of Rights would achieve little or nothing; merely granting rights is not enough to secure individual freedom and empowerment (for example, in South Africa a Bill of Rights existed during *apartheid*).

Illustrative question

1   The government published proposals to abandon the practice of preventing the spread of rabies by quarantining animals being brought into the country and replacing it with a system of vaccination. The proposals aroused both widespread support and opposition and led to the formation of 'pro' and 'anti' vaccination groups (P and A groups). When the P group organised a march and demonstration to express its support, members of the A group marched along opposite them, shouting and jeering, holding up placards showing animals suffering from rabies and depicting members of the P group as animal killers. Scuffles broke out along the length of the march and A group members frequently banded together to threaten both P group members and any bystanders who indicated any support for them. Subsequently, there was a great deal of public criticism of police tactics at the march and also of the behaviour of the A group. Nevertheless, the P group announced that it would be holding another march followed by a meeting in church grounds adjacent to privately owned playing fields (onto which, it was immediately objected, the meeting would spill). The A group then made it clear that it would be present to demonstrate its opposition once again.

Explain what liability arises out of the incidents at the first march and demonstration and consider how the police should deal with the plans by the P group to hold a second march and meeting.   (25)
(London)

This problem question is generally concerned with public order. It is important to examine the scenario from a 'freedom versus order' broad perspective and consider the best ways of controlling the events. Consider the general rule in *Beatty* v *Gillbanks* (1882) that marchers behaving peacefully and lawfully should not be prohibited from marching merely because another group of marchers would oppose them and thus threaten the peace. It is equally important that you are specific on the particular offences which have been committed or may have been committed. Speculate on the possibilities. You should try to cite relevant sections of Acts.

Suggested answer
Freedom of assembly is a fundamental freedom in English law. However, it must be balanced with public order. Like all freedoms, constraints must exist. This question is mainly concerned with constraints imposed by the Public Order Act 1986.

In relation to the first march and demonstration, the conduct of members of the A group in shouting, jeering and holding up placards may well be an offence under s. 4 of the 1986 Act. They are using threatening, abusive and insulting words to members of the P group and to bystanders. They are also displaying abusive and insulting signs to the members of the P group. In both cases, it is likely to cause fear of violence or to provoke violence, and indeed, scuffles break out along the route of the march. Similarly, offences under s. 4A and s. 5 have probably been committed. These are summary offences.

If members of either group have used or threatened to use unlawful violence towards another in such a way as to cause a person of reasonable firmness present at the scene to fear for his personal safety then the offences of affray, violent disorder or even riot may have been committed. The scuffles suggest this may be the case. The particular offence committed would depend upon proof of numbers involved. Under s. 3 (affray), only one person need use or threaten violence towards another. However, the tendency of A group members to band together to threaten P group members and bystanders also raises the possibility of the more serious offence of violent disorder, for which there must be at least three persons present together using or threatening unlawful violence (s. 2). If it could be proved that 12 or more persons used violence together for a common purpose and caused a person of reasonable firmness to fear for his personal safety, there is a possibility that the indictable offence of riot has been committed. It is also worth noting that there may well have been instances of obstruction of the highway (common law and s. 137 Highways Act 1980) and significant breaches of the peace. The police would have had powers of arrest and dispersal in consequence of the commission of the offences and the occurrences of breach of the peace.

In relation to the proposed second march and demonstration, the police should be careful not to restrict the freedom of expression of the essentially law abiding P group merely because another group intends to be disruptive and to behave in an unlawful manner (*Beatty* v *Gillbanks*). Whilst taking account of the need to preserve public order, the police should try to apply measures designed to minimise the threat from the A group rather than to constrain the P group. Even so, the police might use their powers under s. 14A, in order to prevent the meeting spilling over into private grounds. Under s. 11, the police will expect notice of the march and can then consider whether the route poses any particular problems and can decide what conditions, if any, to impose. For example, the police superintendent may authorise random stop and search for offensive weapons or dangerous instruments in order to forestall trouble from the A group (s. 60 Criminal Justice and Public Order Act 1994).

Practice questions

1 I had a long record of petty theft and burglary but had never been known to be involved in any violence. One Saturday night the police were called to investigate a stabbing in a fast food shop. Three men had run away after the stabbing and witnesses described one of them in a way which approximated to I's description. This information was relayed to Police Constable (PC) J, who was on foot patrol in the town centre some two miles away. He saw I walking down the street with K and immediately took hold of I's arm and told him to turn out all of his pockets. I refused and K sought to free him before giving up and running off. PC J then dragged I into a doorway and searched him thoroughly whilst a crowd gathered and laughed at I. Finding nothing on I, PC J told him that if he did not reveal K's identity and address, he could expect some rough treatment in the future. I gave PC J the information and both then went round to K's house, where I was forced to pretend that he was alone so as to get K to open the door. As soon as K did so, PC J burst in and searched the house. He found a number of car radios with their serial numbers obliterated and seized them all, despite K's protests that they were in a room which he rented out and that he knew nothing about them. I and K were then kept at the police station for 36 hours, during which they were permitted only one brief interview with the duty solicitor, and were questioned for long periods of time about the stabbing and the car radios. Eventually, both were released without charge when three men were arrested for the stabbing and K's lodger gave a satisfactory account of his possession of the car radios.

Explain whether the police were legally entitled to act as they did and consider whether I and K have any remedies. (25)

(London)

Pitfalls

A common pitfall is to be vague on the relevant provisions of the Police and Criminal Evidence Act 1984 (PACE 1984). It is important to identify in a plan all the possible breaches of PACE 1984 in order to gain maximum coverage of the issues. A good answer would refer to the relevant sections. Another weakness is to ignore the instruction to examine possible remedies.

Key points

❶ Examination of whether PC J had grounds to stop and search I under ss. 1 – 3 PACE 1984. PC J probably had reasonable grounds to suspect that he would find offensive weapons or blades on I because of the information but the search was carried out in breach of Code provisions which could form the basis of a complaint to the Police Complaints Authority (PCA).

❷ Examination of whether PC J's entry into K's house and seizure of the car radios is lawful under ss. 17 – 19 and 32 PACE 1984. There is no genuine consent and no other grounds to make it lawful therefore the seizure of the radios is also unlawful.

❸ Examination of whether the arrest of K and I is lawful under s. 25 PACE 1984. The presence of the car radios raises a reasonable suspicion that an arrestable offence has been/is being committed, probably justifying arrest.

❹ Examination of whether the detention and questioning of I and K is lawful under Codes of Practice and s. 58 PACE 1984. Requirements about breaks and refreshments, and access to the solicitor have been contravened.

❺ Examination of the possible remedies available to I and K including an action for unlawful arrest and associated trespass to the person, trespass to premises and false imprisonment, a complaint to the PCA which could result in criminal and/or disciplinary proceedings.

2 Including in your answer an explanation of any reform(s) which you believe to be desirable, write a critical analysis of the protection of fundamental rights and freedoms within English law.

(25)

(AEB)

Pitfalls

You must try to construct a coherent answer. It is more sensible to consider reforms after having explained and illustrated the method of protecting rights and freedoms within English law. Providing an adequate explanation of the notion of residual freedom does not mean writing a *list* of laws which restrict freedom. When evaluating reforms, it is essential to recognise there is significant resistance to enacting a Bill of Rights and you should consider other possibilities.

Keynotes

1. Explanation of residual nature of freedoms and contrast with positive rights.

2. Illustration by reference to one or more freedoms, indicating the nature of constraints which delimit the scope of the freedom(s) (the greater the range of freedoms discussed, the less the degree of detail required).

3. Examination and assessment of methods of asserting the freedom or freedoms discussed above, e.g. civil action, criminal prosecution, tribunal actions, ombudsman, including the European Convention on Human Rights.

4. Assessment of the protection of rights and freedoms within English law.

5. Identification of possible reforms, i.e. piecemeal, Bill of Rights.

6. Explanation and evaluation of piecemeal reform.

7. Definition of a Bill of Rights and a discussion of problems of determining potential content, including incorporation of the European Convention on Human Rights.

8. Implications of adopting a Bill of Rights.

9. Arguments for and against a Bill of Rights for the UK.

10. Assessment of whether any reforms are necessary or desirable.

CHAPTER 9

GENERAL PRINCIPLES OF LIABILITY

Units in this chapter

Chapter objectives

This chapter explores two key principles which underpin liability in crime, tort and contract: individual responsibility and fault liability. The concept of individual responsibility in both crime and tort is discussed. The chapter examines the meaning and importance of fault as a requirement of liability and analyses the arguments for and against fault liability. Alternatives to fault liability are also discussed. The chapter assumes prior knowledge of the relevant substantive areas of law. It should be read in conjunction with Chapters 5 and 7.

9.1 INTRODUCTION

One of the most basic functions of law is to specify the situations in which a person may be legally liable for his acts or omissions. There are certain general principles which underlie liability in crime, tort and contract. These principles are perceived by judges and legislators as fundamental to any branch of law. They have long been at the root of liability in English law and embody morality and justice. They may be summed up in two propositions. First, only those persons who are morally blameworthy, or at fault, should be held liable. Secondly, individuals bear responsibility for their conduct. These are frequently expressed as 'no liability without fault' and 'individual responsibility'. It is important to note that they are *principles*, rather than *rules*. Therefore, there are exceptions. Sometimes a person may be held liable when he is not the actual wrongdoer, or without being at fault. The exceptions are based on *policy considerations*. The connections between principles and policy is evident when examining this topic.

9.2 INDIVIDUAL RESPONSIBILITY

Liability in criminal law assumes a notion of individual responsibility or autonomy. This means that criminal wrongdoing is assumed to be the product of choices freely made by an individual and is not in some way 'pre-determined' by events or factors outside the individual's control ('determinism'). If this assumption is not made, the foundations of criminal liability in fault and blame and the associated sentencing aims are severely undermined. More generally, if the broad aim of the criminal justice system is to discourage undesirable conduct, it has to use methods which assume that individuals can in principle achieve compliance. Of course, some defences in criminal law (such as insanity, automatism and duress) recognise that the individual had no significant freedom of choice and serve to absolve from liability. Since the general aim of imposition of liability in the civil law system is in some way to compensate the victim of a wrong, it is not so imperative that the principle of individual responsibility be observed. Even so, liability in tort is usually based on acts and omissions for which individuals bear responsibility and defences exist which acknowledge that the individual is not liable for conduct outside his control (for instance, for the act of a 'stranger' in *Rylands* v *Fletcher*) or which limit liability by attributing part of the responsibility to the alleged victim (contributory negligence).

Though not an inevitable corollary of the notion of individual responsibility, it might further be assumed that the individual is liable for his conduct only, and not for that of any other person. This is largely true of criminal liability, where even liability as a secondary party is dependent on the individual's *own* conduct in assisting, encouraging or procuring commission of the offence by the perpetrator. Even so, there are limited circumstances in which criminal liability may be imposed for the conduct of others (vicarious liability). In civil law, once again, the focus on the interests of the victim dictates that there is much more scope for the application of the vicarious liability principle.

9.3 FAULT LIABILITY

9.3.1 CRIMINAL LAW

Expression of fault

Fault is expressed in many ways in criminal law. When explaining how fault is embodied within the rules of law, in order to illustrate arguments, reference should be made to cases already learned. Fault is expressed through:

- The *actus reus*: a **chain of causation** must exist between the defendant's conduct and the event. If the chain of causation is broken, for example, by poor medical treatment (and the original wound is no longer an operating cause), then the defendant will not be liable, since he is not 'to blame'. Generally, the defendant must *voluntarily* commit the *actus reus*. If the defendant was not in control of his body, for example, because he was being attacked by a swarm of bees whilst driving his car, he may not be liable. He will be able to plead the defence of automatism. In such a situation he is not 'at fault' and the law will not blame him for his conduct (see Units 5.2 and 5.3).

- The *mens rea*: the defendant's degree of fault is expressed through the concept of *mens rea*. The most blameworthy *mens rea* is intention. If a person kills another, and intends to kill and is unable to plead a defence, he will be convicted of murder and will receive a mandatory life sentence. Subjective recklessness, where the defendant foresees the risk but takes it regardless, is more blameworthy than objective recklessness. If the reasonable person could have foreseen the risk, irrespective of whether the defendant did, then he will be objectively reckless. Gross negligence requires the defendant to have behaved extremely carelessly. It is a stricter test than that imposed in civil law. A person who kills another due to gross negligence (and is unable to plead a defence) will be convicted of manslaughter. The sentence will be at the discretion of the court (see Unit 5.2).

- Defences: the essence of a defence is that it excuses or justifies the defendant's conduct. Defences are legally recognised excuses which remove the defendant's blame. A defence may negate *all* of the defendant's fault. For example, if the defendant kills whilst using reasonable force to protect himself, he will not be liable. Of course, if he were to use excessive force, he would be at fault and therefore liable. Similarly, if the defendant is involuntarily intoxicated, he may not be liable. However, voluntary intoxication is treated quite differently in law, and will rarely be a defence. This is because the defendant bears some responsibility in becoming intoxicated in the first place. If a defendant successfully pleads insanity, he will not be *punished* (although he may be compulsorily detained in order to receive *treatment*). Partial defences remove part of the defendant's blame. The defendant still bears some responsibility for his conduct and he will be convicted of a lesser offence. For example, a defendant who successfully pleads diminished responsibility or provocation to a charge of murder will be convicted of manslaughter (see Units 5.3 and 5.7).

- Sentencing: the degree of the defendant's fault is a factor taken into consideration when passing a sentence (see Units 4.1 and 4.2).

Exceptions to the principle of 'no liability without fault'

Crimes of strict liability do not require *mens rea* to be proven (see Unit 5.4). Almost all strict liability crimes have been created by Parliament, though one or two exist at common law. The courts will presume that *mens rea* is a requirement of liability but sometimes they are prepared to dispense with the requirement (see guidelines in *Gammon* v *Attorney-General of Hong Kong* (1985)). A person may be convicted of a crime even when he is not necessarily at fault. However, the statute creating the strict liability crime often provides specific defences which may incorporate an element of fault into the offence. There are few crimes of absolute liability. In very limited circumstances, a person may be liable for the crimes of another but there is no general principle of vicarious liability operating in criminal law (unlike civil law).

Should a person be convicted of a crime without being at fault?

When evaluating whether fault *should be* important, it is essential to keep in mind the aim of criminal law, that is, to secure compliance with standards of behaviour. Criminal law focuses on the offender. It may appear to be unfair to punish a person for conduct which is not his fault. However, arguments in favour of strict liability exist. They include:

- most strict liability crimes are 'quasi-criminal' (or regulatory) where no stigma is attached to a conviction;
- the prosecution's task in proving guilt is easier when it does not have to prove *mens rea*;
- therefore proceedings are quicker and cheaper. In general, people are more likely to plead guilty to a strict liability offence;
- it is easier to convict companies of crimes of strict liability since it is particularly difficult to prove that a company has *mens rea*;
- a higher standard of care is imposed;
- certainty in law is achieved.

However, arguments against the imposition of strict liability exist:

- it is manifestly unjust to convict a person of any crime and punish him when he is not to blame or at fault in any way;
- the law may be imposing a standard of care too high to be attainable.

9.3.2 TORT

Expression of fault

Fault is a requirement of liability in most torts. The plaintiff has the burden of proof and usually must show that the defendant was at fault in some way. Careful examination of the rules of law in each tort reveal the fault requirement (see Chapter 7):

- Negligence and occupiers' liability require the defendant to have failed to exercise reasonable care. The defendant is not required to act perfectly, but must have failed to reach the standard of the reasonable person. The defendant will only be liable for harm arising from conduct which could reasonably be foreseen. Again this is measured against the reasonable person.
- Trespass to land, person and goods requires the defendant to have acted intentionally.
- Defamation generally requires the defendant to be at fault. Innocent publication is recognised as a defence. Also, if the defendant acts maliciously (with intention) many defences fail, such as fair comment and qualified privilege.

Exceptions to the principle 'no liability without fault'

There are two main exceptions operating in the law of tort (see Unit 7.10). These are:

- Strict liability torts, such as product liability under the Consumer Protection Act 1987, liability for dangerous animals under the Animals Act 1971 and, to some extent, the rule in *Rylands* v *Fletcher* and nuisance, neither of which enquire as to the cause of the escape or interference complained of. The defendant need not be at fault in this respect. There are few strict liability torts.
- Vicarious liability, where the employer is liable for damage caused by the torts of employees committed during the course of their employment.

Should we enable victims to be compensated without proof of fault?

When evaluating whether fault should be important in the law of tort, it is essential to keep in mind the purpose of tort, that is, to compensate (or provide some other remedy for) the victim. Tort focuses on the victim. Arguments favouring strict and vicarious liability exist. These include:

- Loss distribution: both strict and vicarious liability enable the victim to be compensated by a sizeable section of the community through insurance payments rather than by one person.

- More victims are compensated by the imposition of strict and vicarious liability.

- A higher standard of care is created, particularly in relation to hazardous activities by imposing strict liability in relation to such activities. Also strict and vicarious liability encourage safety in the work place and accident prevention.

Arguments against the imposition of strict and vicarious liability include:

- it is unfair and unjust (morally) to impose liability on an individual who is not blameworthy;

- the law of tort acts as a deterrent and this purpose would not be fulfilled;

- such liability imposes a too high standard of care;

- insurance burdens on businesses, in particular, are increased;

- these forms of liability still require victims to find someone to blame and prove causation. Victims still have to make use of legal procedures.

Alternatives to fault liability in the law of tort

The aim of the law of tort is to compensate victims. It is argued that the current system, which is heavily dependent upon proof of fault, is not achieving this aim. The tortious system is often compared to a 'lottery'. There are some big 'winners' with the majority of accident victims being 'losers' and receiving no compensation. The tortious system is also very expensive to operate. The Pearson Commission (1978) found that for every £100 awarded in compensation, costs amounted to £85.00. They also discovered that 88% of accident victims (defined as those who were forced to take three weeks or more off work as a result of their injuries) received no compensation whatsoever. Such information has led for calls for reform of the current system. There are two main reforms that have been proposed. These are:

1. *The creation of more strict liability*: this is the approach favoured by the European Union. Piecemeal reform, by imposing strict liability in more and more areas of tort, would result in more victims receiving compensation. However, as stated above, whilst strict liability reduces the victim's burden of proof, making it easier to prove his case, it still requires use of lawyers and the legal system. Therefore it does not remove all the disadvantages associated with civil procedure.

2. *No-fault liability schemes*: radical reform could be achieved by creating a no-fault liability compensation scheme. The **Pearson Commission** proposed a limited no-fault system of compensation. The Commission was set up in 1973 in order to investigate the system of obtaining compensation for personal injuries. The Commission's most radical proposal related to personal injuries received as a result of motor vehicle accidents. They recommended a state-run system administered by the Department of Social Security whereby compensation would be payable, if a motor vehicle was involved in the accident, irrespective of whether anyone was at fault. The cost of such a scheme would have been met by a levy on petrol of 1p per gallon. Levels of compensation would have been similar to those paid by the Industrial Injuries Scheme. Since the scheme was to run alongside the tortious system, victims would probably have gained more compensation from tort, if successful in court. These proposals were never adopted. A more comprehensive no-fault compensation scheme operated in New Zealand during the 1970's and 1980's. Compensation was paid to accident victims at 80% of a weekly wage although lump sums were available to all for permanent physical disability, pain,

suffering, disfigurement and loss of enjoyment of life, medical expenses, and death. The scheme was subsidised by a combination of a levy on employers (those employers with a good safety record were charged less as an incentive, and those with poor safety records charged more), vehicle licences and general income tax. Unfortunately, the scheme was abandoned in 1991 due to the recession in New Zealand. However, it provided a model to other countries, and many argue that a similar sort of scheme should be adopted in the United Kingdom.

Arguments for and against no-fault liability

A no-fault compensation system would:

- be proportionally cheaper to administer;
- be less like a lottery;
- concentrate on injury, not cause;
- compensate all victims irrespective of fault and regardless of cause;
- relieve the burden on the civil courts.

However, disadvantages of such a system include:

- it is a move away from individual responsibility and may encourage people to take more risks;
- it does not serve to act as a deterrent;
- it would not highlight dangerous practices;
- it would give less money to successful victims;
- it would be dependent on employers' contributions and income tax and may place excessive burdens on the employers and the public.

Illustrative question

1. (a) To what extent may liability in criminal law and in tort be imposed without proof of fault? (12)

   (b) Discuss the arguments for and against the imposition of such liability. (13)

   (AEB)

Tutorial note
This essay question is divided into two parts: the clue to the length of answer required is the mark allocation. Roughly equal amounts of time should be spent on each part. As with most two part questions, part (a) is mainly description and part (b) requires evaluation.

Suggested answer
In (a) the meaning of fault in this context should be explained. Emphasis on 'no liability without fault' as a general *principle* of liability in English law should be made. The exceptions to the principle should be discussed. This should focus on strict liability offences in criminal law and strict and vicarious liability in tort. The answer should define strict liability and explore the situations when the courts are prepared to dispense with the *mens rea* requirement, examining the guidelines given in *Gammon v Attorney-General of Hong Kong*. Categories of strict liability offences should be explained and illustrated with cases. Strict liability in tort should be examined, with particular reference to product liability, *Rylands v Fletcher* and nuisance. Finally, the answer should explain the elements of the doctrine of vicarious liability. Cases should be used to illustrate how it has been developed and applied by the courts.

In (b) the arguments for and against imposition of strict liability in criminal law should be discussed, using cases to illustrate these arguments. Similarly, arguments for and against the imposition of liability without fault in tort should be explained and illustrated. The question requires assessment of these arguments. The advantages and disadvantages should be weighed up. Some reference to alternatives, particularly no-fault compensation schemes for personal injury, may be useful when evaluating the arguments. A conclusion should be reached as to whether the existence of no-fault liability is desirable in crime and/or tort.

Practice questions

1 How do the courts ascertain when the imposition of strict liability for a criminal offence is justified? (50)

(*UODLE*)

Pitfalls

This question requires an explanation of the *approach* adopted by the courts to determining whether an offence or any element of the offence is one of strict liability. A danger in answering this question would be *only* to explain and illustrate the meaning of strict liability. The wording of the question does not specifically call for an evaluation of the approach though some evaluative comment may be desirable. A mere evaluation of arguments for and against strict liability would not answer the question.

Key points

❶ Definition of strict liability.
❷ Explanation of the presumption of statutory interpretation that fault is essential requirement of liability in criminal law (*Sweet* v *Parsley*).
❸ Explanation of the circumstances when the court would be prepared to dispense with *mens rea*; discussion of the guidelines in *Gammon* v *Attorney-General of Hong Kong*.
❹ Illustration of the above.
❺ Some evaluative comments on those guidelines.

2 How satisfactory is the present system whereby compensation for personal injuries arising from a negligent action depends on proof of fault? Are there any alternatives? (50)

(*UODLE*)

Pitfalls

The question requires the discussion to focus on the tort of negligence. The examiner presumes that fault is an essential requirement of negligence, and this should be discussed. A potential danger is to discuss the tort of negligence in detail, rather than focusing on the fault requirement. There is also a danger that this question may be answered by extensive discussion of the alternatives, instead of explaining and evaluating the importance of fault in the tort of negligence first.

Key points

❶ Definition of fault in this context.
❷ Discussion of how fault is expressed within the tort of negligence.
❸ Explanation of the exceptions to the principle, such as vicarious liability and strict product liability.
❹ Evaluation of the arguments for and against the fault requirement.
❺ Explanation and evaluation of alternatives, including strict liability and no-fault compensation schemes.

TEST RUN

In this section:

Test Your Knowledge Quiz

Test Your Knowledge Quiz Answers

Progress Analysis

Mock Exam

Mock Exam Suggested Answers

■ This section should be tackled towards the end of your revision programme, when you have covered all your syllabus topics, and attempted the practice questions at the end of the relevant chapters.

■ The Test Your Knowledge Quiz contains short-answer questions on a wide range of syllabus topics. Your should be aware that it may contain questions which are not part of your syllabus. You should attempt all relevant questions without reference to the text.

■ Check your answers against the Test Your Knowledge Quiz Answers. If you arc not sure why you got an answer wrong, go back to the relevant unit in the text: you will find the reference next to the answer.

■ Enter your marks in the Progress Analysis chart. The notes below will suggest a further revision strategy, based on your performance in the quiz. Only when you have done the extra work suggested should you go on to the final test.

■ The Mock Exam is set out like two real exam papers. It contains a wide spread of topics and question styles, as used by the examination boards. You should attempt Paper 1, no matter what syllabus you are studying. Your approach to Paper 2 depends upon your syllabus. If you are studying one specialist area (e.g. UODLE, NEAB) you should attempt questions on your specialist area only. You are advised to answer at least one problem question and one essay. If you are studying more than one specialist area (e.g. AEB, London), you should attempt Question 1 from two of the three sections, your choice depending on which areas you have studied. Read the instructions carefully. Attempt the papers in the time allowed, and without reference to the text.

■ Compare your answers to our Mock Exam Suggested Answers. We have provided tutorial notes to each, showing why we answered the questions as we did and indicating where your answer may have differed from ours.

TEST YOUR KNOWLEDGE QUIZ

1   Identify all the courts which administer *civil* law.

2   State the differences between a *lay* and *stipendiary* magistrate.

3   Identify all the *statutory* schemes which provide free or subsidised legal advice and/or representation.

4   State two differences between the work of a solicitor and the work of a barrister.

5   Identify two groups of people who are ineligible for jury service and two groups of people who are excused as of right.

6   Name the informal and formal stages a Bill goes through before it becomes an Act of Parliament.

7   What is meant by parliamentary sovereignty?

8   What do *ratio decidendi* and *obiter dicta* mean?

9   Describe and distinguish between Regulations, Directives and Decisions.

10 In relation to the historical development of equity, explain the significance of the Judicature Acts 1873–75.

11 List the main types of sentences available for adult offenders.

12 Explain what is meant by *actus reus*. When can an omission be sufficient for the *actus reus* of a crime?

13 Identify the elements of the defence of provocation? What is the effect of successfully pleading this defence?

14 Explain what is meant by '*invitation to treat*'. Illustrate with a case.

15 Differentiate between a condition and a warranty.

16 List four ways a contract may be discharged.

17 Identify the elements of the tort of negligence.

18 State three differences between private and public nuisance.

19 Differentiate between libel and slander.

20 Distinguish between a rights-based approach and a freedoms-based approach to protecting civil liberties.

TEST YOUR KNOWLEDGE QUIZ ANSWERS

The chapter and unit which explains the answer given is noted in brackets after the answer.

1   County court (including small claims procedure), magistrates' court, High Court, Court of Appeal and House of Lords. (Unit 1.1)

2   A lay magistrate is unqualified in law, unpaid, part-time and usually sits on a bench of three, whereas a stipendiary magistrate is qualified in law, paid, full-time and sits alone. Stipendiary magistrates sit in larger cities. (Unit 1.4)

3   Legal Advice and Assistance (Green Form Scheme), Duty Solicitor Scheme, Criminal Legal Aid, Civil Legal Aid, Assistance by way of Representation. (Unit 1.7)

4   A solicitor deals with the public directly and does mainly paperwork. A solicitor can only represent a client in the higher courts if he has a full practising certificate. A barrister specialises in advocacy and has full rights of audience. A barrister does not deal with members of the public directly. (Unit 1.2)

5   The clergy and those involved in the administration of justice (such as lawyers, judges, the police) are ineligible for jury service. Members of Parliament and the Armed Forces are excused as of right. (Unit 1.4)

6   The informal stages are the idea stage, consultation stage and drafting. The formal stages are first reading, second reading, committee stage, report stage, third reading, the other House and Royal Assent. (Unit 2.1)

7   Parliament is the supreme law-maker. It can make any law and repeal any law, although it cannot bind its successors. Judges must apply law made by Parliament. They cannot question its validity. (Unit 2.1)

8   *Ratio decidendi* is the binding rule of law based on the material facts of a case. *Obiter dicta* is things said in passing, not strictly based on the facts of the case. *Obiter dicta* is not binding, but can be persuasive. (Unit 2.2)

9   Regulations, Directives and Decisions are all secondary legislation of the European Community. Regulations are immediately binding on all member states, Directives are binding in policy and leave implementation to the member state and Decisions are binding on one member state, company or individual. (Unit 2.3)

10 The Judicature Acts 1873–75 merged the administration of common law and equity. Both can be administered in all courts. (Unit 2.4)

11 Imprisonment, community sentence (probation, community service, curfew, combination order), fine, absolute and conditional discharge. (Unit 4.1)

12 *Actus reus* means guilty conduct. An omission may form the *actus reus* if the defendant was under a duty to act. A duty may be imposed in a parent/child or equivalent relationship, if the defendant voluntarily assumes a duty of care, if the defendant created the danger, under a contract of employment or if there is a statutory duty. (Unit 5.2)

13 The defendant must be provoked by words and/or conduct; he must have a sudden and temporary loss of control; and a reasonable person would have acted in a similar way in the defendant's position. A defendant who successfully pleads this defence to a charge of murder will be convicted of manslaughter, allowing the judge discretion as to which sentence to impose. (Unit 5.7)

14 Invitation to treat means invitation to others to make offers. In *Fisher v Bell*, it was held that goods on display in a shop are an invitation to treat. The customer makes the offer which the shop may accept. (Unit 6.2)

15 Conditions are the more important, fundamental terms whilst warranties are the less important ones. When a condition is breached the innocent party can choose whether to affirm or repudiate the contract. When a warranty is breached the innocent party may sue for damages only. (Unit 6.4)

16 Performance, agreement, frustration, breach. (Unit 6.7)

17 The defendant must be under a legal duty of care, he must have breached this duty, and the plaintiff must have suffered damage as a result of the defendant's breach. (Unit 7.2)

18 Private nuisance protects a person's use and enjoyment of land and is a tort only. Only one person need be affected. Public nuisance protects public rights and is a crime and a tort. A number of people must be affected. (Unit 7.4)

19 Libel is defamatory material in a permanent form, is actionable *per se* and it may be a crime. Slander is defamatory material in a transitory form, is usually only actionable on proof of damage and is only a tort. (Unit 7.7)

20 Rights are positively expressed. They are often declared in and protected by a constitution and are entrenched. They are enforceable by reference to a special court. Freedoms are negatively expressed. They are residual and enjoy no special protection. (Unit 8.2)

PROGRESS ANALYSIS

My total mark is ....out of 20.

If you scored 0–5

You need to do some more work. Examine the contents page again, and if any topics look unfamiliar, make a note and go back over that chapter. You will then have a further revision plan to work from. You will need to attempt the Test Your Knowledge Quiz one more time before you are ready to go on to the Mock Exam.

If you scored 6–10

You need to do a little more work to fill in the gaps in your knowledge. Look back at those questions you answered incorrectly and aim to revise all those topics again. If you don't think you'll have time to do this, look through the Practice Questions at the end of each chapter, and the notes on points to include. You should then attempt the Test Your Knowledge Quiz again before you attempt the Mock Exam.

If you scored 11–15

You are just about ready to attempt the Mock Exam, but to get the best out of it, you might like to be a little more confident about your recall of some topics. If you have time, look through the Practice Questions at the end of each chapter. This should tell you which syllabus areas are still unfamiliar. You should also identify the questions you got wrong and read the relevant chapter again. You should then be ready to go on to the Mock Exam.

If you scored 16–20

Well done. You have a sufficient grasp of the syllabus topics to get real value out of attempting a Mock Exam in exam conditions. It is still worth going back to the specific Unit referred to in the Test Your Knowledge Quiz Answers for any questions you got wrong and reassure yourself that there is no real gap in your knowledge.

MOCK EXAM

Paper 1   Time allowed: 3 hours

Answer *four* questions. All questions carry equal marks.

1 The jurisdiction of the High Court is both civil and criminal and both original and appellate. (25)
   Discuss. (NEAB)

2 'Equity developed to remedy the deficiencies of the common law. It has no role in our present day legal system.'
   How accurate do you consider this statement to be? (25)
   (UODLE)

3 (a) What part is played by juries and lay magistrates in the resolution of civil and criminal cases? (10)
   (b) Examine critically the arguments for and against the use of *either* juries *or* lay magistrates in the English legal system. (15)
   (AEB)

4 What reforms could be suggested for improving the legal aid and advice system? (UODLE)

5 (a) Discuss the options open to a sentencer, explaining what these different sentencing options are intended to achieve. (15)

    (b) Comment on how a sentencing court will decide on the most suitable disposal for an individual offender. (10)

    (NEAB)

6 Consider whether there are areas of private morality which are not the law's business. (25)

    (London)

7 How do the English courts deal with apparent conflicts between EC law and domestic law? (25)

    (London)

8 'Courts have never been held back by the doctrine of precedent. It is plain to see that, despite its demands, they have developed the *common law* whenever necessary.'

    Making use of appropriate common law examples, explain the operation of the doctrine of precedent and consider the validity of this assertion. (25)

    (AEB)

9 Consider the effectiveness of the Law Commission in promoting changes in the law. (25)

    (London)

10 'The English courts must follow the European pattern. No longer must they examine the words in meticulous detail. No longer must they argue about the precise grammatical sense. They must look to the purpose or intent...' (Lord Denning in *Bulmer v Bollinger* (1974))

    To what extent do you agree that judges should use the European purposive approach when interpreting statutes in the English courts? (25)

    (UODLE)

Paper 2   Time allowed: 3 hours

Answer *either*: Question 1 from two of the three sections

    or: Questions 1 and 2 and *either* 3 or 4 from any one section.

Contract section

1 The April edition of *Quickbyte*, a magazine for computer games enthusiasts, contained a large central section advertising a 'Computer Games Fayre' to be held in June and included a prominent statement by Highjump Ltd that the author of their best selling game would sign copies of the game to be supplied free of charge to the first 20 persons to present three coupons from previous editions of *Quickbyte*.

    Susan read the magazine and attended the fayre. However, though she had taken three coupons along with her, she was unable to get the autograph and free game because at the last moment Highjump Ltd had decided not to exhibit at the fayre and had published a notice to this effect one week before the date of the fayre in a weekly general interest computer magazine.

    However, at another stand at the fayre, Susan won a competition to find the most successful player of a particular game. The prize was the option to purchase from Richard a reduced-price disk containing a very popular computer game. She bought the game without noticing that a display copy of the disk indicated that intending purchasers should first read the important details supplied with it. These details disclaimed all responsibilities for any damage that might be caused by any faults in the disk.

    When Susan used the disk, she found that it contained data which made the game unplayable and which damaged programs already installed in her computer. These programs had to be re-installed at a cost of £200.

    (a) Examining the rules on formation of contract, explain whether Susan has any rights against Highjump Ltd. (10)

    (b) Taking into account the disclaimer in the information supplied with the computer disk, consider whether Richard is in breach of any contract with Susan. (15)

(c) Assuming that Richard is in breach, consider what remedies would be available to Susan. (10)

(d) How could Susan obtain advice about her legal position? (5)

(e) Explain what machinery exists for the resolution of contractual disputes of this kind of value and consider how satisfactory it is. (10)

(AEB)

2 Hillview Farm Limited made an oral contract for the purchase of 20 tons of early seed potatoes from Growmore Seeds Limited, a company they had dealt with for many years. The seed potatoes were delivered together with a standard form invoice which had been agreed between the Seed Trade Association and farmers' organisations. On the front of the invoice in bold print was 'For Conditions of Sale see reverse'.

Clause 3 in the contract states … Any complaint as to quality, description or suitability of seeds, bulbs, corms, tubers, trees or plants (hereinafter referred to as Seeds or Plants) or non-delivery of the correct quality in accordance with the contract must be made to the seller within three days of delivery and if made verbally confirmed in writing within ten days.

Clause 6 states … we will at our option, replace the defective seed or plant, free of charge to the buyer or will refund all payments made to us by the buyer in respect of the defective seed or plant and this shall be the limit of our obligation. We hereby exclude all liabilities for any loss or damage arising from the use of any seed or plant supplied by us and for any consequential loss or damage arising out of such use.

The reason for the three day provision was that seed potatoes are extremely perishable and deteriorate very quickly if not stored correctly.

Growmore Seeds Limited had on some previous occasions made 'ex gratia' payments in excess of the seed cost in circumstances which they thought to be justified.

Hillview Farm Limited planted the potatoes and the crop completely failed. It was discovered after tests that the reason for the failure was partly caused by the seed potatoes being contaminated with a virus which could not be detected by normal inspection and partly caused by seed potatoes not being early seed potatoes as ordered but a less hardy variety which should be sowed much later in better weather.

Advise Hillview Farm Limited as to the legal basis of any action it may wish to pursue and whether it can claim for the loss of the expected value of the crop on the open market. (25)

(NEAB)

3 The ideas of laissez-faire in the law of contract have been gradually eroded by statute. Discuss some of the incursions of statute law to control contractual agreements. (25)

(NEAB)

4 Is it correct to say that every untrue statement which induces a contract will amount to a misrepresentation in law? (25)

(UODLE)

Crime section

1 Anna had become wholly obsessed by the belief that it was wrong to exploit animals for any purposes. She had been ridiculed for her views for many years during which, she now felt, she had campaigned without success, and she had recently become very depressed. She was convinced that the whole system of exploitation was underpinned by finance from the banks. Consequently, she decided to stage a dramatic robbery at her local bank.

She went to the bank armed with a shotgun and forced Erica, the manager, to come out of her office to listen to her speech about animal exploitation. During the speech, a bank customer shouted, 'She is just one of those stupid animal rights idiots.' Hearing this, Anna moved in the customer's direction with the shotgun raised but Erica obstructed her and in the struggle that followed Erica was shot and killed.

Anna then rushed outside and got into a taxi which was just about to drive off with a passenger. Sitting in the back seat, she held the gun to the passenger's head and told Ben, the taxi driver, not to stop for any reason. Ben drove through red traffic lights at a road junction and collided with a cyclist, Christine. Christine later died from her injuries.

(a) Discuss Anna's criminal liability for the death of Erica. (15)

(b) Discuss Ben's criminal liability for the death of Christine. (15)

(c) If Anna and Ben were tried for offences of unlawful homicide, explain which courts would deal with them, including any appeals which might be made. (5)

(d) Anna's problems were associated partly with a desire to bring a particular cause to the attention of the public. Explain and discuss the approach of English law to support for, and protection of, freedom to do so. (15)

(AEB)

2 *X* ran a small restaurant which boasted that all food used in the cooking was 'as fresh as the dawn'. One day, having been let down by her supplier, *X* drove to a nearby farm, and picked some wild mushrooms growing on cattle pasture, and also picked some flowers from a walled section of the farm. That evening, she was told by some diners who were leaving the restaurant that the bill was to be paid by *Y*, who was then in the toilet. When *X* confronted *Y*, he denied that he was the one to pay the bill and, after an argument, *Y* ran off, but was apprehended by a passing police officer.

With what offences, if any, might *X* and *Y* be charged? (25)

(London)

3 Consider the proposition that individuals should be able lawfully to consent to the infliction of non-fatal physical harms upon themselves. (25)

(NEAB)

4 In what circumstances is the imposition of strict liability for a criminal offence appropriate? (25)

(UODLE)

Tort section

1 Nathan and his very large number of friends are all addicted to watching sport on television. He frequently invites them to his house where they tend to stay until the early hours of the morning. There is always a lot of shouting and cheering and they often drink and talk in the garden and sometimes take a television out there. People in neighbouring houses are disturbed by this noise and the noise when they leave. Also there are frequent arguments over car parking and access.

To make it more convenient to watch programmes in the garden, Nathan installed a supply of electricity to an outbuilding by running a cable to it from the house. Though he buried the cable in the ground, he did not use the materials or method required by law and he did not have the installation properly checked. Subsequently, he engaged Owen, a gardener, to install some fencing. Whilst drilling holes for fence posts, Owen cut through the cable and was electrocuted and seriously injured. This incident was witnessed by Nathan's neighbour, Richard, who collapsed with shock.

Though he was using the supply to the outbuilding to power his machinery, Owen had not asked Nathan about the electricity cable and Nathan had not attempted to mention it to him.

(a) Discuss what legal action Nathan's neighbours might pursue in respect of the noise and inconvenience and consider how effective any remedies available might be. (10)

(b) Consider whether Owen may be able to recover compensation from Nathan for his injuries. (15)

(c) Assuming that Owen were able to do so, explain whether Richard could also recover compensation from Nathan. (10)

(d) Assuming that Owen has little money, how might he be able to pay for legal *advice* about his case? (5)

(e) To what extent is the influence of policy considerations evident in the rules of law which you have discussed in examining the cases of Owen and Richard? (10)

(AEB)

2 Adrian has been employed for five years by Daily Deliveries Ltd as a deliveryman. It is a term of Adrian's employment that he may not carry any person other than employees of Daily Deliveries Ltd on his van. In fact, since his employment started, Adrian has been helped on Saturdays, and during school and college holidays, by his son James who is aged 19. James has never been employed by Daily Deliveries Ltd and is aware of the restriction in Adrian's contract of employment. Last month James was helping Adrian as usual when, owing to Adrian's negligent driving of the delivery van on their lunch break, there was an accident in which James was seriously injured.

Daily Deliveries Ltd has now told James that the Company has no liability to pay damages to him.

Advise James.   (25)
(UODLE)

3 It has been argued that 'there is no need for a law to protect privacy; the existing law of defamation achieves this'. Does the law of defamation successfully protect privacy?
(25)
(UODLE)

4 In relation to the concept of nervous shock, Lord Justice Oliver has stated that he could not 'regard the present state of the law as entirely satisfactory or as logically defensible' and concluded that only 'considerations of policy' made it explicable.

Is Lord Oliver's view justified?   (25)
(UODLE)

MOCK EXAM SUGGESTED ANSWERS

Tutorial note

It is very important in a law exam to cite cases and statutes where appropriate. In particular, in Paper 2 when explaining the law, you *must* refer to the sources of the law. Do not simply cite a case name, give some indication that you understand the case by referring to the facts, the decision and the *ratio*.

Paper 1

1 The civil original jurisdiction of the High Court: each of the three Divisions.
The civil appellate jurisdiction of the High Court: the Divisional Courts.
The criminal appellate jurisdiction of the Divisional Court of Queen's Bench Division.
There is no original criminal jurisdiction.

2 Describe the deficiencies of the common law and the development of Equity. Describe the role of Equity today, for example, equitable remedies. Finally, consider whether the statement is accurate, in the light of your answer.

3 (a) Describe the *role* of juries and *lay* magistrates in civil matters, then their role in criminal cases. Do not include other material, such as how juries are selected or the social background of magistrates.

(b) Choose *either* juries *or* magistrates and give arguments for and against their use. This is the point to discuss issues of selection, training, general competence. Make sure you examine the arguments critically. For example, it is said that the jury is not competent to decide complex issues in fraud trials — where does that criticism come from? How valid is it? If juries were not used in fraud trials, would the alternative be any better?

4 First, describe the system as it exists in both civil and criminal cases for both advice and assistance and legal aid. Then consider the criticisms that have been made and suggest reforms. Do not be tempted to make up ideas for reform on the spur of the moment. Either refer to reforms that have been suggested by others or, if you have an idea of your own, make sure it is one you have thought out thoroughly and can explain convincingly.

5 (a) Explain the sentences that are available and for each sentence explain what aim might be pursued. For example, imprisonment may be used to deter, to reform, to punish and to protect society; a fine is a punishment and a deterrent. Be sure to explain the full range of sentences.

(b) Explain the use of antecedents, including the relevance of past offences. Explain mitigation. Explain the use of pre-sentence reports and victim impact statements. Explain tariffs and guidelines from the Court of Appeal. Finally, draw these elements together and consider how they impact upon each other and which are likely to be given precedence in making a sentencing decision.

6 Draw a distinction between legal rules and moral rules. Explain how the law is based on moral rules upon which there is general consensus. Choose an area upon which there is not a general consensus and explain the basis upon which lines are drawn as to what is the law's business and what is not. This is often best done by examination of a case such as *R v Brown and Others*: make sure you know your case thoroughly enough to give your discussion a firm basis.

7 Explain the rule that where there is conflict, EC law prevails, with reference to the European Communities Act 1972 and relevant cases. Consider the benevolent interpretation approach as well as the final solution of suspending an English statute, as in *Factortame*. Consider what the courts would do if Parliament expressly stated that a statute was to overrule EC law.

8 Explain how precedent works: the hierarchy of courts, the *ratio* as the binding element of a decision and the reporting system. Choose one or two examples that can be used to demonstrate how the common law has been developed. Any area of substantive law is fine, but do be sure to use *common law* examples, not cases about the interpretation of statutes.

9 Explain the work of the Law Commission. Give examples of changes in the law that have been the result of Law Commission reports. Consider why many Law Commission reports do not result in legislation and conclude by deciding whether the Law Commission can be described as 'effective'.

10 Explain the various approaches to statutory interpretation: literal, golden, mischief. Illustrate each with a case and then explain and illustrate the purposive approach. Consider what the consequences would be if English statutes were always interpreted purposively: what would have happened in the cases you used to illustrate the traditional rules? Would the result have been better or worse? Consider the difference in drafting styles between UK and EC law. Conclude by answering the *to what extent* question.

Paper 2

Contract section

1 (a) Explain the distinction between an offer and an invitation to treat. Explain revocation of offer. Apply the rules to Susan's situation.
(b) Explain the relevant rules from the Sale of Goods Act 1979 and Unfair Contract Terms Act 1977; apply them to the facts.
(c) Explain the remedies for breach of condition and damages for consequential loss.
(d) Consider the sources of advice available (solicitor, CAB, trading standards) and the means of financing advice (private funding, legal advice and assistance).
(e) Describe, compare and evaluate small claims in the county court, arbitration and mediation.

2 Describe the statutory terms implied into a contract between businesses: Sale of Goods Act 1979 and UCTA 1977. Consider whether clauses 3 and 6 were incorporated into the contract, with reference to the common law rules on incorporation. Note that clause 6 is a limitation clause and the consequences of that. Apply the law to the facts.

3 Explain what is meant by *laissez-faire*. Choose some examples of statute law in contract and discuss how they control what the parties may do. If would be a good idea to compare the rules relating to contracts between businesses and consumers with those between two businesses.

4 Avoid the temptation of beginning with a conclusion. Explain the law on misrepresentation, drawing out the circumstances in which an untrue statement inducing a contract does not give rise to an actionable misrepresentation.

Crime section

1 (a) Discuss the *actus reus* and *mens rea* required for murder and the defences of provocation and diminished responsibility. Apply the law to the facts.

(b) Discuss the offence of gross negligence manslaughter and the defences of duress and duress of circumstance. Apply the law to the facts.

(c) Remember to begin with the magistrates' court (for committal proceedings), then Crown Court (as these are both indictable offences), appeals to the Court of Appeal and House of Lords.

(d) Explain the residual nature of English law on freedom of speech and give specific examples of restraints on that freedom. Compare this with an approach based on a Bill of Rights and explain the role of the European Convention on Human Rights.

2 Explain the law with regard to theft, especially what constitutes 'property', and making off without payment — think about the *mens rea* required for this offence.

3 Consider the defence of consent in relation to the different degrees of harm required for different offences. Reference to decided cases and the Law Commission's work on the topic would enhance the quality of your answer.

4 Explain what is meant by strict liability in criminal law. Discuss when its use is appropriate and when it is not.

Tort section

1 (a) Explain the tort of private nuisance and the relevance of public nuisance. Apply the law to the facts. Describe the remedies of damages, injunction and self-help and consider their relative effectiveness.

(b) Discuss the law relating to occupiers' liability, especially with regard to the standard required in relation to a tradesman, and negligence. Apply the law to the facts.

(c) Discuss the law relating to liability in negligence for nervous shock. Apply the law to the facts.

(d) Notice that the question is about paying for legal *advice* (not representation): discuss the statutory and other schemes for obtaining advice — note that the question is about *paying* for advice, so free advice schemes are not relevant here.

(e) Explain what is meant by *policy considerations* then discuss perhaps two rules of law you have already explained with reference to the policy issues evident in those rules. For example, the different rules relating to duty of care in negligence for cases of physical injury and cases of nervous shock.

2 Briefly explain the law on negligence, but concentrate your answer on vicarious liability. Note that James knew about the restriction — can he be *volenti*?

3 Explain the law of defamation, then consider whether it protects privacy. It would be relevant to consider how accessible defamation actions are to ordinary people, given that there is no legal aid, as well as looking at the substantive rules relating to defamation.

4 Explain the law on nervous shock. Consider whether the law is satisfactory and whether it is logically defensible. Then consider the policy considerations that could explain why the law is what it is. Conclude by stating whether you find Lord Oliver's view justified.

INDEX